The Gothic Sublime

SUNY Series on the Sublime
Rob Wilson, Editor

The Gothic Sublime

Vijay Mishra

State University of New York Press

Production by Ruth Fisher
Marketing by Nancy Farrell

Published by
State University of New York Press, Albany

Printed in the United States of America

For information, address State University of New York Press,
State University Plaza, Albany, NY 12246

Library of Congress Cataloging-in-Publication Data

Mishra, Vijay.
The gothic sublime / by Vijay Mishra.
p. cm. — (SUNY series on the sublime)
Includes bibliographical references and index.
ISBN 0–7914–1747–6 (alk. paper). — ISBN 0–7914–1748–4 (pbk. : alk. paper)
1. Horror tales, English—History and criticism—Theory, etc. 2. English fiction—18th century—History and criticism. 3. English fiction—19th century—History and criticism. 4. Gothic revival (Literature)—Great Britain. 5. Romanticism—Great Britain. 6. Sublime, The. I. Title. II. Series.
PR830.T3M53 1994
823'.0872909—dc20 93–147
CIP

10 9 8 7 6 5 4 3 2 1

To Nalini
a gift of scholarship

kālo 'smi lokakṣayakṛt pravṛddhaḥ

Bhagavadgītā 11.32

I am become death, shatterer of the worlds.

As quoted by J. Robert Oppenheimer (1945)

Contents

Acknowledgments

I would like to thank, first of all, my wife Nalini and my children Rohan and Paras for their unflinching support and encouragement during the long years I have spent writing this book. The shape of this book owes much to research I undertook at Oxford, and in that context I should especially like to thank Professor David Punter of Stirling University; Professor Thomas Docherty of Trinity College, Dublin; Mr. Jonathan Wordsworth of St. Catherine's College, Oxford; Professor Christopher Norris of the University of Wales College of Cardiff; and Professor Paul Hamilton of the University of Southampton. Although I have not been able to do full justice to their manifold suggestions, I'm deeply aware that without their help this book would have been much the poorer.

Of the many libraries in which I have worked, I should like to mention, in particular, the Bodleian, the British Library, the Victoria and Albert Museum Library, the Ashmolean Museum Library, the University of Wales College of Cardiff Library, and the Murdoch University Library in Perth. The staff of these libraries have always been extremely generous with their time.

Lord Abinger gave his permission to quote from and use photographic specimens from the Shelley-Godwin papers deposited in the Duke Humfrey's Library of the Bodleian. The Huntington very generously provided me with a microfilm of Richard Brinsley Peake's *Presumption*. Ms. Cynthia Baker of Murdoch University decoded my chaotic handwriting and spent many weeks producing a perfect typescript. Ms. Sally Garratt of the University of Wales College of Cardiff typed the concluding chapter, made final corrections, and reinserted commands lost during the transfer of the manuscript from one disk to another. Ms. Diana Clegg, Secretary to the English and Comparative Literature Program at Murdoch University, has tirelessly retyped the many changes I have since made to the original manuscript.

My ideas were considerably modified through interaction with the members of the Centre for Critical and Cultural Theory, University of Wales College of Cardiff. I would like to thank Professor Catherine Belsey for inviting me to the Centre during the autumn of 1989, and the staff of the School of English Studies for making my stay in Cardiff so very pleasant.

The book could not have been written without financial help from Murdoch University and St. Catherine's College, Oxford, and an ORS award made by the British Government. At my own university I would like to thank in particular my friend Bob Hodge, who has helped me out with a number of classical allusions in my source texts. I am also indebted to a former colleague, John Frow, who encouraged me to undertake research in this area when I gave lectures in his Period Study course in 1983–84. Students of my Narrative Fiction class at Murdoch University have taught me more than they would care to admit. The combination of strong textualism with theory is a direct result of my interactions with students and colleagues in the English and Comparative Literature Program at Murdoch University, where, thankfully, theory and interdisciplinary studies continue to be encouraged.

Of the many scholars whose work on the sublime I have used in this book, I would like to place a special word of thanks to Rob Wilson, general editor of the SUNY Series on the Sublime, who has been of enormous help to me throughout this past year. His splendid work on the American Sublime is the impossible ideal to which I have falteringly attempted to aspire. At the SUNY Press itself I would like to thank the editor Carola Sautter and the production team—Ruth Fisher, Jan Brittan, and Nancy Farrell—for their patience and commitment to this book.

A deep regret, however, colors my acknowledgments. My father died as this book in its original form was coming to a close. As I stood next to the furiously burning pyre, I was struck by a sense of the sublime that was not unlike Lord Byron's feelings on the shores of Viareggio as Shelley's body was being cremated. He had noticed, as I did then, how much brighter and purer the fire was when fueled by the human body itself. Much of this book is informed by the sublime as the dissolution of the self in death. My father would have understood the specifically Hindu nature of that connection.

Vijay Mishra
Murdoch University, Perth

Introduction
Reading Others Reading the Gothic

A book entitled *The Gothic Sublime* invites comparisons with at least two key critical studies of the Gothic, both relatively old. The first book is Montague Summers' historical survey *The Gothic Quest* (1938), the second Devendra P. Varma's enthusiastically written *The Gothic Flame* (1957). These are not the best books on the Gothic for contemporary readers and they have been superseded by critical studies by David Punter, Coral Ann Howells, Elizabeth Napier, and Eve Kosofsky Sedgwick. The early studies of Summers and Varma, however, use the words *quest* and *flame* (not *sublime*) to define the Gothic in ways that, in terms of their syntagmatic positionings at any rate, echo the project of this book, even though my reading of the Gothic parts company from theirs quite dramatically. For both these writers the Gothic confirmed a lost sense of the numinous, as they draw, quite self-consciously, attention to the possibility, in the Gothic, of some redeeming, religious experience that realist texts, with their closer links with shifts in capital and the individualism of the bourgeoisie, had clearly sacrificed. Devendra Varma is positively lyrical in his identification of the Gothic with the search for "absolute spiritual values":

> Primarily the Gothic novels arose out of a quest for the numinous. They are characterized by an awestruck apprehension of Divine immanence penetrating diurnal reality. This sense of the numinous is an almost archetypal impulse inherited from primitive magic. The Gothic quest was not merely after horror—a simple succession of ghastly incidents could have satisfied that yearning—but after other-worldly gratification.[1]

Varma is clearly after a "mystical interpretation of life" that would, finally, make the Gothic sublime a version of the religious experience. The Gothic subject in Varma's reading thus finds in the supernatural the sublime as the object of an essentially spiritual quest. That such a reading went against the quite subversive, at times profoundly skeptical, readings of religion in the Gothic texts themselves, Varma seems not to have registered. In this version of the

Gothic/religious sublime the subject itself is defined in unproblematic terms. And since the "meaning" of the Gothic is now legitimated through the unsaid Absolute Signified (God), Gothic texts become quite orderly narratives linked intrinsically to some ideal logos.

Varma, of course, inherits this reading from Montague Summers' epilogue, "Surrealism and the Gothic Novel," in which Summers mounts a vigorous defense of the Gothic against what he sees are the mistaken appropriations of the form by the avant-gardists. In a remarkable echo of Lyotard's discovery of the "logic" of postmodernism in the eighteenth-century theories of the sublime, the surrealists (in Montague Summers' argument) claimed to have found their precursor in the "sublime" of the Gothic. Such a proposition strikes Summers as utterly preposterous, because the collapse of the categories of dreams and reality (the basis of the surrealists' claims to a discursive anteriority in the Gothic) went against Summers' own reading of the Gothic as a genre that dealt with the continuing search for the divine in men. The Gothic flame is then a beacon that guides the human spirit through history and prevents humankind from precisely the excesses and absurdities that the moral Right has traditionally associated with surrealism. "An aristocrat of literature"[2] like the Gothic novel demands deference and respect, not indiscriminate poaching as found in André Breton's writings. Essentialist as he was, Summers therefore argued that Gothic ruins, for instance, were "a sacred relic, a memorial, a symbol of infinite sadness, of tenderest sensibility and regret"[3] and not, as André Breton's surrealism seems to suggest, dream corridors into the unconscious. As we can see from the selective use of "sacred," "relic," "memorial," and "infinite," the Gothic is being carefully framed in a discourse of the religious sublime. Not surprisingly, Summers refused to read Walpole's claim that *The Castle of Otranto*, the Gothic precursor text, originated in a dream in anything but purely pragmatic terms. Repeating his well-known words to Rev. William Cole, Walpole had written to Rev. William Mason apologizing for the haste with which he had composed his slight novel.

> . . . I published The Castle of Otranto with the utmost diffidence and doubt of its success[. . . .] Your praise is so likely to make me vain, that I oblige myself to recollect all the circumstances that can abate it, such as the fear I had of producing it at all . . . ; the hurry in which it was composed; and its being begun without any plan at all, for though in the short course of

> its progress I did conceive some views, it was so far from being sketched out with any design at all that it was actually commenced one evening, from the very imperfect recollection of a dream with which I had waked in the morning. It was begun and finished in less than two months, and then I showed it to Mr. Gray, who encouraged me to print it; this is the true history of it; and I cannot but be happy.[4]

Writing here emerges as a defiant act of "gaming," a subversive play with the received definitions of the work of art which had come to be seen largely in terms of principles of harmony and form. The attractiveness of such a confession to the avant-gardist (whether defined as surrealist or postmodern) is not difficult to see. But this very legitimate interpellation of the surrealist subject through a retrospective or regressive reading of an earlier artistic form is violently resisted by Montague Summers, who in fact parodies Gothic narratives themselves in his pursuit of the hidden agenda of the surrealists, who become, for Montague Summers, creatures of the labyrinth in need of exorcism. The agenda at work in Summers' vituperative criticism soon becomes clear. Like many critics of postmodernism, Summers read surrealism as an extremely dangerous, communist phenomenon. Since at the height of Stalinism all versions of authoritarianism were associated with communism, the surrealist was defined as an ungodly, latter-day Jacobin, hell-bent on destroying civilized society. "If Surrealism is knit to Communism," wrote Summers, " it can have nothing to do with the Gothic novel, nor indeed with romanticism at all."[5] It is ironic that Summers should have mounted an attack on surrealism from behind the shaky defenses of the Gothic when the Gothic is perhaps least equipped to advance a conservative attack on the avant-garde. Nevertheless, Summers' critical discourse on the Gothic and the metaphorics of the quest and the flame generally are symptomatic of the manner in which the Gothic had been appropriated to serve specific ideological ends. The current postmodern interest in the sublime in one way brings the argument begun by André Breton full circle. The literary reception of the Gothic is thus a field of knowledge that periodically repeats itself, and in doing so echoes a familiar postmodern conception of textuality—that in fact texts "deconstruct *themselves* by themselves." Furthermore, the procedures used by Montague Summers in his panic defense of the Gothic through an ethicopolitical framing take us to the very heart of a Gothic signifying practice as they bring to the foreground precisely the question of what constitutes critical judgment. Like Samuel Monk's Romantic sublime, the Gothic, too, caught the century "somewhat off its guard."[6] To the positivities of the aesthetics of beauty the Gothic sublime brought a dangerous, negative principle of nontranscendental subjectivity. Montague Summers placed a lid on this frightening knowledge, and Devendra P. Varma saw it as the impossible object of the Kantian Idea. The historical negotiation of the Gothic as a text of barbarism, what Walter Benjamin felt was a necessary concomitant of all texts of civilization, is a narrative that we must now use as a stepping stone for theorizing the Gothic sublime in this book.

Contemporary readings of texts are, within limits, probably the most exciting. Since critical perspectives are still being formed and an historical sense is often absent (especially for outrageously radical texts), the criticisms quite unpretentiously and with disarming familiarity quickly undercut any sense of presumption that an author might have harbored. In reading how others read the Gothic we shall begin with the Gothic precursor text itself before looking at how the Gothic, as a total discursive system, was read. As far as *The Castle of Otranto* is concerned, Horace Walpole, its author, was himself one of the earliest readers of the Gothic form. Recalling his scattered responses to this founding text of the Gothic over some twenty years, Walpole wrote to Hannah More, energetic member of the Blue Stocking Circle, on November 13, 1784, protesting about the likely effects of his magical romance on poor Mrs. Ann Yearsley, a poet better known as the "Bristol Milkwoman."[7]

> What! if I should go a step farther, dear Madam, and take the liberty of reproving you for putting into this poor woman's hands such a frantic thing as The Castle of Otranto? It was fit for nothing but the age in which it was written, an age in which much was known; that required only to be amused, nor cared whether its amusements were conformable to truth and models of good sense; that could not be spoiled; was in no danger of being too credulous; and rather wanted to be brought back into imagination, than to be led astray by it—but you will have made a hurly-burly in this poor woman's head which it cannot develop and digest.[8]

In Walpole's own words, the Gothic text is "a frantic thing," amusing but not in any manner connected with the real world. The Enlightenment breeds a callous disregard for constant vigilance as the imagination invites excitement of senses. Unfortunately for poor Mrs. Yearsley, she does not have the security of the Enlightenment—something extraordinary seems to have happened in the past twenty years about which Walpole remains silent—and may well find the Gothic "hurly-burly" difficult to digest. The retreat into a "ludic" conceptualization of the book is not unusual; Walpole often retreats into descriptions of his work as a "trifle" or "a trifling romance" or even "my idle" in his voluminous correspondence. But he was acutely aware of the open-ended nature of his own "trifle," the fact that what his slight work had started was a particular discursive practice to which additions could always be made. In 1796, frail and bedridden, Walpole was wildly enthusiastic about Bertie Greatheed's drawings depicting episodes from *The Castle of Otranto*[9] because they reinforced his idea of the text as an object that could continue to be expanded, through dramatic adaptations, paintings, and so on. Walpole's deconstruction of his own work fissures the presumed homogeneity of the literary text: this early Gothic already heralds a theory of textual heterogeneity.

Other readers had been even more ambivalent toward the Gothic than Walpole. It was all very well if the text were simply a translation from some obscure Italian work, as Walpole originally pretended it was. "This is a mere translation, and I am not really responsible for this gibberish" is how Walpole addressed his readers.[10] Conned by the so-called translator's artless guile, the imperious John Langhorne, writing for the *Monthly Review*, felt that the work was written with "no common pen," and was assuredly a "work of genius, evincing great dramatic powers."[11] But once the hoax was exposed, the bruised ego of Langhorne poured scorn on Walpole, calling the work "false," "preposterous," and forgivable only as a "translation" from a "gross and unenlightened age." "It is, indeed, more than strange," wrote Langhorne, "that an Author, of a refined and polished genius, should be an advocate for re-establishing the barbarous superstitions of Gothic devilism!"[12] Langhorne's second reading, in fact, had been foreshadowed in the *Critical Review*'s initial reading of *The Castle of Otranto* as a text "composed of . . . rotten materials" and full of "monstrosities."[13] Since "Gothic devilism" was synonymous with the much-maligned "primitivism" associated with Bishop Hurd (who supported a return to an ethnic English literary archive), it is hardly surprising that contemporary critics with their classical bias heaped such scorn on the text.

In terms of literary reception, perhaps the single most important moment in the critical history of *The Castle of Otranto* occurred with Scott's generous introduction to the 1811 Ballantyne edition of the work. In the Harvard University copy of this edition, which has extensive notes in Scott's own hand, the holograph notes speak of Walpole as someone who disclaimed the "pursuit of fame" and "who did not mean to descend into the common arena."[14] Scott makes careful discriminations throughout this essay, conscious of the work's weaknesses but also aware of its compositional features. Twice in this essay he refers to "a peculiar species of composition" (varied to a "new species of literary composition"[15]) marred in places by "injudicious repetition," which seem to remain consciously uncorrected. Since the broader genre in which this "literary composition" finds form is "romance," it follows, for Scott at any rate, that a "mysterious obscurity" should inform this text. Yet "obscurity" should not become far "too frequent"; nor should it be completely explained (as one finds in Radcliffe) since the magic of "romance" is lost if one knows that behind every "lion's mask" there is a real man. This is about as close as we get in contemporary criticism to the aesthetics of the sublime. Yet insofar as Scott insists upon the "romance" paradigm and quotes, approvingly, Walpole's letter to Madame du Deffand in which he claimed he had composed *Otranto* in "defiance of rules, of critics, and of philosophers," Scott does seem to suggest the level of textual difference implicit in Walpole's text and its special place in the genre.

The nineteenth century consigned Walpole to oblivion, and in doing so effectively buried the genre of the Gothic as well. Even Hazlitt, an otherwise generous man, found "no peculiar originality of mind, or depth of thought"[16] in Walpole. Thomas Babington Macaulay rose to great rhetorical heights to condemn Walpole's "extravagant nonsense": ". . . none but an unhealthy and disorganised mind could have produced such literary luxuries as the works of Walpole."[17] And in spite of Leslie Stephen's reference to Walpole's "versatile, and original intellect,"[18] no one seems to have taken him seriously. In his 1893 biography of Walpole, Austin Dobson summed up the attitude when he wrote, "Autres temps, autres moeurs,—especially in the matter of Gothic romance."[19]

"A bundle of contradictions," proclaimed Leslie Stephen's renowned daughter Virginia Woolf much later. And "did not gossip whisper," continued she, "that he was not his father's son, and was there not, somewhere deep within him, an uneasy suspicion that there was a blot on his scutcheon, a freakish strain in his Norfolk blood?"[20] Earlier, in 1921, however, Woolf had considered more specifically the curious phenomenon of *The Castle of Otranto* in her review of Edith Birkhead's *The Tale of Terror*. Though she refused to acknowledge the high claims being made on behalf of this genre by Edith Birkhead ("It would be a fine exercise in discrimination to decide the precise point at which romance becomes Gothic and imagination moonshine,"[21] she wrote), she does acknowledge that the psychological effects produced by the texts may have a direct bearing on those contemporary writings which explore the "ghosts within us."

Virginia Woolf had clearly detected an urge "obscurely hidden in the psychology of the human race,"[22] but neither Edith Birkhead nor the general literary historians of this form—Railo, Tompkins, Summers, Lévy, and Varma among them[23]—pursued this dimension in any serious fashion. Birkhead was centrally concerned with connecting *The Castle of Otranto* (and the Gothic generally) with an entire literary history of the supernatural that included, with the courtesy of J. G. Frazer's paraphrase, *The Epic of Gilgamesh* as well. The other critics followed more or less the same argument and unproblematically wrote their Gothic literary histories in the hope of constructing a master narrative of the Gothic that would take us to the very beginnings of fiction. Only in Mario Praz's comparative study of versions of the satanic myth in Romantic culture[24] and in Wylie Sypher's astute Marxist reading of the Gothic writers' "innocent" grasp of the banalities of bourgeois existence without any real understanding of the underlying antagonistic social relations do we find attempts at reading the Gothic theoretically. Outwardly more hostile toward bourgeois morality, the Romantic artist attempted a "resolution by simplification" (recall Byron's amorality and Shelley's selfishness, for instance), whereas the Gothic writers, less aware of these contradictions and more inhibited in their social consciousness, concealed them in their writings, and in so doing exposed the bourgeois order much more effectively.[25]

Up till now the Gothic had been represented as an alternative novelistic genre, a kind of degenerate literary form that should best be treated as a minor diversion, or, as with Summers and Varma, defiantly connected to a version of the sublime as positive, confirmable desire. By the early sixties André Breton's connections between the Gothic and the avant-garde and Varma's own acceptance of this proposition in *The Gothic Flame* gets reformulated as a theory of evil itself: the Gothic is basically a Manichean form that dares to raise the necessity of evil. The most elegant formulation of this proposition appeared in the 1962 essay of Lowry Nelson, Jr. Borrowing his crucial archetypes from Edith Birkhead's 1921 study, from Railo, and from Praz's *The Romantic Agony* ("Guilt-haunted wanderers," "Byronic figures," "Faust," "Don Juan"), Nelson penned his argument in prophetic terms:

> it could be claimed that the development of the gothic novel foreshadows the future interest, both in art and science, in hidden workings, contradictory impulses, irrational and gratuitous evil, the intimacy of love and hate, whose effects are so diversely seen (whether expressed or suppressed) in Balzac, Dickens, Browning, Baudelaire, Dostoevsky and their heirs.[26]

The first major critic to use this strategy was Robert D. Hume, who in 1969 claimed that the term *Gothic* may be extended to include *Wuthering Heights, Moby Dick,* and Faulkner's *Sanctuary*.[27] Although these may be considered "extensions" of the Gothic, the works of Poe, Hawthorne, and Charles Brockden Brown are actually "part of the original Gothic tradition," wrote Hume. The aesthetic basis of Hume's claim comes straight out of Coleridge's *Biographia Literaria*. Slightly amended, the argument goes something like this: unlike Romantic writing, which imaginatively reconciled "discordant elements," "Gothic writing" functioned within "opposites" without any desire toward reconciliation. In short, whereas "Romantic writing" affirmed "Imagination," "Gothic writing" was a product of "Fancy." It was this transposition of Coleridgean doctrine onto what, to many, seemed a tendentious historical distinction, that led to a heated debate between Hume and Platzner in the pages of the *PMLA*.[28] The counterattack from Platzner, however, was based on the retrieval of the metaphysical "quality of evil" in Gothic texts to distinguish the Gothic vision from other types of "fantasy literature." The debate is interesting even if the battle was fought within the parameters of an essentially humanist critical practice.

It was left for later critics to explore the theoretical claims implicit in the Hume/Platzner debate. Echoing Ortega y Gasset, Robert Kiely, for instance, examined the negative effects of an intertext that would produce anti-institutional discourses. One strategy of subversion Kiely detects in the Gothic is the implicit transfer of the center of texts from the humanist essentiality of character to architecture. Space becomes more important than the consciousness, as being, that constructs the world.

> Believable relationships—sexual or otherwise—are impossible, not because the state is tottering with corruption, but

> because the essence of individual identity has been dislodged from its human centers and diffused in an architectural construct which seems to have more life than the characters who inhabit it.[29]

Kiely returns to Kenneth Clark's 1928 monograph entitled *The Gothic Revival* in which Clark connects Gothic architecture to the eighteenth-century excitement with graveyard poetry and ruins, as well as symbolically linking two discourses, the literary critical and the architectural. Kiely's key term—the dislodgement of human centers—was, however, examined by Coral Ann Howells in *Love, Mystery, and Misery.* In this work she followed the consequences of what happened when a surplus of "emotion" or "sensibility" took over discourse; when, in fact, the "world of nervous breakdown from which Pamela and Clarissa were saved" was no longer subject to control and threatened to destroy the very "stability of the external world," asserting as this new genre does "the power of the irrational over the rational."[30] In the Gothic novels this world is "interiorized" and transformed into a private domain of neurotic sensibility. Everything here is extreme: "extreme sensibility," "febrile temperament," excessive "anxiety," "repression" and so on. Women who occupy ambivalent "spaces" throughout totter toward the verge of sexual collapse and exhaustion. No wonder "the dread of sex runs right through Gothic fiction and is basic to many of its conventions of anxiety and terror."[31] Howells does not name her sublime but her reading of the Gothic very clearly demonstrates, at least for the women characters, an ever-present terror of rape and confinement that may be connected with this trope only as its dreaded negation, the threatening but very real underside of a female sublime. Where the masculine sublime (and the category of the sublime has always emphasized a male subject) saw in the unpresentable an impossible idea, but one that it nevertheless wished to embrace, however fleetingly, as its Romantic versions tell us, a female sublime reads the unpresentable as the horrifying threat of violation.

The sublime as its obverse, as powerlessness, leads William Patrick Day to read Gothic anxieties in terms of an essentially modern dilemma of the failure of self-definition. There is a central monomyth that underlies the Gothic, and this is expressed through a single "reference" text that the Gothic tales repeat with minor variations. The central monomyth is a composite, androgynous, Faustian figure who in one of his sexual roles (as strong Faustian male, or as passive female) is dragged into the Gothic underworld from which escape, theoretically at any rate, is impossible. If release does take place, as in *The Castle of Otranto* or in Radcliffe's romances, or if the outcome is tragic, it has little effect upon society, since the character's life has not been able to transform the world. The idea of changing the world is not countenanced because human will cannot alter a world drawn up as a dream landscape.[32] In other words, since the world is all maya in the first instance and cannot be interpreted, the issue of the self transcending human limitations and claiming to change the world does not arise.

The ideas canvassed thus far go back to the Lowry Nelson, Jr. project, which in fact finds its most schematic articulation in David Punter's 1980 work on the literature of terror.[33] Though Punter does not use the term, what clearly emerges from his study is that the Gothic is a "scriptible," open-ended form that periodically disrupts the literary canon from Walpole to Pynchon. Punter does not go on to make the obvious connection between the Gothic (Walpole) and the postmodern (Pynchon) through Lyotard's postmodernity as the "threat of nothing further happening,"[34] but he is nevertheless very conscious of the remarkably transgressive nature of Gothic texts. Two key concepts that Punter uses to explore this thesis are *taboo* and *alienation*. "Taboo" is used within a psychoanalytic hermeneutic to indicate the levels of possible transgressions in the texts; "alienation" is read through a Marxist hermeneutic to mean alienation from products of labour, from the natural world, from a "sense of human-ness" and from one's own self. In short, the disjunction between "work value" and "use value" irrecoverably fractures the psyche of capitalist man. Punter finds many examples of "alienation" in the tales of "terror" without trivializing either the complex uses of the term *alienation* or extending it to incorporate every kind of social disjunction. It is Punter's awareness of the underlying complexity of the form and its massively overdetermined existence that leads him to recognize the essential ambiguity of the Gothic:

> The central contradiction, however, from which all the others flow, is this: that Gothic can at one and the same time be categorised as a middle-class and as an anti-middle-class literature.[35]

This, as Punter demonstrates so admirably, is the "central dialectic of Gothic fiction": massively deconstructive but, like Cressida, timid as a "virgin in the night" (these are Troilus' words, not Cressida's!).

The dialectic ultimately explains why this "form of fiction . . . continues to flourish . . . despite efforts to lay the ghosts to rest."[36]

There is, then, a double alienation at work in Punter's reading as the subject is cut off from productive activities of the body and the mind: one is master of neither one's labor nor one's intellect. If there is any form of possible transcendence it is one that, according to Linda Bayer-Berenbaum, "deals with the nature of . . . a transcendence that at first appears to be most alien to modern thinking."[37] The Gothic, Bayer-Berenbaum continues, is marked by a negative transcendence that is "primarily evil,"[38] a point which Elizabeth MacAndrew had also made in her 1979 study of the Gothic.[39] Reformulated as an excess in the Gothic, the negative transcendence in question expresses itself through an anti-institutional ideology that connects the genre with (counter) revolution and anarchy as the tyrant is paradoxically endorsed. "In its most basic implication," continues Linda Bayer-Berenbaum, "the Gothic quest is for the random, the wild, and the unbounded,"[40] as she connects Gothic literature with the restless energy of Gothic architecture, where fleeing gargoyles were aimed at frightening away evil spirits. In the words of Wilhelm Worringer, the peculiar aesthetic demand of the architecture leads to an "activity to which we submit against our will."[41] The architectural design is active, soaring, complex, like the vast, confusing narratives of the Gothic that often parody the linearity of realist texts. Bayer-Berenbaum speaks of Gothic creation as "incomplete" because "in the end there is no pattern, no answer."[42] She does not connect her reading specifically with the Gothic sublime, but her concept of the unbounded nature of the Gothic quest mirrors the mind's confrontation with a horror that is contrary to the momentary freedom given to the imagination in the Romantic sublime. Although Bayer-Berenbaum does not make it explicit, it is clear that in the Gothic the law of reason does not (dare not?) impose its moral principle; instead, the submission to the sublime is against our will, and transcendence is the bliss of pure negation.

A different critic of the Gothic (but probably the most influential in recent times) is Tzvetan Todorov, whose *Introduction à la littérature fantastique*[43] appeared in 1970. It established the importance of a systematic genre theory to a discussion of any variety of the fantastic by drawing attention to the fact that thematic critics of the Gothic had ignored the langue, the underlying system, in favour of the parole, the surface literary instantiations. The emphasis on the langue led Todorov to construct a hierarchical system of theoretical and historical genres into which "evanescent genres" may be easily absorbed. The fantastic is the middle or intermediary genre in a tripartite system of the "marvellous," the "fantastic" and the "uncanny." Where the first accepts the laws of the "supernatural" and the third the laws of the "natural world," the middle genre remains precariously sandwiched between the two. Whereas it is easy enough to demonstrate the supernatural operating in the "marvellous" and through psychoanalysis (though Todorov himself disapproved of this), the peculiar narrative of the "uncanny," it is much more difficult to establish the precise limits of the "fantastic." To account for the effect of the "fantastic" on the reader Todorov employs a version of reception theory by suggesting that there is an "ideal" reader of the "fantastic" whose reactions mark moments of indecision in the text. In other words, the dilemma is articulated through a version of the statement "I nearly reached the point of believing." The "fantastic" is thus a genre that is constructed "upon" this moment of hesitation or indecision. There is a kind of restraint imposed upon thought through repetitive use of linguistic modalities ("nearly," "seemed," "almost," etc.) that reinforce this indecision. Furthermore, it is assumed that this directive to the ideal reader also stipulates a nonpoetic and nonallegorical reading of the text. In other words, the rhetoric of allegorical correspondence, which would lead to the construction of a stable semantic universe, is replaced by a theory of reception based on a mental state, for the moment, unable to make a decision based on the competing claims being made in the text at crucial moments of textual significance. Though, as a structuralist, Todorov is concerned mainly with the inner "design" or "deep structure" of the texts, he nevertheless sees the importance of the reader in any theory of the fantastic. The category *reader* has been curiously missing from most of the major studies of the Gothic though, to be sure, Tompkins was aware of the large body of women readers for whom many of the "popular" late eighteenth-century novels were written. For Todorov, as I have said, the fantastic leads "a life full of dangers, and may evaporate at any moment."[44] Given these generic determinations and the significance of the "hesitating" reader, the historical Gothic does not belong to this genre. It belongs to the two adjacent genres of the "marvellous" and the "uncanny." By implication, then, Todorov reduced the Gothic to two "less interesting" genres that reflect two distinct branches of the Gothic: the first affirms the supernatural (*The Castle of Otranto, The Old English Baron, The Monk, Melmoth the Wanderer*, etc.), whereas the second confirms the rules of the "natural order" (*The Mysteries of Udolpho, The Italian*, etc.). Mary Shelley's *Frankenstein* and *The Last Man* would presumably make this neat taxonomy slightly suspect.

Todorov had veered clear of the psychoanalytic hermeneutic, a fact that, perhaps, accounts for both his strength and weakness. Although it allowed him to keep his generic structures relatively discrete, it led him to a total blindness toward the very obvious play of the self and other/nonself going on in the "fantastic." This blindness is corrected in Rosemary Jackson's study entitled *Fantasy: The Literature of Subversion*.[45] There are three distinct kinds of "inscriptions" going on in this work. The first relates to the elements of "madness" and the carnivalesque that draw upon the theories of Foucault and Bakhtin, respectively. The second is a shift toward the "polyphonic" nature of the fantastic, which Jackson borrows from Bakhtin's reading of the novel as an essentially dialogic form.[46] Here the "fantastic" is seen as a text with a multiplicity of voices, with a certain "structural indeterminacy" that eschews easy, unequivocal closure. The third is Freudian psychoanalysis as it is mediated in the discourse of Jacques Lacan. Through these three forms of inscriptions Jackson advances a complex theory of subversion that keeps the specificity of the "fantastic" as a "total" generic form (she does not adopt Todorov's typology, for instance), as well as "grounding" it in modes of material, human cognition (she does not, like Eric Rabkin,[47] insist either upon "alternative realities" or upon a mutually exclusive literary discourse, a "subcreation," as Tolkien defined fantasy[48]). In spite of these procedures, Jackson ends up advancing a "riot" or "surplus" of conflicting concepts of "subversion," so much so that I am not sure whether "fantasy" is not simply another word for "metafiction." There is thus no attempt to control what Umberto Eco has called these "structurally possible worlds."[49] Everything, in a way, may be deemed "subversive" in an all-embracing theory of fantasy. The specificity of the Gothic, either philosophically or historically, needs to be established first before its effects can be fully documented.

There is another kind of subversion in the Gothic that is detected by Eve Kosofsky Sedgwick in her remarkable study of male homosocial desire. She writes, "the Gothic novel [is] . . . an important locus for the working-out of some of the terms by which nineteenth- and twentieth-century European culture has used homophobia to divide and manipulate the male-homosocial spectrum."[50] There is, she observes, a later sub-group of the Gothic—*Caleb Williams, Frankenstein, The Confessions of a Justified Sinner* among them—whose plots might be likened to Freud's case studies, notably those of Dr. Schreiber and the Wolf Man. As we point out at some length later in this book, a work such as *Caleb Williams* is "emplotted" on the principle of the subject's persecution under the compulsion of another male. This subgroup brings to the fore the importance of "homophobic thematics"[51] to the construction of the Gothic novel. Apart from the explicit or implied gay tendencies of Walpole, Beckford, and Lewis, the Gothic novels themselves mark out homophobic plots through an almost paranoid reading of the male psyche.[52] What is finally suppressed are utterances that must remain repressed, commands that are "unspeakable," and narratives that cannot express their own epistemological basis. The homosocial sublime too finds its proof texts in the Gothic.

The Gothic as a locus for, or a literary archive of, cultural and historical trends finds its most articulate summation in Roland Paulson's brilliant study *Representations of Revolution.*[53] In his chapter on the Gothic he argues, persuasively I think, that Gothic narratives of the son killing his father to become, in turn, even more repressive (the paradigm case is Ambrosio in Matthew Gregory Lewis' *The Monk*) are recast as metaphors of the French Revolution itself.

> The gothic did in fact serve as a metaphor with which some contemporaries in England tried to understand what was happening across the channel in the 1790s. (217)

As a dark metaphor of the mind or, more accurately, as the symbolization of the repressed structures of the unconscious, the Gothic is a ready medium through which a reality (such as that of the French Revolution) may be sublimated and fears about it rechanneled through the discourses of art. Ronald Paulson, therefore, continues:

> I do not think there is any doubt that the popularity of gothic fiction in the 1790s and well into the nineteenth century was due in part to the widespread anxieties and fears in Europe aroused by the turmoil in France finding a kind of sublimation or catharsis in tales of darkness, confusion, blood, and horror. (220–21)

In the *Reflections on the Revolution in France,* Edmund Burke had in fact troped the Revolution as a false sublime, the sort of sublime that he had associated in his aesthetics (*A Philosophical Enquiry into the Origin of Our Ideas of the Sublime and Beautiful*) with the negative, blinding force of dazzling light. In other words, ordinary light (the beautiful) can also blind if it becomes too intense. The beautiful, then, becomes its very opposite, a false sublime, destructive and terrifying. Paulson demonstrates that Burke's personalization of the Revolution as the humiliation of the beautiful in the figure of Marie Antoinette and the corresponding masculinization of femininity by the women of Bastille (in some cases men disguised as women as it turned out) work precisely on the principle of this analogy about the effects of light. Revolution transforms the beautiful (Marie Antoinette) into the sublimely Gothic terror of disorderly men and women. Even as Paulson makes the connection between the narrative structures of the Gothic and their appropriation by writers, conservative and Jacobin alike, it must be stressed that Gothic texts are no straightforward sources of structures that one finds in a revolution, though the image of a Gothic patriarch fending off attempts by upstarts or misguided aristocratic princes to infiltrate the castle is an immensely powerful symbol of both empowerment and its absence. Contradictory as the image is, it is true that for Burke, as Mary Wollstonecraft recognized only too well,[54] the Gothic was a thoroughly systemic archive for the false sublime.

Nevertheless, it is true that the Gothic was an available discourse, especially dominant after 1789, that could be used as a highly mediatized allegory of the Revolution. The classic texts of the tyrant father and the rebellious son (*The Castle of Otranto, The Monk, The Italian*) speak of characters with strong oratorical skills who fail in the end because their desire is in excess of what the spectators can accept. The Gothic, in the words of Ronald Paulson, "offered a form in which inexpressible, hitherto unthinkable aspects of the human psyche could be symbolized and silenced" (223). At the same time the symbolization is done in a narrative in which logic and linearity are replaced by mystery and circularity: "the gothic describes a situation in which no one can understand or fathom anyone else's motives or actions" (224). That these are features also of the sublime obscurity of Burke is not surprising since the Gothic fed on Burke's aesthetics but also turned it on its head. The false sublime of the dazzling light is in fact the metaphor of the Gothic sublime after all and it is here that the use of the Gothic genre as a metaphor of the Revolution creates some difficulty. Unless the reader knows that ideologies function through the principle of inversion (what you see is not what the world really is) it is difficult to see how the Gothic could also have been read as a way of explaining a revolution that both Thomas Paine and Mary Wollstonecraft read along radically different lines to Burke. For them the French Revolution was the triumphant blasting of an impossibly reactionary ideology. It was the old régime that was the authoritarian law of the father against which a Wordsworthian Vaudracour (in the 1805–1806 *The Prelude*) would rebel unsuccessfully. It is the double discourse of Burke that Paulson recognizes and in so doing demonstrates the ideological uses and abuses of the Gothic form in the debates about the French Revolution in England.

The foregoing resume is not meant to be comprehensive, but it does help us establish the different ways in which the Gothic has been historically reconstituted. In some instances, as in Birkhead and Varma, the Gothic is a prior moment of the surreal in art or, conversely, a genre capable of sustaining a multiplicity of functions. Without claiming for the Gothic those "profound realizations about human consciousness" that Elizabeth R. Napier rightly castigates some critics for doing,[55] what one misses from these prior readings (and this is by no means an original observation) is an examination of the ways in which the Gothic itself re-theorized a particular form of aesthetic speculation. In other words, at the heart of Gothic discourse is the crucial problematic of the presentation of that which had previously been thought presentable as the mind now struggles to find an adequate image of its own dissolution (we anticipate here Benedict's question in Walpole's *The Mysterious Mother*: "Is my poor language nauseous?"). This failure is not a failure of consciousness, as Elizabeth Napier suggests,[56] rather, it is a failure that is part of the design of the sublime insofar as the sublime threatens our very capacities of cognitive judgment. The nonpresentability of the idea is a consequence of an acute disjunction between the signifier and the signified that puts into doubt the meaning-making capacity of linguistic signs themselves. In Walpole that disjunction had occasionally erupted through verbal ruptures in words such as "disculpate" (28), "being comprehensive" (31), and "wonnot be" (107), all of which were read by editors either as malapropisms or stylistic lapses.[57] We, therefore, cannot make the Gothic determinate, we cannot impose limits upon it, since our judgments cannot be based, finally, upon a particular historical, political, or social imperative. I think that this is where so many critics of the Gothic including Scott, Summers, and Punter go wrong, but Praz gets it right because he senses its radically different aesthetic designs. For Praz, the key to the profound otherness of the Gothic is to be located in an anti-realist architectural code made famous by the dramatic, but frightening, etchings of the mid-eighteenth-century Italian architect Piranesi. But just as Piranesi takes us to an abyss that incapacitates our powers of cognition and impedes our sense of aesthetic gratification in the sublime object, so, too, does the condition of the postmodern block our judgment as we are pushed into the phase of the doomed desire to pass beyond the hyperreal. This is a conjunction that I do not wish to establish in an unproblematic fashion. It is not that the historical Gothic is a precursor of the postmodern sublime, but that the postmodern definitions of the Gothic (recall Jackson and Sedgwick in particular) have uncanny resemblances (like the shock recognitions in the invisible depths of the dream-tangle) with Lyotard's readings of the postmodern sublime. As far as I am aware, the Gothic has not been read systematically through a hermeneutic that effectively considers this form as an earlier moment of the postmodern. To make the Gothic speak to us here and now we must return to Walter Benjamin's blasting open of the continuum of history. We do that through a postmodern intervention and a reading of the sublime not as a simple aesthetic category arising out of a delight with terror, but as the fundamental faculty of the imagination, which grasps the essence of the Gothic before reason supervenes and effectively silences it. This act of censorship is precisely what the Gothic refuses to accept, and it is at this point that the Gothic sublime is effectively the subject's entry into the abyss as it faces the full consequences of the failure to transcend. Where the Romantic sublime, finally, has the triumphant subject, the Gothic sublime is a version of the Lacanian Real as *"the embodiment of a pure negativity"*[58] into which the subject inscribes itself as an absence, a lack in the structure itself. Robert Kiely spoke of the subject in terms of the dislodgement of human centers. In the sublime object of the Gothic the subject is the site of a non-transcendental aesthetics. It is this basic problem of being hostage to the unpresentable that is the concern of this book as the erstwhile metaphors of quest and flame are now re-imaged as the Gothic sublime.

1

Theorizing the (Gothic) Sublime

"Whether some things that men think they do not know, are not for all that thoroughly comprehended by them; and yet, so to speak, though contained in themselves, are kept a secret from themselves? The idea of Death seems such a thing."[1] This passage occurs in Melville's *Pierre or The Ambiguities* at a crucial moment in the lives of Pierre and Isabel. It is a moment when Pierre has been effectively disinherited, and he must now face up to the consequences of his own ambiguous relationship with his half-sister. The things that men know, that are contained within, yet inexplicable; known, and yet not known, such as the idea of death, signify that sense of boundlessness and indeterminacy that threatens the definition of the subject. In short, Pierre reads Death as the abyss of the sublime. Regardless of the specific avatar of the sublime (as mechanically rhetorical or dynamically natural), it is always an overglutted sign, an excess/abscess, that produces an atmosphere of toxic breathlessness. The Gothic maidens retreat to the misplaced security of the pastoral sublime, the postmodern subjects to the oxygen mask. The terror—that final substratum of the Gothic sublime—remains the same. Melville's *Pierre* stands at the receiving end of an entire aesthetic of the sublime as the eighteenth century read the idea, as Kant and the post-Kantians expanded it, and as the Gothic enriched it by transforming this aesthetic into a psychology. In this respect *Pierre* anticipates, as the Gothic texts did, the sublime as a moment of entry into the unconscious, the "unplumbable," the tangled depth of the dream-text that surfaces in life only as certain effects like that of the "uncanny." In the classic formulation of Kant (to which all theorizations of the sublime return) the effects are the consequence of the mind's confrontation with an idea too large for expression, too self-consuming to be contained in any adequate form of representation, but which idea, as representation, in a momentary surrender of the law of reason the mind nevertheless grasps. The desire to present that which is unpresentable, that which is sublime, in the first sustained burst of capital in the second half of the eighteenth century also troped itself into a literary phenomenon subsequently designated "Gothic." The sublime empowerment of the Gothic, in Melville's American version, constructs an unnameable dread (*das Unform*), a kind of a symbolic blockage, that threatens subjectivity itself.

It is this premonition of the Longinian *hypsous* that leads to Pierre's mental disintegration and the writing, on his part, of two books. One is a public book—if it ever finds a publisher—but the other is a kind of "primitive elementalizing" (304) that, of course, "can not be composed on the paper, but only as the other is writ down in his soul" (304). Like a "vast lumbering planet," this book "revolves in his aching head" (305). When both Lucy and Isabel offer to be Pierre's "amanuenses" (349) for that "vile book" (348) that somehow always remains unfinished, Pierre replies: "Impossible! I fight a duel in which all seconds are forbid" (349). The ambiguous feelings that constitute this inner writing, and the total incapacity of a second to understand it, are such that they are "entirely untranslatable into any words that can be used" (353).

Pierre or The Ambiguities is Melville's sublime, a powerfully fractious rendition of the program of the sublime as Kant, the post-Kantians and the Gothic read that concept. For we know that in Kant's moment of the sublime, and especially in the negative sublime, discourse itself breaks down as reason struggles with imagination for ascendancy: what can be grasped is not equivalent to what is meaningful. The resultant discourse—a ruptured discourse—can come from either the signifiers (the objects) that cannot be grasped or the signified (the mind), which in itself is overwhelmed by the highly overdetermined characteristics of this "colossal" experience. What this leads to is a failure in representation through a massive disturbance as the texts, in trying to present the unpresentable, veer toward collapse. This is also the postmodern condition for which the Gothic, it seems, is a kind of traumatized earlier moment. Without wishing to collapse the different stages of capital and the legitimate linkages between the postmodern and late commodified capitalism (that is, without wishing to collapse different historical moments) the rhetoric of the Gothic sublime may be seen as somehow anticipating the postmodern. It is here that the return to the sublime on the part of key theoreticians of postmodernism (notably Jameson and Lyotard) needs to be clarified because its rebirth "in the panic-stricken and commodity-glutted aesthetics of postmodernism"[2] is under the injunction, under the sign, under the (dis) guise of the Gothic.

Whence the attractiveness of the term? In recent years we have used (and abused) every possible association of the word sublime: the Romantic sublime, the American sublime, the Indian sublime, the nuclear sublime, the Arctic sublime, the female sublime, the imperial sublime, the post-Kantian sublime, the postmodern sublime, the textual sublime, the religious sublime, the Oedipal sublime, the oppositional sublime, the Euro-American sublime, the Enlightenment sublime, the genetic sublime, the moral sublime, the technological sublime, to name a few. In all these sublimes there is clearly some understanding of limits or boundary implied in the descriptors that act as markers of containment. At the same time it is clear that the varieties of sublime indicated in this list demonstrate what David Morris has called the impossible quest for "a single, unchanging feature or essence."[3] Regardless of the historical or periodic positioning of a specific sublime (say, the Arctic sublime, with its emphasis on the European sense of disempowerment in the face of the Arctic void and the kinds of knowledges, both human and barbaric, the voyages in search of the Northwest Passage symbolized[4]), the central problematic of the sublime is still a relic of the old questions about what we mean by the sublime: is it "apprehension or comprehension, syntagmatic or paradigmatic, infinite or limited"?[5] To borrow Steven Knapp's ideas for a moment here, we always ask ourselves three fundamental questions: what is the nature of the sublime object (the text), who is the agent that produces this object (the author), and what is the nature of the spectator (the reader) who encounters the object?[6] Depending on our ideological position, we may well have radically different answers. Before theorizing the female sublime, Patricia Yaeger, for instance, called the sublime a genre of "questionable use . . . old fashioned, outmoded, concerned with self-centered [male] imperialism." Nevertheless, even as the sublime celebrates its phallocentricity (though some of the great practitioners of the Gothic sublime were women), for Yaeger the sublime's very real sense of empowerment and transport, of authority, makes it a "genre the woman writer needs."[7] The female sublime is ideological and critical, since it draws its strength from a critique of a sublime male subjectivity. But this subjectivity itself may be turned on its head through the "what if" question: what if the sublime object were to "leak into the subject," as Peter de Bolla asks?[8] What if the triad of Knapp's questions were to collapse only into an endless subjectivity, both in the political and ethical sense of the word? What if there is nothing but effects of subjectivity, constructions of the object whose validity, whose reality (as the Lacanian Real, so to speak) were to reside only in consciousness? The shift from the rhetorical/natural/ideological to the psychological is clearly implicit in these questions. It is at this juncture that we can make our initial intervention on behalf of the Gothic, without in any way suggesting that any sublime (whether Gothic or Romantic, whether American or Indian, whether nuclear or postmodern) can be wholly original or different. We are in fact tracing a genealogy (of the Gothic sublime) that can't possibly have a genealogy (origins, histories, and so on); we are talking about an adjective that transplants or supersedes the noun substantive, and this is clearly not one.

Our aim, therefore, is to theorize a Gothic sublimity that corresponds to the textual evidence. We need to articulate the Gothicness of the Gothic sublime, both in terms of its difference from and affinities with what may be collectively termed versions of the Enlightenment sublime. We shall give these versions the generic title of "the historical sublime." Our key concept will be the idea of surplus, excess, or spillage that surrounds the discourse of the sublime. There has been an historical tendency to read the Gothic sublime as the natural sublime, as an object-based sublime that excluded the affective subject and the rhetorical trope (language). Though we know that this has never been the whole story of the sublime, Gothic or not, the tendency to read it thus is linked to a need to specify the historical moment of the Gothic through a citation of Gothic special effects (a kind of early version of the technological sublime) in which secret, hidden vaults, and the general hyperreality of the Gothic dreamscape, were seen as somehow signifying something very special about the Gothic. To an extent, the symbolic linking of the Gothic to metaphors of the labyrinth is heuristically essential for an adequate theory of the Gothic. However, the cataloging of objects of terror is only part of the total story, because it insinuates a Gothic exclusivity that does not exist. To shift from Gothic terror (a critical dominant for so long) to the Gothic sublime means that we can intervene into the Gothic through a much more pervasive and contradictory aesthetic. In other words, we now break the boundaries of the Gothic by using it to challenge the received wisdom of the sublime itself. The bold claim that we would want to make is that no sublime, not even the Gothic sublime, is pure in terms of either discursivity or phenomenality. All sublimes are contaminated, though some sublimes are less contaminated (but equally contaminable) than others. Our working definition would then take some such form as the following. The Gothic sublime is not a definitive form in its own right; it is a symbolic structure, historically determined though not rigidly constrained by the dawn of capitalism, around which a host of other sublimes intersect. The Gothic tropes the sublime as the unthinkable, the unnameable, and the unspeakable, always making it, the sublime, and its basic forms (the rhetorical and the natural) both incommensurable with each other and in excess of language. The phantasmagoria of the Gothic sublime, as the projection of a psychic terror, finally leads to the unpresentability of death itself. It is not what the Gothic sublime *is* that is crucial, it is what it *effects* that is its essence.

Any idea that is in excess of language signifies the death of its own medium of representation, that is, of language itself. In narrative theory, as Foucault tells us, "writing so as not to die . . . is a task undoubtedly as old as the world."[9] The "postmodern"/"postmortem" phrase ("In the nights of prenativity and post-mortemity," wrote Joyce in *Ulysses*[10])—writing so as not to die—gestures toward a sublime capacity involving our consciousness about language itself. For speech is marked by a compulsion toward its own self-dissolution, its own nirvana, that narrative attempts to circumvent by prolonging through writing.

> Perhaps there exists in speech an essential affinity between death, endless striving, and the self-representation of language. Perhaps the figure of a mirror to infinity erected against the black wall of death is fundamental for any language from the moment it determines to leave a trace of its passage.[11]

Language, therefore, acts out the procedures and processes of this deferral or postponement—the prolongation of the moment of death when speech is consumed by silence. The great epic poets, the singers of great tales—these minstrels, through their glorification of personality and a conception of utterance as endless repetition indeed got around the compulsion toward death by effectively stilling narratives. The *Mahābhārata* is replete with the name of the subject followed by the verb *to say,* hence *arjuna uvāca,* "Arjuna said." Again, in another twist of Odysseus' autonarrative, Demodecus recounts to the Phaecians, in Odysseus' own presence, Odysseus' tale, already a thousand years old.

The epic poets' "self-enclosed expression" of the glory of the work they transmitted comes to an end more or less at about the same time as the beginnings of late eighteenth-century tales of terror. In the "languages" that make up the tales of terror we discover an uncanny image of language itself. "These simple languages . . . ," writes Foucault, "are curiously double"[12] because they mirror their own mortality in the act of writing. Thus, Sade's "pastiche of all the philosophies and stories of the eighteenth century,"[13] written to no one from the confines of his prison walls, expresses the boundless doubling and redoubling of language. Where epic certainty had once prolonged life through the device of the twice-told tale, the tales of terror now turn inward and become regressive. The prolongation becomes a matter of reaching outward toward a form that is curiously double because it can only repeat a desire for the unpresentable without ever finding any adequate image for it. The language of the Gothic now presages not the prolongation of life but its opposite: we speak so as to die. A text such as Maturin's *Melmoth the Wanderer* that seemingly prolongs itself through the device of the tale within the tale (a narrative mediatization that is not uncommon in the Gothic generally) nevertheless can no longer construct the certainties of the epic narrators for whom writing could prolong life. The *Mahābhārata,* for instance, never comes to an end. Contemporary reviewers of *Melmoth the Wanderer* sensed this schism in the narrative when they spoke of a "diseased imagination" obsessed by "unwholesome recreations" carrying an "exploded predilection for *impossibility.*"[14] Earlier, William Beckford's *Vathek,* with its wildness and extravagance, its orientalist flavor and Arabian Nights narrative—*Vathek* anticipates Salman Rushdie—had had the same doubling effect. But the doubling, this inward turn of the narrative, occurs through a curious process of inversion, through a construction of a parallel, almost parodistic, text that mirrors, critically, the self-enclosing, functional claims of the narrative. The Gothics "were not meant to be read at the level of their writing or the specific dimensions of their language; they wished to be read for the things they recounted, for this emotion, fear, horror, or pity," writes Foucault.[15] Foucault inserts into the texts of the Gothic a form of reception aesthetics in which the "rabble of the senses" momentarily questions the primacy of reason. In their emphasis on emotions and feelings, the Gothic texts, like parasites, release a poison that consumes the host and confronts it with its own self-evident though inferior logic. A profane daemonization of space (sacred or otherwise) takes place as the castles, for instance, undergo remarkable degrees of sexual and social contamination. The reader senses an *Es Spukt hier* effect, the haunting effect of the religious visibility/invisibility that Mircea Eliade detects in the believer's construction of the initial sacred space.[16] The haunting presence/absence of the uncanny inscribed in the Gothic, and its seemingly paradoxical endorsement of death, is seen by Foucault as the real agenda of the Gothic. It is this agenda that underpins the Gothic sublime.

Foucault's archaeology of faked immortality through the endless deferrals of the epic has its other side in the frightening mortality of writing in the Gothic sublime. The epic was built on a teleology; the Gothic passes the sublime, unresolved, to future generations. In a deconstructive echo of the postmodern, the Gothic becomes a force field that intervenes into the continuum of history and blasts it open. What this procedure implies is a kind of an aesthetic rendition of history that now requires us to go beyond theories of orderly narratives to those of the sublime. Since, as we have already seen, all versions of the sublime in Western thought, at any rate, have the same starting point, we need to construct a history of the sublime so as to make more meaningful our claim that the Gothic sublime insinuates a postmodernity in its undermining of a realist economy of meaning. To make this somewhat difficult connection possible, I would like to isolate the major trope of the Gothic—the sublime—and read it with a view to establishing its resonances with the postmodern.

The sublime has now become a trope that is somehow antianalytic, suprasensible, and beyond the grasp of our cognitive faculties. Rereading it in the light of religious philosophers such as Mircea Eliade and Rudolf Otto (who preferred to use terms such as "hierophanic vision" and "the numinous") one begins to sense the "sublime" (here in quotation marks) as a kind of a radical Other, the perennial underside, of materialist politics and sociology. In many ways, then, the postmodern (mis) appropriations of this term signal also a remarkable disenchantment with scientific paradigms and theories of knowledge, in that the sublime allows us a freedom (in both the intellectual and interpersonal spheres) from the highly organized world that, increasingly, we inhabit. The constitutive features of this world and the significance of the sublime in coming to terms with it are best summarized by one of the foremost postmodern theorists, Fredric Jameson:

> a new depthlessness, which finds its prolongation both in contemporary "theory" and in a whole new culture of the image or the simulacrum; a consequent weakening of historic-

> ity, both in our relationship to public History and in the new forms of our private temporality, whose "schizophrenic" structure (following Lacan) will determine new types of syntax or syntagmatic relationships in the more temporal arts; a whole new type of emotional ground tone—what I will call "intensities"—which can best be grasped by a return to older theories of the sublime. . . .[17]

Jameson connects the postmodern sublime with the third stage of capital (he follows Ernest Mandel here), where the reality of social and economic institutions is "only dimly perceivable." In this stage capital is "hypermobile" and "hyperflexible" as dispersed production under the sign of global transfers of capital now displaces the old-fashioned monopolistic capitalism that frames the later eighteenth-century Gothic. The sublime then becomes a metaphor of that which is beyond the "capacity of the normal reading mind" faced with the complexities of the digital information networks of the third "decentered global network."[18] The final aim of Jameson's project is to offer a theory of the fractured nature of postmodern or technological subject in terms of an equally disfigured and dehumanized multinational capitalism. For this reason "older theories of the sublime" are dragged out in an act of pseudopanic to explain the subject "blissed out before feats of postmodern commodification."[19] The bliss in question here is, of course, a negative bliss, a terrifying bliss whose analogue is not simply the general trope of the sublime but the more specific trope of the Gothic sublime and its subsequent avatars. Because the Gothic is the absolute negative of this bliss, the linking of the genre of the Gothic with postmodernity has a different order of social payoff. The Gothic sublime and the sublime of late capital are linked by the definitions of the subject. A bourgeois individualism that produced through its imperial apparatus a tea-drinking culture in the eighteenth century[20] now finds itself in the grip of the American postcolonial drug overlords. The analogy may sound obscene, but both are linked to similar histories of dispossession and colonization. Peter de Bolla has in fact made a very strong case that the discourse of debt in the mid-eighteenth century crossed with that of the sublime to construct a subject as " the excess or overplus of discourse itself: as the remainder, that which cannot be appropriated or included within the present discursive network of control."[21]

The literary Gothic of the late eighteenth and early nineteenth centuries was one example of a seemingly barbaric document, to use Walter Benjamin's phrase,[22] that is also the occluded text of the postmodern. It offers in a stark, uncompromising form a textuality (recall Jameson's summary of the discursive features of the postmodern) in which many of the current issues surrounding experimentation, the affirmation of discontinuous histories, the fractured subject, radical and unstable epistemologies, the distrust of *grands récits*, ideological commitment, and legitimation had already been played out. All these features recall Lyotard's definition of modernity in the *locus classicus* text for contemporary debates on the postmodern:

> Modernity, in whatever age it appears, cannot exist without a shattering of belief and without discovery of the "lack of reality" of reality, together with the invention of other realities.[23]

The "'lack of reality' of reality" has a familiar Gothic ring about it. Nietzsche had called this nihilism, and enthusiastic postmodern critics have endorsed the equation. For a good critic of postmodernism like Arthur Kroker, the connection may be underlined through a reading of Giorgio de Chirico, "the painter of postmodernism *par excellence*."[24] Seen from Kroker's perspective, what Chirico's paintings demonstrate so clearly is the impossibility of the real, the "representable." As *the* artist of nihilism Chirico "understood the full consequences of Nietzsche's accusation that in a world in which conditions of existence are transposed into 'predicates of being,' it would be the human fate to live through a fantastic inversion and cancellation of the order of the real. Commodity into sign, history into semiurgy, concrete labor into abstract exchange, perspective into simulation."[25] Chirico poses the rupture of Western consciousness, a nihilism that is both "the limit and possibility of *historical* emancipation."[26] In Chirico's *Landscape Painter* Kroker sees precisely those features that are the hallmarks of postmodernism: the impossibility of representation, humanity's imprisonment in the dead empire of signs, the end of power, truth, history, and nature as referential finalities, the "metamorphosis of society into a geometry of signs."[27]

Nietzsche, Chirico, cynical history, the end of the emancipating quality of history, the logic of the sign, our existence only within the sign itself (with the possibility of the "beyond the sign" articulated so forcefully in *The Will to Power*)—these are the loci of the postmodern, the discourses of which permeate culture at every turn.[28] The heterogeneity of elements, language games, as well as the triumph of local determinism, in the postmodern social formation, make it impossible for us, as subjects, to unify, in one image (as V. S. Naipaul does) the multiplicity of narratives that bombard us from all sides. It is for this reason that appeal to the sublime becomes an uncanny repetition of the Gothic situation we have already sketched. Hence Lyotard's return to the sublime: "it is in the aesthetic of the sublime that modern art (including literature) finds its impetus and the logic of avant-gardes finds its axioms."[29] In Lyotard's summary the defining characteristic of the sublime is a "strong and equivocal emotion." The "equivocality" of this emotion is a result of the origin of the sublime in pain. Unlike judgments on beauty, which are a matter of consensus as the mind creates stable harmonies, the sublime is a radically different sentiment. Before we proceed any further, we must quickly historicize the sublime so that we can ground our own readings of the Gothic in an identifiable and discrete body of knowledge.

"As a power to make trouble for categorizing procedures,"[30] wrote Donald Pease in an exemplary essay, the sublime has come to be seen as a thoroughly independent, defiantly disruptive, trope not unwilling to make trouble in the realms of aesthetics, rhetoric, or politics. "Theories of beauty," as one of the great critics of the sublime, Samuel H. Monk, had also noted, "are relatively trim and respectable; but in theories of the sublime one catches the century somewhat off its guard, sees it, as it were, without powder and pomatum, whalebone and patches."[31] Monk's remarkable study points out in great detail the complexity of the diverse theories of the sublime in the eighteenth century, and the dangers of reducing the sublime to the formulations of any one aesthetician. The crucial moment that marked the beginnings of interest in the sublime was Boileau's translation (1674) and re-reading of Longinus' *Peri Hypsous* ("Sublime"). Having defined the sublime as a

> certain power of discourse which is calculated to elevate and to ravish the soul, and which comes either from grandeur of thought . . . or from magnificence of words. . . .[32]

Boileau rewrote the rhetorical sublime as the effect of subjectivity. Such was the impact of Boileau's translation that the original Greek text of *Peri Hypsous* was regularly printed and between 1710 and 1789 no fewer than fourteen editions were available.[33] The commentaries that these editions spawned, however, indicate that the eighteenth century was not particularly interested in total definitions. Instead we find a much greater interest in specific effects, in thematizations of the sublime, and in the whole question of emotional intensities. The key figure in the English theorizations of the sublime is, of course, Edmund Burke. However, it seems unlikely that Burke's singular achievement would have been possible without the intermediate work of John Dennis.

In both *The Advancement and Reformation of Modern Poetry* (1701) and in its incomplete sequel *The Grounds of Criticism in Poetry* (1704) Dennis expanded Boileau's reading of the sublime as residing in a great artist's mind to make a series of correlations between the sublime, the highest art, and the expression of the greatest passion. These three (the sublime, great art, and passion) are connected, finally, through a theory of association. The theory itself is never made explicit (Dennis did not have a sophisticated aesthetic discourse that he could use for his theory) but the "associationist" move on the part of Dennis took him to what he called "Enthusiastic Passions," which were "admiration, terror, horror, joy, sadness, and desire."[34] These "enthusiastic passions," however, imply a hitherto undertheorized connection between the sublime and terror. The paradox of pleasure arising from the seemingly unpleasurable—from terror, from pain, from the grotesque and ugly, in short, from the body itself—was not only enormously fascinating to the English mind, but also intellectually frustrating, since contemporary neoclassical theories could not account for it. Dennis' use of the concept of the sublime to explain the inexplicable, the "excessive," the "Other," is the first clear statement about how terror escaped from the order of neoclassicism by aligning itself with the lawless sublime. It is as though the "narrative of terror" is the first of our language games that could not coexist unproblematically with the grand narrative of a neoclassic epistemology. Dennis was, however, unhappy with a broad semantic class called "terror." He therefore divided it into "Common Terror" and "Enthusiastick Terror" so as to be able to distinguish between the religious and nonreligious sublime. "Enthusiastick Terror" may sound to us a rather peculiar phrase, but Dennis wished to use it to designate the human state of mind confronted with the wrath of God as the most intense moment of the sublime.[35] Eighteenth-century meanings of "enthusiastic" and "enthusiasm" were closely aligned to their original Greek root as signifying "possession by a god, supernatural inspiration, prophetic or poetic frenzy," or "pertaining to, or of the nature of, possession by a deity" (*Oxford English Dictionary*). It is in this semantic context that Dennis' use of "Enthusiastik Terror" should be considered. In making the connection between terror, religious awe, and the sublime through the centrality of emotion, Dennis foreshadowed Edmund Burke's reduction of the individual subject to the effects of a particular structure of emotion based on an unresolved tension between a scientific empiricism on the one hand and a psychological idealism on the other.[36] The technology of the sublime in Burke is terror.

By the time Burke published his essay in 1757, the sublime had become more or less absorbed into the English language.[37] Longinus' *Peri Hypsous* was readily available in the original, and English translations of the original or of Boileau kept the debates alive. Edward Young ("The Complaint, or Night Thoughts on Life, Death and Mortality"), Joseph Warton ("The Enthusiast: or the Lover of Nature"), and Mark Akenside ("The Pleasures of Imagination"), among other poets, drew on contemporary readings of the sublime, which by now had incorporated, after Addison and John Baillie (author of the posthumously published *An Essay on the Sublime,* 1747), the related concepts of the "unbounded" and the "immensity of [its] views."[38] In Akenside's "The Pleasures of Imagination" we read:

> From the womb of earth,
> From ocean's bed they come: th' eternal heav'ns
> Disclose their splendours, and the dark abyss
> Pours out her births unknown.[39]

In this version of the sublime the effects of horror come from castrating amphibian females. The vision is in fact quite frightening, because birth is imaged as an act of perversion from the womblike ocean's bed and from the dark abyss. At the same time the Gothic pouring forth of splendors, which are to be read as negative delights, fails to arouse the intensities of terror one associates with Edmund Burke. It is only in Burke that the subject actually faces the pleasures of impotence transgressively offered by the sublime.

The source of (negative) pleasure for Burke is pain, and it is on this basic dichotomy of pain and pleasure that Burke constructs a series of eight emotional effects which, as Craig Howes' summary shows very clearly, follows from two mutually exclusive sensationist positions. Pain generates self-preservation, terror, and the sublime, while pleasure "enlists the social passions" related to society, love, and the beautiful.[40] These are what in Sanskrit poetics one would call the effects of *rasas,* aesthetic states that are mental correlates of real emotions (*bhāvas*) in the world outside.[41] The primacy given to terror, however, underlies a much more pervasive belief in Burke about the ruling passions of the sublime, for which terror was the only real source. But Burke's sensationist aesthetics have no room for mediating categories, since emotions and their mental transformations are absolutely identical, as *rasas* and *bhāvas* are not. It is here that Burke's principle of terror as the source of the sublime lacks that daemonization of the spirit and its sublimation that are the hallmarks of the Gothic sublime.

> Whatever is fitted in any sort to excite the ideas of pain, and danger, that is to say, whatever is in any sort terrible, or is conversant about terrible objects, or operates in a manner analogous to terror, is a source of the *sublime*; that is, it is productive of the strongest emotion which the mind is capable of feeling. (39)

Even as Burke defines the experience of the sublime through the technology of terror, he still works with absolute categories, since his terror and sublime are somehow ideas that require no mediation whatsoever. There is no intransigence in these terms, they become the secret, veiled characteristics of the occluded hero of the sublime who is, for Burke, God. The empowerment of language that Burke especially endorses (at the expense of pictures) associates the most powerful feelings with a Burkean deity who, finally, confirms that the effects of sublimity will not lead to the construction of Akenside's monsters. The same sense of absolutism is to be found in Burke's definition of "Astonishment":

> The passion caused by the great and sublime in *nature*, when those causes operate most powerfully, is Astonishment; and astonishment is that state of the soul, in which all its motions are suspended, with some degree of horror. In this case the mind is so entirely filled with its object, that it cannot entertain any other, nor by consequence reason on that object which employs it. Hence arises the great power of the sublime, that far from being produced by them, it anticipates our reasonings, and hurries us on by an irresistible force. Astonishment, as I have said, is the effect of the sublime in its highest degree; the inferior effects are admiration, reverence and respect. (57)

The capitulation of the subject in the face of the "passion" of astonishment, it seems, is a profoundly religious experience that connects the passage directly with the devotional sublime. Since for Burke the object of astonishment remains the unnameable presence of God, the sublime in this theorization cannot possibly connect the subject itself with the will to dominate. In this regard, as Adorno recognized, there is a greater complicity with domination in Immanuel Kant, because in linking the sublime with power he pushed the subject beyond Burke's fundamentally consensus aesthetics to reimage the procedures of thinking the unthinkable. In this version of empowerment, the subject, as "an epistemological entrepreneur,"[42] must remain constantly active and forever vigilant.

Whereas the beautiful in Kant, writes Paul de Man, "is a metaphysical and ideological principle, the sublime aspires to be a transcendental one, with all that this entails."[43] It is this hidden agenda of the transcendental that leads Kant to qualify the sublime with the adjective *absolutely* so that the phrase would broach no comparison whatsoever. Admittedly, the sections in the *Critique of Judgement* that deal with the sublime (Part 1, Book 2, sections 23–28) are among the most difficult and unresolved passages in Kant generally. This is largely because Kant's aim, to paraphrase Donald Pease, is to authenticate the discipline of aesthetics without erasing the subject that the sublime ("an outrage to our imagination") proposes to disrupt.[44] Kant had in fact observed:

> For the beautiful in nature we must seek a ground external to ourselves, but for the sublime one merely in ourselves and the attitude of mind that introduces sublimity into the representation of nature.[45]

Terry Eagleton most certainly has this passage in mind when he writes:

> In the presence of beauty, we experience an exquisite sense of adaptation of the mind to reality; but in the turbulent presence of the sublime we are forcibly reminded of the limits of our dwarfish imaginations and admonished that the world as infinite totality is not ours to know. It is as though in the sublime the 'real' itself—the eternal, ungraspable totality of things—inscribes itself as the cautionary limit of all mere ideology, of all complacent subject-centredness, causing us to feel the pain of incompletion and unassuaged desire.[46]

Sublimity in this definition is not a quality intrinsic to the object, as one finds in the rhetorical sublime (an essentially aesthetico-stylistic category) or the medieval *sublimitas* and *humilitas,* which were "ethico-theological categories"[47]; rather, it is profoundly, principally, and preeminently a state of mind contemplating its own supersensible being. In Kant's classic formulation:

> *The sublime is that, the mere capacity of thinking which evidences a faculty of mind transcending every standard of sense* (98),

the demonstrative *that* clearly alludes to infinity as a whole, a fact which explains Kant's rather austere thesis. Imagination fails to satisfy reason's demand for totality and yet, it seems, it is reason that leads imagination to the condition of the sublime because it wishes to enter, momentarily, into a pre-Oedipal chaos, the realm of the Lacanian *imaginary,* which it, as law, cannot countenance.

Consequently, the experience of the sublime pushes the imagination to crisis point, to a point of exhaustion and chaos. But precisely because of the extreme condition of the imagination—"our incapacity to attain to an idea *that is a law for us*"—we are filled with "RESPECT" (105). This reverence arises from a failure to grasp what reason has established as law, that is, the transformation of everything into an absolute whole. Reason must totalize; the sublime gestures toward the unattainable. Now this is the cause of a fundamental contradiction or confusion that gives rise to an ambiguous state of pleasure and displeasure. Displeasure, because the imagination fails to deliver the absolute, that is, unqualified magnitude (the condition of the sublime), and pleasure, because in spite of this failure the imagination is nevertheless in accord with reason, insofar as it attempts to achieve the aim of the law of reason, which is totality.

> The feeling of the sublime is, therefore, at once a feeling of displeasure, arising from the inadequacy of imagination in the aesthetic estimation of magnitude to attain to its estimation by reason, and a simultaneously awakened pleasure, arising from this very judgement of the inadequacy of the greatest faculty of sense being in accord with ideas of reason, so far as the effort to attain to these is for us a law. (106)

The feeling of the sublime as an alternation is also a sign of its essential mobility. It is not a feeling that arises out of static or *"restful"* contemplation; on the contrary, it has a certain kinetic energy, a vibration, a motion, "a sense of power"[48] that explains why it is attracted *and* repelled by the same object. This vibration, alternation, or simply energy is a consequence of precisely those forces which give rise to the sublime. The imagination wishes to grasp the unimaginable, the limitless, the nonpresentable, and is driven to limits, to excess, as a consequence. Unchecked, such an excess might well be symptomatic of madness or other mental disorders; halted and checked, it becomes part of a crucial ambiguity that is at the very heart of Kant's reading of the sublime. This check, and the consequent paradox, comes from the human faculty of reason, which finds nothing unusual or excessive in this attempt to find a correlate for the unimaginable.

> The point of excess for the imagination (towards which it is driven in the apprehension of the intuition) is like an abyss in which it fears to lose itself; yet again for the rational idea of the supersensible it is not excessive, but conformable to law, and directed to drawing out such an effort on the part of the imagination: and so in turn as much a source of attraction as it was repellent to mere sensibility. (107)

At one level these passages may be mobilized toward a Romantic aesthetics of the sublime, which, historically, has in fact been the case. Yet the furious sense of alternation implied here, the whole question of an almost pathological attraction and repulsion, goes well beyond Romanticism and connects directly with the Gothic. Much of what is implied here is the shock of the new that one associates with postmodernism. The sublime may be read with this function in mind. The kind of compensatory movement that follows the initial moment of shock, the play between what Neil Hertz has termed the "mental overload" and release, between "confusion and assurance," between the processes of attraction and repulsion, "the drama of the imagination's collapse and reason's intervention,"[49] can be readily mapped onto a Freudian discourse. Imagination, guilty and excessive, would wish to cancel out the anteriority of the law of reason, the superego, with its interdicts and proprietorial claims. The ego, in turn wishes to displace, through excessive identification and collapse, the father, reason, superego. And this is where the process of the sublime, in the Freudian discourse, becomes so fascinating. The sublime therefore aspires to the condition of pre- or nondifference, to the state of the pre-Oedipal phase, when, in the words of Wordsworth, "the faint sense which we have of its individuality is lost in the general sense of duration belonging to the Earth itself."[50] Wordsworth is remarkably Kantian in his essay ("The Sublime and the Beautiful") and is conscious of the intersubjective nature of the sublime experience when he draws the distinction between viewing a mountain from a distance and situating oneself close enough "yet not so near that the whole of it is visible."[51] Threatened by its formlessness, the "comparing power of the mind" is then suspended in the contemplation of the sublime as the "absolutely great," in comparison with which, as Kant noted, *"all else is small"* (97). "Sublimity, therefore," concludes Kant:

> does not reside in any of the things of nature, but only in our own mind, in so far as we may become conscious of our superiority over nature within, and thus also over nature without us (as exerting influence upon us). (114)

One gains access to the sublime through self-contemplation, unrestrained by other demands or imperatives. In this narrative "the sublime is simply the heightened consciousness of beholding oneself beholding the world."[52] Or else it is the extreme instance of Kant's "lawlessness without a law,"[53] revealing in this memorable phrase a purposiveness without purpose, an antidote to Kant's own uncompromising appeal to abstract reason but, at the same time, a further confirmation of the centrality of the subject, rationally defined through the categories of pure and practical reason, as "sovereign," "buoyantly active, with all the productive energy of an epistemological entrepreneur."[54] The subject may well be sovereign, but he or she is nevertheless pushed by the sublime toward a redefinition of his or her own sovereignty by the need to confront his or her own incompletion in the presence of limitlessness, turbulent and ungraspable. As we have already noted, however, this dual movement, which is marked by an excessive desire followed by its lack, paradoxically confirms the centrality of the subject and his/her capacity to avoid total dissolution in the sublime. The sublime representative of this position is, quite naturally, the mature Wordsworth of *Resolution and Independence*. Put in this manner, the Kantian sublime is defiantly Romantic and raises important questions about how another sublime, the Gothic, which both antedates the Kantian and feeds on it may be defined.

For Samuel H. Monk, with whom we began this section, theorizing the sublime more or less comes to an end with Kant; the "eighteenth-century aesthetic has as its unconscious goal the *Cri-*

tique of Judgment."[55] This is no throwaway line since after the *Third Critique* we find philosophers quite self-consciously using Kant as their point of departure. Schopenhauer makes this connection explicit: "My line of thought, different as its content is from the Kantian is completely under its influence, and necessarily presupposes and starts from it."[56] The same indebtedness may be seen in Schiller and Hegel as well. In matters of the sublime Kant then becomes the grand patriarch who dominates the scene. One,therefore, speaks under a kind of Kantian interdiction. But since the sublime in Kant had, however contradictorily, a transcendental presence, it is not identical with the Gothic sublime, for which the primacy of reason cannot be taken for granted. In this respect Schiller's connection of the sublime with "the *pure daemon*"[57] in us, as both an ontology and a phenomenology, Hegel's incorporation of negativity in the miserable corporeality of the Real, and Schopenhauer's decisive rewriting of the sublime through the nirvana principle (an oceanic consciousness that is clearly linked to the Indian sublime: *ahaṃ kṛtsnasya jagataḥ prabhavaḥ pralayas tathā*, "I am the origin of this entire universe and its dissolution," said Krishna to Arjuna in the *Bhagavadgītā*) begin to shift the sublime toward the Gothic. The daemonic in us (Schiller) and the oceanic sense of dissolution (Schopenhauer) are clearly linked to the impossible object (the Lacanian Real or the Hegelian supersensible Idea) that leads us to the paradox of representation at the heart of the sublime. In the words of Slavoj Žižek:

> The Sublime is therefore the paradox of an object which, in the very field of representation, provides a view, in a negative way, of the dimension of what is unrepresentable.[58]

There is, then, an epistemological inadequacy, a negativity that governs the sublime. The impossible representation of the idea, in its negation, proposes the incomparable greatness of the Thing in question as it also connects the imagination with pain. Not surprisingly, for Kant there was "no more sublime passage in the Jewish Law than the commandment: Thou shalt not make unto thee any graven image . . . " (127).

If we take Kant's metaphorical analogy seriously, then for the Gothic, as for Melville, the impossible idea, the "no more sublime passage," is the idea of death itself, since death is quite beyond representation. The mind introjects the fear of death (for Burke the cause of absolute terror) and the subject defines itself in terms of this absolute negativity (which cannot be imaged). It is here that the Gothic becomes one of the key texts of the sublime and the effective literary source of the "uncanny" as sublimation. In Schopenhauer's oceanic manifestation the sublime is the terrifying metaphor of the confrontation of the desiring self with a world that is ontologically locked into suffering (the Buddhist *duḥkha*). To the rational mind, however, the final horror is that the oceanic sublime is also the end of narrative, and of history, as epic certainty is replaced by Gothic unpredictability. The uncanny logic of this version of the sublime is to be found in the Gothic.

Hence the metaphysics of human superiority espoused by Kant are no longer the conditions of the sublime. Instead, death is embraced contemplatively, and idealism is now tempered by pessimism and human insignificance. Desire becomes a thing-in-itself, and since it is founded on lack (we desire that which we do not possess), the oceanic sublime becomes the desired object. Unless, as Freud qualifies it, the reality principle intervenes, this *nirvana* principle, this death instinct, becomes the goal of life.[59] Freud quotes Schopenhauer approvingly ("For him death is the 'true result and to that extent the purpose of life'"[60]) in his own deliberations on the struggle of the death instinct with the persistent will to live. More extensively argued in his essay entitled "Leonardo da Vinci and a Memory of his Childhood" (1910) Freud introduces the term "sublimation" to mean both Schopenhauer's sublime as exaltation and a process of change borrowed from the scientific definition of the term. The conflicting drives of life and death, therefore, find in the process of sublimation a substitute outlet for these conflicts that, if discharged, would make conscious life intolerable. In the words of Steven Z. Levine:

> The process of sublimation converts the unsayable into the said, the unseeable into the seen; but the underlying drive remains behind in a repressed, unconscious form, ever ready to erupt.[61]

Life and will therefore struggle against the repressed desire for death. In the sublime—and especially in the oceanic sublime metaphorically invoked by all theoreticians of the subject, from Longinus to Schopenhauer—the death instinct is momentarily triumphant. (Schopenhauer had, of course, read this through a very Hindu concept of universal self-extinction and oneness with Brahman; Freud sees in it the essential "truth" of the unconscious itself.)

In other words, in the oceanic sublime we discover the image of a desire to return from the terrors of life to the "inviting tranquillity of death."[62] The latter is what we would call sublimation, a process of displacement and rechanneling, which allows the ego to confront its own relentless, and inevitable, goal, death.[63]

The foregoing very selective outline of the sublime from the eighteenth-century theoreticians through Kant to Freud is meant to demonstrate the possibilities of another narrative of the sublime that remained occluded or repressed. The extraordinary emphasis on the primacy of reason meant that the subject, though scarred, nevertheless emerges from the encounter with the sublime more or less triumphant. Against this I have projected the category of the Gothic sublime as the other, unspeakable narrative of this position, claiming that the triumph of reason (which has its counterpart in the epic's capacity to achieve, through writing, a faked immortality) is not to be taken for granted and that the totalizing grand narrative that is implicit in that claim to triumph is presaged in the Gothic, which shows the far-reaching consequences of narratives that examine a possible history of the period designated in the momentary lapse on the part of reason as it gives imagination total freedom. If we examine that space we find that there is no hope of self-transcendence available, as the subject simply dissolves into the pleasure principle and, finally, death. The narrative of this gap, this lapse, begins with Kant but ends up with the ghosts of the unconscious that Freud lays bare before us. In this respect the Gothic sublime becomes a general field under which another narrative, more like our own postmodern narrative, may be composed. This other sublime, the Gothic sublime, is in many ways the voice from the crypt that questions the power of reason (in Kant a substitute for the law of patriarchy as well) and destabilizes the centrality of the ego in Kant's formulation. It is the voice that wishes to write the narrative of the gap, the infinitesimal lapse, in which reason for the moment gives way to chaos as the mind embraces the full terror of the sublime. The Gothic narrative is to be located at that indeterminate moment of the near-abyss where the subject says, I am my own abyss, and is faced with a horrifying image of its own lack of totality. Where the Romantic version of this narrative reestablishes a totality as the ego under the security of reason embraces the magnificence of storm or holocaust, the Gothic subject has none of the capacities of the supremely confident, overpowering (though often insecure) Romantic ego: "We Poets in our youth begin in gladness;/ But thereof come in the end despondency and madness."

The Gothic's abject failure to totalize brings us tantalizingly close to what Lyotard has called the "abyss of heterogeneity,"[64] history as a series of events that stubbornly resists any totalizing pattern. In this respect Lyotard's selective use of the Kantian sublime as the linchpin of his definition of the postmodern condition is not so much a statement about the power of indeterminacy in the general domain of the sublime as a strategic harnessing of the occluded texts of the Gothic. In other words, the real metatexts for Lyotard are in fact the texts of the Gothic sublime. In Lyotard's reading of the Kantian sublime, the sublime does violence to the imagination, since the passage from speculative reason to its representation in an object commensurate to the idea can only lead to a radical heterogeneity. The heterogeneity is another way of explaining the chasm that exists between the two orders, the idea and its representation, will and action, in postmodern speculations on history. Like Andy Warhol's postmodern image of the Empire State Building in flames, the Gothic sublime is pure Piranesi; not the vast oceans and tempests of Longinus or Kant, but the subterranean passages and the grotesque deformations contained in the dreamscape of the Gothic imagination. The Gothic sublime is the *sub,* not as "up to" (as in *sub* + *limen,* the Latin etymology of sublime), but rather as the *below*, the underneath, of the *limen,* of the limit of one's perception. Clearly, it must be stressed that this possibility of the sublime was not lost on Kant, who was aware, in Paul de Man's words, of the "dialectical complication"[65] of the sublime, since its *Lust,* its peculiar pleasure, implied the ravenous appetite also of monsters and ghosts occluded from consciousness. That Paul de Man retreats into the discourse of the Gothic to explain the lawlessness of the sublime is symptomatic of a tendency in the criticism of the sublime generally, in which the Gothic is invoked but not granted theoretical legitimation. From the depths of the underworld/abyss/unconscious the Gothic invades the discourses of the sublime. We need not go beyond de Man and Lyotard to become conscious of this contamination.

One of the shortcomings of earlier theories of sublimity (Gothic or not) is that they were linked to single-effect theories. In other words, the effect of the sublime was seen through either geographical categories (landscapes of vastness, the sublimity of storms, the movement of the "lumbering planets") or through psychological categories (the impact on the mind of an extreme emotion attendant on terror). In these single-effect theories the subject's sense of sublime empowerment comes directly from the descriptive force of the adjective that precedes the noun: the Romantic sublime, for instance, is basically an egotistical sublime that consumes in its search for self-transcendence all possible distinctions; the technological sublime deals with special effects and finds its grand metaphors in cinema; the genetic sublime, as in Ibsen, locates sexually determined sources of terror; the Indian sublime seeks to aestheticize the religious experience, and so on. What our study of the Gothic sublime establishes, albeit only partially and problematically, is that all single-effect definitions of the sublime are predicated on the supplanting of the force of the sublime by its preceding descriptor, without recognizing that it is the very nature of the sublime that it cannot be contained. To add a descriptor to the sublime is to frame it; it is to establish formal limits to the sublime. Although these heuristic limitations are often necessary, what must be stressed is the regressive assimilationist force of the term *sublime*. It is not that the word *Gothic* in the phrase *Gothic sublime* progressively assimilates the sublime into its own domain; on the contrary, it is the sublime that regressively colonizes its descriptor. In the final analysis this is the terror of the sublime, the frighteningly contaminative force of the impossible idea itself. To collocate with the sublime, to cohabit with it, is to be faced with an instance of radical incommensurability. Of all the sublimes, the Gothic sublime (in this specific collocation/cohabitation) is most aware of this incommensurability and the inherent problems of self-transcendence. The Gothic subject never self-transcends, in this sense. Its self-empowerment, as the subject under the sign of the Gothic, always implies subservience to the trope. There is a pleasure of impotence in the face of the sublime: the sublime castrates, it humiliates by its (phallic) grandeur.[66] If, as Rob Wilson points out in his masterly study, one version of the American sublime is to be read "as a sign of national grandeur and collective empowerment,"[67] then the Gothic sublime is a collective disempowerment under the sign of patriarchal power. Where the American sublime harnesses patriarchy toward its positive (divine) ends, Gothic sublimity is incapable of harnessing that force because the subject under patriarchy is continually defined in terms of lack. In this respect the Gothic sublime is indeed Harold Bloom's countersublime, impossible to imagine without repression.[68] The sublime, as an imaginal construct, may be troped by its descriptor, but not framed by it; it is the impossible *ergon* without a *parergon*.

The classic text here, of course, is Derrida's reading of the Kantian sublime in *The Truth in Painting* (*La vérité en peinture*)[69]

Why, then, the retreat from empiricism in the Gothic sublime? The question might be answered once again by looking at the attractiveness of the sublime to postmodern theorists. The attraction has clearly a lot to do with a belief in the end of a totalizing Reason (with its grand narrative or legitimating myths) in favor of "reasons" and in a basically antifoundational conception of knowledge that has come with a critique of theories of universal knowledge per se. The trope that becomes important is no longer the trope of the beautiful, a determinate conceptualizing of the aesthetic, but the sublime, which eludes any kind of representation through "categories of analytic thought."[78] The Gothic sublime may be read as a category of the postmodern, insofar as the postmodern is also marked by the problematizing of what had hitherto been an uncritical identity of language and the world. Though almost artless in its simplicity—that as the latent underside of any literary history or discursive formation the Gothic signifies a break in the continuum of history—the argument of this book, nevertheless, requires us to develop strategies that would both express the nature of the Gothic sublime and connect it to the historical postmodern. For the literary historian of the Gothic the text in which this noncorrespondence took decisive form was a slight work by Horace Walpole. The Gothic sublime finds its proof text in this work.

2

The Precursor Text

"The German critic Walter Benjamin," writes Terry Eagleton, "dismissed the view that all literary works were equally 'readable' at all times."[1] At the heart of Benjamin's argument is our capacity to blast open the "continuum of history."[2] As historical readers we return to those texts which speak to us across the historical divide in much more urgent tones. This is because, as Habermas points out, "the authentic moment of an innovative present interrupts the continuum of history and breaks away from its homogeneous flow."[3] The innovative moment—like our own postmodernity—can therefore anticipate the future, but only by remembering "a past that has been suppressed."[4] In Eagleton's words again, we forge "conjunctures between our own moment and a redeemed bit of the past, imbuing works with retroactive significance so that in them we may better read the signs of our own times."[5] The conjuncture between the moment of the Gothic and our own postmodernity (which I accept as a cultural field intrinsically linked to the nature of late capitalism) is something that has not been adequately theorized with reference to specific literary texts. The argument I have advanced is that the postmodern trope of the sublime as a category that captures the disjunction between the idea and its representation, and the uncanny horror of recognition that this disjunction entails, has had its antecedent in the Gothic. The origin of the sublime in terror (or the horror inflicted on the subject) is the epistemological basis of all sublimes. To rephrase Edmund Burke, we love and enjoy what we can control, what we can mold closer to our hearts' desire (the beautiful). Against this we are compulsively and negatively attracted to what subjugates (the sublime). In the Kantian/Romantic sublime the power of subjugation is still under the control of the law which knows that the disturbance caused by the mind's confrontation with the sublime is only momentary. Soon afterward this very subjugation is transformed into power as a sense of self-transcendence replaces the sense of awe and human insignificance. It is at this point that the Gothic parts company with what may be called the historical sublime. The Gothic celebrates both the power of the sublime and the self's willingness to be subjugated. The will to power, in this negativity, is thus linked to a desire, a will, to be subjugated in the first instance. The Gothic places its faith in the sublime and takes an enormous risk, because for the Gothic there is no such thing as the aesthetics of the beautiful, there is only the superabundance, the terror, of the sublime. It is this risk that leads to an insoluble and contradictory thematic core in the Gothic texts as they fail to put the lid back on the mysteries that have been released. In reading a number of texts of the late eighteenth and early nineteenth centuries we can arrive at a structure of the sublime that needs Kant for theory but alters the ontological basis of the experience of the sublime, which impossible object, as the Real, now makes subjectivity itself impossible. It is in this respect that analogies between the postmodern and the Gothic sublime may be fruitfully made. In other words—and in spite of the vastly different nature of the relationship between capital and labor between the two "moments"—the postmodern sublime may now be given a more precise historical grounding than Jameson's generalized program of a return "to older theories of the sublime" to account for the culture of the simulacra that he associates with the postmodern condition. It is important to stress that the key theorist whose reading of subjectivity allows us to radically re-read the Gothic in this fashion is Sigmund Freud. Two narratives, then, collapse on each other: the narratives of the Gothic uncanny and the uncanny resemblances between the Gothic sublime and the postmodern.

There is a scene in Jane Austen's *Northanger Abbey* that may be used as our point of departure.[6] At Bath ("in the Pump-room one morning," to be precise) Catherine and her friend Isabella are discussing the current fashion for popular Gothic romance. Their primary text is Mrs. Ann Radcliffe's *The Mysteries of Udolpho,* which Catherine has been reading frantically all morning. She has reached the episode of the "black veil" when, in a thinly disguised parody of contemporary reading habits, Jane Austen's Catherine indulges in the artificial shock-effects so characteristic of Radcliffe's Gothic romances. Catherine in fact prefers not to know what is behind "the black veil" and adopts the posture of a mock romance reader by looking for clues that might support her hunch that the figure behind the black veil is indeed Laurentina (Laurentini in Radcliffe). In many ways this is precisely Emily's position in *The Mysteries of Udolpho.* Laurentini's "black veil" is one extreme of the spectrum of "veils" we find in Radcliffe's texts—from the unveiled Emily to the partially veiled Ellena to the completely veiled Laurentini. To gain access to the face behind the veil is often the aim of the hero and the villain alike. In Emily's desire to see the face behind the veil, she, too, participates in the economy of desire for the Other, as Catherine, the reader, does as well.[7] In drawing the attention of her own ladies to the mystery of the black veil, Jane Austen takes us to the very heart of the symbol of the veil that signifies the twilight zone of representation between the real, the known, and the unknown. Her commentary also constructs the Radcliffe texts as a seamless corpus, a continuum in which the first text will be constantly rewritten. But in Catherine's immediate response to the titles suggested by Isabella—that she would read them only if they are "all horrid"—we get another interpretation that requires a commentary.

Familiarity, teasing, ludic resistance, aleatory narrative, and parody—the playing out of games with texts—are the characteristics of Catherine's complex responses to Isabella's encyclopaedic knowledge of the Gothic. She would read the other novels only if they are "all horrid." "Horrid," however, is not just "horrible" (its primary meaning) but also horrifying and shocking; it is the genteel, the civilized semantics of the unspeakable, the sublime. Strange things will happen in the Gothic as it teases and waylays the reader by offering her desires that will not be fulfilled. "Are you prepared to encounter all the horrors that a building such as 'what one reads about' may produce?" asks Henry Tilney, later on in chapter 20. *Northanger Abbey* has read its Gothic extremely well, and read it in a most postmodern fashion, playing with the source text, parodying it and modelling its own realistic discourse to accommodate, but not legitimate, the source text's narrative. In the process, however, *Northanger Abbey* crystallizes the code in which the source text is written and demonstrates a fundamental truth about the Gothic: there can be no *grand récit* here, since all master narratives are suspect. Behind Catherine's "horrid" novels reference stands an anxiety of influence that would take us to Horace Walpole's *The Castle of Otranto*.[8] It is a text that we will read, analytically, later on in this chapter, since it constitutes our principal precursor text. But first the ground must be cleared through a pragmatic examination of the first of the key terms in the Gothic sublime, the word *Gothic* itself.

The *OED* has an extensive entry for the word *Gothic,* which covers a whole range of meanings and associations from primitive social behaviour (Gothic barbarism) and vernacular literary discourses (medievalism, as opposed to the classical, popularized by Bishop Hurd's studies[9]) to architecture (the arched window form) and writing (the black letter). Gradually three significant constellations of meaning evolved which A. E. Longueil, writing so many years ago, termed "barbarous," "medieval," and "supernatural."[10] In these definitions the Gothic emerges as an antirational and anti-Enlightenment genre to be read in totally adversarial terms. Reading it as a generic register of self-conscious defiance is not incorrect, though the degree to which it was oppositional requires closer scrutiny, something that unfortunately is beyond the scope of this book. But Sir Walter Scott was certainly conscious of this historical reading when, in defense of the Gothic, he suggested that Walpole had in fact contributed to the rescue of the Gothic from "the bad fame into which it had fallen, being currently used before his time to express whatever was in pointed and diametrical opposition to the rules of true taste."[11] At the same time the Gothic (whatever values we may wish to read into the word), with its presumed origins in the vernacular, seems to be implicitly resisting the colonization of reality by the aesthetic orders of the grand artistic forms of literature and architecture. This point is made by D. H. Lawrence in *The Rainbow*, when he refers to Will Brangwen's love for the Gothic: "So he had turned to the Gothic form, which always asserted the broken desire of mankind in its pointed arches, escaping the rolling, absolute beauty of the round arch."[12] Perhaps this sense of rebelliousness explains many of the contrived shock effects we find in the literary Gothic.

The *OED* constructs a syntagm of historical examples through which a word has evolved, but as the supplements to the *OED* so clearly indicate, the evolution itself cannot be completely documented. Words, by definition, cannot be tied down to specific meanings, and even the citation of historical instantiations are no more than an attempt to prevent excess of meaning from spilling over into the totally inaccessible realm of chaos. These citations may be read as "anchoring points" or, as Lacan once said about nodal items in a dream-text, *"points de capiton,"* which enable us to grasp "meaning" for a moment before it is lost in discourse.[13] In citing the *OED* I simply wish to indicate the historical construction of meaning. But the trajectory of the word through history (although limited) is in itself a principle of hermeneutics—the hermeneutics, indeed, of the word as in fact the carrier of human consciousness. When applied to literature the word *Gothic* triggers a predictable set of images—ghosts, subterranean passages, creaking doors, skeletons—as well as a specific narrative form that often reads like a collection of fragments, a prototypical "tissue of past citations."[14] This predictability persuaded G. R. Thompson to suggest that in literature the Gothic should be replaced by the term *Dark Romanticism,*[15] where the dominant trope is a counter-sublime.

It could be argued that the Gothic works on at least two levels. The first is the intertext of generic abstraction: the conventions of romance that, finally, act as a censor to the Gothic, selecting, organizing, controlling, even redistributing a certain number of quite distinct procedures, but conscious nevertheless of the essentially problematic nature of the genre. *The Castle of Otranto,* for instance, was subtitled simply "A Story" when it was first published anonymously. It is not too difficult to replace "A Story" by "A Romance," thereby giving it an immediate (and legitimate or safe) generic anchorage. At the same time this "safe anchorage," through the imperialism of generic conventions, may be uncritically appropriated to deny Gothic texts a specificity that "restores to language its active energy."[16] This takes us to the second level of meaning. The Gothic must be seen in terms of its intrinsic instability, in terms of its serious doubts about the unproblematic possibilities of representation, in fact, as a discourse that moved, to use a Roland Barthes phrase, "in its historical impetus, by *clashes.*"[17] In the immediate context of the Gothic, such a "clash" might be considered in terms of a "counter-factual scenario" that would show the probable discourse situation in the second half of the eighteenth century if the Gothic had not so daringly exploded on the scene. In such a scenario we might conceivably draw a picture of the novel and romance (as Clara Reeve in particular defines these terms) dividing the literary domain between them. These genres would have then crossed over into each other's domains, giving rise, finally, to some other radically different form. The discourse that underpins the signifying practice of the Gothic must, therefore, be approached "in terms of the struggles traversing it, so that the contradictory modes in which it exists as a whole can be studied."[18] Frederick Garber makes the same point when he demonstrates that the confrontationist design of the Gothic enables the "separate identities" in a text to exist alongside each other. The Gothic becomes "the site of constant collisions"[19] against the essentially humanist conception of authorship and subjectivity that had in fact imposed an imaginary continuity and an unproblematic relationality (between art and life) on an underlying (and quite normal) tendency toward discontinuity and decenteredness. In claiming a realistic basis for the novel form ("The Novel is a picture of real life and manners, and of the times in which it is written,"[20] wrote Clara Reeve), critics in the second half of the eighteenth century were clearly closing it off as both the legitimate genre of the times and superior to everything else. This struggle for generic control, as we shall see later, found its most dramatic expression in what may be called the catastrophe of *The Castle of Otranto.*

Central to any Western theory of discourse as a social phenomenon locked into and colluding with the multiplicity of institutional and social practices that give it shape and form is a theory of "authorship." The concept of authorship, which parallels bourgeois notions of ownership, is closely tied up with a whole host of sociopolitical and economic factors such as individual ownership of property, legal bequests, and so on. It is not necessarily a "natural" way of identifying either a text or property, as may be seen from its almost total absence from Sanskrit aesthetics, for instance. It has been historically constructed and seems to have acquired a very special meaning in the eighteenth century. As Michel Foucault has pointed out in his influential essay "What Is an Author?" the "author function" is an historical agreement[21] that seems to have coincided with the rise of the novel. Such was the value placed on authorship that Clara Reeve, probably in exasperation, wrote, "Perhaps there is not a better Criterion of a merit of a book, than our losing sight of the Author."[22] In a paradoxical endorsement of the author function, however, the middle years of the eighteenth century produced a curious phenomenon in literature with Macpherson's "Ossian," Chatterton's "Rowley," and Walpole's "Muralto," all nonexistent names on whom authorship was artificially foisted. Between 1760 and 1763 James Macpherson, in fact, claimed that his collections of "literal" translations were from the ancient Gaelic of a third-century Scottish poet, Ossian, son of Fingal. The results were sensational. For almost a generation authors on both sides of the channel (Goethe included) saw in these poems of "Ossian" those "sublimely bleak, stormy, monochrome landscapes"[23] that became a hallmark of Gothic writing.

A much more relevant concept than the "author function" for my argument is Foucault's invaluable concept of "founders of discursivity." My earlier comments may now be read through this radical notion of founders of discursive orders. In short, the classic authors of English realism, Defoe, Richardson, Fielding, and Smollett among them, were, collectively, founders of a particular form of discursivity. The form of representation they adopted highlighted *vraisemblance*. Yet it also reflected a major epistemological shift in Western thought that clearly, after Descartes, privileged consciousness as the "purveyor" of truth. As Ian Watt has noted, "[it was] as defiant an assertion of the primacy of individual experience in the novel as Descartes's *cogito ergo sum* was in philosophy."[24] In retrospect, it is a paradox that historically Realism itself was an act of "defamiliarization" [*ostranenie*] that opened up new literary possibilities: "when art cannot advance," writes Alastair Fowler, "it requires deliverance by the noncanonized."[25] It is as a founder of discursivity that Horace Walpole's *The Castle of Otranto* is of such great significance in our study of the Gothic sublime. In superimposing this concept of Foucault on our Gothic precursor text, I wish to distinguish, along with Foucault, authors who influence others through the "radicalness" of their style, authors such as Laurence Sterne and James Joyce, and those who are endlessly rewritten. In this argument Lacan and Althusser, for example, would be read as "authors" who rewrite Freud and Marx, respectively. Since the "rules for the formation of other texts" are immanent in Freud and Marx, these masters indeed become the "authors" of Lacan and Althusser too. Not surprisingly, we hear these discourses readily identified as Freudian or Marxist. This argument carries enormous weight, because unlike "influences" (the kinds of novelistic influence Sterne's *A Sentimental Journey* had on Henry Mackenzie's *The Man of Feeling* or the latter on both Charlotte Smith and Frances Burney) we are in fact speaking about "divergences" and "differences" too. The insights that both Lacan and Althusser, for instance, bring to the body of human knowledge are finally to be placed against the backdrop of the psychoanalytical and Marxist discourses themselves.

Horace Walpole, in other words, not so much "influenced" subsequent writers as actually founded a discursive practice that may be called Gothic (in literature) in much the same way in which Freud's or Marx's discourse may be deemed Freudian or Marxist. Anyone writing in the "style" of the Gothic, therefore, simply extended that particular practice and, in effect, "colluded" with it in an act of complicity. Our precursor or founding text, *The Castle of Otranto,* presents itself as internally ruptured and discontinuous, and endorses a very postmodern claim about its own lack of originality. First published in 1764 (the date given in the first edition is in fact 1765) as a translation from the "Original Italian of Onuphrio Muralto, Canon of the Church of St. Nicholas at Otranto by William

Marshall," the title triggers, for the historical reader, a particular chain of literary facts and figures. Consider a few examples: *Letitia; or, the Castle Without a Spectre* (1801), *The Castle of Wolfenbach* (1793), *Edmund; or, the Child of the Castle, a Novel* (1790), *Seymour Castle; or, the History of Julia and Celia* (1790), *The Castle of St. Donat's* (1799), *The Castle of Santa Fe* (1805), *The Castle de Warrenne, a Romance* (1800), etc. What these titles endorse or affirm is the centrality of the castle itself in these narratives. The realist novel, one recalls, had preferred "history" and "adventures" (markers of temporality) over symbols of space, since its concerns are pre-eminently with questions of origins, both of the subject and of the genre. The symbol of space, this castle, is not, as one would expect from a spatial referent, ambiguity-free, since its meaning implicates sites of power (in feudal structures, for instance, but also in chess, where, as a verb, it is a particular movement of overlap between the king and the rook), as well as its absence in the real (one builds castles in the air). The castle is therefore an "immense structure of possibility," as Norman Holland and Leona Sherman[26] have pointed out, designated, in the main, in the locative case and largely uninterpreted. In Holland and Sherman's "gendered" response, the castle becomes a complex site on which many meanings are superimposed. As they probe its significance, they become conscious of its immense plurality. The castle is a signifying chain that draws into itself the human body, the ruthless father, the yielding mother, as well as the thematics of sexual transgression. As a "potential space," the castle thus creates possibilities into which the subject enters, both as reader of the text and character in the narrative. For "castle" is a *mise-en-scene*, a nightmare house, a site of sexual, genealogical and psychological struggles, a physical space that will accept, in psychoanalytic parlance, infinite residues of unconscious material. A space is where "games" may be played, but the castle may confine, threaten, symbolically castrate, or make impotent all within its walls. Holland and Sherman see the castle as representing "a markedly untrustworthy Other," ambivalent but terribly attractive to whoever comes within its orbit. As an instance of space, therefore, the castle cannot generate a narrative by itself; it cannot be the center of consciousness, reflecting and coming into contact with reality. It is like Jeremy Bentham's Panopticon, a prison house, which "used," in Foucault's words, "a form close to that of the castle—a keep surrounded by walls—to paradoxically create a space of exact legibility." But it is also, as Foucault affirms (with a decisive "Absolutely") "the areas of darkness in man that the century of Enlightenment wants to make disappear."[27] In his extraordinary examination of discipline and punishment, Foucault had, in fact, written comprehensively about the phenomenon that, after Bentham's study, he called "Panopticism." Panopticism, for Foucault, was the mode of dissociating the seer from the seen. In the design of the Panopticon, which has a central tower overlooking a semicircle, with cubicles that extend the whole width of the building, Foucault discovers an architectural form capable of sustaining domination and power by its mere design. Given such a design, he writes, "in the peripheric ring, one is totally seen, without ever seeing; in the central tower, one sees everything without ever being seen."[28] There is a kind of gaming implicit here, a "playing with the pieces"[29] in the hyperreal castle complex that is not dissimilar to the postmodern aporetic situation, because there is no way in which the gaze of the two crucial subjects in the Panopticon might be reconciled, might be made commensurable to each other.

In fact, the Panopticon is a seemingly orderly version of Piranesi's radically postmodern architectural drawings. In transforming Piranesi's "ruined prisons, littered with mechanisms of torture" into a "cruel, ingenious cage,"[30] the Panopticon offers a "gaze [of the supposedly rational subject] that objectifies and examines."[31] The transformation certainly endorses order and power, but it cannot totally displace the Gothic horrors on which it has been superimposed. Since Piranesi's Gothic visions cannot be controlled so easily (it is after all "unpresentable" in precisely the way in which Lyotard defines it as beyond rational articulation), what the Panopticon demonstrates, however paradoxically, is the desire for the adequate image and its lack, an impasse that the Gothic transforms into its own narrative situation and into an epistemology of the sublime. The realm of supersensible ideas becomes an escape chute to avoid what the Marquis de Sade called the compulsive "violence of reason." The logic of the Panopticon, then, is predicated on the need to contain the socially aberrant (the madman, the convict, the political radical) through a simulated form (since the Panopticon, as Bentham conceived it, never found actual representation in reality) that emphasizes the incommensurability between the idea and its presentation. The narrative of the Gothic sublime is bound up with these crazy architectural projects. Its compulsive attraction to the realm of darkness is a form of therapy based on the assumption that experiencing the unknown is the best cure for the return of the repressed. Whether in this way the Gothic sublime dispelled those fears outright is something we shall never know.

In a recent review essay David H. Richter argued that the history of the Gothic (which we seem to understand, and define, intuitively) "cannot be told as a single coherent story."[32] "The form that story takes," he adds, "depends on one's underlying conception of genre." The underlying conception of the genre of the Gothic implicit in my argument is that it is a genre of fissure and fracture, a kind of an antilanguage, which heralds and foreshadows the postmodern. It excites us because in this genre we recognize forms of textuality that constitute the postmodern. One of the most obvious characteristics of the Gothic is its radical rereading of the grand eighteenth-century discovery of character. There is nothing of that bourgeois essentiality of character at work here. "Character"—the central discovery of the Enlightenment novel, the "novelistic norm," the spectacle that binds the viewers to an objectified presence of themselves like a specular filmic image—has little place in a theory of the Gothic where stylized figures are much more abundant. Instead of "social persons" who are carriers of consciousness, the Gothic characters are disfigured, fragmented, disembodied voices, physical residues, ambiguously placed between logical and psychological reality. "Characters" are shadowed by others and their individuality, their radical difference or uniqueness, dismantled through a technique of duplication or uncanny repetition. The triumph of this mode of characterological fragmentation is William Godwin's *Caleb Williams*, which we discuss at length in chapter 4. As Ronald Paulson has shown in a masterly essay, character in the eighteenth century was considered either as a "personality developing in time" (as in the novel) or as "an identity which exists in terms of a certain action—a crime—committed at a particular time" (as in a legal definition that satire, too, appropriates).[33] But whereas satire, a moralizing form, requires the reader to "face the acute problem of our political or metaphysical destiny,"[34] the Gothic transforms character into a grammatical subject and, furthermore, rends it apart and redistributes it. This becomes clearer if we shift our ground from the castle, the architectural space, to its owner, the site of the construction of the novelistic universe, in Walpole's *The Castle of Otranto*.

Manfred, the terrorizing patriarch, is presented as an agitated and high-strung occupant of a castle that he cannot contain within his consciousness—so much so that the castle will begin to have an independent existence. As the site of the primal scene, it is a space resonant with possibilities, since it is here that the real drama of humanity will be enacted. The battlements therefore replace Hamlet and the Ghost; the Castle of Elsinore becomes *Hamlet* the play; the Inn at Upton easily displaces *The History of Tom Jones*. The shift in focus from the priority of character to the imperative of space (the hyperspace) clearly alters the nature of the reading process as the underlying assumptions of the master genre of romance (on which Gothic narratives are invariably superimposed) are radically subverted. This seems to be the logic of the "new" narrative in which the castle does not stand for Manfred within the rhetoric of metaphor, but constantly displaces him in an endlessly metonymic chain of repetition (because he is both *present* and *absent*). We enter the rhetoric of metonymy, which bypasses the obstacles of censure and implicates the return of the repressed. In short, "*The Castle of Otranto*" negates "The House of Manfred" by marginalizing the owner, by reducing him to a trace, a cypher. Since what surfaces as a consequence is the "castle," it acquires the force of the "Other" toward which all else must gravitate. All those who enter it forego prohibition as the libido is allowed a relatively higher freedom of "play." Everyone, including Hippolita, is implicated. The friar Jerome confesses his own sexual transgression on entering the castle; both Isabella and Matilda discover "passion," which they don't really comprehend, and so on. In the words of Caroline Spurgeon, a "strange *disquietude* of the Gothic spirit"[35] prevails over the castle like a "concealing" and "concealed offense":[36] lovers become "lechers," reality, the horrors of the repressed. The Gothic is centrally a discourse of instability, of the impossibility of representation. Like "laughter" and the "carnivalesque," it is always on the verge of madness, the state of the complete dissolution of logic and categories of "difference." The castle threatens to turn inward on itself, "encrypting," if need be, all its occupants. The various underground passages are relics, traces, metonyms in fact, of the larger "encrypting" potential of the castle.

The origin of the novel in a dream as the scene of writing (a fact not lost on Montague Summers) is thus implicit in the text, and it comes as no surprise when we chance on precisely this fact in Walpole's letters. In a letter to Rev. William Cole dated March 9, 1765 Walpole had written:

> Shall I even confess to you what was the origin of this romance? I waked one morning in the beginning of last June from a dream, of which all I could recover was, that I had thought myself in an ancient castle (a very natural dream for a head filled like mine with Gothic story) and that on the

> uppermost bannister of a great staircase I saw a gigantic hand in armour. In the evening I sat down and began to write, without knowing in the least what I intended to say or relate. The work grew on my hands, and I grew fond of it. . . . In short I was so engrossed with my tale, which I completed in less than two months, that one evening I wrote from the time I had drunk my tea, about six o'clock, till half an hour after one in the morning, when my hand and fingers were so weary, that I could not hold the pen to finish the sentence, but left Matilda and Isabella talking, in the middle of a paragraph.[37]

The citation of his own dream as the source of inspiration (one is struck by the imagery of nightmare and the peculiar intensities of his rhetorical tropes) is largely at odds with the realistic terms in which the novel had hitherto been written. We return to the questions posed by the surrealists a century ago. Is the work constructed as free associations after a dream? Is it the strange narrative of the unconscious glimpsed only through dreams and parapraxes? George E. Haggerty reformulates the problematic into another question: "What manner of prose narrative most effectively embodies a nightmarish vision?"[38] "Gilly" Williams' complaint to George Selwyn that this was a "feverish" dream[39] connects *The Castle of Otranto* to Freud's commentary on dreams in *Die Traumdeutung*. Peter Conrad has a similar reading in mind when he writes, "*Otranto* is an essay on the epistemology of that enfevered imagination, forever interrogating the precise status of all its visions."[40] Is it, then, automatic writing, "in defiance of rules," as Walpole wrote to Madame du Deffand,[41] the unmediated obsessional discourses in a dialogic narrative situation between the analyst and the analysand, a case history like Dora's where the source text is invariably the italicized *ur* text? If uncontrolled, not premeditated, does the discourse bring us closer to the language of the unconscious itself? And do we sense here echoes of Freud's own frustration in his failure to adequately record for publication "the history of a treatment of long duration"?[42] Can Walpole, too, by extension, be immune from transference and countertransference and avoid being implicated in the very neurosis he proposes to cure? Is the signifying practice of the Gothic, as its primary precursor text offers us, precisely this? Is postmodernist writing similarly constructed—a signifying chain where the signifieds always slip under, are erased, confounding referentiality? Is this, after Lacan, that schizophrenic tendency that the alarmist detects in postmodernist writing? But we know that dreams, however, cannot reconstruct history since the memory of dreams is finally unplumbable (at some point, Freud noted, a dream is uninterpretable). A text originating in dreams signals its simulative status. In other words, since it is not based on any original, it is pure simulacrum. The narratives of the Gothic function on a different order of similitude, because the sublime object cannot be grasped in all its totality. Instead, what we are confronted with is the triumph of the sublime, Piranesi's enfevered imagination and threatening etchings, the spatial fictions of the Panopticon.

The Penguin edition of *Three Gothic Novels* (which includes *The Castle of Otranto*) has Fuseli's "The Nightmare" on its cover, and Mario Praz in his introductory essay to this collection discovers the "origin" of Walpole's dream in Piranesi's *Carceri*.[43] In doing this, is Praz, too, offering a "symptomatic reading," treating the author so that he could be cured by confronting the "truth" behind Piranesi, who, Praz writes in another work, can "be described as 'Gothic' in a wider sense than that of a mere imitation of style"?[44] The search for this "truth" takes us to Piranesi's (1720–1778) obsessive, often laudanum-induced "exercises in spatial composition."[45] Here is more than just a psychological connection; in fact, we enter into the realm of an English fetish for Piranesi's drawings, which English tourists in Rome and Venice bought at ludicrously cheap rates to adorn the halls of their country houses for the next two centuries. In what Jonathan Scott has called "the turbulent splendour of the [young] artist's vision,"[46] Piranesi's inventive architectural designs (especially of stage prisons), his errors in perspective and excessive geometric forms, in short a "systematic criticism of the concept of 'center',"[47] tended to enter into and fracture those very laws of classical antiquity that, technically, architecture had so steadfastly upheld. In Piranesi's vision, the perspective is often that of the "mole" seeing huge, ruined colonnades from below, disturbing the presumed sanctity of an objective (or correct) point of view. In the Ashmolean Museum, Oxford, copy of the *Carceri* (Prisons) and *Le Antichità Romane* (Antiquities of Rome),[48] we get an unsettling sense of ruins, a sense of "wings" cut off in mid-flight, sections collapsing, a pending doom, with vegetation challenging art through cracks and hollows. In the "prison drawings" the central image is often of torture, with occasional epigraphs summoning up the texts' relationship to prison lore in the form of a Kafkaesque allegory. One epigraph in the *Carceri* reads *ad terrorem increscen(tis) audaciae,* next to which is inscribed *infame scelus (arbo)ri infelici suspe(nde)*[49] In one of these a man's ankles are tied by ropes to a rotating wheel which in turn is being pulled by a jailer. A riot of characters in abysmal states occupies the drawing, and groups of people, similarly confused, look down on the torture chamber.

Going through these etchings in the *Carceri* in particular, one becomes conscious of the Gothic sense of architecture (a sense that seems to respond to Piranesi's somber designs, his chaos of subterranean structures, huge pulleys, and so on) and the likely visionary resonances between our Gothic writers and Piranesi. In looking at architecture (and whatever life remained to be seen) through Piranesi's etchings, the Gothic writers probably compounded, and confused, the fictions on which Piranesi's own visions were based. The shadowy figures and forms (with an exceptionally heavy alternation of shade and sunlight, reflecting an etching technique where the acid was allowed to bite in a fraction longer for the desired effect), the horror, the spikes and dungeon chains, all added to the feverish somberness of Piranesi's probably strained, definitely obsessive, perhaps deranged, imagination. All the fragmentation and dismantling, the "disarticulation of organisms,"[50] however, reveal, in the words of Sergei Eisenstein, "no less emotional flight"[51] than those found in much more structured historical precedents. Layers and layers of levels—in an almost infinite series of architectural profusion, or madness—flow in and out of his drawings. And for all that the view remains from below—hellish visions indeed! Pulleys and chains, huge, clanging door knobs, the network of heavy wooden stairs, rafters, beams, and walkways suspended in the air often camouflage and belittle naked human beings with their hands tied behind and ready to be impaled by the active aggressiveness of the architecture. Yet the *Carceri*, like the *Antichità*, remains ultimately monotonous, a desperate compulsion to repeat the mind's subterranean horrors.[52] The look of horror is evident in Felice Polanzani's (1700 to c. 1783) portrait of Piranesi that adorns the *Antichità*, but which originally appeared in 1750 as a sort of frontispiece for another work (*Opera varie*). It shows a head gazing at the onlooker from atop a huge slab of stone, on which has been placed a bound collection of his etchings. This figure of Piranesi from the bust above, dwarfed as it is by his name and occupation carved into the slab itself, dares the onlooker to enter the world of the etchings he has bequeathed to history. The etchings, of course, speak not of history, but of their daemonization by the spirit as it makes its journey "through a maze of tangled paths."[53]

"The sublime dreams of Piranesi,"[54] as Horace Walpole called them, invade Gothic discourse at every step. In Piranesi's "grandeur" and "wildness," in his fantastic juxtapositions and architectural boldness, in his Gothic sublimities and discontinuous montage, we discover conventions that were taken up more comprehensively by later Gothic writers, notably Beckford and Maturin. In Walpole that feverishness, that intensity of experience, the sense of "I and the Abyss" are lacking; nor does he possess Piranesi's obsessive capacity for the negative sublime. As the symbol of the negative avant-garde (the fragmented subject, the sacralization of banality), Piranesi prefigures the postmodern tendencies of the Gothic, those tendencies which are marked by the mind's confrontation with its own dissolution, and the dissolution of history where it, history, becomes a nightmare. To read Walpole through Piranesi requires a postmodern strategy that would enable us to carve open and rip apart the hidden text, the text that is disavowed by Walpole.

Walpole's dream, then, is the hidden text that can generate, in Freudian terms, a commentary such as *The Castle of Otranto*. But the commentary is presented in the first edition as an unauthored text, which Walpole has simply translated. We enter into the realm of gaming, writing as hoax and play, and the abrogation of authorial responsibility. Walpole disavows authorship in the preface to the first edition, under the influence, no doubt, of the "Ossianic" fashion for the literary hoax (which in this case doesn't quite come off). At one level this act of distancing would permit the construction of alternative worlds whose truth conditions need not be validated by the author him- or herself. As translator or reader of a discovered text (most Gothic narratives are mediated narratives of this kind), the "author" proclaims him- or herself to be an objective reader of the text. And even though Walpole confesses authorship a few months later, in the second edition of the novel (where he calls his work "a new species of romance"), the pattern of collusion and quasi-legitimation through framing gets firmly established as it becomes one of the basic characteristics of Gothic narrative. The text speaks the unspeakable by transgressing acceptable norms, but the transgressions themselves must be framed in such a way that they do not suggest any real onslaught on decorum or censorship. The text allows the surfacing of the repressed by creating a disequilibrium, but at the same time it wishes to hide its own procedures by framing the narrative and by adopting recognizable generic principles. In both—in the account of the dream and in the account of the writing itself as translating and editing—the text's mimetic pretensions are done to excess. These strategies are part of the general principle of illusion underpinned by the narrative of the uncanny on which *The Castle of Otranto* operates.

The narrative of the uncanny is, however, linked to a genealogy that, as in all romance, is in itself a narrative. The "grid" of the family tree forms a kind of a deep structure on which the plot, which Robert Kiely called "part obstacle course, part free-for-all, and part relay race in which the participants run through a cluttered labyrinth passing the baton to whomever they happen to meet,"[55] is superimposed. Like the Oedipus myth, where genealogy is utilized to startling ends, here, too, it is genealogy that carries the plot, which in turn is really a riddle. The Oedipus myth invades the text in another way, as transgressive sexuality threatens to destroy genealogical purity. Since the implied pollution of blood must be avoided at all cost, the novel constructs its narrative situations in the shadow of this censorious law. Theodore's relationship with Matilda is doomed since both trace their ancestries back to Alfonso the Good—even though in the case of Matilda, her great-grandfather Don Ricardo's claim to unproblematic descent from Alfonso the Good was based on a spurious claim made for the sake of political legitimacy.[56] Manfred's own desire for Isabella, the betrothed of the ill-fated Conrad, again threatens order and genealogical purity and must be neutralized.

Not surprisingly, the novel in fact begins with a kind of family tree. "Husband," "wife," "son," "daughter," "sterility," "heir" are words that occupy a central place on the first page. But the only person who is qualified in a positive, though slightly ominous, fashion is the daughter: "the latter, a most beautiful virgin." Against Matilda's virginity, Manfred is purely "titular," Conrad, the brother, is infirm and sickly, and Hippolita, Manfred's wife, though amiable, is of little consequence because of "her own sterility" for giving Manfred "but one heir." The "beautiful virgin" is, however, not the object of Manfred's pride. Instead, it is the miserable Conrad who is Otranto's darling, and though three years younger than his sister, it is Conrad who is about to be married off first. His bride-to-be is Isabella, a lady whose marriage had been "contracted" on his son's behalf by Manfred and who had been already "delivered" into the Otranto household. All this is narrated in fewer than twenty lines. It is only afterward that we are given an obscure, and for the moment unintelligible, prophecy as the reason for this overhasty marriage. The cryptic prophecy was in fact an interdiction: *"That the castle and lordship of Otranto should pass from the present family, whenever the real owner should be grown too large to inhabit it"* (15–16). Such is the force of the genealogical sublime that the supernatural event occurs on the day of the marriage, as Conrad is struck down by the force of a gigantic helmet. The origin of this helmet remains a mystery—all that we know is that it has an uncanny resemblance to the helmet on the head of the statue of Alfonso, the patriarch of Otranto. There is, then, an immense disequilibrium created at the very beginning, which would generate startling consequences. Theodore, who alone can restore the old order, will have to be granted a legitimate genealogy, even though this would mean tracing him back to Alfonso through his mother and not his father (who was a monk).

The primacy given to genealogy is so strong that the search for a return to a genealogical equilibrium is disrupted or punctuated on several occasions by the sources of terror, which are largely symbols of the otherworldly or the supernatural. At crucial moments the plumes of the helmet wave, the portrait either descends and walks or simply sighs, three drops of blood fall from the nose of Alfonso's statue, which grows enormous in size, and so on. Apart from the collapse of the walls (which destroys the profane space of the castle) the most direct manifestations of the marvellous are related to situations in which women are being sexually threatened. Forms of sexual transgression, through a symbolic exchange of daughters on the part of both Manfred and Frederic, emphasize the correspondence between the marvellous and the threat to genealogical purity. The marvellous or the supernatural, in short, acquires its greatest force whenever radical sexual transgressions are underway. The genealogical and the sexual sublimes invade the realms of the Gothic sublime and give it its possible narratives.

The fear of "incest" destabilizes sexual behavior by threatening cultural norms. In *The Castle of Otranto* even natural passion is read as guilt: ". . . eradicate this guilty passion from thy breast," warns Father Jerome, to which Theodore replies, "Guilty passion . . . can guilt dwell with innocent beauty and virtuous modesty?" Clearly, Father Jerome is reading the word guilty to mean an attack on proper genealogical transmission—the Houses of Ricardo and Alfonso are, after all, related by blood, and Theodore has an uncanny resemblance to Alfonso's portrait. Related to this seemingly unholy desire is the whole question of the exchange or barter of women. Since only women, as Terry Eagleton says, are commodities on "the sex and property market"[57] (the sexuality of Manfred and Frederic has "no price, no exchange value"), Hippolita's acquiescence to the designs of Manfred is curiously ambiguous. Her endorsement of Manfred's plans demonstrates her ambivalent position as the carrier of two radically divergent ideologies—the dutiful wife is also the powerless woman. At the same time her "sterility" (the fact that she cannot produce another son) symbolically makes Manfred impotent. Hippolita is thus a site of sets of contradictions surrounding power and patriarchy that permeate all levels of the text and which lead to quite unsettling forms of sexual representations in the text. Earlier on in the narrative we read:

> But come, lady, we are too near the mouth of the cavern; let us seek its inmost recesses: I can have no tranquillity till I have placed thee beyond the reach of danger. (73)

Isabella recognizes the sexual innuendo of the "mouth of the cavern" and sounds horrified when she replies, "Alas! what mean you, sir?" The text attempts to naturalize this discourse into an interrogative of apprehension, but only succeeds in postponing the real implications of the language. Seduction here still wishes to retain its mystery, its magic, so that it does not collapse into an undifferentiated obscenity.[58] In a replay of this encounter, Manfred ends up stabbing his own daughter Matilda "into the bosom" (104). The Gothic clearly wishes to recharge language with its hidden meanings, to connect it with a vast repertoire of unconscious associations. In plunging the dagger into his own daughter's bosom, Manfred seeks out the place of taboo, and in a horrifying moment confuses daughter with mistress. The deed is done in the shadow of the moon. The moon is not only a sign of things to come ("this moon will not be out without our seeing some strange revolution," says the fool Jaquez) but also the backdrop of desire. It is, after all, the "moon-beams" that expose Matilda's bosom and fill the mind of the austere priest Ambrosio in M. G. Lewis' *The Monk* with an impossible passion, the unpresentable sexual sublime.

The Castle of Otranto is the central text (or moment) of the Gothic precursor text. Its radical difference might be located at three levels. The first is its challenge to accepted forms of fictional representations. In daring to represent the unpresentable—both at the level of the outwardly supernatural and the inwardly uncanny—Walpole puts into relief the whole question of what constitutes reality and how it is (or might be) represented. This question, which for some empiricists is an ontological given, and is defined by them in terms of an absolute distinction between the physical and the metaphysical, is at the very core of the Gothic sublime and postmodernism.[59] The nostalgia about the impossibility of presentation (the classic version of the sublime) now gets reinforced by what Lyotard, in defining the postmodern sublime, said is "the putting back into an endless play the presuppositions which are at work in all work."[60] The logic of the endless play is to be found in the gradual conceptualizing of the Gothic by its own writers as a single heterogeneous text that constitutes a self-contained and autoreferential intertext, an intertext very much in Julia Kristeva's sense of the word.[61] Linked to this reading of the sublime is our second crucial difference, which we have already located in the Gothic texts' conscious doubling of character. Character is not rendered organically through social processes; instead, it enters into an imaginary series where specular identifications or confusions are the norm. Manfred/Frederic, Matilda/Isabella, Theodore/"Alfonso" draw on each other's descriptions and betray (if not actually encourage) identity, rather than individuality and difference. Using Roland Barthes' classes of narrative, we can see that the entire discourse of *The Castle of Otranto* is largely an interplay of *catalyses* (the merely chronological) and *informants* (pure data).[62] This play on *catalyses* and *informants* suggests an evasion of the full psychological complexities of characters as carriers of consciousness. Characters become cyphers, marks on paper, in a narrative of duplication and redundancy. Thus, Manfred's continued references to his "story" ("you are acquainted with my story," "my story should be no secret to you," "my story has drawn down the judgments," and so on[63]) uncannily echo every one else's stories as well. To read the Gothic is to understand the logic of the uncanny. Finally, as a case history the Gothic cannot be written down because each subsequent text will attempt its own reading of the initial Gothic scene. As the texts write out or expand on the possibilities inherent in the original moment of the Gothic, the cleavage between language and representation becomes progressively more acute as, in a conscious departure from Ann Radcliffe's retrospective explanations, the elements of the supernatural get absorbed into the overall definition of the Gothic sublime. The supernatural ceases to be shocking or "horrid" (in Jane Austen's sense of the word) as it now acquires an agenda quite different from those attributed to it by contemporary readers. What is at work here is no less than a radical retheorizing of the Longinian/Burkean sublime as the texts, anticipating Kant's demarcations of the domains of the mind (where aesthetic judgment appropriates an almost autonomous space for itself), project a vision of the world that the mind can grasp only if it forgoes for the moment the law of reason. The compromise that the imagination makes in the process for this passing privilege, in narrative terms, gets transformed into the condition(s) of the subject as it is attracted and simultaneously repulsed by the object of the sublime in an economy of evil and the dissolution of the self. The forced unity of romance that one finds in Walpole and Radcliffe has its counterpart in the total lack of the self-transcending subject in M. G. Lewis, Mary Shelley, and Charles Maturin. Not surprisingly, in the Gothic antiheroes become much more interesting than heroes even though, for political purposes, the superficial ideology of the text continues monotonously to affirm, on the whole, the triumph of good over evil.

Without repeating our theoretical insights, we can now move toward the principle of Gothic heterogeneity by enlarging our precursor text through the examination of a more direct example of sexual transgression and disturbance of the social order in the Gothic sublime. We can do this through a more or less pragmatic reading of some key texts. This part of our narrative commentary also begins with a letter. On April 15, 1768, Horace Walpole wrote to George Montagu:

> I have finished my tragedy, but as you would not bear the subject, I will say no more of it, but that Mr Chute, who is not easily pleased, likes it, and Gray who is still more difficult, approves it. I am not yet intoxicated enough with it, to think it would do for the stage, though I wish to see it acted. . . .[64]

More detailed information about the date of its composition and Walpole's subsequent responses to this tragedy (up to 1791, when it was finally published) are to be found in the *Yale Walpole*.[65] In the "fragments" entitled "short notes" we discover that the tragedy was in fact begun on December 25, 1766 and finished on March 15, 1768. Unlike *The Castle of Otranto*, this tragedy, which he called *The Mysterious Mother*,[66] took longer to compose, but then, as we are told in the "short notes," he did lay it "aside for several months." There is a long saga surrounding its publication. A few copies, about fifty in all, were printed at Strawberry Hill between 14 June and 6 August 1768, and there is some evidence that it might have actually been staged in 1778, had not Sir John Hawkins, the influential magistrate friend of Dr. Johnson, objected to the theme. The play, printed by Dodsley in 1781, had to wait another ten years before it was released.[67] Whatever his feelings toward *The Mysterious Mother* when he first wrote it and privately printed fifty copies for distribution, his subsequent reaction to the play was always couched in the most negative of terms. It is not uncommon to find phrases like "inexcusably disgusting," "the subject of which is so disgusting," "disgusting tragedy," "so horrid," scattered throughout his correspondence. What is this strange tragedy, the likes of which, in drama at any rate, English literature has barely seen? Byron had this tragedy in mind when in his preface to *Marino Faliero*, he called Walpole the "'Ultimus Romanorum,' the author of the Mysterious Mother, a tragedy of the highest order, and not a puling love-play."[68] Just over a century later Peter Burra echoed Byron's enthusiastic comment by calling it "the greatest play of the century."[69]

Walpole himself was, however, less impressed. In a carefully written postscript to the play in his posthumously published *Works*, Walpole admits that the play is "revolting" in its theme. In this postscript he also gives an account of the real events on which the tragedy was based.[70] This point was recognized by Mrs. Barbauld in her preface to *The Castle of Otranto*, published in the British Novelists series. Elaborating on a play the subject of which she considered "so disgustingly repulsive," she added, "The story itself is in the *Gesta Romanorum*, and in Taylor's *Cases of Conscience*; and as in a play it never could be acted, it had better have remained in the form of a story."[71]

Some sixteen years before the play opens, the Count of Narbonne was accidentally killed. That same night his son Edmund, then sixteen, went to bed with his paramour Beatrice. The following day Edmund's mother banished him from Narbonne. The play itself opens with the return of Edmund and a young soldier named Florian, in whose mind seems to linger a forewarning (from someone "like the tenant of some night-haunted ruin") that he should not go into this castle. Inside the castle is the Countess, who has been mourning her "son's birth" (1.5) and two scheming priests (Benedict and Martin) who are suspicious of the Countess's "boundless passions" (1.3) and who want to "sift" her "secret sin." There is some "untold tale," some "mystery" surrounding these "mould'ring castles," some strange event that makes an "orphan girl" shudder at the thought of going past the church porch where they say "the count [of Narbonne] sits" (2.2). The atmosphere is heavy and exhausting, and for sixteen years it has been like this, says Friar Martin:

Sixteen fatal years
Has Narbonne's province groan'd beneath the hand
Of desolation—for what crimes we know not!
(2.2)

Struck by the demeanor of Edmund's friend Florian, the Countess encourages the liaison between her favorite orphan Adeliza and this young man. Unknown to the Countess, however, Adeliza has fallen in love with Edmund, who finally confronts his mother in person with this information toward the end of Act 3. The language here is pure Gothic as the encounter replays a forbidden memory. Alone and seemingly trapped within the confines of her delirium, it is now "passion's crime," "convulsions," "madness," "conscience," "phrenzy" that shoot through a barely intelligible discourse. Her images are those of "ravishing." In a clear echo of the scene in which Manfred stabs his own daughter Matilda, the Countess screams in agony, "I know the foe—see! see! he points his lance!/He plunges it all flaming in my soul" (4.4). Lost in "eternal anguish," this is no common "shame" or "guilt," this is the very return of the repressed, the confrontation with the uncanny in the special language of the Gothic sublime. Language henceforth must be "unriddled," and this is precisely how Benedict falsely conveys to Adeliza and Edmund what he says is "the Countess's wish." "Is my poor language nauseous?" (4.6) complains Benedict. This is a strange description of language—"nauseous." Yet that is exactly what has happened to the Countess' discourse itself. Later on, Ambrosio's language (in Lewis' *The Monk*), too, will become "nauseous," a hateful memory trace rather than the full-bodied medium through which we define our own existence. "Nauseous" is a "prison-house" that not only "delimits" and "confines" but also condemns the subject in a "musty," "smelly" dungeon of the unconscious.[72] Language here has become nightmare, and the sublime, nauseating. So the marriage of Adeliza and Edmund is a "business dispatch'd," their nuptials are "blasted e'er accomplish'd" (5.1). Benedict's language (5.5) is strong with sexual innuendos, suggesting a "revenge" that is both political (clergy over state) and sexual—the countess is an object of imaginary sexual gratification for these highly repressed (and oppressive) yet privileged friars, because they have access to confessions.

The countess speaks of a "disturb'd" brain, of reason "guilty" and "unhinged," and of her life as a strange "book of fate." Sixteen years after that dreadful night when her husband died hunting a stag and she herself had taken Beatrice's place in her son's bed, the narrative of the Oedipus complex reenacts itself. Her own son has married their daughter. Genealogy begins to sound like a riddle as, confused and delirious, the Countess asks "am I not in my castle?" Yes, she is no longer in "her castle": the walls that make up that space have collapsed. Language can only repeat itself when the "secret" is unravelled. It cannot say any more without either becoming redundant or retreating into silence. And it has been a very "wordy" exercise so far—no real drama, no action, only "words, words, words."

> Confusion! phrenzy! blast me, all ye furies! . . .
> . . . quick unsay
>
> The monstrous tale—oh!
>
> (5.5)

Such knowledge splits open the "Globe of the world," dissolving "mother," "mistress," "daughter," "sister," "wife," "husband," into "the pillar of accumulated horrors" (5.6). As Edmund the "polluted son" exclaims, it is an "execrable" truth from which release is possible either through the violent murder of the mother or through suicide. He attempts to do the latter, but his mother stabs herself first. Before she does so, she asks Edmund to conceal the "truth" from the world: a lid must be placed on "prohibitive" truth. Adeliza, who swoons before the secret of her birth is told, is sent to the "holy sisters" while Edmund himself gets ready to "welcome the sabre/That leaves no atom of it undefac'd!" (5.6). The incestuous sublime is an impossible idea incapable of becoming part of real historical processes. Edmund's suicidal option confirms that the self is so totally castrated that it cannot claim any form of empowerment under the sign of the sublime. It becomes obvious that Gothic discourse now begins to explore radically different means by which the unutterable may be articulated as the mind struggles to offer a determinate judgment on the (sublime) experience itself.

The Mysterious Mother is another moment of the Gothic precursor text in that it expands themes less explicitly articulated in its first moment, the moment of *The Castle of Otranto*, the "founding" text of this discursive practice. When Robert Jephson dramatized *The Castle of Otranto* he called it *The Count of Narbonne*[73] effectively reading *The Castle of Otranto* through *The Mysterious Mother*. In Jephson's version "Otranto" becomes "Narbonne"; Conrad, Edmund; and Matilda, echoing Adeliza, Adelaide. Unaware of the existence of *The Mysterious Mother*, the early reviewers of the play simply read it as a dramatic transformation of *The Castle of Otranto*.[74]

The argument for a heterogeneous Gothic, which parallels Lyotard's own appeal to the Kantian sublime as "a principle of ultimate 'heterogeneity,'"[75] becomes clearer if we recall how the changes in names of characters in Jephson's play enable *The Mysterious Mother* to function as a screen between the play and *The Castle of Otranto*. The latter thus becomes a text that is not just the pages between the covers of the novel, but all three texts. Again, there is a "textual" invasion, a "takeover" that destroys the "unity" of the text. More dramatic consequences arise if we actually examine the play further. Isabella becomes an absent signifier now, in that she is only pursued through various labyrinthine passages offstage. Her plight is narrated to Raymond, Count of Narbonne, but she may well be a figment of his imagination. She is, in fact, a kind of a "specter," which is never grasped nor represented on stage. Similarly Conrad, who is now Edmund, has just fallen off his horse ("That curs'd Barb . . .") which was Narbonne's "fatal gift" to him. We recall the death of the Count of Narbonne in *The Mysterious Mother*, who dies while hunting a stag. Did he, too, fall off a horse? We begin to read *The Count of Narbonne* as a kind of a metatext or a commentary on *The Castle of Otranto*. Has the father killed his son for fear that he might usurp his place in his wife's embrace? He certainly does kill Adelaide/Adeliza at the end of the play. This kind of dissemination of textual signifiers (character, space, time, narrative) finally takes us back to our initial question: who, in fact, is Manfred, Prince of Otranto in the first instance? Can he possibly be retrieved? Is he the signifier in a text published in 1764 or is he a signifier with multiple associations? Does he not become Raymond, Count of Narbonne, as well as the dead husband of the "Mysterious Mother"? And in retrospect are not Hortensia and Hippolita both implicated in the crime of the Countess of Narbonne? Although there isn't in Jephson the same overcast, heavy imagery that permeates *The Mysterious Mother*, there are strong hints of sexual transgressions, and a similar use of a metonymic discourse that, again, connects us with the language of dreams and the structure of the unconscious. Raymond's fear of impotence and sexual envy takes the form of a verbal contrast between Theodore's "tough arms" and "force" against Isabella's "delicate hands," "weak, soft and yielding to the gentlest touch." Before he stabs his daughter

Adelaide, his language acquires a directness that even *The Mysterious Mother* might have found excessive:

> Arise grim Vengeance, and wash out my shame!
> Ill-fated girl! A bloody Hymen waits thee.
> (5.10)

The hymen that "divides and joins" must be cruelly raped so that the phallus may demonstrate its ultimate domination. In *The Castle of Otranto,* where the censorship was much stronger, the dagger was plunged "over her [Matilda's] shoulder into the bosom." What convention makes the articulation of "Hymen" permissible, and what is the source of its fascination in the Gothic sublime? Is it that, finally, the Gothic sublime is the repressed semantics of a pre-Oedipal urge toward dissolution that surfaces, in the texts, purely as effects of the uncanny? Or are we seeing the reimaging of the sublime in such a radically different manner that the sublime object of the Gothic leaves a bad aftertaste in our mouths? Is the nostalgia for nondifference also, like Gothic language, nauseous?

Walpole himself did not read *The Count of Narbonne* in anything like this fashion. In fact in a letter to Robert Jephson written on January 27, 1780, Walpole warmly praised the manuscript of *The Count of Narbonne,* commenting on the author's success in making "so rational a play out of my wild tale."[76] In the same letter Walpole says that he "cannot compliment the author [Clara Reeve] of *The Old English Baron,* professedly written in imitation, but as a corrective to *The Castle of Otranto.*"[77] Two years previously, in a letter to Rev. William Cole (August 22, 1778) he had called the work "the most insipid dull nothing you ever saw," since it is so entirely "stripped of the marvellous."[78] Similar sentiments were expressed to Rev. William Mason to whom, too, he had written, "any trial for murder at the Old Bailey would make a more interesting story."[79] Yet in spite of Walpole's disapproval, it is *The Castle of Otranto* that was the departure point for Clara Reeve.

Like *The Castle of Otranto, The Champion of Virtue*[80] (the original title of *The Old English Baron*) was offered to the reading public as a translation of a "manuscript in the old English language." With the permission of the owner, who also happened to be a friend, it was claimed that the "editor" simply translated this document into modern English.[81] Furthermore, even in the first edition, the work's indebtedness to *The Castle of Otranto* was explicitly stated. A more detailed indebtedness to Walpole is expressed in the preface to the second edition, to which I must now turn my attention. The work's anonymity is now lost and, echoing Walpole's own preface to the second (1765) edition of *Otranto,* Clara Reeve finds vindication in the public's enthusiasm for the work. In a much more explicit, and extended, fashion the intertext is now foregrounded:

> This Story is the literary offspring of the Castle of Otranto, written on the same plan, with a design to unite the most attractive and interesting circumstances of the ancient Romance and modern Novel. . . .[82]

Her disagreements with the intertext, though not major, are nevertheless not inconsiderable, especially since Ann Radcliffe was to endorse them, if not in her critical practice, at least in her fiction, a point picked up by the *Critical Review*'s comment on Mrs. Radcliffe's *The Romance of the Forest* in 1792: "The greater part of the work resembles, in manner, the Old English Baron, formed on the model of the Castle of Otranto."[83]

Clara Reeve's almost parodistic rendition of the precursor text, her conscious appropriation of the earlier moment of the Gothic and its feminization, leads to what Frank Kermode called "a problematical abdication of authority and control."[84] This abdication, which Reeve herself had raised in her theoretical piece, *The Progress of Romance*, endorses writing as an anonymous activity, an *écriture,* discontinuous and indeterminate, "unsutured," to use a term common in current cinema criticism. The claim that the reconstruction will be only partial because the manuscript being "edited" is itself barely legible, gradually becomes intrinsic to the genre itself. The precursor text, as argued here, therefore loses its bondage to specific authors, since each "author" embeds his or her text in this radically new genre, which began with *The Castle of Otranto*.[85] The Gothic thus becomes a literary terrain that extends the metonymic relationships between "self," "site," and "other." In Clara Reeve the dominant signifier, "the castle," continues to be read as in *The Castle of Otranto,* as mere space without actually being predicated. Of the sixty-nine or so occurrences of the actual word *castle* in *The Old English Baron* (it occurs around sixty-five times in *The Castle of Otranto*) what continues to be emphasized is its descriptive emptiness, its refusal to be "interpreted." The plot of the novel, which revolves around predictable questions of genealogy ("excessive" genealogy in the case of Baron Fitz-Owen; "problematic" genealogy in the case of the usurper and the current Lord

Lovel; "negative" genealogy in the case of Sir Philip Harclay; and "reconstituted" genealogy in Edmund's) seems to contradict the symbolic emptiness of the space of habitation, the castle. Yet in its very excess, this genealogy cannot generate a complex narrative and relapses simply into a confirmation of Edmund Twyford's antecedent. Like a black hole, the castle absorbs history into its own emptiness.

What marks off the various versions of the primary precursor text are levels of uncanny duplication at work in the Gothic. Read as the recognition that nothing further ever happens, that all history has always already been played out and that the subject is simply locked into an incessant series of repetitions, the Gothic rewrites the sublime and prefigures its theorization as the "Uncanny." Behind this stands a linguistic gulf that separates the word and its referent. For someone like David B. Morris, the literary genre that participates in this exchange, schism or gulf, and expands its symbolic possibilities, is the Gothic novel.[86] Nevertheless, in his reading of this practice Morris continues to construct the Gothic sublime as an extension of the Romantic sublime, which he defines, after Thomas Weiskel, as "that moment when the relation between the signifier and the signified breaks down and is replaced by an indeterminate relation."[87] Weiskel's examination of the Romantic sublime is a bit more complex than that, but for Morris the definition suggests a fracture or disjunction between word and image, an instability in our construction of meaning, which distinguishes the Romantic sublime from the eighteenth-century discussions of the subject, covering the period from Boileau to Dennis. Against the "fundamentally affective and pictorial" eighteenth-century sublime, we now have a defiantly hermeneutic and, arguably, prophetic and visionary reading of the exalted image. Morris' essay is interesting because it deconstructs the slightly more complex conjunction of forces that produced the Gothic novel. For instance, it is not simply a matter of the Gothic novelists using Burke as the source book of terrifying objects and examining their effects on the mind. More important, what Morris suggests is the connection between the Gothic image as the image of sublime impossibility and Freud's metapsychological insights. The Gothic sublime radicalizes the Romantic/historical sublime by treating terror as an effect of an object linked to the whole question of selfhood itself. A regressive narrative of the backward glance—captured so well in Isabella's anticipatory recognition of the real import of Manfred's demand—now displaces the prophetic and the visionary that Morris continues to connect, after Montague Summers and Devendra Varma, with the Gothic.

Freud's great text of the sublime as it shapes the Gothic is his essay entitled "The 'Uncanny.'"[88] Freud introduces a psychologically based theory of terror in which the subject is confronted with terror stemming from anxieties within the self. Against Burke's concern with a largely empirical account of terror, framed, moreover, in a discourse empowered by a sublime deity, Freud advances the idea of conflicting instinctual impulses that lack the absolute mimeticism of art and life. In the peculiar logic of attraction/coincidence/repulsion that underpins Freud's essay we begin to understand why the sublime (as an effect of terror that produces an uncontrollable emission or excess) is of such consequence to the Gothic novel. It is for this reason that

> A critical approach which reduces Gothic sublimity to the familiar inventory of ghosts and dark passageways cannot help us understand what was both profoundly innovative and yet also deeply inadequate in Burke's account.[89]

Burke's account of terror, as we have noted, failed to examine adequately its psychological dimensions (or grounds). At best, he could only offer a pseudoscientific explanation: "the radial fibres of the iris"[90] are agitated when one confronts terrifying objects. Now in the Gothic novels themselves, this contraction of the muscles of the iris (if we wish to follow Burke's science here) is superseded by a more thoroughgoing understanding of the unconscious yearnings and desires that underlie the subject's response to the terrifying. In this way the Gothic is a "testament to how much he [Burke] and his age were unable to explain about the sublime."[91]

As we have seen in the founding text(s) of the Gothic discursive practice, terror and the sublime are reached through an excessive (and self-consciously monotonous) use of the rhetorical devices of exaggeration (hyperbole) and repetition. These two devices reinforce two substantially different but interrelated concepts. Exaggeration is signalled in these texts primarily through absurd or excessive emotions, through the self-conscious expansion of the founding text, or through the language of sentimentality (whose triumphant texts were Henry Mackenzie's *The Man of Feeling* and Goethe's *Werter*). Repetition, the other rhetorical trope of the Gothic, has often been cited as a weakness in the composition of the Gothic novel (imprisonments, escapes, and much else besides are repeated at least twice, sometimes three times); however, it connects with a version of history where past and present commingle or interpenetrate. More significant, the repetition of events demonstrates, in David B. Morris's words, "an unknown or buried pattern, for which the curse on Otranto is a gaudy symbol."[92] Repetition also leads to duplication, to reality as "mirroring." Events repeated confound the chronological discreteness of history and their presumed noniterability. Reality mirroring questions the formal grounds by which character difference is designated. Character, in its most important use, its legal use, is normally read as social and historical difference. In the nonrealist discourse of *The Castle of Otranto,* resemblances and the narrative of circularity implicate the very logic of the uncanny and of the unconscious. The logic of the uncanny enables us to read into the Gothic sublime a narrative that has always been part of its hidden side. We get this immediately in *The Castle of Otranto,* where the death of young Conrad under the weight of a gigantic helmet reads like a sudden, nonsequential nightmare event, which is then extended even further with Theodore's immediate connection of this helmet with that on the head of the statue of Alfonso. Without any transition, the next segment recounts Manfred's attempted rape of Isabella, who a moment before would have been his daughter-in-law. Since there is no time here for a full-blown, realistic subject to develop, the question of a consciousness capable of self-transcending (as in the Romantic sublime) does not arise. Because the subject does not know what it is doing—the entire narrative of conscious control and motivation is missing from here—its desire is constructed through a series of unrelated effects; in short, desire becomes a function of the "Uncanny." At this point we need to offer a commentary on Freud's essay on the "Uncanny" so as to complete our theoretical account of the Gothic sublime.

In the basically etymological section of his essay on the "Uncanny," Freud anticipates his own position by quoting approvingly a quotation from Gutzkow, and another from Schelling. Gutzkow had quoted *"Oh, we call it 'unheimlich'; you call it 'heimlich.'"* And Schelling had added, *"'Unheimlich' is the name of everything that ought to have remained . . . secret and hidden but has come to light."* Freud comments:

> In general we are reminded that the word *'heimlich'* is not unambiguous, but belongs to two sets of ideas, which, without being contradictory, are yet very different: on the one hand it

> means what is familiar and agreeable, and on the other, what is concealed and kept out of sight. (345)

The words used for *heimlich/unheimlich* ("canny/uncanny") in the English translation undergo a similar process of ambiguation. At two points in their respective citations in the *OED* the meanings of "canny" and "uncanny" overlap. Consider the second meaning of "canny" as "cunning, artful, wily" against the third meaning of "uncanny" as "unreliable, not to be trusted." If the meanings are superimposed on each other, then the essential difference between the two words implied in their first dictionary meanings is totally lost. Again, when we examine their fourth respective entries, a similar (uncanny!) correspondence emerges. "Supernaturally wise, endowed with occult or magical powers," proclaims "canny"; "as being associated with supernatural arts or powers," replies the "uncanny." From around 1850 the meaning of "uncanny" as "mysterious, weird, uncomfortably strange or unfamiliar" has been on the ascendant.

It is not too difficult to see why the uncanny, with its intrinsic ambiguity and its emphasis on the surfacing of the hidden, should take us back to the debates about the postmodern sublime.

> There is no question, therefore, of any intellectual uncertainty here: we know now that we are not supposed to be looking on at the products of a madman's imagination, behind which we, with the superiority of rational minds, are able to detect the sober truth; and yet this knowledge does not lessen the impression of uncanniness in the least degree. The theory of intellectual uncertainty is thus incapable of explaining that impression. (352)

"There is no question, therefore, of any intellectual uncertainty here," writes Freud. Though Freud is specifically referring to Jentsch's explanation of the uncanny experience as a moment of doubt (one recalls Todorov's defiantly nonpsychoanalytic theory of the fantastic here), the theory of intellectual uncertainty is also a theory of the experience of the sublime. Freud advances two interrelated ideas in his essay at this point. The first is that the movement of the uncanny in Hoffman's "The Sand-Man" uncovers two crucial mental processes: the fear of castration which, displaced, transformed, is represented as the gouging out of one's eyes, and the notion of the compulsion to repeat. The fear of castration takes us to the threatening figure of the patriarch, whereas the compulsion to repeat expresses itself through the peculiar logic of attraction and repulsion.

Central to both these concepts—threat of castration and compulsion to repeat—is the theme of the double. This theme, with its variant in the Gothic, was originally an insurance or guarantee against death. In time, however, the double "becomes the uncanny harbinger of death" (357). The double then carries with it residues of a more primitive moment in the development of the subject when "the ego had not yet marked itself off sharply from the external world and from other people" (358) and had not quite entered the realm of difference. In other words, there is a strong sense of self-extinction in the phenomenal world that marks the experience of the repetition of the same thing (initially as an identification with the object in a mirror, but later in the projection of the self onto others). The source of uncanny feelings (the phrase is Freud's), such as unsuspected recurrences and involuntary repetitions, is now read by Freud through a discourse that has close parallels with the entire German tradition of the sublime, from Kant to Schopenhauer. Freud, therefore, gives the uncanny a firmly subjective dimension. He uses phrases such as "we do feel," "their uncanny effect," but what is different is the explanation of this feeling. The pre-Freudian sublime had considered responses to the sublime through aesthetic categories of taste. Furthermore, it had advanced the idea of the incapacity of the mind to comprehend the phenomenon even when reason demanded total "comprehensibility." With Freud, however, the effect of the uncanny is explained through an inner, unconscious compulsion to repeat. The subject is therefore formed not through conscious and rational thinking, but is itself a complex site through which the unconscious represents itself. Let us give this a sharper focus by juxtaposing two definitions:

> Whatever is fitted in any sort to excite the ideas of pain, and danger . . . whatever is in any sort terrible . . . is a source of the *sublime.* (Burke, *Enquiry,* 39)

> . . . whatever reminds us of this inner "compulsion to repeat" is perceived as uncanny. (Freud, "The 'Uncanny,'" 361)

The source of terror now regresses into a trace, a memory, a recollection that is firmly located in the unconscious because underlying Freud's "compulsion to repeat" is the crucial psychoanalytic theory of repressive anxiety. In fact, the point of the uncanny (recall Schelling again) is that the old, the hidden, the repressed reappears. One class of things that constantly undergoes this process is the "frightening" (Burke's terrible). Now, whether the original itself was frightening is inconsequential; what is important is that the repressed effect of it is. The uncanny, as the moment of the release of the repressed, is the moment of the unpresentable as well. In narrative it erupts as the double at the level of the look and as a synchronous moment of "I have been there before" at the level of thought. (In a curious fashion, as Freud himself acknowledges, psychoanalysis, which seeks to explain the source of our feeling of the uncanny, is itself "become uncanny" [366]). Of course, the place where we've been before, the womb, is the ultimate source of the uncanny. The *unheimlich* here, as Freud says, is "what was once *heimisch,* familiar" (368) where the prefix *un-* is the sign of repression.

Just as everything that is frightening is not the source of the sublime, so, too, everything that has been repressed is not the source of the uncanny. The theme of the double, the repetitions, the many moments of synchronicity, and so on in fairy tales, for instance, do not lead to the effect of the uncanny because they do not, for the subject, induce a return of the repressed. In fact, the event or object that gives rise to feelings of the uncanny is directly related to a confirmation, in that object or event, of a prior, discarded belief. This class of the uncanny parallels Kant's "mathematically sublime," in that there are elements of duration, extension, chronology, limit, and so on involved here. The second class of the uncanny, with its "repressed infantile complexes, . . . the castration complex, womb phantasies, etc." (371) might be likened to Kant's "dynamically sublime," which deals with ineluctable intensities. The classes—both Freud's and Kant's—are not discrete, since there is a considerable level of overlap between them. Nevertheless, Freud advances a relatively neat definition of the uncanny:

> an uncanny experience occurs either when infantile complexes which have been repressed are once more revived by some impression, or when primitive beliefs which have been surmounted seem once more to be confirmed. (372)

In Freud's own usage (*Das Unheimliche*) the play on the double and its examination leads to degrees and levels of self-reflexivity in which Freud himself is firmly implicated.[93] Indeed, the double constructs a *mise-en-âbime* pattern of receding narratives that can only lead to an abyss. So the essay repeats itself at many levels, drawing on life and fiction, myth, dreams, and phantasms. In the essentially fictional discourse that Freud adopts, analyst and analysand, author and reader, get enmeshed in a narrative of the pursuer and the pursued, with a consequent confusion of identities. Freud's own uncanny reference to the number 62 (his age) is presented through the fictional second person "you" as the reader's phantasmal encounter with that number. The irreducibility of the *Unheimliche* and the *Heimliche* leads Freud to a peculiarly androgynous semantic theory of the two in one. But this very insight, the doubling and "returning" of meaning, "the infinite game of substitutions, through which what constitutes the elusive moment of fear returns and eclipses itself again," in Hélène Cixous' words,[94] is at the very core of the Gothic sublime. Cixous, in fact, delineates four significant clusters of "doubling" that Freud systematically pursues: manifestations of the double ("telepathy," substitution, recurrence, return of the repressed); researchers of the double (Otto Rank, Hoffman, Freud, E. Jentsch, the poet Heine); anecdotal examples (tales, recollections); and thematic doubling ("each theme is the double of another theme").[95]

Two further points raised by Cixous require a gloss here. The first of these deals with mortality and the uncanny figure of the Ghost; the second is the reading of fiction through Freud's *Unheimliche/Heimliche.* Our relationship to death is itself an instance of the *Unheimliche* since, in life, it has no representation. In death, death represents itself, but the moment of death denies life access to it. This irreducibility of death, its defiance/denial of the principle of the eternal returning (everything else returns except death) is what characterizes its peculiar attraction and its dread. Burke had recognized this as an instance of the sublime since it is a "cause of terror" (57). With ghosts, however, the mind represents the uncanny return of the dead and finds a mode of representation that for the subject, when alive, had always been impossible. The many versions of Alfonso's ghost (often indicated only metonymically, through the gigantic helmet) are thus a return of the genealogically repressed, since Manfred's lineage is that of a usurper.

For Freud, fiction has a special relationship to the *Unheimliche:* ". . . there are many more means of creating uncanny effects in fiction than there are in real life" (373). The line between fiction and life or reality is therefore as problematic, as complicated, as obscure as that which connects the *Unheimliche* with the *Heim-*

liche. As Freud's own examination of fiction proceeds, both of these—the *Unheimliche* of reality *and* of fiction—interpenetrate, flow into each other, and confuse all prior distinctions between literature and life. One of the key themes of the uncanny in the Gothic is the theme of incest, because it introduces an *Unheimliche* terror based on biological doubles: father and daughter; mother and son; brother and sister. To quote Cixous slightly out of context here, "it 're-presents' that which in solitude, silence, and darkness will (never) be presented to you."[96]

With Freud's redefinition of terror as the return of the repressed (Schopenhauer's *nirvana* principle is the mediating category here) we enter a domain of the sublime that allows us to read our precursor text(s) in a much more sophisticated fashion. But more important, as Harold Bloom has pointed out, "The 'Uncanny'" and *Beyond the Pleasure Principle* are "the only major contribution that the Twentieth Century has made to the aesthetics of the Sublime."[97] The sublime is one of Freud's major repressed concerns; it is also a creative moment explicable in terms of catastrophe theories of creation. Harold Bloom once again:

> I would venture one definition of the literary Sublime (which to me seems always a negative Sublime) as being that mode in which the poet, while expressing previously repressed thought, desire, or emotion, is able to continue to defend himself against his own created image by disowning it, a defense of *un-naming* it rather than *naming* it.[98]

Gothic terrors are therefore drawn from the deepest recesses of the psyche, in short, from the unconscious (Freud's *das Unbewusste*), the realm of the repressed. But since the unconscious is also the place of the uncanny (and of the sublime), it is the labyrinthine site of the *mise-en-âbime*, of images that constantly regress and reduplicate, of compulsive repetitions into which entire human history is locked and from which alone the "subject" speaks. Crucial to this version of the sublime is death (the aim of life is, after all, death) and it is only in the ghost (in the supernatural) that the "unrepresentability" of death in life (to experience death is to die) is made a possibility. This is the next great theme of the Gothic, but like the theme of the double, it repeats an earlier moment, an already occurred event.

But as we have seen already, Gothic death is no longer the same object that for Burke was the source of terror and therefore of the sublime. Death as the sublime in the Gothic is the uncanny-sublime; it is the always recurring/repeating presence that threatens the subject with the image of his or her own impossible representation: Dracula cannot see himself in a mirror—death has no way of representing itself. Yet in the Gothic, death is troped through the supernatural machinery and used as the uncanny image of love itself. Even though in the case of Frederic's desire for Matilda we are considering a negative *Lust*, it is worth recalling that he stumbles on a cowled skeleton in his search for Hippolita precisely when he needs her as a go-between. More dramatically, in Matthew Gregory Lewis' *The Monk* the ghostly, bleeding nun exchanges places with Agnes and offers herself as Don Raymond's bride instead. Feelings of disgust as well as desire commingle, and yet it is sublime in its terrifying mystery as the repressed returns. Cixous had referred (after Freud) to the "uncanniness of the repressed and the uncanniness of the surmounted."[99] These surmounted beliefs are represented in the supernaturalism that we find in the Gothic novels. It is not a question of whether the events themselves are true or not; rather, it is a question of their power over the mind and their ultimate source in the unconscious. "Since almost all of us still think as savages do on this topic," Freud explains, "it is no matter for surprise that the primitive fear of the dead is still so strong within us and always ready to come to the surface on any provocation" (365). In the Gothic, ancient and residual beliefs always return to haunt us; from these there is no escape.

David B. Morris' argument that Gothic fiction actually revised and rewrote the eighteenth-century sublime may be seen as a tendency that was intrinsic to theories of the sublime in the first instance. The mind's failure to grasp the sublime is now transformed into an uncanny experience of that which lies outside consciousness. In the autoreferential discourses adopted by the Gothic, the sublime as "the infinitely unpresentable which spurs us to yet finer representations, the lawless masculine force which violates"[100]—the central concern of Burke—is taken a step further. In "regressing" the sublime, Horace Walpole, for instance, returned to the unconscious for tropes, uncanny figures, fragmented narratives that function as substitutes, doubles, or surrogates of this unknown. Death in the figure of a corpse or a skeleton cannot be read allegorically (as in realist texts), as representing or symbolizing itself; on the contrary, the figure, the uncanny presence of the impossible apprehension in life, endorses the ultimate otherness of death and our own failure (of the will) to know. Where Burke had adopted a discourse full of eloquence to designate the sublime ("Whatever is fitted in any sort . . ."), Gothic sublimity articulates that which cannot be articulated, or named, and in the process transforms the experience into something like a primal scream (or swoon). The Gothic precursor text(s) therefore trouble us through their uneasy relationship with language and reality, and through their uncanny intrusions into those areas which lie outside language.

In the negative sublime—the sublime that connects Burke with Lyotard's postmodernism—the superego is all anxiety, as it initially threatens and then collapses the ego's own equilibrium. It is at this point—the point so brilliantly mapped out by Kant—that reason turns to imagination with an offer that it, imagination, cannot refuse. It encourages the imagination to possess the object, only to warn it of the impossibility of possession. Consequently, imagination is asked to renounce this fantastic desire to possess and conform to the dictates of reason. What reason offers as compensation (for the loss of desire, what it itself lacks) is an alternative power, different but greater than the loss of desire. But in that momentary wish to possess, in that twilight zone of indeterminate, frenzied, and chaotic excitement, the (Kantian) sublime comes into being. This is the imperial, the grand narrative of the sublime, without which there is no point of departure for any study of the sublime. No matter what our sublime—whether it is the genealogical, the incestuous, or the textual—we have to return to Kant as our point of departure. But what the Gothic precursor text(s) now express is the figure of the rational subject as it looks back at reason for permission to possess what is clearly the illicit, the obscene object. The nod that it requires assumes both an essentialist definition of the subject and the subject's capacity to accept that the freedom, the leeway, is only momentary. In the Gothic sublime the question one asks deals with this grand narrative of the sublime, but the emphasis is different: what are the consequences of reason's loss of control, of the lack of return from the cognition of the sublime, if the subject does not keep his or her side of the bargain? As David Carroll points out, "Kant makes 'being hostage' to the unpresentable bearable, so to speak, by regulating its nondetermined, 'subjective,' characteristics in terms of an Idea."[101] In other words, the regulating principle of the Idea (which is in itself sublime, since it has no corresponding object) functions as a grand, controlling narrative that legitimates, finally, the primacy of the subject in the first instance. The Romantic sublime would not be possible if this primacy were not firmly in place in the first instance. Against this the Gothic sublime offers a minor narrative without a grand controlling principle. It critiques the historical sublime with a further extension of the "what if" question. In the process it leaves the subject scarred and without the semantics of the controlling Idea. The horrifying knowledge here is that the sublime is like a black hole, it drags the subject into its abyss, into its pure negativity. The politicoethical dimension therefore becomes a matter of contingency, of culture-specific, narrowly historical contexts, from which we operate as social beings. It is for this reason that the Gothic sublime is its own precursor. It is also a sublime that the postmodern condition understands well as its own double.

3

Gothic Fragments and Fragmented Gothics

There is a class of Gothic texts that I would want to refer to as symptoms of the form insofar as it raises problems hidden "by the completeness of works that have attained the status of 'texts'."[1]. If in literary terms transcendence always implies a way of totalizing so that the work of art itself triumphs over the contradictions rendered in the social formations depicted in the text (the Marxist sublime), then the extreme version of its negation would be texts that are so ruptured, so rent apart, that they signify the ultimately uncanonizable in literature. These barely theorized Gothic symptoms (or texts) signify, discursively, the impossibility of any order of the *a priori*, whether thematic or structural, and resist the inscription of the Real in them by foregrounding features that Jameson was to describe as characteristics of postmodernism: "new types of syntax or syntagmatic relationships." I have in mind those extreme instances of Gothic fragments that Robert D. Mayo believed belonged to a "distinctly different genre."[2] The paradigmatic text of this form was Mrs. Barbauld's "Sir Bertrand," which spawned countless imitations in the magazines. In all these fragments the aim was simply to arouse fear, astonish, and delight,[3] and as fragments they were inconclusive narratives. But we need not commit ourselves totally to Mrs. Barbauld's definition of the Gothic fragment, because fragments are really versions or symptoms of the extreme otherness of the Gothic sublime, which emerges, in these fragments, as the embodiment of what Slavoj Žižek has aptly called the "void, the emptiness created by the symbolic structure" implicit in the fragments.[4] My use of the term *fragment* is, therefore, slightly different from its traditional generic definition (as in Mayo, for instance). Apart from "Sir Bertrand," all the other texts discussed in this chapter are fragments only insofar as they characterize a particular type of tendency in the Gothic. Wordsworth's *Gothic Tale* and Byron's "A Fragment" were simply left incomplete by their respective authors. Mary Shelley's *Mathilda,* in its manuscript form, strikes one as a kind of a palaeographic sublime in which a daughter's agitated writing (the marks of ink on paper, writing as pure signifier) draws on the handwriting of the absent historical father, William Godwin. Goethe's melancholy sublime, *Werter,* is a text that invades these fragments and offers a prior model, a simulacrum, sets of "intensities," that infiltrate the discourse of the Gothic by entering its interstices and providing it with a narrative of nostalgia and loss.

Polidori's narratives, notably *The Vampyre* and *Ernestus Berchtold,* comprise another type of "fragment" we discuss here. *The Vampyre* is a conscious writing out of a fragment, a re-working of a precursor, that in turn becomes itself fragmented as a text written in the shadow of Byron. *Ernestus Berchtold* is a horrifying tale of incest, in many ways even a cruel text, as it terrorizes the mind of the reader with a narrative that aims at radically lifting the censorship of the superego and indeed, making its claims to a superior moral ground redundant. Polidori's attempts to give form, find a totality, through a perverse writing that encourages capaciousness and plenitude, are symptomatic of the genre of fragments, as we use that term here. In this respect *Ernestus Berchtold*'s realist design and formal patterning simply hide its fissures, its incapacity to "contain" its themes within narrative. The thematic core of this text, an extreme form of incestuous coupling, the absolute *imaginary* relation, as defined by Lacan, is then played out in *Mathilda,* the text with which this chapter ends.

In both Byron and Polidori, the narrative on the theme of Calmet's vampires introduces a "love-crime,"[5] the rape/death of a woman on her wedding night. This murder and violation is related to a perverse fascination, on the part of the narrator, with the vampire-hero (developed more fully in Bram Stoker's *Dracula*) who is "sick unto death." The sublime vampire gets recast as Frankenstein's monster who will also violate Frankenstein's bride on her wedding night. The conjunction of love and death that we noted with reference to Walpole and Matthew Gregory Lewis takes a more extreme form in these fragments as the life force, through the structures of the "Uncanny," duplicates itself in its absolute opposite, the principle of death. Gothic fragments and fragmented Gothics are thus explorations of a psychology that threatens the subject with another form of the sublime. This sublimity is marked either by the sentimentalist's obsession with death (in a version of the proto-oceanic sublime), as in *Werter* and *Mathilda,* or by the victim's fascination with a (heroic) representative of death. As we examine the texts, it should become clear that the two versions (the sentimentalist and the heroic) in fact collapse into one another, dissolving all these texts into fragments of the Gothic "unspeakable," the absolute negation of the soaring, ultimately defiant, subject of the positive Romantic sublime.

One of the underlying characteristics of these fragments is the desire for the Other which is, however, never fulfilled. Because desire is insatiable, it is indicated in the Gothic fragments either by an incapacity to complete the narrative ("I almost reached my destination" form) or by a failure to work through the moment of trauma. These fragments are therefore marked by constant deferrals, reformulations, tautologies, recurrences, return to beginnings, repetition, exhaustion, excess, and so forth, as the thinking self is invaded by the desiring self. Desire, of course, cannot be fulfilled or represented, since we don't really know,in Žižek's words, "What desire should I desire?"[6] In short, the form that the narratives take is predicated on a Gothic sublime that, like the Lacanian Real, escapes inscription. But the subject's orientation in terms of this sublime points to its own lack as a signifiable entity. It is this lack that drags the subject (as the ideal ego) to the theme of incest, which is one of the grand narratives of the *imaginary* identity of self and Other through the metaphorics of the double and the mirror. The suture implied here of this impossible act of totalization can only lead to an even further regression. Again, the subject in the Gothic sublime ceases to soar; the mind fails to supply it with the technology of transcendence because, in spite of the intervention of the law of reason, the attraction of dissolution in the sublime is so overpowering that the subject does not metaphorically glance back at the Law for permission for this momentary fascination with the sublime. The abyss is embraced, but not contemplatively, as in the Indian sublime.[7]

There are, then, two distinctive themes that we must isolate here. The first of these, as found in its archetype, Mrs. Barbauld's "Sir Bertrand," precludes the kinds of writing one associates with the literary work of art; the second relates directly to the discourse of sentimentalism as "a new type of emotional ground" (the phrase again is Jameson's). The sentimental sublime coexists with the Gothic for obvious reasons. First, its sense of excess in the crucial domain of emotions and their representation highlights precisely a characteristic that is endemic in the sublime—the relationship between emotions and the presented world. So Radcliffe's heroines would describe nature at length, and repetitively, because the threat of rape over them can only be deflected, inversely, on a nature that is the very opposite of the heroine's confused feelings. Second, the melancholic character, a totally "vertiginous being," instead of contemplating the objective world, so that his or her mind is embalmed, hystericizes it; he or she transforms the world into symptoms of his or her own repressed desire. In this respect, as we have said before, the Gothic sublime is an archesublime voraciously feeding on other sublimes. The exemplary text of sentimentalism is, of course, Goethe's *Werter* (1774).[8]

Let us, then, examine Mrs. Barbauld's fragment first as an example of the genre. Mrs. Anna Laetitia Barbauld (née Aikin) was an essayist and writer of extensive prefaces on the works of contemporary novelists. However, she did dabble in theory, and wrote the definitive Gothic fragment, "Sir Bertrand," a work that produced, as we have noted already, imitations with monotonous regularity during the late eighteenth century, "often with only slight or superficial modifications."[9] In her essay entitled "On Romances, an Imitation,"[10] Mrs. Barbauld argued that reading was essentially therapeutic, since it smoothed the "agitation of a ruffled mind with images of peace, tranquillity, and pleasure" (43). Yet the mind's equally intense delight, or absorption, in "misery" and "imaginary fears" (44) must be acknowledged as "a kind of paradox of the heart" (44), whose validity resided (as with the dreamlike quality of escapism) in their being "universally felt." The universalizing move here is linked, after Burke, to morality, because the "horrors" make us understand better "our own lot" by "beholding pictures of life tinged with deeper horrors" (44). Mrs. Barbauld is conscious of the argument of "refined selfishness," where the reader never believes that his or her own mind can lead to the miseries depicted in fiction. At heart Mrs. Barbauld remained a sentimentalist.

This point takes us directly to Mrs. Barbauld's second essay and her fragment "Sir Bertrand."[11] The core of this essay (which acts as a preface to the fragmentary tale) is the eighteenth-century (and largely Burkean) concern with pleasure and the paradox of pleasure arising from scenes in themselves rife with affliction. Mrs. Barbauld's argument is clearly an extension of her earlier essay on Romance, and based on the entire English tradition of sensationist theories of pleasure and pain. In this essay she writes that "human afflictions" are "a source of pleasure" (119) because these afflictions lead to a meditative condition, a reflective personality, which makes us, the readers, better than we are. Thus, instead of fleeing "from them with disgust and horror" (120), we return to them. Yet there is another order of fiction, which she defines as that order in which "horror" is not connected to moral ends, because it cannot possibly lead immediately to a state of higher awareness or understanding.

Toward the end of this essay Mrs. Barbauld offers "Sir Bertrand, A Fragment" as a practice demonstration of her theories: "The following fragment in which both these manners are attempted to be in some degree united, is offered to entertain a solitary winter's evening" (127). This "Fragment" opens with a knight (Sir Bertrand) alone on the "dreary moors before the curfew" (127). In the dark, he cannot move, fearful of the many "pits and bogs" (128) gaping to drag him and his horse down unawares. Through the thick clouds the moon is "a faint glimmering of light" (128). In such a night he lies on the ground, only to be excited by the sound of a "distant bell" (128), the source of which was marked by a "dim twinkling light" (128). Moving cautiously toward this source, he comes to a moat from which "by a momentary glimpse of moon-light" (129) he sees "a large antique mansion" in a state of considerable ruin and disarray (129). Sword in hand, he lifts the latch of the gate. The huge door creaks, and, predictably, closes behind him "with a thundering clap" (131). Ahead he sees a "pale bluish flame" (132), which moves through the usual halls, staircases, galleries, and further stairs into "a lofty gallery" (134) in which stands a large figure thrusting forth "the bloody stump of an arm" (134) and brandishing, menacingly, a sword. In desperation Sir Bertrand strikes at this figure, which vanishes, dropping a "massy iron key" (134). With this he opens a "brazen lock" (134) and finds himself in "a large apartment" (134) at the end of which is a coffin resting "upon a bier, with a taper burning on each side of it" (134). About "six paces" from the coffin, he pauses, because "a lady in a shrowd and black veil rose up in it" (135), stretching her arms toward him. Sir Bertrand quickly clasps the veiled lady in his arms; she responds by lifting up her veil and kissing "his lips" (135). Immediately the whole building shakes "as with an earthquake" (135), and Sir Bertrand falls "into a sudden trance" (135). Upon recovering, he finds himself "seated on a velvet sofa" (135) in a magnificent room. A sumptuous banquet, music, a lady of "incomparable beauty" (136), "gay nymphs" (136), all extraordinary in themselves, complete the scene. The lady advances toward Sir Bertrand and falls on her knees to thank "her deliverer" (136). She then leads him to the banquet, the music continues, and Sir Bertrand is without words. At this point the narrative comes to an abrupt end with the "final" sentence still incomplete:

> After the banquet was finished, all retired but the lady, who leading back the knight to the sofa, addressed him in these words:—(136–37)

Mrs. Barbauld's contrived ending of this romance is clearly designed to shock readers, or at least it is an invitation to them to complete the text. At the same time, any act of completion reverses the hierarchy of the sublime and the beautiful in this particular aesthetic economy. For, whereas the beautiful presupposes a harmony in our consciousness about the relationship between the self and the object of cognition, the sublime can only proclaim an incommensurable dissonance. What is equally important is the semantic ground of the genre as it locks itself into the language of sentimentalism, which, like the *limen* (the root of the word sublime), works on the "maximum amount of stimulus or nerve-excitation required to produce a sensation" (*OED*). So the next component that feeds into these fragments (as more than a genre, in Mrs. Barbauld's sense of the word) is, of course, the discourse of sentimentalism for which our proof-text is Goethe's *Werter* (1774).

Like Henry Mackenzie's extremely popular *The Man of Feeling* (1771), Goethe's novel also spawned many imitations, including a stage play by Frank Reynolds in 1786.[12] The strategic placing of *Werter* at this point is aimed at demonstrating the way in which the Gothic takes to those discourses that work with notions of emotional excess. Sentimentalism shares with Gothic fragments precisely a capacity to defy, as in the Lacanian *imaginary*, the laws of the rational-symbolic. In *Werter* sentimentalism is clearly the dominant discourse, as the novel's early letters are marked by a strong sense of solitude and mental agitation. We are left with a picture of a man who is both ill at ease with the world and dissatisfied with himself (*Weltschmerz* as well as *Ichschmerz*). The melancholic state of being, in the literature of sentimentality at any rate, is seen as a virtue, since it heightens or sharpens, as the argument goes, the hero's responses to and awareness of his or her predicament. The theory is clearly based on a notion of reader response not unlike the theory of aesthetics in Sanskrit dramaturgical treatises (the theory that textual unity is directly related to its power to evoke a direct emotional response) called *rasa*. In *rasa* theory, a text is read through a prescribed set of emotional "classes" such as love, hate, horror, and so on. But unlike sentimental literature, in which there are direct correspondences between "textual emotions" and real, lived emotions, the Sanskrit theoreticians, notably Bhamaha, Abhinavagupta, and

Mammaṭa, developed a theory based on the aesthetic correlates of emotional conditions. In other words, a scene of horror (say, the Gothic descriptions in Wordsworth's *Gothic Tale*) would achieve a unity not because it evokes the condition of dread in the reader (which is true, but which is deemed a primary emotional response only) but because it is a play on an "abstract," aesthetic concept of "horror" that, in its essence, is signified through another term. The unity of a scene is therefore related to the ways in which this abstraction is manipulated, especially insofar as the writer in question has added to the received repertoire or radically reread it. The ideal reader thus never cries after a pathetic scene or is filled with "real," lived dread after a horrifying one. He or she considers these scenes in terms of the possibilities of representation inherent in the abstract, aesthetic condition of that mode of expression. Naturally, the level of detachment implied here is an ideal, since it is no more than a frame of reference. But I think this is precisely where *rasa* aesthetics and sentimentalism come together—both are essentially reader-oriented, and both consequently require a strong historicist and intersubjective perspective to correct their seeming subjectivism.

As we have already noted with reference to Radcliffe, sentimental heroes seek the refuge of the pastoral whenever they are in trouble. Werter, the melancholic sublime, too, finds the innocence of the pastoral endearing, especially since his painting skills are limited to the depiction of idyllic scenes of nature and family life. The growing melancholy (and sentimentality) of Werter suddenly takes a different turn after he meets Charlotte, a young woman already engaged to a certain Albert. After some clearly ambiguous gestures from Charlotte, he is finally convinced that she loves him (105), only to find soon after Albert's return that Charlotte's affections for her betrothed remain unaffected by Werter's presence. In a characteristically sentimental fashion, Werter takes refuge in nature, in the "craggy mountains," in the "flight of a sea-bird" (152), and in the "immeasurable waters" (153). To the sentimentalist, however, nature only triggers opposite effects: "instead of prospects of eternal life, a bottomless pit is for ever opened before me" (154). Racked by the pangs of love (and remorse) Werter feels "degenerate": he can't think, and concludes, "I see no end to these torments but the grave" (165).

In volume 2 this abiding love takes the form of a misguided belief that only he, Werter, could make Charlotte happy. The rising tempests within, his essential instability—"My sensations change with the rapidity of lightning" (68) he writes—lead to the poetry of

Ossian and a discourse full of sound and fury. "Impetuous whirlwinds," "spirits of our ancestors," the roar of waters (78), "plaintive sounds issuing from the deep caverns" (79) are the raw images of the romantic lover. These outer correspondences reflect a gradual obsession with death, with possession, and a brooding mind incapable of interpreting signs: language as a system of communication is itself placed under considerable strain. The sentimentalist is affected by even so much as a minor disturbance, a narrative or event that might remotely parallel events in his own life. When such a temperament is greeted by an accusing "Werter, you are indeed very ill" (111), the sentimentalist retreats even further into his world of haunting echoes and possessive spirits as the repressed returns through the "Uncanny." In short, Werter's already tenuous hold on his mind is now being lost. What was originally a normal, if pathetically ineffectual, desire for a woman becomes, through a meditation on sacred love between brother and sister, tinged with echoes of incest. Even as he endorses the greater bliss of sisterly love, he still dreams of her in his arms. The duplication of the self in the image of the sister again turns sentimentalist discourse into the language of the *imaginary*. Like Pierre and Mathilda, Werter too finds entry into the *symbolic*, into the law of difference, impossible to accept. They are all doomed from the start to find adequate representations in the mind of the impossible object of the sublime.

In the end the narrative, too, cannot be continued without appropriate editorial emendation or commentary. And this is what happens as the "editor" pieces together for the reader the rest of Werter's tragic life. Convinced that in death alone he can possess Charlotte, Werter decides to end his life. Before shooting himself with pistols borrowed from Albert but which had been handled by Charlotte, Werter writes in his letter to Charlotte: "I wished to receive my death from your hand, and from your hand I am going to receive it" (172). He orders the fire to be lit, and a pint of wine to be brought. As the clock strikes twelve, he shoots himself: "the clock strikes twelve—I go—Charlotte! Charlotte! Farewell! Farewell!" (182). In spite of its obvious weaknesses—its central narrative is far too thin, many of the episodes are clearly padded, with little reference to Werter's central dilemma—*Werter* is a major work in this mode, with some extremely fine touches, as may be seen in the detail with which Werter's last moments are described:

> When the surgeon came to the unfortunate Werter, he was still lying on the floor, and his pulse beat: but the ball going in

above his eye, had pierced through the skull. However, a vein was opened in his arm, the blood came, and he still continued to breathe. (183–84)

What we discover in the Gothic is that the discourse of sentimentalism becomes interconnected with the genre, so that the Gothic sublime itself is articulated through the kinds of emotional excesses one associates with this form of writing. The theory of the "generic fragment" and the discourse of sentimentalism as features of the Gothic sublime in fact intersect in a little-known narrative poem of Wordsworth that was partially composed, but never published nor completed, between 21 March and October 1796. Though some elements of it made their way into *The Borderers,* it was not until 1940, when de Selincourt pieced it together and gave it the title *Fragment of a Gothic Tale,*[13] that its existence became known. In spite of what may be called its palimpsestic status, this fragment is of enormous interest to us because it signifies what the crazed version, the underside, of the Romantic sublime in fact was. It is also a proof text of a crucial ambiguity in Wordsworth's poetics (that "awful mystery," to use Peter Burra's early phrase[14]) that explains why Romantic transcendence is articulated in such fragile terms in Wordsworth. What we sense here is a panic situation, in which to complete the fragment would have meant subjecting the self to the powers of the sublime without ever returning to the equanimity of reason. The panic situation expresses itself in the verse that hides the murderous intentions of the stripling by projecting desire onto the ruined castle and its shady inhabitant(s). To complete the text would have meant that retreat from the nontranscendental (Gothic) sublime was not possible; the refusal to complete is, therefore, a refusal to be complicit with the unspeakable. So at precisely the point when the murder of the father figure is about to take place, Wordsworth stops abruptly and "does a Mrs. Barbauld." But the textual wounding, as the incomplete text, leaves a scar that surfaces again and again in Wordsworth, notably in the figures of the poet who meets the Leech Gatherer, and the pastoral swain who becomes the phallic destroyer in "Nutting." The repressed, as the mutilated text, returns as its uncanny double to haunt the Romantic sublime throughout. It is here that the unproblematic claims to transcendence on behalf of Wordsworth (a genius who was "a pure emanation of the Spirit of the Age"[15]) must be critically examined, because what the Gothic discourse did was make sublime empowerment a kind of schizophrenic terror as well.

The fragment as it survives begins with a strong narrative, as two people wind their way over a loose plank. The sound of the waves from the chasm below may be heard by the "blind man" as he walks with his "hand on the other's shoulder." The opening images are classic Gothic: two people make their way up a cliff, the winds howl furiously and a "horseman gallops by" in panic. The catalogue of the sublime at this juncture comes straight out of a long-established repertoire of sublime objects. Then suddenly, like a Piranesi etching in which the subject views the world from the eye of a mole, an image erupts from below as the young man sees a castle precariously perched on a cliff:

> Like some grim eagle on a naked rock
> Clapping its wings and wailing to the storm.
> (ll. 23–24)[16]

The castle hangs, "perch[ed]" like "a dim-discovered form!"—a veiled object toward which the travellers move their "laborious steps." The sublime gradually gets objectified as a certain lack as we detect a shift away from Walpole and Radcliffe's spatializations of the Gothic to the effects of the object on the viewer. In the process the castle ceases to be totally available to consciousness. The castle is not ours to occupy, as mysterious figures claim priority in this relic of the unconscious. And relic it is in more than one sense of the word. The "touch of time" had "split with ruined deep" and yet, haughtily, the towers, "though shattered" stood "as in their prime" (ll. 67–70). What version of the sublime do we get here, if not the castle as its own lack, as its own "unimaginable" (l. 67)?

But then Wordsworth gives it a further twist, because the "sulphurous bolt of terror" breaks through the sinews of the blind man for whom the sublime has not been a matter of sight (as it is for the murderous stripling) but of sound. Thus, the effect of the sublime now gets transformed into a negative empowerment from within, as the blind man "shuddered to life's inmost source" (l. 89) through "the darkness of his brain" (l. 90). The apparatuses of Gothic architecture are pursued further, as the stripling and the blind man make their way to a "dungeon" (l. 96). The dungeon where the sailor finds momentary repose, unaware of the stripling's murderous designs ("'For work is here which none may overlook'") had since been smothered over by nature. And the vault, given its "smoothness," to the blind sailor is "security"; without its visual Gothic signs, the "vault" becomes for the old man-child a womb, the repository of desire:

Methinks I could almost be happy now
(l. 108)

The "security" of the vault (which is always ambivalent: a refuge for Matilda in *The Castle of Otranto,* but also the place of rape) allows the sailor to relapse into "sentimentalism":

A Poor useless man and better with the dead.
(l. 135)

The blind sailor's "moral weeping," to use R. S. Crane's apt phrase,[17] writes its narcissistic history as a form of escape from reality. But "moral weeping" has its own precursors here, notably in Henry Mackenzie's classic *The Man of Feeling* and Goethe's *Werter.* However, the discourse of sentimentality does not produce those sudden changes in narrative that one finds in Indian popular cinema (a very colonial genre that feeds on English sentimental discourses), for instance. Instead, the retreat into sentimentality that would move the Gothic sublime into the sentimental sublime (a shift in the hierarchical status of these two sublimes) is arrested because for the youth, the blind sailor's sentimental discourse were "words of blood" with the opposite effect of serving to nurse "purpose most foul with most unnatural food." The received discourse of sentimentalism is thus ruptured by "impulse horrible" and "black regret." The desire to murder continues to be deferred through grotesque images borrowed from the classic fragment of Mrs. Barbauld. She had written about "the bloody stump of an arm"; Wordsworth expands these images of the dishevelled flesh with exposés of a cutlass "to staunch the blood of recent wound" (l. 39), "a hand of fleshly hue" (l. 159) and an arm "that bled as from a recent wound" (l. 170). All these metonymic references relate to a figure who is dimly perceived by the youth in the ruined castle. The wounded sentinel of the ruined castle is never seen, though the glimpse of the hand makes the "stripling light of soul" (l. 180). The Gothic supernatural is, after all, a projection of the stripling's own disturbed state of mind. The absence of ghosts, however, does not remove anxiety, as the glimpse of a star high above "the dungeon's roof" continues to send "to his fluttering heart a momentary dread" (l. 194).

In Wordsworth's Gothic fragment, however, there is no certainty, no will to power, no Romantic spirit attempting to triumph over nature, no control over the conflicting pressures of total detachment and complete identification (the extremes of the *sym-*

bolic and the *imaginary*). Instead, as the youth reaches the dungeon's mouth to see nature turned silent, the tempest gone, and the moon "her lustre spent"—all of which now convince him that it is time to murder the sailor—a sudden "uncouth horror" is heard:

> Such rending peal as made the vault rebound;
> Nor whelming crash it seemed, or shriek or groan,
> But painful outcry strange, to living ear unknown.
> (ll. 210–12)

What the stripling hears in this Gothic landscape is a kind of a primal cry, not like the sound of a "crash" or of "shriek or groan," but a "painful outcry" (l. 216). His "outcry strange, to living ear unknown" is thus a kind of unmitigated, unpolluted, "pure" (though "negative") sound that the sailor, too, hears; it is a "controlling point," a kind of a proto-spot-of-time or memory-of-place, which now distorts perception and brings back images, incoherent, inexplicable, dreadful:

> And all which he, that night, had seen or felt
> Showed like the shapes delusion loves to deem (teem?)
> Sights that obey the dead or phantoms of a dream.
> (ll. 219–21)

The fragment, then, works through the fragmented nature of a consciousness linked to phantoms and dreams. In Wordsworth's version of the Gothic sublime, the Gothic is seen in psychological terms as a haunting spot-of-time or memory-of-place from which there is no return. Where the ruins of Tintern Abbey are a source of strength, a power that drags the mind back from the brink of collapse, the Gothic is all collapse; there is no dragging the mind back, there is only an absolute negativity. There is no uplifting, only a vertiginous plunge into the depths, into the dungeons of the unconscious. Through the narrative of a version of parricide, Wordsworth's Gothic tale demonstrates the absolute otherness of the Gothic as the subject under interdiction, as the fragmented self defining its own subjectivity only in terms of a lack in the symbolic order itself. Wordsworth would continue to deploy Gothic conventions in his verse but the experience of the *Fragment of a Gothic Tale* was sobering. Later he would transform Gothic dread into a positive Romantic sublime, though it is clear that elements of the Gothic would always stalk Romantic transcendence, the dark side pursuing what it sees as an abrogation of the original design of the sublime. In this respect Wordsworth's fragment is like a palimpsest, a relic of what Mary Shelley in *The Last Man* was to call the "Sibylline leaves." Its status is, therefore, like that of a dream fragment, which, after all, is the ontology of the literary Gothic anyway.

Mrs. Barbauld's theories of romance and her reading of the Gothic were probably crucial for the development of the Gothic. Wordsworth's *Gothic Tale,* as we have seen, inscribes itself quite consciously into the formal narrative conventions of Mrs. Barbauld's fragmentary tale. Wordsworth's tale remains a fragment through no conscious design on his part; Mrs. Barbauld, on the other hand, exploits the illusions of the incomplete manuscript text that formed the basis of many subsequent Gothic texts and which, though in a more or less completed form, Horace Walpole, too, had used to such remarkable effect. Mrs. Barbauld, unfortunately, is concerned only with the formal dimension of a fragment, with the "materially" incomplete text. As a consequence, she fails to put her own theory into practice, since the fairy-tale dimension of her Gothic fragment left little room for Gothic terrors. Wordsworth knew the genre's specificity better; he knew its psychology; and he knew, above all, the highly uncertain and ambiguous nature of the Gothic. In reading the *Gothic Tale* in this light we become conscious of the value of Gothic fragments to any adequate retheorizing of the Gothic sublime. Gothic marginalia thus confirm from another perspective the ideology of the precursor text.

As indicated at the beginning of this chapter, we continue our narrative of the Gothic through readings of texts that are historically (and genealogically) interconnected. In fact, the vast bulk of the rest of this book will deal with texts written by members of the Byron-Shelley circle. Since William Godwin is closely linked to this circle through Mary Wollstonecraft Godwin Shelley, it could be argued that he, too, may be included in this collective group. At any rate, we can now historicize our readings of "fragments" more effectively, because our texts belong to a much more manageable literary archive with quite self-conscious inscriptions of one text into a prior intertext. On the immediate question of Gothic fragments as defined earlier, we begin with a reading of the two "vampire texts" of Lord Byron and Polidori.

Byron's physician Dr. John William Polidori (whose excessive gambling led him to commit suicide at the age of twenty-six) is remembered chiefly as the person who left behind a brief account of the night of June 16, 1816, when five individuals, three singularly gifted, began to write their ghost stories.[18] Two of them—Claire Clairmont and Percy Bysshe Shelley—defaulted; Byron produced an outline of a tale about a vampire-villain, whereas the remaining two, Mary Godwin Shelley and Polidori, in fact completed their tasks. Though we know very little about the reactions of the members of this group to each others' compositions, Byron is reported to have said to Mary Shelley, "You and I will publish ours together" on the night of the telling of the ghost stories.[19] Later, in a letter dated April 27 (1819) to Mrs. Maria Gisborne (née Reveley), who was an old acquaintance of both William Godwin[20] and Thomas Holcroft, Mary called the plot of Byron's (Polidori's) story "very dramatic & striking."[21] What Mary Shelley and Polidori finally completed are by no means equal, and comparisons between *Frankenstein* and *The Vampyre*[22] are often made only to complete an extended footnote. We return to Mary Shelley's *Frankenstein* later in this book. My aim here, however, is to examine the nature of Gothic fragments further through Polidori's and Byron's versions of the vampire tale.

Byron's own fragment (under the title "A Fragment") first appeared as an appendix to the first edition of Byron's *Mazeppa, A Poem*.[23] It begins as a letter dated June 17, 1816 (which corresponds exactly to the day after the telling of the ghost stories referred to by Polidori), but the story itself is located in the century before, though how far before we can't be at all certain. The opening words, "In the year 17—," constitute a common literary device, which we encounter in *Frankenstein* as well. This is followed by the first-person narrator declaring that he set out to travel through "countries not hitherto much frequented" (59) with a friend, Augustus Darvell. An older person, the latter was, we are told, a man of fortune who belonged to an "ancient family." He has, however, a strange attraction about him, a capacity, charismatic no doubt but probably fiendish, to draw people toward him even though one always feels terribly uncomfortable in his presence. One is never sure, after all, whether his behavior has a cause—"ambition, love, remorse, grief" (61)—or whether it is "a morbid temperament akin to disease" (61). As Byron proceeds from the simple and totally explicable elements of romance to the unconscious world of the Gothic his account of Darvell becomes more and more complicated: "these were so contradictory or contradicted" (61). It takes the narrator, ultimately, to an equation so crucial in the Gothic between mystery and evil:

> Where there is mystery, it is generally supposed that there must also be evil: I know not how this may be, but in him there certainly was the one, though I could not ascertain the extent of the other. (61)

In spite of Darvell's aloofness, their differences in age, and the obvious presence of an abiding, uncomfortable enigma, the narrator is drawn to him. The attraction, in a replay of the uncanny recognition of one's own double, is so powerful (though implicitly doomed) that the narrator is not satisfied until Darvell agrees to be his travelling companion. Attracted by Darvell's "shadowy restlessness" (62), he finds himself in a dreadful predicament when Darvell asks him to take an oath:

> This is the end of my journey, and of my life—I came here to die: but I have a request to make, a command—for such my last words must be—You will observe it? (66)

The command in fact is, on the surface, innocuous enough: "conceal my death from every human being" (66). After some hesitation, he swears to do so, and Darvell looks considerably relieved. He dies uttering, "Tis well!" (68) and asks the narrator to bury him that evening at the spot where an ominous bird was perched (68). Having bound the narrator to an oath full of alarming possibilities, an oath that is fraught with self-extinction as it traps the subject into the *imaginary* realm of duplication or nondifference, the fragment ends with the words:

> Between astonishment and grief, I was tearless. (69)

Since the Gothic is an already-told tale, a relic of the already-occurred event, in some ways these consciously incomplete Gothic fragments demonstrate a feature of the genre that is part of its occluded structure. In short, the fragment is itself a theory of the Gothic as it exposes the hidden agenda of the form. All dream texts are similarly incomplete fragments that require efforts of interpretation before they can be completed. To read the Gothic fragment is thus tantamount to reading the real, repressed Gothic form. Of course, we can construct, even without the help of Polidori, the inevitable ending of the narrative. In Byron's outline of the story—glimpsed from references in Mary Shelley's journals and letters, and in Polidori's own *The Vampyre* and diary—Darvell returns from the dead to seduce the narrator's own sister. And the enigma, the evil force, that binds the plot here is the oath which cannot be broken. Because of this she can't be forewarned that Darvell (as his name suggests) is the *devil himself*. The narrative inversion/perversion here is interesting because Darvell's interdiction turns around to haunt the honorable, realist subject. Where Darvell knows the true nature of the Gothic narrative (that honor is an ideological device), the narrator, trapped in the discourse of realism, mistakes illusion for truth. The positive sublime finally constructs a world that is meaningful; the negative Gothic sublime, only the mutilated and castrated subject who willingly submits.

The complete version of this narrative is to be found in Polidori's *The Vampyre*. The figure of Darvell now functions as the sign of the loss of individual identity, of difference, as in fact the sublime object of the Gothic Other, the object of desire. As we see repeatedly, what the Gothic subject desires is the death of selfhood, a guilty absorption in the censored object. The Gothic narrative here plays on a version of the theme of the Faustian pact, an attraction to the Other, from which there can be no escape. Literature has many versions of this pact, but all seem to be a variation on the pact with the Devil. Polidori takes up this theme and transforms Byron's Darvell/Devil into a vampire. This transformation and the reasons for it are explained in Polidori's introduction. His starting points are stories about "the dead rising from their graves, and feeding on the blood of the young and beautiful" (xix). Drawing on an account in the *London Journal [The Thursday Journal]* of March 1732, Polidori recounts the case of a Hungarian who was "tormented by a vampyre" (xx), but who attempted to get rid of the vampire by "eating some of the earth out of the vampyre's grave, and rubbing himself with his blood" (xx). The source of the *London Journal*'s information was Augustine Calmet's work on vampires.[24] Polidori might have been familiar with English translations of Calmet's work, though it is more likely that he came to Calmet through reviews in the periodical literature.

For the purposes of our analysis the crucial section of Calmet's work may be found in volume 2, chapters 7–35 (29–131). Apparently in Moravia it was common enough "to see men who had died some time before, present themselves in a party, and sit down to table with persons of their acquaintance without saying anything; but that nodding to one of the party, who would infallibly die some days afterwards" (29). These specters, when driven through with "stakes," would utter "very loud cries, and a great quantity of bright vermilion blood" would flow from them (31). If we compare Calmet's observations with Polidori's introductory remarks in *The Vampyre*, it soon becomes clear that he is either quoting directly from this text or, as I think more likely, quoting extracts from Calmet cited elsewhere. In a region in the vicinity of Transylvania the Heyducq people call the ghosts from the dead vampires who suck the blood of the living to nourish themselves. While the victims debilitate, and perish, these vampyres "fill themselves with blood in such abundance that it is seen to come from them by the conduits, and even oozing through the pores" (37). The life of a certain Heyducq, Arnald Paul (Polidori's "Arnold Paul" in his introduction) is then recounted. This Arnald Paul was crushed to death, but some weeks later inexplicable "vampyre" deaths occur, which recall to the people's mind Arnald Paul's own claim that in the frontiers of Turkish Serbia, he had been visited by vampires. He'd cured himself (since those sucked by vampires in turn suck others on their death) "by eating earth from the grave of the vampyre, and smearing himself with his blood; a precaution which, however, did not prevent him from becoming so after his death, since, on being exhumed forty days after his interment, they found on his corpse all the indications of an arch-vampyre" (38) (Polidori in fact quotes the entire passage verbatim.) The Hadnagi, or bailiff, ordered that sharp stakes be driven through his heart. But when the stake was pierced through his body he uttered "a frightful shriek, as if he had been alive: that done, they cut off his head, and burnt the whole body" (38).[25] The vampire, being neither dead nor alive, contains within him both the principles of life and death (Eros and Thanatos) and parodies the religious belief in life after death. The vampire is a ghastly/ghostly parody, a monstrous subversion that mocks a fundamental tenet of Christianity: that Christ alone returned from the dead.

Drawing on Calmet, Polidori is able to fill out the general outline of Byron's narrative. Whereas the relationship between Darvell and his victim (Lord Ruthven and Aubrey, in Polidori) remains unchanged, we are given a fuller account of Lord Ruthven's disturbed state of mind: there is a "curse on him" (34) and there is something "supernatural" (36) about his person. Such is the strength of this sublime object that during the continental journey Aubrey refuses to accept that his beloved Ianthe was actually murdered by Lord Ruthven (the "Vampyre") even though a dagger left behind perfectly matches one of Lord Ruthven's sheaths. Since the Father's Law (Lord Ruthven is another version of the Gothic patriarch) must be obeyed, Aubrey can only relapse into a state of delirium, from which he recovers only to be led by Lord Ruthven toward his own death in an Orientalist fantasy. As in Lord Byron's "A Fragment," the dying Ruthven extracts a terrible promise. "I would do any thing," says Aubrey (54), and binds himself to Ruthven by taking an oath.

> "Swear!" cried the dying man, raising himself with exultant violence, "Swear by all your soul reveres, by all your nature fears, swear that for a year and a day you will not impart your knowledge of my crimes or death to any living being in any way, whatever may happen, or whatever you may see." —His eyes seemed bursting from their sockets: "I swear!" said Aubrey; he sunk laughing on his pillow, and breathed no more. (55)

Although Ruthven's demand does not have the "Orientalist" promise of numerological fulfillment—this Orientalist fantasy/promise would unlock a different or alternative meaning, if pursued far enough—it corresponds nevertheless, in essence, to Darvell's demand in Byron's "A Fragment." There is clearly a much older, and complex, tradition of narrative based on "enigmas" of this kind; though here one of the discoveries of that narrative—promise followed by pact and exchange—is not explicitly stated. The silence is a pact based on notions of honor and friendship, but Aubrey gets nothing in return, and, in fact, loses not only his beloved (which he has done anyway) but also his sister. The promise is thus ambiguously directed at a ritual, an exchange, through silence, of a sister. But the exchange remains one way only; unlike Faust's pact, where knowledge is imparted, and unlike the godly promise of a beatitude, all we get is a fiercely binding promise, and its own equally inexplicable logic.

Polidori's narrative then moves toward the sacrifice of a sister whose desecration and rape by Lord Ruthven anticipates the sister/bride's rape by the Monster in *Frankenstein*. Because the oath has such binding force (an interdiction, a taboo, a threat) it subverts the logic of the superego. Instead of controlling the libido, it releases it; the sister is offered as a sacrifice and Aubrey becomes an accomplice in this act of barbarism. It is only after the deadly hour of the oath has elapsed that Aubrey narrates his tale, only to die immediately afterward. By then "Lord Ruthven had disappeared, and Aubrey's sister had glutted the thirst of a VAMPYRE!" (72).

Contemporary periodical literature by and large ignored Polidori. When there is a reference to this tale, it is in the context of Byron's works. Thus, when *Mazeppa* and *Don Juan* were reviewed in the July 1819 issue of the *Monthly Review*,[26] Polidori is mentioned in passing with reference to *Mazeppa*. The only significant contemporary examination of Polidori's *The Vampyre* is to be found in the *Monthly Review* of May 1819, which gives an account of the plot together with copious quotations. Thus, the ten pages devoted to the book—technically one of the longer reviews in the journal that year—hide a singular disinterestedness in the work itself. In fact, the reviewer seems to be more interested in the scientific literature on "vampyres" than in the special problems of either demonology or fantasy. Thus, Polidori's "error" in describing the vampire antihero (a "deadly hue, which never gained a warmer tint") is set against scientific accounts that refer to the complexion of "vampyres" as "florid, healthy, and full of blood." Echoing the critical discourses on *Frankenstein,* which was reviewed by the same critic in April 1818, the reviewer argued that works like these "produced . . . for a temporary and social purpose" cannot be subjected to close critical scrutiny.[27] The concept of peripheral or marginal writing, or *"terrorist"* writing, as one reviewer called it,[28] has always been set against books of permanent value in periodical literary criticism. The use of the term *terrorist,* which is italicized for both emphasis and, perhaps, semantic deviation, is used here in the satirical sense in which it was used by a correspondent to refer to Ann Radcliffe's "fashion to make *terror* the *order of the day,* by confining the heroes and heroines in old gloomy castles, full of spectres, apparitions, ghosts, and dead men's bones."[29]

Polidori's tale of obsession and demonology was not new—Calmet had done the background work and Byron had effectively written the plot. But he did combine in his works the two essential characteristics of the Gothic that go back to Walpole: horror and incest. In Walpole these two themes made their way into a heterogeneous set (*The Castle of Otranto* and *The Mysterious Mother*). By a neat repetition of the same process, in Polidori the two themes are distributed through *The Vampyre* and *Ernestus Berchtold.* The levels of genealogical duplication and uncanny identifications that signify the order of the *imaginary* become a powerful feature of Polidori's narratives. The sublime, as we begin to understand it in these fragments, now takes the form of the kind of unities of self and other theorized in Lacan. Polidori's little-known tale of double incest is about as good a proof-text of this theory as any. We therefore turn to *Ernestus Berchtold* next.

The epigraphs to Polidori's *Ernestus Berchtold*[30] juxtapose two radically different poets, Dryden and Byron. From Dryden a passage from "Oedipus" is quoted; from Byron, a passage from "The Giaour," one of Polidori's favorite poems. The theme of the novel is thus implicit in these two quotations—Dryden's predictable condemnation of humanity trying to unravel (much to its grief) the mysteries of "heavenly justice," Byron's much more passionate concern with individual guilt and transgression. In the introduction, Polidori concedes his own lack of talent as a writer. He "cannot boast of the horrible imagination of the one, [Mary Shelley] or the elegant classical style of the latter [Byron]" (vi). Polidori is also conscious of the criticism directed against supernatural tales—that they are not realistic, their moral vision is blinkered or flawed, and so on—but he would nevertheless want to defend his own work by the old trick of claiming that the actions of the characters are not different from those found in everyday life.

Incestuous coupling has a peculiar fascination for the Gothic, since the consequence of this coupling is not, as in realist fiction, a matter of moral anxiety; rather, the consequence is "structural" in that it threatens and splinters human history through an alternative history that is pre*symbolic*. As in Walpole's *The Mysterious Mother,* the tale of incest becomes indistinguishable from the Gothic of horror because both begin to share the same concerns about history, that is, an urge (though admittedly "failed") toward the dissolution of difference, and a confrontation, in representational terms, with the extremes of experience. The incestuous sublime thus repeats an essential feature of both the unity of the self and Other in the *imaginary* and the subject's plunge into the horrifying abyss of personal genealogy in which the distinctions so carefully made in *The Castle of Otranto* collapse. Since genealogy is the true narrative of *Ernestus Berchtold,* we shall summarize the narrative through a genealogical chart:

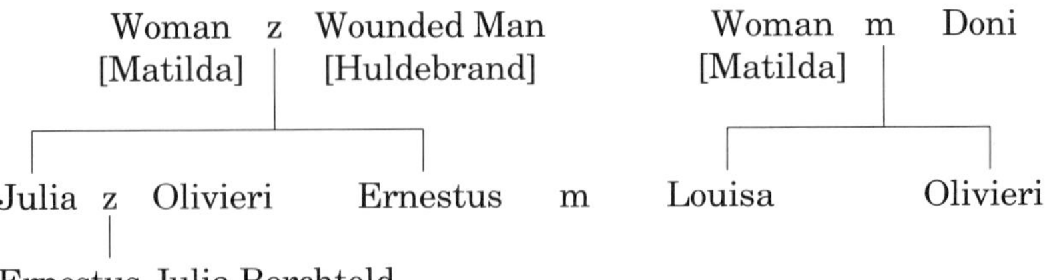

[z = extramarital relationship]

The formal marriage of Ernestus and Louisa is paralleled by the illicit union of Olivieri and Julia, who are also half brother and sister. This genealogical duplication is then extended to cover a duplication in the narrative procedure itself. Doni, the father of Louisa and Olivieri, writes down his secret life (which includes a Faustian pact with an Arab based on the exchange of happiness for money) as a way of lifting the lid on his dark and unspeakable history. The narrator, the character Ernestus, finally leaves Doni's manuscript with the person to whom the text has been narrated all along because he is unable to articulate this "real [but monstrous] history," of which he is a source and a participant. He therefore tells the narratee, or the infra reader:

> I cannot tell you more; read that damning tale, and then you may know what I dare, nay, dare not rest on. My history is quickly ended. (222–23)

As in the Gothic generally, there are two histories at work here. One is the history of the grand narrative, the history of events that may be quickly and decisively plotted. The other is history as unspeakable genealogy that transforms human history into a pathology, as indicated in the final words of the novel (which are in fact Doni, the father's):

> But you married; I dreamt of happiness, on Louisa's birthday accompanied you to your room, and the demon's threat I found had indeed been fulfilled. Your mother's portrait was Matilda's. Olivieri had seduced, you married a daughter of Matilda, of Matilda's husband, and I was the murderer of her father. (275)

Such is the frightening nature of this admission that the passage cited above, composed in a slightly awkward syntax, is part of a coda to the text, given ostensibly as documentary evidence without any authorial/editorial intrusion. This coda, entitled "The Life of Count Filiberto Doni," insinuates an objective history that the Gothic cannot possibly accept. The unspeakable genealogical sublime fragments, rips apart, shatters the Gothic by writing out the narrative of the *imaginary* ideal in the double, the sexual relationship of the frighteningly harmonious whole. In all these Gothic fragments and fragmented Gothics the agenda is the same: not the subject's momentary entry into the sublime under the law of reason, but his dissolution in a version of the oceanic experience.

This reading was, of course, totally lost on the contemporary reviewers. In the February 1820 issue of the *Monthly Review*,[31] for instance, *Ernestus Berchtold* is damned with faint praise: the work is "gloomy and sceptical," but Polidori is encouraged to write more since "he is capable of writing in a higher and purer strain." In the preface to the novel, Polidori had covered himself by claiming that the characters were all under a demonic influence. Clearly, Polidori had consciously told a lie; he had repressed in his critical preface the real, disturbing, narrative of his work by doing precisely what so many other Gothic writers had done before: issuing a disavowal that contradicts the text itself. The *Monthly Review*, however, continued to read Polidori in largely realist terms by rebuking him for adopting an apparatus (the exchange of knowledge for wealth with the mysterious Arab) that added nothing more to the text.

> The story displays considerable powers of imagination, but conveys merely irrelevant hints at supernatural agency; so that, in the explanation which follows it, we are surprised to find how busy the evil spirits have been in producing misfortunes which we had been satisfied with ascribing to the influence of evil passions.

The fascination with "evil passions," notably incest and "evil spirits," has been one of the more powerful underlying themes of the Gothic. Indeed, as we found out in Walpole's *The Mysterious Mother*, these themes are the underside, the soft underbelly, of the surface horrors of all Gothic texts. In Polidori, as in Mary Shelley's *Mathilda*, the conjunction of the two makes explicit the final and unremitting "horror" of the Gothic. It was a theme that had been played out by Polidori in a poem entitled "Chatterton to His Sister."[32] The construction of an imaginary sister for Chatterton allowed Polidori to enter into the theme of an illicit passion, which surfaced much more explicitly in the Ernestus-Louisa/Julia-Oliviera affairs some months later. Polidori had subtitled his *Ernestus Berchtold* "The Modern Oedipus" with a view to connecting it with the subtitle of *Frankenstein*: "The Modern Prometheus." If there is a work of Mary Shelley's with which it might be aligned comfortably, it is not *Frankenstein* but *Mathilda*, a startling tale of desire and incestuous passion that Mary composed in 1819.[33] We enter into this text by exploring two kinds of archives. The first is what may be called the archive of the palaeographic sublime, which is made up of documents in which writing as a pure signifier masks a hidden narrative of a daughter writing down, in an image of the father's style, not only her own work but fragments from her father's compositions (see manuscript specimen from *Mathilda* and William Godwin's autobiographical fragment). Anyone who has gone through the Abinger Shelley-Godwin papers in the Duke Humfrey's Library of the Bodleian is struck by the feverish nature of Mary Shelley's handwriting. What is striking here, moreover, is a young hand (compared to father Godwin's more mature writing) that echoes, graphologically, her father's autobiographical fragments and letters, often by writing them out herself. As in the Lacanian *imaginary*, which is the psychic economy of the Gothic generally, the absence of the law of difference in these copy-texts of the father implies that identities between self and the name (of the Father) would only lead to increasing levels of confusion. The subject cannot name herself without simultaneously naming the father, and the father, too, feels threatened by the upstart daughter. In the Gothic, therefore, we do get an excess of specularity as ill-formed egos—sometimes produced as residual effects of the Gothic apparatus as in Wordsworth's fragment—are drawn into an abyss constructed around a narrative of endless duplications. The dissolution that this necessitates is thus countenanced without a full, symbolic, awareness of its consequences. There is, then, a fascinating crossover of history and discourse in the Mary Shelley version of the Gothic sublime. Her fictions mirror a repressed sublime in life itself, which may be best examined through a reading of the next archive: Mary Shelley's own personal trauma before the composition of *Mathilda*. It is a procedure to which we will have occasion to return in later chapters.

Between the publication of *Frankenstein* (March 1818) and the death of Shelley (July 1822) Mary's life reads like a litany of calamities. Barely a year old, Clara Evcrina died in September 1818. Their first child, William, died nine months later, in June 1819. This second death, so soon after the first, left Mary almost inconsolable: "—May you my dear Marianne never know what it is to loose [*sic*] two only & lovely children in one year—to watch their dying moments—& then at last to be left childless and for ever miserable," she wrote her friend Marianne Hunt.[34] Shelley, too, was deeply affected by this and confided to Leigh Hunt on 15 August that though Mary turned to her father during these trying years, she received from him scarcely the kind of support she needed.[35] In fact, it was at moments such as these that Godwin demonstrated a singular lack of affection, and selfishness. There is a very unusual

79 is no longer, and what I most dreaded in
this world is come upon me. In the 47
despair of my heart I see what you
cannot conceal: you no longer love
me. I adjure you, my father, has not
an unnatural passion seized upon
your heart? Am I not the most miserable worm that crawls? Do I not
embrace your knees, and you most
cruelly repulse me? I know it - I see
it - you hate me!"

I was transported by violent
emotion and rising from his feet, at
which I had thrown myself I leant
against a tree, wildly raising my eyes
to heaven. He began to answer with
violence; "Yes, yes, I hate you! You
are my bane, my poison, my disgust! #
Oh! no," And then his manner changed, and
fixing his eyes on me with an expression
that convulsed every nerve and member
of my frame - "You are none of all
these; you are my light, my only one,

Manuscript of *Mathilda* in Mary Shelley's hand, pages 79 and 80. Abinger Shelley-Godwin Papers: Dep. d. 374/1, Duke Humfrey's Library, the Bodleian, Oxford.

80 my life.— My daughter, I love you!'" The last words died away in a hoarse whisper, but I heard them and sunk on the ground, covering my face ~~and almo~~ almost dead with excess of sickness and fear: a cold perspiration covered my forehead and I shivered in every limb— But he continued, clasping his hands with a frantic gesture:

"Now I have dashed from the top of the rock to the bottom! Now I have precipitated myself down the fearful chasm! The danger is over; she is alive! Oh, Mathilda, lift up those dear eyes in the light of which I live. Let me hear the sweet tones of your beloved voice in peace and calm. Monster as I am, you are still, as you ever were, lovely, beautiful beyond expression. What I have become since this last moment I know not; perhaps I am changed in mien as the fallen archangel. I do believe I am for I have letter of Godwin's that is quite extraordinary in its content and history. This letter survives in Mary's hand on paper watermarked 1839.[36] The original was written on October 27, 1818. The surviving manuscript must have held a special significance for Mary, since at the end she adds a postscript beginning "The loss of my infant daughter; who died at Venice," which she then cancels. From Godwin came no real feeling, and no real sympathy either. He speaks more like a philosopher, and very much less like a father as he considers death simply as a "trial of your constancy & the firm-ness [*sic*] of your temper that has occurred to you in the course of your life." We get a similar lack of compassion in Godwin's letter to Mary on the death of her first child William Shelley.[37] It is clear from this letter that Mary had not received the level of support she had expected from her father. In fact, Godwin's own letter begins with a reference to Mary's complaint precisely on this score: "Your letter of August 19 is very grievous to me, inasmuch as you represent me as increasing the degree of your uneasiness & depression." As in the earlier letters, Godwin is just not able to share in Mary's considerable grief, and relapses into philosophical explanations. At one point in this letter he almost accuses Mary of excessive sentimentality: "But you have lost a child: & all the rest of the world, all that is beautiful, & all that has a claim on your kindness, is nothing, because a child of three years old is dead!"

Some of these crucial letters survive, in fact, in Mary's hand. To others Mary adds postscripts or marginal notes. There is, then, a "re-covery" of the initial moment of trauma through the act of writing and semieditorial commentary. In an impassioned journal entry of October 1822, not long after the death of Shelley, Mary compares her present state with the moment of writing *Mathilda*: "Before when I wrote Mathilda, miserable as I was, the *inspiration* was sufficient to quell my wretchedness temporarily."[38] There is also a looking into a father's thought processes by becoming a father's amanuensis. A later return to the original scene of trauma is paralleled by writing "out of one's system" through fiction. In this respect *Mathilda*, begun in August 1819,[39] is contiguous with the moment of trauma. Initially titled *The Fields of Fancy*,[40] this tale was completed a month later. It was clearly written during a period of intense agitation, and in an advanced state of pregnancy (her fourth child, Percy Florence Shelley, was born on November 12, 1819 and the manuscript of *Mathilda* is itself dated "Florence. Nov. 9th 1819"). It is a tale of an incestuous passion that, as is the case with so many of these fragments, again takes us back to Walpole's

The Mysterious Mother. Mathilda, the revised work with a new title, remained unpublished mainly because Godwin, who was instrumental in the publication of many of Mary's later works, felt uneasy about this tale. He considered the subject matter of the story "disgusting and detestable,"[41] and, seemingly proper as he was, he suspected that much more might be read into it.

We know that Mary read the works of her parents assiduously and, even though she had no memory of her mother, she often imaginatively reconstructed her mother's death. Upon William Godwin's death she zealously guarded the letters of her parents. We are also told that years later she would read at the grave of her mother in St. Pancras' churchyard.[42] It is possible that she was familiar with her parents' wish for a son and probably knew that even before her birth both William Godwin and Mary Wollstonecraft had named their unborn child "William." In two letters written on June 6 and June 10, 1797 respectively, Mary Wollstonecraft appeals to Godwin by invoking William's name. Part of the letter of June 6 reads:

> I was not quite well the day after you left me; but it is past, and I am well and tranquil, excepting the disturbance produced by Master William's joy, who took it into his head to frisk a little at being informed of your remembrance. I begin to love this little creature, and to anticipate his birth as a fresh twist to a knot, which I do not wish to untie.[43]

The mother's love for Godwin that Mary Wollstonecraft confesses in the later sections of this letter is "confirmed" by the child's own movements in the womb. But unknown to the mother (and father) their baby is not a boy, but a girl who, as the twenty-two-year-old writer of *Mathilda,* must surely have wondered how her mother (and father) had responded to the birth of a baby girl. The complex ways in which Mary's life interacted with her parents' letters and manuscripts, and her several pregnancies between 1815 and 1819, necessitate a reading of her from beyond the frames of the texts she writes. Text and context collapse as personal history invades the autonomy of the aesthetic, imbricating the two in forms of knowledge no longer accessible to us simply through an objective literary criticism. Thus, versions of psychobiographies become important tools of analysis. Three years after the composition of *Mathilda,* and soon after Shelley's death, Mary confessed to her friend Jane Williams, "Until I knew Shelley I may justly say that he [Godwin] was my God—& I remember many childish instances of the excess of attachment I bore for him."[44] This, then, is the second related archive of one of three versions of Mary Shelley's Gothic sublime we shall read in this book.

An essential ambiguity or ambivalence at the heart of our archives—adoration of the father followed by a daughter's aggression toward him—takes us back to *Mathilda*, our final Gothic fragment. As U. C. Knoepflmacher observes, "*Mathilda*'s passive withdrawal clearly stems from parricidal wishes,"[45] a point that is more or less endorsed by a number of recent commentators. But *Mathilda* is also a rewriting of the "nature of love-sensibility,"[46] a productive feature of sentimentalism itself, that one finds in Goethe's *Werter*, a work that functions as another of Mary Shelley's generic intertexts here. What is crucial, it seems, is the "taming" of aggressive/parricidal impulse through a form that gives the illusion of excessive sensibility. In other words, the central theme of *Mathilda*, incest, is couched within a contradictory discourse at once innocent and subversive.

Mathilda is a highly intense work, in some ways much more intense than *Frankenstein*. It is also, as I've suggested already, an extremely personal work that self-consciously connects itself with two primal myths of civilization: Oedipus, and "the primal crime of mankind . . . parricide."[47] Mathilda narrates a "sacred horror" so polluted and polluting, so "nauseous" that its own correlative is the dying Oedipus: "and Oedipus is about to die" (2). She reconstructs the moment of this pollution in a state of agitation and on the verge of death ("I know that I am about to die"), but even as she composes she is horrified by her recollections, which, of course, become that much more meaningful, through the semiotics of the original handwritten text. "What am I writing?" she indirectly asks her friend Woodville (Mary Shelley toyed with "Lovel" and "Herbert" as possible names before settling on Woodville), to whom the text is addressed. And through writing Mathilda proposes to cure herself, explain away the cause of her "solitary life," her "impenetrable silence" (2). Yet this "writing" echoes ever so clearly William Godwin's *Caleb Williams*. Caleb's tale had to be told because his life as a "theatre of calamity" necessitated urgent expression in words. The intertextual debt that we foreground at this point is not a matter of coincidence or conjecture; it is a matter crucial to our understanding of the Godwin-Mary Shelley texts and their versions of the Gothic sublime.

An "only relick" of a letter and a miniature portrait are the slender threads that unite Mathilda with her father, who left her sixteen years ago. She is rejected by her father because her mother, Diana, died during childbirth. In this letter her father had stated his wish to become "a wanderer, a miserable outcaste—alone! alone!" (18). In a clear reference to Mary Shelley's own life, Mathilda copied this letter again and again so as to keep the "memory" of her father alive. For sixteen years she had been in the care of an aunt, her father's half-sister, believing herself to be an unwanted, unloved child. In this state of seclusion (and exclusion) her father's letter and the miniature portrait she wore "exposed on [my] breast" (29) are her only comfort. She is also sustained by the imaginary hope that this will be the icon of recognition, having already fantasized her father's first words on their reconciliation to be "my daughter, I love thee!" (29).

Soon after her sixteenth birthday, however, this vain hope is indeed fulfilled. Her father sends letters to his half-sister indicating his ardent "desire to see [my] Mathilda" (31). The encounter itself is equally dramatic. On the day of her father's arrival she gets lost in the wood, then jumps in a boat and rows across the lake to meet him. In a moment she is "in his arms," and only then does she begin "to live" (35). Thus begin her few precious months of happiness. But this happiness, she writes, was simply a calm before a much more tumultuous event recounted in the context of banishment from paradise:

> I disobeyed no command, I ate no apple, and yet I was ruthlessly driven from it. (42)

The father is of a poetic frame of mind, and prone to wild and "unearthly" thoughts (not unlike a sentimental hero)—these are Mathilda's descriptions of her father before they move to London two months after her aunt's death. A casual interest in her on the part of a young man in London is the catalyst that triggers a remarkable change in Mathilda's father's attitude toward her. He begins to show a "coldness" and detachment that Mathilda glosses as "diseased," "incomprehensible," an "unknown horror," and so on. The horror of the unspeakable, the unpresentable, is couched in a highly ambiguous discourse of love, threat and, finally, rape. He takes Mathilda to his Yorkshire estate, where he shows her rooms in which her mother lived: "there was something strange and awful in his look that overcame me," she writes (59). Affected by his condition, Mathilda feels deeply involved and blames herself for her father's frame of mind. "I shall enjoy the ravishing delight of beholding his smile" (67), she ponders in this highly ambiguous language. "Ravishing delight" in the context may be innocent enough; but its resonances, given Mathilda's premonition immediately after ("I gained his secret and we were both lost for ever"), connect with an underlying discourse of desire that effectively marks the moment of the return of the repressed.

Yet the constant writing out of the encounter in the language of the *imaginary*, with its fragmentations, its metonymies, leads to an increasingly ambiguous expression of the nature of her relationship with her father. Her language knows more than she does about its cause, and hence the seemingly innocent and yet inwardly destructive nature of her discourse. "Am I the cause of your grief?" (75) she asks, and receives an almost complete (and explicit) confession.

> Yes, you are the sole, the agonizing cause of all I suffer, of all I must suffer untill I die—Now, beware! Be silent! Do not urge me to your destruction. I am struck by a storm, rooted up, laid waste: but you can stand against it; you are young and your passions are at peace. One word I might speak and then you would be implicated in my destruction; yet that word is hovering on my lips. Oh! there is a fearful chasm; but I adjure you to beware! (75–76)

Like Oedipus, however, Mathilda must know the ultimate cause, the truth that would cure both father and daughter. The perseverance on the part of the daughter is such that even the father is struck by it. She demands to know, inviting in the process ruin and damnation. Finally she threatens with the ultimate: "you no longer love me" (79), and receives after some tentative moves, the final, uncluttered, unqualified admission: "—My daughter, I love you!" (80).

Truth can wound as the youngest daughter of Mne. Seraphim understood as well. "Why a little curtain of flesh on the bed of our desire?" is the final question that Thel hears from the "hollow pit" after encountering the world of sexual difference and reproduction in Blake's poem. And Thel's response is one of horror: she screams and returns to the vales of Har:

> The virgin started from her seat, and with a shriek
> Fled back unhindered till she came into the vales of Har.[48]

Mathilda too flees in horror—("I tore my hair, I raved aloud")—a half-crazed young girl comforted by the unspeakable whose language is "nauseous" and whose cry is simply, "Was my love blamable?" (103). "Nauseous" and "blamable": words that connect *Mathilda* with Walpole's *The Mysterious Mother*. Once "this guilty love" is confessed the text enters the realms of "discursive redundancy"; once the unspeakable, the unpresentable, the sublime, in short, has been given utterance, the text exhausts its narrative. What follows is predictable enough to any reader of the Gothic. The truth of the Gothic sublime is of such devastating magnitude that, like the vampire-figure of Byron/Polidori, it drags you into its own vast negativity. One plunges into it; one never triumphs over this version of the sublime.

Fear of footsteps approaching her chamber ("Was not that sacred?" [91] she asks) is followed by a fierce dream in which she pursues her father, who leaps into the sea from a huge cliff. Guilt-ridden, Mathilda the wronged, like Caleb Williams, becomes the wrongdoer; she now looks for her father, the lawgiver whose Law, in this instance, confounds precisely the decorum that keeps a restless social order intact. In a curious conflation of discourses and confusion of subjects, Mathilda's language ceases to maintain the difference between guilt and innocence. She now *is* the guilty partner because she cannot function without the lawgiver and the Law itself. In search of her father, who has left the estate having confessed in a highly ambivalent letter his unnatural love for her, Mathilda now imagines her father dead, and is willing to be his mistress. "Passion, and guilt, and horror," terms applicable to her father, are now appropriated by Mathilda herself:

> Oh! God help me! Let him be alive! It is all I ask; in my abject misery I demand no more: no hope, no good: only passion, and guilt, and horror, but alive! alive! (114)

But dreams in the Gothic discourse have an uncanny element of reality; they are not simply premonitions but the "already occurred event" seeking confirmation in the "real" world. Mathilda's dream thus finds an uncanny confirmation as, during a torrential rain, she finds the body of her dead father in a cottage next to the "overhanging beach."

Delirious and confused—the guilt of unnatural passion complicated by the primal crime—Mathilda, conscious of her "father's guilt" in her "glazed eyes" (128) contemplates suicide but rejects it, since it would "violate a divine law of nature" (145). For two years she seeks peace of mind in pastoral surroundings away from her original home, conscious of the fact that she can now respond only to those possessed with the purest sympathy. This sympathy finally comes from Woodville,[49] a poet whose own history is marked by grief: his betrothed, Elinor, had died before they could get married. At twenty, then, Mathilda finds a little peace, but even this is momentary. An "unlawful and detestable passion had poured its poison" into her ears and there was no escape, as Mathilda realises, from her past except in death:

> In truth I am in love with death; no maiden ever took more pleasure in the contemplation of her bridal attire than I in fancying my limbs already enwrapt in their shroud: is it not my marriage dress? Alone it will unite me to my father. . . . (219–20)

The peculiar logic of the metaphors—bridal attire and shroud—encourages an even more intense reading of Mathilda's subliminal desire, a pouring forth on paper, a writing out of one's own pain, a giving birth to yet another monster, the monster of one's own desire, the articulation of that which has been repressed. At twenty, Mathilda explains (Mary Shelley herself turned 20 in 1817):

> Almost from infancy I was deprived of all the testimonies of affection which children generally receive; I was thrown entirely on my own resources, and enjoyed what I may almost call unnatural pleasures, for they were dreams and not realities. (220)

Two ages, sixteen and twenty, are so very rich in meaning for Mary Shelley/Mathilda. At sixteen Mary eloped with Shelley; at sixteen Mathilda confronts the fact of incestuous love. At twenty Mathilda's life comes to an end, at twenty Mary Shelley completed *Frankenstein*. Though the analogy is imprecise—*Mathilda* was written two years later, when Mary was twenty-two—life invades fiction and fiction invades life. Dispirited and sick, with those haunting lines of Wordsworth already written down ("Rolled round in earth's diurnal course/With rocks, and stones, and trees"), Mathilda's own text comes to a close. Addressed to her friend Woodville, the final few lines take her back to "the only being I was doomed to love" (224) and to the exhaustive three months in which the manuscript was composed. In the end the guilt of love destroys Mathilda as she can only wait for death with a frightening sense of foreboding. For the female Gothicist this is the truth behind the sublime: the Law of the father makes "nauseous" love itself. Not surprisingly, the metaphorics of the oceanic sublime saturate the text in the end.

Mathilda is the last of our Gothic fragments or fragmented Gothics, and marks a decisive shift toward the beginnings of a strongly articulated female Gothic (sublime) that had been in the making since Clara Reeve, Mrs. Barbauld, and Mrs. Radcliffe, among other women writers. But this fragment of a Gothic, as a manuscript text (the palaeographic sublime), now takes us to female appropriations of the sublime as a primarily masculine trope. The bliss of the sublime draws on the dangerous sublimes of Polidori and Byron, on the disastrous productions of sentimentalism, and finally on the power of the negative *Lust*, the attractiveness of the principle of death, prefigured in our vampire narratives. These Gothic marginalia are the uncanonical texts of the Gothic through which we gain a glimpse into the real narratives that the completed texts often hide. As texts of the *imaginary* they are in fact texts/fragments in which the grand narrative of the eighteenth-century sublime and its "troping" into a Romantic orthodoxy are persistently undercut. Since they are counternarratives without any real aesthetic function in the public sphere, they become all the more honest renditions of the real agenda of the Gothic. As a manuscript text with two archives of the kind I have outlined, *Mathilda* becomes the ultimate symptomatic Gothic fragment, a literary model of text and criticism, through which scholarship, from our own vantage point, now rereads the Gothic. The emphasis placed on the fragments discussed in this chapter generally may also be seen as an example of critical terrorism, the drawing together of marginal works into the mainstream so as to explode the constructions of a Gothic canon. As such, these fragments are as close as we get to literary texts that theorize their own coming into being. Like Thel, for whom the order of the *symbolic* through the Law of the father is such an astounding "truth" that she must reject it, these Gothic narratives now retreat into the *imaginary*. What propels the narrative is the push toward specular identifications and an attraction to one's own dissolution in a version of the sublime. Since this sublime cannot be grasped (because it has no "adequation"), Gothic fragments gesture toward it through a form that plays out the extreme alterity of its existence. Fissured texts drag the self into their own interstices through narratives of circularity and repetition in a replay of the essential economy of the *imaginary*.[50] This frightening truth is the improbable basis of the Gothic sublime, as the historical sublime gradually gets shifted toward the uncertainties of Freud and the postmodern.

❧ 4 ❧

Unstable Text/Unstable Readings: William Godwin's *Caleb Williams*

The enduring quest for the Gothic and its sublime object gets progressively more difficult to define or contain in a purely critical endeavor. Like all studies of the sublime, procedures of containment of this colossal, unthinkable Thing, in the domain of the literary, are primarily heuristic, since readings are aimed at pursuing specific effects of the sublime and its avatars. Clearly, the Gothic sublime gets articulated in a number of not necessarily complementary ways, but there are certain key themes that continually recur. All these themes deal with the question of the subject as a lack in the structure itself. In some ways this very lack, which is a constituent feature of the ultimate negativity of the Real (which is not presentable), now overcompensates for its failure to positively "subjectify" by retreating into its own vertiginous recesses, where it finds tropes that confirm the subject's endless search for its double. It is here that Gothic subjectivity locks into the economy of the pure *imaginary*, an impossible ideal in which differences cease to exist. The Gothic fragments thus become our most theoretical texts, because they explore themes of incest and desire with a compulsiveness that is narrativized through an absolute fixation on the ungraspable Other best exemplified in Byron/Polidori's vampire tale. As an extension of the kinds of historical and archaeological strategies foreshadowed toward the end of the previous chapter, I would like to frame the guilty subject (there is no Gothic subject without guilt) in a reading of a text that, by and large, has been interpreted as a political text. I have in mind Mary Shelley's father's classic *Caleb Williams*.

The history of the composition and publication of *Things as They Are; or the Adventures of Caleb Williams* is well known. First published in 1794, a year after Godwin's principal philosophical work, *Enquiry Concerning Political Justice,*[1] it quickly became something of a cause célèbre that underwent successive reprints in 1796 and 1797. Contemporary readers read it as a powerful Jacobin novel written to repeat, in fictional terms, the author's own radical political philosophy. A preface penned on the day on which Thomas Hardy, a member of the London Corresponding Society, was arrested for high treason (May 12, 1794) was suppressed by the publisher for fear that Godwin, too, would be arrested and the problematic fictionality of his text considerably undermined. The preface was, however, incorporated into the 1796 text, its political immediacy lost with the arrest and successful prosecution of the original dissenters. In the preface Godwin had observed:

> What is now presented to the public is no refined and abstract speculation; it is a study and delineation of things passing in the moral world. (xix)[2]

Two months before, during the trial of Joseph Gerrald, "the ablest theorist of the L. C. S. [The London Corresponding Society],"[3] Godwin had been unflinching in his support of the dissenters (see manuscript specimen from William Godwin's "Draft of an Autobiography 1794–95" and "Letter to Miss Holcroft").[4] Gerrald was convicted and transported to New South Wales in May 1795, where he died five months later.[5] In this context Godwin's growing fears on account of the original preface were therefore genuine, for only the year before, Pitt fell short of prosecuting the author on the grounds that radicals could ill afford to pay £1.16.0 for *Political Justice.*

Yet the establishment's literary response to the text was anything but dramatic. The *Critical Review,* for instance, was more interested in its plot than in its politics.[6] Since it believed that fiction should reflect truth and virtue, the *Critical Review* advised the author that the novel should have been entitled "Things as They Ever Have Been!" The *British Critic* came out more openly against a work that it felt could only compromise the aesthetic domain through its shameful celebration of the political:

> When a work is so directly pointed at every band which connects society, and at every principle which renders it amiable, its very merits become noxious as they tend to cause its being known in a wider circle.[7]

The emphasis on Godwin's own political persuasion is not uncommon. In fact, the *British Critic* continued to read Godwin's other works, *St. Leon* (reviewed 1800) and *Fleetwood* (reviewed 1805) along much the same lines. The political sublime in literature had not been an English strength, a fact that is certainly reflected in the periodical literature even of the revolutionary 1790s where, curiously enough, what was preferred was the ideology of the beautiful because it reinforced a nostalgia for a Burkean order under the sign of the divine or, again in Burkean terms, contained conflict within the economy of the Oedipal stage. Desire for the security of the Mother was certainly less threatening than the imperious, castrating law of the Father. The political as the grotesque (or Gothic) threatened the establishment's conception of the aesthetic. Happy with the novel of manners, or with texts that uncritically represented social mores (their definition of "life"), the reviewers were clearly ill at ease with a text that was a powerful critique of existing social values. The artistic strengths of the work, however, came across most powerfully in the *Analytical Review*'s ambiguous reading of "this singular narrative,"[8] what Anna Seward was to call "a novel without love, or intrigue . . . without ruined castles, and haunted galleries,"[9] in terms of its departures from the usual comedy of manners through a "minute dissection of characters."[10]

The commercial success of the book was such that within two years George Colman, the Younger, published *The Iron Chest,* a play in three acts.[11] The ease with which the novel was transformed so successfully into another literary genre is testimony to the imaginative power of a very basic plot around a pursuer and the pursued, extended over three books. Falkland,[12] a rich country squire, relentlessly persecutes his servant Caleb Williams because the latter, out of sheer curiosity, uncovers Falkland's deepest secret by looking into a forbidden chest. The fact is that Falkland is a murderer. In the published version of the ending, Falkland finally confesses his murder in a court of law and the two are reconciled. In the more powerful manuscript ending to which I return later, there is no confession, let alone any hope of reconciliation. The sublime dements Caleb as he struggles to keep language and thought together. For the moment, however, we are concerned only with the published version, because this is the only version that has had an historical readership until very recently. In George Colman's play, then, there are two iron chests: the first is the mysterious portmanteau of Sir Edward Mortimer (Falkland), the second a "trunk" (the word "chest" is reserved for Mortimer's portmanteau) that belongs to Wilford (Caleb). It is in the second chest, that is, in Wilford's "trunk," that the secret of Mortimer's crime is discovered. In his

104

~~bert Merry, Dr Joseph Ritson * insertion~~

1794

The year 1794 was memorable for the trial of twelve
persons under one indictment upon a
charge of high treason — some of these persons were my particular friends; more
than half of them were known to me —
this trial is certainly one of the most memorable epochs in the history of English
liberty — the accusation, combined with
the evidence adduced to support it, is ~~cer-~~
~~tainly~~ not to be exceeded in vagueness & in-
coherence by any thing in the annals of
tyranny* — the name of the man in
whose mind the scheme of this trial was
engendered was Pitt — Mr Horne Tooke
was apprehended on the 12th of May —
the novel of Caleb Williams was then ready for publication, & appeared about a fort-
night after — in the following month I
paid a visit to Mr Merry at Bracon Ash,
near Norwich, & to ~~#~~ my friends & relatives in Norfolk, whom I had not visited
for twelve years — in October I went into
Warwickshire on a visit to Dr Parr, who
had earnestly sought the acquaintance & intimacy of the author of Political Justice —
my position on these occasions was a singular one — there was not a person almost to be
met with in town or village who had any acquaintance with modern publications, that had not heard
of the Enquiry concerning Political Justice, or that ~~or who~~ was not
acquainted in a great or small degree with
the contents of that work — I was no where

* — it was an attempt to
take away the lives of men
by a constructive treason, &
out of many facts no one
of which was capital, to
compose a capital crime

Manuscript of Draft of an Autobiography 1794–95 in William Godwin's hand. Two leaves paginated 104–7. Leaves watermarked 1807. Abinger Shelley-Godwin Papers: Dep. c. 531, Duke Humfrey's Library, the Bodleian, Oxford.

105)

imagine calculated to render me a more capable servant of the public — &, as I was
averse to the expenditure of money, so I was
not inclined to earn it but in small portions
— I ~~can~~ considered the disbursement of money for the benefit of others as a very difficult
problem, which he who ~~has~~ {has} the possessor of it
~~was~~ {is} bound to solve in the best manner he ~~could~~ {can}
~~&~~ but which afford~~ed~~ small encourage{ment} to any
one to acquire it, who {has} ~~had~~ it not — the plan
therefore I resolved on was leisure, a leisure
to be employed in deliberate composition, & in
the pursuit of such attainments as afforded me
the most promise to render me useful — for years
I scarcely did any thing at home or abroad
without the enquiry being uppermost in my
mind whether I could be better employed for
general benefit; & I hope much of this temper
has survived, & will attend me to my grave —
The fame in which I found myself, exalted my
spirits, & rendered me more of a talker than
I was before, or have been since, & than {is} ~~was~~ a-
greeable to my natural character — certainly
I attended now & at all times to every thing
that was offered to me, {in the way of reasoning & argument,} with the sincerest desire
of embracing the truth, & that only x — in this
year I wrote the principal {part} of the novel of Caleb
Williams, which may perhaps be considered as
affording no inadequate image of the fervour of
my spirit: it was the offspring of that temper
of mind in which the composition of my Political Justice left me — in this year I acquired
the friendship of many excellent persons, Thomas
Wedgwood, Richard Porson, Joseph Gerrald, Ro-

x insert) — the Enquiry concerning Political Justice was published in February a stranger — the doctrines of that work (though, if any book ever contained the dictates of an independent mind, mine might pretend to do) coincided in a great degree with the sentiments then prevailing in English society; & I was every where received with curiosity & kindness — If ~~xxx happy~~ to temporary fame ever was an object worthy to be coveted by the human mind, I certainly obtained it in a degree that has seldom been exceeded — I was happy to feel that ~~the distinction I received~~ this circumstance did not in the slightest degree interrupt ~~dis turb~~ the sobriety of my mind

On the sixth of October, the day after that on which I left London for Warwickshire, the grand jury found a bill of indictment against the twelve persons who had been accused before them — among the names in the indictment were included not only the persons known to me who were already in confinement, but also that of my friend Holcroft & others who were at large — Holcroft immediately surrendered himself, & was committed to Newgate — he wrote me word of his situation, & requested my presence — I left Dr Parr on Monday, the 13th, who would not part with me, till I had promised that in the following summer I would come & make up the visit which, as he kindly said, was so untimely broken off — I reached town on Monday evening, & having fully revolved the subject, & examined the doctrines of the Lord Chief Justice's Charge to the Grand Jury, I locked myself up on Friday & Saturday, & wrote my Strictures on that composition, which appeared at full length in the Morning Chronicle of Monday, & were transcribed from thence into other papers. — During the progress of these trials I was present at least some part of every day. — Hardy's trial lasted eight, & Horne Tooke's six days. — Among the many atrocities witnessed on that occasion, perhaps the ~~greatest~~ most flagitious was the speech of the attorney-general, now lord Eldon, at the close of the trial of that extraordinary man. — In his peroration he burst into tears, & intreated the jury by their verdict ~~on that occasion~~ to vindicate his character & fame; he urged them by the consideration of his family to cooperate with him in leaving such a name behind to his children as they should not look upon as their disgrace. — It was in the close of this year that I first met with Samuel Taylor Coleridge, my acquaintance with whom was ripened in the year 1800 into a high degree of affectionate intimacy.

1795

This & the following year were employed in revising my two works of Political Justice & Caleb Williams, without my performing any new literary labour. — My bookseller then played an injudicious part in deferring so long the printing an octavo edition, because a certain number of the quartos remained on his hands. — The work in reality principally addressed itself to, & was most likely to become a favourite with, persons in the middle classes of society, for whom the price of the quarto was too great. — The consequence of this overstrained prudence was that incorrect ~~editi~~ & imperfect editions were printed in Ireland, & (as I am told) in Scotland & America. — In revi-

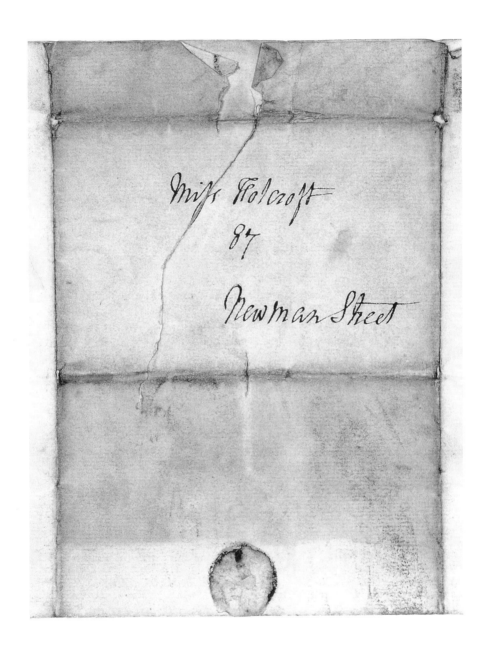

Manuscript of letter to Miss Holcroft (but directed to the Lords of the Privy Council), dated October 9, 1794, in William Godwin's hand. Abinger Shelley-Godwin Papers: Dep. c. 531, Duke Humfrey's Library, the Bodleian, Oxford.

To the lords of his majesty's most honourable privy council

William Godwin of Chalton Street Somers Town desires to be admitted to visit Thomas Holcroft, now a prisoner upon a charge of high treason, the said Thomas Holcroft having expressly signified to William Godwin his desire to confer with him.

Oct. 9. 1794 William Godwin

I beg the favour of you to communicate the following to Mr. Marshal, or any other person that may be thought proper.

I see by the Chronicle just received that Mr. Holcroft is in custody. I am of course unwilling to quit Hatton without some prospect of ~~m~~ usefulness, & there seems to be an uncertainty as to the admission of friends to visit him. At the same time I will make any sacrifice with chearfulness to his smallest benefit or consolation. This letter will arrive time enough for an answer by Friday post, which I shall receive on Saturday.

For God's sake inform me whether I can have admission to him, or be of consolation to his family. I will set off at an hour's notice. Deliver the inclosed yourself in person, unless Mr. Erskine should direct otherwise, & let me have the precise answer at all events state to Mr. Erskine that I am Mr. Holcroft's principal friend, upon whom he chiefly depends, & that I prefer his happiness to every earthly consideration.

Let me hear satisfactorily or unsatisfactorily by return of post; but perhaps you should not summon me to town without the possibility of some small benefit.

Thursday
Oct. 9. 1794

haste to frame Wilford for stealing, Mortimer inadvertently places, it seems, the entire contents of the "chest" into the "trunk." What is exposed, in the words of Fitzharding, Mortimer's brother and judge, is "a paper / Of curious enfolding—slipt, as 'twere / By chance, within another." A knife is also found with "Marks of blood on it." Finally, there is a manuscript entitled *"Narrative of my murder of—"* that unequivocally exposes Mortimer's crime. In Colman's hands the play is characteristically late eighteenth century, its immediate intertexts being Schiller's *The Robbers* (English translation, 1792) and the German drama of August von Kotzebue, notably his Pizarro plays. Not surprisingly, the *British Critic* called it "feeble and uninteresting; tediously lengthened out" and rather dull.[13] Nevertheless, even though Colman tried to eschew all political controversy by emphatically denying any interest in Godwin as a political philosopher, it is difficult to see how the two texts could have been separated. The very first act, for instance, gives an extremely pathos-ridden and sentimental account of the Rawbold family illegally living off the beasts of the landed gentry because they have been forced out of their jobs. But the difficulties of transforming a novel into a play, in this instance, were considerable. Mrs. Elizabeth Inchbald, in one of the many subsequent editions of this play, reflected on the "adverse fortune" of *The Iron Chest* by drawing attention to the difficulties posed by a text such as *Caleb Williams,* which allowed "no representation in action" of its "finer details."[14]

As we have seen in our account of the Gothic precursor text(s), adaptations from one genre into another or textual expansion and reinscription within the same genre are not uncommon. In fact, textual dissemination and multiplicity are crucial to a heterogeneous formulation of the Gothic as a composite text in the first instance. A Gothic text is therefore all its textual variants, as well as all its transformations into other semiotic systems. Another type of heterogeneity takes the form of conscious authorial commentary on the original moment of composition. In the 1832 preface to the "Standard Novels" edition of *Fleetwood* (1805),[15] Godwin does precisely this. The urgent political tones are muted, the restlessness of the syntax replaced by a more controlled reflection. In fact, Godwin here becomes very much a first reader of his own text, emphasizing psychological states and foregrounding "fictitious adventure" in favor of political enactment or dogma. It is a clear instance of an historical reading—the torrid lives of Mary Godwin Shelley and the poet behind him, a Whig sinecure just around the corner[16]—in which one detects a marked shift in Godwin. Moving from context to text Godwin points out that *Caleb Williams* was conceived in reverse order, with the final book "invented" first (a method which Dickens was to approve of in his note to Edgar Allan Poe[17]). Although there is nothing particularly original about this claim—most authors construct their narratives backwards—the fact that the original ending was altered just before the book went to press does indicate that the text, in its final form, disrupts the claims made about it in the preface. The implied sense of an ending based on a conceptualization of a character who, in the end, will internalize the positions of both self and Other, is therefore a false promise. In this respect the surviving manuscript ending is a Gothic fragment in its own right as it returns, like the textual repressed, to haunt claims made about the text by William Godwin. Thus, Godwin does not tell us the whole truth, even in his own retrospect (this preface was composed for the 1832 edition), but uses the claims about inventing the ending of the work first to emphasize the feverish nature of the text's composition. After this observation, however, what Godwin claims about the book is something of a nonsequitur. Godwin continues:

> I will write a tale, that shall constitute an epoch in the mind of the reader, that no one, after he has read it, shall ever be exactly the same man that he was before.[18]

The conceit comes across powerfully in this passage but the boast has more than just an element of truth because what Godwin emphasizes is simply a version of Hazlitt's oft-quoted remark that "no one that ever read it [*Caleb Williams*] could ever forget it."[19] As Godwin continues, the implied preeminence of narrative is seemingly undercut by the workings of a "metaphysical dissecting knife" to show why characters behave in a particular fashion. There is a mild contradiction at work here, since it is never too clear in the work when such a dissection and "laying bare" of characters triumphs over the primacy given to narrative ordering by William Godwin.[20]

This emphasis on the narrative—on the plot, in fact—is conspicuously present in the intertexts Godwin specifically cites in his preface. They include *The Triumphs of Gods Revenge,*[21] with its strong image of the omnipresent eye of God pursuing the likes of the scheming Hautefelia and the treacherous "Apothecary" Le Fresnay, and the many versions of the tale of Bluebeard. The latter intertext explains the once fashionable reading of Caleb and Falkland along "gendered" lines: Caleb is the inquisitive wife of Falkland/Bluebeard who discovers that the "blue chambers" contained headless bodies of Bluebeard's previous wives.

In the two separate accounts of the composition of *Caleb Williams* left behind (in the date list for the composition of *Caleb Williams* and in his diary), Godwin does not mention the books that he specifically cites in the preface to *Fleetwood*. The date list omits all reference to other readings.[22] The diary, however, documents in some detail texts that Godwin read while writing *Caleb Williams*.[23] Among these were: *The Mysterious Mother*, various plays of Shakespeare, *Sir Charles Grandison, Gulliver's Travels, Anna St. Ives, Roderick Random, Ferdinand Count Fathom, Hugh Trevor, A Simple Story, Colonel Jack, The Mysteries of Udolpho, Clarissa, A Philosophical Enquiry . . . Sublime* (mentioned a few weeks after *Caleb Williams'* publication). When we recall this list we become aware of the various competing discourses that were at work on the relatively homogeneous narratives of the texts Godwin cites in the preface. The two "lists" in fact draw us toward a reading of *Caleb Williams* that cannot be a simple endorsement of the program outlined in his preface. Moreover, what the preface fails to theorize is the Gothic sublime as human object perceived by an hysterical individual for whom the object is both a source of fear and an obsessive necessity. Thus, textual politics is mediated by a discourse seeking full self-expression but failing to do so. This version of the Gothic sublime is more powerfully present in the unpublished manuscript ending of *Caleb Williams* in which Godwin duplicates the figure of the Gothic hero by presenting us with a character who totally fails to self-transcend, and a narrative that, like a Gothic fragment, is without closure. If we want a textual analogy of this form we will have to go to Dostoevsky's *Notes from Underground*. The sublime for Caleb is a retreat into the vertiginous depths of the self. Hysterical and totally consumed by the desire for a fictive unity with Falkland (a version of the voyeuristic spectacle of cinema), Caleb expresses the sublime through the metaphorics of oceanic dissolution. Why Godwin changed his mind on reflection and turned to the seductive but illusory harmony of the Gothic as romance (the ending of the published version) might be explained by the frightening truth of the sublime contained in the first version.

The designation given to *Caleb Williams* in the final paragraph of the preface to *Fleetwood* is characteristically eighteenth century in its self-effacement. Godwin calls his work "this mighty trifle," invoking the rhetorical understatement of Walpole who also called his *The Castle of Otranto* a "trifle." His daughter Mary, as we shall see later, called *Frankenstein* "my hideous progeny," where the literary work is no longer a "trifle," an amusement, but an act of conception, creation, and reproduction, a release of one's child into history. But the "trifle," the understatement—for it must be so after the preceding eight pages of almost unrelieved self-aggrandizement—also leads to a different kind of knowledge or awareness. Though couched again in the rhetoric of understatement, there is a self-analysis going on here that leads to a degree of uneasiness, to a confession:

> How many flat and insipid parts does the book contain! How terribly unequal does it appear to me![24]

Though the dissenter and political reformer Joseph Gerrald had read the book in a night and awoke, the following morning, "refreshed," the fact remains that Godwin was concerned about the fate of his text. Will it remain, as he anxiously asks, a "trifle," a romancing of life read by boys and girls "without chewing and digestion?"

The relative merits of the competing claims made by Godwin and his readers about the value of *Caleb Williams* may be elaborated through the Gilfillan-De Quincey debate. In his "Literary Portraits," Rev. George Gilfillan of Dundee (1813–1878) had apparently written about *Caleb Williams* that it "is in every circulating library, and needs more frequently than almost any other novel to be replaced."[25] Thomas De Quincey took up Gilfillan's remarks in his own notes on "Gilfillan's Literary Portraits," in which he strongly disputed Gilfillan's assessment of *Caleb Williams* by referring to the number of editions of *Caleb Williams* actually published (nothing remarkable here, he protested) and by suggesting that even if readers were indeed inclined to read the work, this would be explained away in terms of the popular vulgarity of taste. De Quincey, in fact, saw "no merit of any kind" in the novel and added that contrary to rumour, the majority of people disliked *Caleb Williams*.[26] What is worse, continued De Quincey, William Godwin himself had no artistic integrity whatsoever, since he wrote with an eye to the expectations of the reading public. For instance, since the public would not accept the hanging of the hero (the "hero" here is Falkland), Godwin simply found a way out of this by granting him a reprieve in the end. Beyond artistic integrity, it is suggested, there is also the question of mediocre artistic ability for Godwin.[27] De Quincey cites the case of the contents of the mysterious trunk and suggests that unless Falkland had actually soaked Tyrrel's head in brandy and left it there, there could be nothing more in the trunk that could have incriminated Falkland any more. De Quincey had obviously read *Caleb Williams* in realist terms, and there may well have been touches of personal acrimony coming through in his hostile criticism. The personal bias notwithstanding, De Quincey's extended reading of Godwin through Gilfillan is a useful point of entry into modern readings of *Caleb Williams*.

"A schism, which is really perplexing, exists in this particular case . . . ,"[28] De Quincey had written, and it can be legitimately argued that readings of *Caleb Williams* have continued to reflect something of that schism. More recently, *Caleb Williams* has been read variously as manifesting a "schizophrenic tendency" (D. Gilbert Dumas), as a "moral fable" (Rothstein), as a "symbolic statement of the author's relation to God" (Walter Allen), as a "study of morbid pathology" (Charles Edwyn Vaughan), as an "attack on the Calvinist conception of a benevolent, omnipotent deity" (Angus Wilson), or as the expression of a man "peculiarly sensitive to the spiritual terrors and despairs that lay beneath its [the text's] intellectual composure and certainty" (Angus Wilson), as a quasi-referential or historically specific text where Falkland has strong affinities with Edmund Burke (Boulton, Butler, McCraken), as a Calvinist study in the psychology of rebelliousness and consequent guilt (Storch), as "an allegory of Protestant, not to say Dissenting, history" (Kelly), as a transposition onto fictional characters of Garrick's Richard III or Kemble's Coriolanus (celebrated stage performances of the period) as one of "the earliest fantasies of dualism" (Jackson), as a text about possession and ownership dialectically examined (Kiely), as a "confessional genre" (Furbank), as an allegory of humankind trapped in the doomed nightmare of history (Harvey), as an example of the literary use of Gothic horrors to symbolize social issues (Gross), as a "romancing histor[y]" (Rothstein), as a critique of *Political Justice* (Balfour Elder), as an exploration of "the relationship between subject and master" (Paulson), and, finally and least productively, as a text simply representing some of the contemporary literary sentiments about Gothic horror.[29]

When we expand on the foregoing commentaries, what we find are echoes of the redoubtable Leslie Stephen's reference to *Caleb Williams* as a "monstrous hybrid . . . which gains its interest by a fortunate confusion."[30] Both P. N. Furbank and Rudolf Storch, for instance, read *Caleb Williams* variously as a study in a guilt situation, obsession, or neurosis, with both political and psychological ramifications.[31] Godwin's own fling with Sandemanian and Calvinist thought clearly influenced his conception of guilt, election, and damnation. But the confused readings of psychology we get in William Godwin are part of a not as yet fully articulated reading of character in the available discourses. Rudolf Storch, for instance, points out that eighteenth-century character analysis just did not have the range of discourses available to it through which intense psychological relationships could be developed. Given this restriction or limitation, it is indeed surprising to see how radical Godwin's text in fact turned out to be.

Another kind of limitation was put forward by James T. Boulton, who argued that Godwin's style was not "lived" but laconic, limpid, and far too generalized. Sometimes Godwin's prose had "no actuality, none of the vivid concreteness that comes from genuinely felt experience."[32] His prose is consequently "loose-limbed," its movement "lumbering." Beyond questions of style, Boulton, however, reads *Caleb Williams* as a political text, and implies in his reading, I think, that a fictive text that foregrounds ideology above all else or is in fact written to express a particular scheme or scenario, a philosophy or politics, is bound to suffer artistically. It will never, in the final analysis, be able to manipulate point of view (ironic, objective, historical, epic, and so on) so essential to undercut the claims made by the characters themselves. Consequently, Boulton reads *Caleb Williams* as a political text in a similar fashion to P. N. Furbank. Boulton, however, is careful not to leave it at that and adds later that "the form of the novel," as well as "the symbolic person" of Burke, should be taken into account in interpreting *Caleb Williams*.[33] This acknowledgment—that the novelistic form has its own laws which mediate between art and history—is a crucial corrective to Boulton's political reading of the text. It is an acknowledgment that gestures forcefully toward the discursive complexity of the fictional form and its essential dialogism.

B. J. Tysdahl was conscious of textual instability when he argued that there is ultimately no "complete thematic unity" in *Caleb Williams* because it had to be "seen as two or three different novels. . . ."[34] This is an astute argument whose clear ramifications Tysdahl does not follow through. Instead he falls back on William Empson's seventh type of ambiguity to explain why *Caleb Williams* expresses "a fundamental division in the writer's mind."[35] Ambiguity, then, permits Tysdahl to bring the various fragments of the text together. Thus, in this argument, the fact that *Caleb Williams* is two or more texts does not make it an "unstable" text; it simply shows that the author was able to hold together a multiplicity of meanings through a "Keatsian negative capability." What Tysdahl does comes extremely close to the heart of the problem of *Caleb Williams*—that it is constructed around competing discourses whose demarcations remain visible—but misses the point by invoking the principle of ambiguity as unity. An unstable text such as *Caleb Williams* is multilayered in a different way. It examines states of being, varying psychological positions, and at the same time suggests the impossibility of its own existence. Textual instability also marks the text as a mirror of its own lack of certitude. We return to Foucault's reading of the Gothic discourse as marking the end of epic certainty, since it now mirrored the death of language. The world is no longer available to us as an object of pure mimesis; the subject searches for self-definition in a depthlessness that, in an echo of the simulacrum as the image, ceases to have a direct relationship with reality. It is because of the inherent instability of a text (the sort of instability, though untheorized, recognized by the best commentators on Godwin) and its existence within a multiple temporality that ultimate, unproblematic reconstructions or recuperations of meaning are not possible. As postmodern readers aware of the "existence" of a text in the interface between a dialectical process of historical determinations and reader actualizations, we construct appropriate heuristic models or "project hypotheses about the patterns in which [the text's] elements cohere,"[36] to read the text. In the rest of this chapter I propose to do precisely that. I construct, in effect, two heuristic models, both interrelated and mutually dependent, so as to "misprision" my text (I borrow this term from Harold Bloom,[37] though I should wish to emphasize the legal meaning of this term as "the concealment of one's knowledge of treasonable intent"—the point being that I am going to radically "misread" the text, but would nevertheless conceal this misreading). In doing so I should like to situate *Caleb Williams* first within the matrix of a theoretical history and, second, within a particular discourse that I have called the discourse of the Gothic sublime. The rest of this chapter is therefore divided into two subsections: "From Order to History" and "*Caleb Williams* and the Gothic Sublime."

From Order to History

The last years of the eighteenth century, writes Michel Foucault in *The Order of Things*, were "broken by a discontinuity similar to that which destroyed Renaissance thought at the beginning of the seventeenth."[38] In Britain that "discontinuity" was characterized by a "gradual process of transformation" that led to the emergence of a "manufacturing system operating under capitalistic ownership and control."[39] The mutation of "order" into history (the shift from hierarchical and fixed class structures to a much more fluid social system) was directly linked to the growth of a wholly new mercantile and entrepreneurial class. But more importantly, the economic shift that came with the notions of the "empire" and the "colony" also made "man" the central object of study. Before the late eighteenth century, in the order of things, "man" had no special privileges. This becomes clear when we recall that even when the totality of classical order had been gradually fractured by a persistent dissociation of the unity of "sign" and "resemblance" (the almost photographic system of representation through the rhetoric of "emulation," "analogy," "sympathy," and so on), there had been no radical subversion of the descriptive system itself. Language, for instance, continued to be discussed in terms of its progressive powers of assimilation and change. What marks this radical transformation of order into history is in fact the *épistème* of "organic structure": "it subordinates characters one to another; it links them to functions; it arranges them in accordance with an architecture that is internal as well as external."[40] The changes in natural history (vitalism, organic wholes instead of mechanism), in the analysis of wealth (Adam Smith and the new concept of labor, 1776) and in general grammar (the study of comparative philology, the discovery of the analogous nature of verbal inflexions between the Sanskrit and Latin verbs *to be*, the discovery of internal morphophonemic relations in language, etc.)—these changes led to the final overthrow of "representation," which, as Foucault says, "lost the power to provide a foundation . . . the links that can join its various elements together." This "absolutely essential displacement" finally "toppled the whole of Western thought."[41]

Through this *épistème* of organic structure and inner relationality, exemplified best in the law of grammatical inflexions, let us consider, within our first heuristic model, the relationship of *Caleb Williams* to its immediate history. At the risk of some slight oversimplification I should like to offer the following transmutation of Foucault's *épistème*. If order is perceived as history, then abstract man now becomes political man. The *épistème* of organic structure, relationality, and process already referred to underlie any archaeology of those discursive practices that constitute and signify our reading of history: this archaeology is precisely the field of consciousness that might be called "political man." In my first model, the first part of a dialectical reading of the text, I propose to place *Caleb Williams* in this historical context. The second model, arising out of the first, takes us to *Caleb Williams* as a text of the Gothic sublime.

Who is the abstract man, and what are his rights? For an answer we must go to the great pundit of Western liberalism, John Locke, and his *Second Treatise of Government* (1690). Locke defined the rights of abstract man, based on an initial contract with God that goes back to Edenic Man, in terms of

> a state of perfect freedom to order their actions and dispose of their possessions and persons as they think fit, within the bounds of the law of nature, without asking leave, or depending on the will of any other man.[42]

The American Declaration of Independence (1776)—a surprisingly Lockean document, and understandably so—called these rights "self-evident truths." Within the framework of a more urgent and sharper rhetorical focus, the document spoke of "inalienable rights," among which may be included "life," "liberty," and the "pursuit of happiness." This is the polemic of order, not of history.

Against Locke's "abstract man" (the definition persists in Berkeley, Hume, Hobbes, and Condillac, for instance) the last decades of the eighteenth century pits the "political man." For our purposes, the growth of this historical concept (for political man is history) may be punctuated by the works of Rousseau, Edmund Burke (both in his stand against Warren Hastings and in *Reflections on the Revolution in France*, 1790), Mary Wollstonecraft (*Vindication of the Rights of Woman*, 1792) and William Godwin (*Enquiry Concerning Political Justice*, 1793). Although the essential confluence of "Reason" and "the pursuit of happiness" (rationality imposes restraints because the higher good is humanity's goal) is never seriously threatened, what is problematized is precisely Locke's "state of perfect freedom" insofar as the ideology of "power" and the fetishization of institutions inhibit and ultimately pervert and corrupt the individual. As "political man," the individual is now a subject who enters the realm of ideology. Rousseau's memorable first sentence—"Man is born free; and everywhere he is in chains" (*The Social Contract*, 1, chapter 1)—juxtaposes the two, showing that institutions coerce the individual; abstract rights (of being born free) cannot be seen outside the context of what Blake called the "mind-forg'd manacles" of oppressive history. So Mary Wollstonecraft speaks of power corrupting the powerful as it enslaves the weak. And before reason (either of Locke or of Rousseau) can be allowed to assert itself, the institutions of power must be put down. Humankind, therefore, enters history. Yet at precisely this point, Edmund Burke, who had earlier defended the rights of Chait Singh of Benares and the Begums of Oudh against Hastings on the grounds that since the Indian body politic was also representative of the principles of human order, sanctioned by age-old social structures and traditions, tyranny (in this case the sublime as colonial terror) of whatever kind was intolerable because it denied the sanctity of natural rights, in his *Reflections* claimed that since man had imperfect reason he was incapable of formulating blueprints of change that would take account of all human relationships and activities. Faced with the bourgeois truism that if institutions were overthrown, the state would also disappear, Burke denied that man could redeem himself through his own efforts. Yet these essentially Lockean invocations of the greater good and a vague "contract" based on original promise (which, ironically enough, was written on the occasion of yet another revolution, that of 1688) trap people into half-truths and lies. Society, states Godwin in *Political Justice,* is not some vague abstraction, and the state and its laws are not intrinsically virtuous. The sanctity of "natural rights" must be read as the right of the individual toward self-determination; through the exercise of reason, free individuals can reach their own conclusions. To act outside human judgment is to be coerced into acting for the self-interests of others. There is, then, an essential contradiction between the needs of society—freedom—and the action of government, which is to subjugate its people and perpetuate injustice. In Book 5, chapter 15, called "Of Political Impostures," Godwin cites Rousseau's claim (*The Social Contract,* 2, chapter 7) "that no legislator could ever establish a grand political system without having recourse to religious imposture."[43] The phrase *religious imposture* is what we would call "ideology," defined as an "*imaginary* set of relationships" invoked by the ruling classes to legitimate their own power. Burke's "principles of human order" are now seen as principles based on "posturing," for when Burke speaks of "people," he in fact has in mind not "the people" but "a people" who understand the nature of the "true" political sublime based on a governmental apparatus that is both feared and admired. Yet although Godwin, like Caleb Williams, understood both the processes of history ("the genuine purpose of history, was to enable us to understand the machine of society"[44]) and fiction ("Romance then, strictly considered, may be pronounced to be one of the species of history"[45]) and their essential contradictions as processes, he could not, finally, accept Rousseau's case for a conscious lifting of repression at every level. The "nation" itself must be right for the state of freedom, and, as one of his more recent editors, Isaac Kramnick, remarks, Godwin remains a kind of a proto-Marxist historian for whom "the inequalities of property perhaps constitute a state, through which it would be necessary for us to pass."[46]

Where does this lead us to? In a summary fashion the argument thus far seeks to locate the meaning of *Caleb Williams* in a political dichotomy whose central opponents are Burke and Godwin. It does not, however, aim to reduce this antagonism (which was a reversal of early admiration: "I had always been a most ardent admirer of the talents and system of life of Mr. Burke," Godwin had acknowledged[47]) to characterological oppositions in the text. On the contrary, the method isolates an epistemic shift that foregrounds humankind as a legitimate object of knowledge in its own right. In this new narrative organicity, political man, and history become the crucial determinants of intellectual discourses. But the text is not to be confused with any single discourse. The text is a fictional discourse, a fact that needs considerable underlining so as to avoid the kinds of traps that many political readers of the text, in particular, have fallen into. The basic contradictions in the text manifest (carry) the transitional nature of the *épistème* itself; they mediate "practices" that can be closed only through an act of political "imposture"/"imposition."

In *Twelfth Night* Olivia warns Viola not to be "out of your text." I must quickly begin to unveil this text in a systematic manner. The title *Things as They Are; or, The Adventures of Caleb Williams* (the Standard Novels Edition, 1831, drops the first half of the title) juxtaposes two essentially diverging discourses: romance (placing itself in the generic conventions of *The Adventures of*. . . romance rather than *The History of*. . . realistic system) and philosophy (in the tradition perhaps of the "anatomical" studies of Robert Burton or the pamphleteering genre of the dissenters). More formally, the code of dual titles, implying parallel narrative actualizations by the reader, is itself not all that unusual. In fact, Godwin's own title quickly spawned imitations or outright parodies: *The Fair Methodist; or Such Things Are* (1794); Elizabeth Inchbald, *Wives as They Were, and Maids as They Are*, a Comedy, in five Acts

(1797); Thomas Tovey, *Things as They Were, as They Are, and as They Ought To Be*, A Poem (1804), all productions of what the *Critical Review* called a "scribbling age."[48]

Godwin's subtitle is neither ironic nor parodistic. Nevertheless, "Things as They Are" certainly implies a didactic challenge, especially when placed alongside the epigraph to the novel, which ends with the line "Man only is the common foe of man."[49] For if things are what they are, then potentially, things ought not be what they are. If the hero of these adventures is to be pitted against the forces of things as they are, then the latter, the representation of the present state of affairs, may well be symbolic of those forces of repression which restrain, through "impostures," through *imaginary* ideological relations, the individual's will to act. But there is a strange antagonism between "action" and "adventures": "adventures" possess semiotic rules of their own; the hero in adventures is by and large a picaro figure. So already we detect two codes whose meanings must be teased out at length before textual significance may be realized.

Structurally, the text is divided into three books, reflecting both a formal convention and the requirements of the publishing industry, with its network of lending libraries. The first book deals in the main with the narrative of Mr. Collins, in which Caleb Williams is only an observer, a historian, in a way. The other two books deal with Caleb's own narrative. Written in the first person the hero is both an actor and a historian. It is in these two books that Caleb is pursued by Falkland (through his deputy Gines), and it is in them that we discover what Godwin himself claimed in his preface to *Fleetwood* as "the analysis of the private and internal operations of the mind." The narrative is in a way propelled by the revelation of Falkland's guilt and it is this particular revelation that constitutes the inner energy of the text. The trajectory of the narrative must therefore be constantly reconciled to this fact, for once Falkland's guilt is revealed, the pursuer (Caleb Williams) becomes the pursued. In political terms, we immediately become conscious of the fact that Godwin's ideal "free men" (in *Political Justice*) who, through their own "reason," can arrive at their "own conclusion" unhampered by either "coercion" or the restrictions of institutions and "law," cannot be realized in a world that legitimates, as Burke was to approve, the eternal and immutable patterns of master and servant. It is here that bourgeois humanism (in the person of the enlightened Falkland) denies its own idealism: confronted with the threat to the very ideologically mystified foundations of the squirearchy, Falkland must first of all murder Mr. Tyrrel[50] (whose antihumanism he disapproves but whose threat to the honor of the gentry he cannot be seen to condone) and, second, persecute Caleb Williams for daring to have access to knowledge (to be read as privilege) when, by simple class definition, he should be excluded from possessing such knowledge. Within the participants of that class "honor" may be mutilated for survival; outside that class the system closes in on itself to present a citadel of solidarity. And so when Laura Denison, daughter of an enlightened Neapolitan nobleman—Prospero and his Neapolitan connections banished—is confronted with the truth of Caleb Williams she, even as a mother, must reject Caleb because class solidarity must be maintained.

At this level of reading we detect two sets of structural relationships, which may be schematized as (a) the system of persecution and (b) the system of power. In the first the three participants are Caleb, Hawkins, and Emily. In the second the participants are Falkland, Tyrrel and Laura Denison. In both, the second two "items" are really subsets of the first. In the first system all three are effectively "servants" who attempt to define "self" by subverting the established institutional orders. Caleb must sacrifice "knowledge," Hawkins "son" and Emily her "body." The sacrifices are not seen as inalienable rights intrinsic to the definitions of manhood/womanhood, but as commodities that must be bartered in a system of economic exchange. Through the paradigm of power, sexuality, and desire the discourse makes this abundantly clear.[51] Emily is defined as an "unbroken filly" (69), with "the wildness, as well as the delicate frame, of the bird that warbles unmolested in its native groves" (64), who during her fever imagines seeing "Mr. Tyrrel and his engine Grimes" (117). The repressed language of English sexuality—"engine" and "machine" are words for "penis" in the antilanguage of the English lower classes—thus makes its way into Godwin's seemingly respectable fictive discourse. Tyrrel thus gets symbolically castrated—struck by a "sudden palsy" (109)—even as he implicitly condones homosexual rape. Tyrrel mentions to Hawkins "this lad of yours, whom I am desirous of taking into favour" (95). The sexual denotations of "desirous," "taking," and "favour" cannot be overlooked. In other words, Caleb, Emily, and Hawkins act out their roles as persecuted subjects trapped inside an ideology of power and sexual abuse strengthened precisely by those laws of "order and continuity" privileged by Edmund Burke. Like Grimes, they, too, "reverenced the inborn divinity that attends upon rank" (108). In the latter part of the eighteenth century this inborn divinity was no more than an acknowledgment of the power of ownership of property, which had been enshrined into English law as inviolate. Since theft of property was as serious a crime as murder, the theoretical equality granted all Englishmen before the law was mere rhetoric, hollow and without any teeth whatsoever.[52] The second system, as we have said, is effectively one of power. Initially, the assumptions of those who belong to the set of rulers are threatened by none other than Falkland himself, who functions as a benevolent patron from within the comforts of the ruling class. Here he is very much like the Edmund Burke who led the impeachment proceedings against Warren Hastings. To Tyrrel, Falkland explains:

> In the society of men we must have something to endure, as well as to enjoy. No man must think that the world was made for him. Let us take things as we find them; and accommodate ourselves as we can to unavoidable circumstances. (39)

Later he damns the system itself: "he could not prevent himself from reproaching the system of nature, for having given birth to such a monster as Tyrrel" (122). The categories of reproach/criticism function within the established codes of bourgeois liberalism. The *épistème* that produces the humanist categories of "society of men," "endurance," "accommodation," "system of nature"—the *épistème* of order—echoes an ideology that fails to detect the underlying sets of relations which indeed produce them in the first instance. It is when Falkland stands accused that he ceases to appropriate the language of Lockean liberalism in favor of a Burkean defense. "There would be a speedy end to all order and good government, if fellows that trample on ranks and distinctions in this atrocious sort were upon any consideration suffered to get off" (382), exclaims the senior magistrate on hearing Caleb's accusations against Falkland. In one way the murder of Tyrrel makes Falkland a "political man"; the hollow gestures of enlightened humanism are replaced by the almost parodied register of class survival. In Falkland are typified the will to fend off the onslaught of "reason" and knowledge possessed by the almost Godwinian Caleb. In the face of this seeming "anarchy," Falkland becomes progressively tyrannical as Caleb becomes desexualized. His "adventures" repeat the pursuit of Emily by Grimes. The sexual threat to Emily from the "engine Grimes" (117) can be answered, by Caleb, only "with this engine, this little pen" (437).

What the text "uncovers," then, is not just the opposing claims of *Political Justice* and *Reflections* by simply thematizing "hierarchy," "human bondage," and "rank," but rather the very psychology of political behavior insofar as this psychology is now the product of a major epistemic shift in Western civilization. Any reading of *Caleb Williams* must first situate the text in this "matricial" shift from "order" to "history," from "abstract man" to "political man," so that the force of history may be recognized in all its brutal complexity. "Things as They Are" is thus not Richardson's "Virtue Rewarded" or Shakespeare's "What you will"; it is part of the very realm of a complex system of ideologies that confine and determine political man. But this is a reading through only the first model. We must now read it through our second model, emphasizing this time the nature of *writing* itself. This model requires, initially, the mediating form of the precursor text.

There is something cruelly ironic about Godwin's description of *Caleb Williams* in his 1832 preface to *Fleetwood* as "this mighty trifle." The year before, in 1831, Mary Godwin Shelley, whose mother (Mary Wollstonecraft) died on childbirth, reflected on her own work, *Frankenstein,* as "my hideous progeny." "This mighty trifle" and "my hideous progeny" occupy important space in their respective prefaces, separated only by a year. The juxtaposition of these two self-effacing definitions of their authors' major fictive works says more than meets the eye about the respective textual status of their works and implicates them within a web of relationships, bondages, and injunctions both literary and human. The father-daughter bond, articulated more imaginatively in "my hideous progeny," involved, as we have already seen in our reading of *Mathilda,* a complex structure of power and patriarchy from which the sexual dimension was inexorably censored. This ambiguous network may be deemed one of the underlying substrata of the Gothic. It is a pattern, or a core, that is forever transformed into texts, through a kind of a freeplay of the kernel. In the process the Gothic becomes a writerly text made up of a heterogeneous series that cannot be reduced to one text, to one master narrative. At the "head" of this series stands Walpole's *The Castle of Otranto,* the founding text of the Gothic precursor. In other words, the intertext of *Caleb Williams* must be found in a literary practice that transcends the texts of the first model of our reading. Of course, intertextuality must not be confused with the actual citations from previous texts (the theory of influences cannot account for discontinuities); rather, intertextuality is marked by forms of literary practice, ways of conceiving/conceptualizing the world, and methods of reworking both actualized and potential literary forms. To read *Caleb Williams* through the Gothic precursor is to read it finally as a text of the Gothic sublime.

Though the critical discourses I have utilized here were not available to the critics of the late eighteenth and early nineteenth centuries, we can see in their concern with the darker, inexplicable (the gloomy) side of humanity issues that are at the very heart of *Caleb Williams* and which speak to us with an extraordinary urgency. In *The Spirit of the Age*, Hazlitt, for instance, is one of the very first critics to see the center of the text as an endless, and remorseless, duplication of two minds agonized by almost parallel doubts.

> Perhaps the art, with which these two characters [Caleb and Falkland] are contrived to relieve and set off each other, has never been surpassed in any work of fiction. . . . The restless and inquisitive spirit of *Caleb Williams*, in search and in possession of his patron's fatal secret, haunts the latter like a second conscience. . . .[53]

What is being foreshadowed here is the sublime read through the Freudian compulsion to repeat. This compulsion to repeat forms the underlying "*ur*-narrative" of the text. Like the associated self-fulfilling prophecies—Frankenstein's fears about the Monster invariably lead to their confirmation—a narrative of repetition along characterological lines is marked by patterns of dissolution of identity and difference. In what Gavin Edwards has, I think correctly, termed a "badly written" novel[54]—which for Edwards also resembles the avant-garde (and the postmodern)—William Godwin writes a text in which fragmentary narratives and discourses are artificially stitched together in ways that often parody their prior models. The compulsion to repeat affected Godwin, too, since it is the one work of fiction that he recounts endlessly. Let us examine this through Godwin's own manuscripts and notes that have survived.

We read as late as 10 October 1824:

> In a spirit something analogous to this [the composition of *Political Justice*] I wrote Caleb Williams. I said to myself a hundred times, The [*sic*] impression of my tale shall never be blotted out of the mind of him on whom it has once been produced: he that reads it shall never again be as if he had not

> read it. I shall not write for temporary effect: my purpose is, that what I say shall be incorporated with the very fibres (fires?) of the soul of him who listens to me.[55]

There is nothing new in this *Political Justice-Caleb Williams* interconnection. The political imperative of the first clearly stalks the fictive text, and William Godwin has often underlined precisely this point. What I'm gesturing at, through the incidental manuscript evidence, is that *Caleb Williams* becomes, for Godwin, the haunting and haunted "spot of time," his own special omphalos. The author repeats the obsessional narrative of the text, drawing the duplication of Caleb and Falkland toward himself as the absolute signified and gets trapped in its rhetoric of gloom and despair.

There are many references in the contemporary periodical literature that refer to Godwin's works in terms of metaphors of gloom and darkness. Thus, Anna Seward termed *Caleb Williams* "a darkly able" work and affirmed her admiration of both Godwin and Richardson.[56] Other critics of the periodical literature endorse this "gloomy style," referring to it as a tendency in both Godwin and in his fictive characters: "all the heroes of all his novels are inflicted with his malady."[57] The gloom that one associates with the Gothic—the gloom that is really the unleashing of forces inexplicable but compulsively attractive to man, wrapped up, for comfort, in romance nevertheless—now finds expression more centrally at the level of character and, as in the case of Mary Shelley, may be connected to the author himself. In the words of a correspondent to *Blackwood's Edinburgh Magazine*, the "gloomy style" is transformed into a "morbid anatomy" whose development Godwin clearly loves to trace, since he "prefers subjects of disordered organs, which ordinary life and nature do not exhibit."[58] "Generic terms are important—as the eighteenth century well knew—,"[59] James Boulton reminds us, but the use of "disordered organs" mimics, as we have seen, Boulton's own description of Godwin's style as "loose-limbed." The previous month (December 1817), *Blackwood's Edinburgh Magazine* had made the "gloomy" connection more explicit by connecting Godwin with Byron (a very different kettle of fish):

> The poet and the novellist have each given birth to a set of terrible personifications of pride, scorn, hatred, misanthropy, misery, and madness. . . . Gloominess and desolation, and Satanic sarcasm, are the ground-work of their fictions . . .[60]

The "nervous and manly" language of Godwin reflects "an imagination invigorated with the supernatural acuteness of disease."[61] The views expressed here conflate the character of Caleb Williams with that of Godwin. The disease metaphor is then expanded by images borrowed from Fuseli:

> The impression which his story makes upon us is like that of a dismal dream, which we feel to be a fiction, and from which we are anxious to escape, but which sits, with a gloomy pertinacity, inflexible upon our breast, and compells us, in spite of reason and volition, to keep our eyes fixed and stedfast on its gliding phantoms and unearthly horrors.[62]

The literary comparison with which the review begins is certainly not tenable—Godwin did not share Byron's brooding darkness, his spirited love for the somber—but its interpretation of *Caleb Williams* as a discourse locked into the subject's unconscious is central to the problematic of the sublime. Caleb's "gloom" is not just a Gothic convention; it is a feature that connects the subject to a narrative of uncanny repetition and duplication. In this version of subjectivity the sublime pushes one further inward; the mind does not soar but regresses into a morbid pathology of its own insignificance. Like Caleb, the subject is essentially suicidal. Contemporary criticism did not, as one would have thought, connect Godwin's gloomy view of the world with the discourse of madness even though the latter begins to touch on the theories of the sublime. In 1804 Dr. Joseph Mason Cox, for instance, published a treatise in which he demonstrates a morbid fascination with madness ("Diseases of the Mind") even though the account is clearly presented as a contribution to medical science.[63] In Samuel Tuke's description of an asylum for the insane near New York the medical is also couched in the language of social containment through a return to Bentham's Panopticon. The kind of asylum endorsed here is constructed around a definiton of an all-seeing, rational legislator whom the mental "criminal" himself can't see.[64] The model, of course, parallels both *The Triumphs of Gods Revenge* (1621), which was one of Godwin's sources, and Caleb's own fear of being always seen by Falkland.

Caleb Williams and the Gothic Sublime

"But the theme by amplification became nauseous . . ." (60). Tyrrel, who finds Emily Melville's excessive praise of Falkland "nauseous," takes the drastic step of bringing Emily's discourse to an end. The "nausea" is an existential sickness, a sense of ennui with life itself, as well as a moment of irrationality constitutive of the experience of the sublime. Tyrrel brings to an end, quite dramatically, the "appeasing" power of Emily's discourse. Caleb Williams also tells a tale that he himself must bring to an end—and at every point in the text the sublime is in fact rendered through the processes of writing about which Caleb/Godwin seem to be acutely aware. The "mighty trifle" of the 1832 preface to *Fleetwood* is in fact a writing that is self-consciously offered as a process: recall Godwin's own emphasis in the preface on the "private and internal operations of the mind."[65] We must therefore return the text to its "play" of discourse, to what this "mighty trifle" turns out to be: an act of "writing" that explores "presence" in its continual being and the paradoxical "enslaving" of the self that occurs through it. As we read, we get involved in the processes of writing that, in the final analysis, are what unites the pursuer and the pursued, cancelling out subject and object through an endless dialogue with the Other. What we are left with at the end is writing itself, bare and wounded.

The act of writing imputes power to the possessor of words and, therefore, we must seek a further clarification of the question: "What kind of a 'writing' (as distinct from a 'text') is *Caleb Williams*?" The first sentence of the novel reads:

> My life has for several years been a theatre of calamity.

The "writing" is therefore going to be about "my life" (that is, autobiographical or confessional), extended through the metaphor of "drama" to examine my "calamity." This is I. A. Richards' simplest definition of metaphor: "my life" is like a "theatre" in respect of "calamity." The use of the word "calamity," which occurs throughout the text to explain Caleb's state of misery or adversity, takes us to an interesting question about its origins and etymology. Like Godwin's mentor, Rousseau, and the text's narrative model, Eugene Aram,[66] Caleb, too, does a bit of devilling into comparative philology in the comfortable company of the Denisons. Now the word "calamity" had been given a false etymology by Latin writers who related it to the word *calamus*, "straw, cornstalk, etc." The *OED* finds this etymology rather suspect since the suffix added to *calamus* could only have produced the meaning "the quality of being a calamus, reed, or straw," and not "damage, disaster, adversity." The *OED* cites Bacon, who interpreted it to mean a catastrophe (a word used interchangeably with "calamity" throughout *Caleb Williams*) by claiming that "the word *calamitas* was first derived from *calamus*, when the corn could not get out of the stalke."

In a rather uncanny fashion, then, the choice of the word *calamity* to designate Caleb's own condition connects two sorts of "instabilities": an unstable etymology and an unstable autobiography. To give this calamity a form, Caleb uses the extended metaphor of the theatre. Like *The Castle of Otranto, Caleb Williams* also falls under the powerful spell of drama, and especially Shakespearian drama. To select only the obvious examples, we therefore read "Hawkins was so foolishly fond of his son" (96, Lear); "We that are rich" (105, Lear); "I lift the curtain, and bring forward the last act of the tragedy" (108, any Shakespearian play, but notably *The Winter's Tale*); "The law justifies it" (112, Shylock); "for the scene was acted upon too public a stage" (122, any play); "I will watch him without remission. . . . Surely at such a time his secret anguish must betray itself" (173, Hamlet); "sleep no more" (190, Macbeth); "No, I will use no daggers!" (435, Hamlet); "Where is the man that has suffered more from the injustice of society than I have done?" (446, Hamlet); "It is a rank and rotten soil, from which every finer shrub draws poison as it grows" (451, Hamlet), among many more.

The "theatre of calamity" through the Shakespearian intertext, and especially through *Hamlet*, is the "space" in which the agonizing search for the sublime father/truth against the beautiful security of the absent mother must take place. But because this father is a "relic," a fragment of the unconscious, "his truth," the written text about a father's unknowable (to his progeny) biography (the unthinkable phenomenon) hidden in the "trunk," would remain inaccessible to Caleb.

> Mr. Falkland had always been to my imagination an object of wonder, and that which excites our wonder we scarcely suppose ourselves competent to analyse. (411)

This description of Falkland comes close to Kant's definition of the sublime. What Caleb does is use the language of the sublime—the momentary loss of the law of reason and our capacity for self-analysis—to designate the peculiar attraction of Falkland. In this economy of the sublime, analysis will always fail us, though this failure has a special fascination for the subject as he identifies with it in a kind of perverse delight in absolute negativity. As a result Caleb can only endlessly write out his "calamity," and in the process also write himself out as a separate being.

In the opening paragraph, "my life" (which is varied to "my fairest prospects," "my fame," "my own conscience") thus enters semiotic systems of "theatre" and the narratives of persecution and of disaster. Even with these analogies to art, "my life," however, proposes to enter a system of referential validity that would lead to the recovery of the reality behind this life. To achieve "my life" (that which is emotionally recoverable in the real world), Caleb must write out "my story," truer than the discourse of truth, which "will, at least, appear to have that consistency which is seldom attendant but upon truth." In writing out my life as my story, the subject I/my as history—as in "my life"—now enters the realm of fiction. The truth that is history is always fragmented, and lacks consistency; the truth that is fiction (a paradox) will "appear" to have a consistency, since art can "fake" concordances or unities, impose a design, that the lived experience of "my life" cannot. It becomes clear that through "writing," then, Godwin/Caleb invokes a totality that is missing from life. But he can only reflect on that totality, since the act of writing will be anything but unified. Clearly "appear to have" is the crucial corrective to Caleb's conception of the writing of "my story."

The need to claim the truth of fiction, to prioritize it over history and life, is a ploy not uncommon among realist writers. Here, however, the desire to collapse the domains of truth and fiction may be connected quite legitimately with the Lacanian realm of the *imaginary,* in which the simulacra, the fiction, or the hyperreal, mirrors the "real" subject. Because *Caleb Williams* does possess a greater realistic base, the decisive orientation of the Gothic toward the *imaginary* (which is a characteristic feature of narratives of the double anyway) is precisely what destabilises the text itself. Between *The Castle of Otranto* and Melville's *Pierre* stands *Caleb Williams.*

The *imaginary* relations referred to take the form of progressive sets of identifications between Caleb and Falkland. These grotesque identifications or Gothic undifferentiation relate directly to the whole question of what constitutes self-consciousness and how it is defined. Rosemary Jackson's cryptic summation of the relationship between Caleb and Falkland as one of "the earliest fantasies of dualism"[67] foregrounds a much more important definition of self-consciousness and subjectivity advanced by Hegel in his *Phenomenology of Spirit.* In the section entitled "Independence and

Dependence of Self-Consciousness: Lordship and Bondage" (#178–196), Hegel writes:

> Self-consciousness exists in and for itself when, and by the fact that, it so exists for another; that is, it exists only in being acknowledged.[68]

Hegel develops this definition further to show how acknowledgment is essentially dialectical and mutually reinforcing. The dialectic traps both Self and Other, as servant and master, into a condition of mutual dependency. And this trap is the precondition for an endless situation of the gaze and the countergaze without the elimination of either the master or the servant. It is, indeed, the very essence of self-consciousness that the Other's destruction, in death, might be countenanced as an ideal but never actually realized. Falkland cannot kill Caleb, nor can Caleb kill Falkland, yet neither can exist without the other. At the same time their self-consciousnesses, at this level, must remain in the realm of the *imaginary*, since the mutual viewing of each other (in terms of which each is acknowledged and defined) is not the same as what either sees in himself. This essential veiling or collapse of two seemingly independent self-consciousnesses—the master and the slave—is almost programatically present in Caleb, the servant's, relationship with Falkland, his master. In the final paragraphs of *Caleb Williams* one gets a colonized discourse, in which language becomes almost totally identificatory as Caleb confesses his misery as a being-in-itself ("now only that I am truly miserable") as this self slides into "no character": the signifiers *I, me, mine* collapse into Falkland's own pronouns as they become philologically regressive. Falkland is addressed as "thou," "thy," and so forth, and the verbs are inflected accordingly. This linguistic regression reinforces the coalescing of the "Caleb-I" with the "Falkland-I"; the drama of "my life" becomes the drama of "thy life." "I have now no character that I wish to vindicate," exclaims Caleb, and we know, as trained readers of Jacobean tragedy, that in the end Vindice, too, has no one else to vindicate: "Tis time to die when we are ourselves our foes."[69]

The loss of "difference" in the character of Falkland and Caleb through a specular identification of Caleb with Falkland is marked by two processes: one structural, the other thematic. The structural aspect takes the form of an oath; the thematic of "naming." When Falkland confesses his murder, he first dictates an oath to Caleb and then immediately binds him: "I had no alternative but to make you my confidant or my victim" (187). "I shall always hate you," he proclaims, and adds, "I charge and adjure you by every thing that is sacred, and that is tremendous, preserve your faith!" The oath is bound not by the figure of "God" but by a somewhat obscure "that [which] is sacred," qualified parenthetically by the word *tremendous.* This word, with its meaning of "awful" or "awe-inspiring," clearly suggests that Falkland's binding oath is based on an essentially Burkean invocation of the sublime as awe-inspiring. Thus, the Gothic "pact" or "contract" like that demanded by Byron/Polidori's fiendish heroes, is based on a "tremendous knowledge" for which the recipient must pay an enormous price. But the knowledge, which is also, for a fleeting moment, power over the giver of knowledge, quickly becomes a sublime horror, since it would implicate both the giver of the knowledge and its recipient. The oath, then, binds Caleb to a sublime knowledge to which he can never give utterance. It is, to use a word straight out of Gothic discourse, "unspeakable," and ultimately, for the subject, quite beyond representation.

The binding oath has strong implications for the second, thematic, process, the process of naming. In the context of the oath it soon becomes clear that "my life" can acquire value and significance only insofar as it can be named, and only insofar as the act of naming and the name itself are deemed to be important. The process of naming in *Caleb Williams* is compounded by a consciousness about the self that is internal to the text. In other words, the subject of the text, Caleb, appropriates functions of the self that are intertextual, intratextual, and pretextual. What Paul de Man summarizes as the four distinct types of the self ("the self that judges, the self that reads, the self that writes, and the self that reads itself"[70]), which are versions really of the critic, the reader, the author, and the author as reader, collapse in the figure of the character Caleb Williams, since he judges, reads, writes, and then rereads what he has written. At the pretextual level Caleb's name goes back to the Book of Numbers, where he is one of the men "sent to spy out the land (of Canaan)." In fact, God is so pleased with him that he is especially singled out:

> neither shall any of them that provoked me see it: but my servant Caleb, because he had another spirit with him . . .[71]

The singling out by God is also an act of naming, of giving individuality to the person addressed. In *Caleb Williams* the person who names Caleb is Falkland. The context in which this takes place—the discussion on Alexander the Great's name (151)—has a dual significance. The first point to be made is that Falkland calls Caleb by his surname "Williams," a formal enough mode of address between master and servant. But in the context of the discussion on Alexander (about whom Caleb becomes progressively more critical), it is clear that whereas Alexander's surname was "the Great," that of Caleb is the common, Welsh "Williams." The surname, or the Name-of-the Father, the agency of self-judgment, is now employed by Falkland to deny Caleb precisely this capacity of distancing himself from his first name. Nevertheless, and this is our second point, Caleb's intervention into Falkland's reading of history is meant to destroy the fantasy of an imperial history as truth, because even Alexander's history must remain contingent. It is a defense mechanism that comes from Caleb's incapacity to name his own family name, and hence to write his own history. Whereas Falkland alludes to a "primary" history as *the* history, Williams refers to history as "histories," each one of which must be recontextualized into its respective *épistèmes*.

In fact what happens here is that both *naming* and *history* become problematic. Caleb must be named by another; and history, as Kunti, the mother in the *Mahābhārata*, alone knew, cannot finally answer the question of ownership, who names whom and why. Let us explore this by following the trajectory of "my life" as "my name" further. The first moment of "self-naming" occurs when Caleb signs himself off as "Caleb Williams" in a letter addressed to Falkland (210). It is a pathetic letter of resignation or release, but Falkland refuses to release him from the symbolic power that binds Caleb to him through Falkland's right to name: your name threatens my (good) name, your name will always be in the shadow of my own (name). Not surprisingly, Caleb names himself only twice in the entire work, both times in the second half of volume 3. To the old man in whose care the two "officers of justice" leave him self-naming proceeds tentatively: first as "Williams" (343)—Falkland's mode of naming—and only on further scrutiny, "Caleb." Finally, disguised as a Jew (echoing the Gothic "Wandering Jew," the eternal wanderer whom even death does not wish to embrace) and trapped by Gines and Spurrel, he exclaims defiantly, "Well, I am Caleb Williams" (377). Apart from the broadsheet histories of the "Most Wonderful and Surprising History and Miraculous Adventures of Caleb Williams" (371; 417–18) and public-house narratives of "the notorious housebreaker, Kit Williams" (325), Caleb is named no more than half a dozen times. Yet in asserting his first name, once symbolically in a letter, but there, too, disconcertingly, and once only in defiance, what he demonstrates is that he does not possess it—he is not the "owner" of the name. The real owner, as the real "my life" and "my story" (and "his life" and "history") is Falkland. We are now in a position to make significant displacements in the text. Before I formally do this, let me relate the first paragraph of the text, which we have already examined, to the last:

> . . . but I will finish them [these memoirs] that thy story may be fully understood; and that, if those errors of thy life be known which thou so ardently desiredst to conceal, the world may at least not hear and repeat a half-told and mangled tale. (452)

"My life" has become "thy life"; "my story," "thy story." The "truth-value" of "my story" is realized in the "truth" of "thy story" so that Falkland's life may not be a "half-told and mangled tale." "Tale" and "story" are implicitly opposed to the essence of the discourse itself.

We return to the two systems of "persecution" and "power" and find that the focal points of both—Caleb and Falkland—merge into one. Their essential dualism is now seen in terms of the categories of "reflection" and "shadow"; the *symbolic* retreating into the *imaginary*, the specularity of the sublime: Caleb's "I," as I have demonstrated, becomes Falkland's "I"; "he" becomes Caleb's ideal "I." In that respect, even in terms of its own historical temporality, *Caleb Williams* is a subversive text, just as *Political Justice* was a subversive ideology, just as the very *épistème* of late eighteenth-century thought, too, was subversive. On another level, especially through the strong sexual envy of the father figure Falkland and Caleb's barely concealed incestuous desire for the mother figure Laura Denison, the text reenacts a game already played out in the unconscious, and repressed by the very institutions that condemn political man. Thus, when Caleb discovers the truth:

> "Mr. Falkland is a murderer!" said I (188),

the sentence is both true and not true; true because there is a referential quality about it (because knowledge is truth: "My story will, at least, appear to have that consistency, which is seldom attendant but upon truth") and not true because within a hierarchically determined mode of signification

1. This knowledge has no functional value and is therefore useless;
2. This knowledge is not contributive of action, and therefore has no material significance;
3. This knowledge cannot be shared, and therefore it does not liberate; it traps consciousness even further because "I will never become an informer," says Caleb (189); and
4. This knowledge has always been "known"—the scene of writing is retrospective—and therefore has no claim to novelty. Even without writing out his history, so much is hinted at by Collins and presented in the Lucretia/Malvesi/Falkland preamble.

The site of truth, the place of taboo (the exposure or transgression of which condemns the subject, guilty and fractured, to an eternity of wandering) is the "fatal trunk." There are three references to this trunk that I should like to quote:

1. I heard the lid of a trunk hastily shut, and the noise as of fastening a lock. (7)
2. I snatched a tool suitable for the purpose, threw myself on the ground, and applied with eagerness to a magazine which inclosed all for which my heart panted. After two or three efforts, in which the energy of uncontrollable passion was added to my bodily strength, the fastenings gave way, the trunk opened, and all that I sought was at once within my reach.

   I was in the act of lifting up the lid, when Mr. Falkland entered, wild, breathless, distracted in his looks! (181)
3. The contents of the fatal trunk, from which all my misfortunes originated, I have never been able to ascertain. I once thought it contained some murderous instrument or relic connected with the fate of the unhappy Tyrrel. I am now persuaded that the secret it encloses, is a faithful narrative of that and its concomitant transactions, written by Mr. Falkland. . . . (437)

One of the common features of all these quotations is that the contents of the "trunk" are never disclosed. In the first two instances

Falkland's entry into the scene (of knowledge) leaves Caleb in a state of agitation. In other words, the Law of the Father intercedes at these crucial moments to deny the "son" knowledge of the ultimate secret. The attempt to grasp this secret only leads to Caleb's symbolic castration and rejection. The final quotation attempts to reconstruct the contents of what is clearly the unconscious through writing, signifying that the "secret" of the unconscious is a narrative. Falkland's secret is also a tale in much the same way as Caleb's "my story" is a narrative. As processes, Caleb and Falkland's lives can only be rendered meaningful through an interminable writing; the first spelled out in all its plenitude as an historical account, the second (Falkland's "faithful narrative" in the fatal trunk) offered as a narrative that can only be grasped through the kind of radical interpretation one does for a dream fragment. It is this endless writing, on the part of both Caleb and Falkland, reflecting and interpenetrating each other, that takes me to the manuscript ending of *Caleb Williams*.

The original manuscript ending of *Caleb Williams* is to be found in the Forster Collection of the Victoria and Albert Museum Library.[72] It was discovered by D. Gilbert Dumas, who described the manuscript ending at some length in a paper published in 1966.[73] William Godwin's detailed date-list for the composition of *Caleb Williams* indicates that pages 107–117 were composed between April 28 and April 30, 1794.[74] This is identical with pages 107–117 (pages 111–112 are missing) in the Forster collection of the *Caleb Williams* manuscript. Four days later, as the journal entry indicates, William Godwin began writing the first of the final nine and one-half pages that constitute the new ending of the novel. This new ending was completed on May 8. Alongside the May 4–8 entries Godwin wrote "new catastrophe." It is not my wish here to enter into the reasons for the change. What I am interested in is the way in which the manuscript ending is a more powerful rendition of Godwin's Gothic sublime as a form of negative empowerment that traps the subject. And if, as Godwin claimed in his preface to *Fleetwood* (1832), he planned the novel backwards, then surely the manuscript ending is the "end" toward which the novel had been moving all along.

As we have seen, in the published version Falkland confesses his crime and dies three days later. Caleb is overwhelmed by a sense of guilt and becomes convinced that he has in fact murdered his master. But there is some hint of Caleb coming to terms with the sublime object, Falkland, even though this means formally accepting the guilt of a son: "now only that I am truly miserable," writes Caleb (451). In the manuscript ending, Caleb continues to write out his history in the shadow of the sublime Falkland, whose name continues to haunt him (even when he is dead). As his own mind becomes more and more fragmented, he loses control of his own self. This "more likely agony, insanity, and death" is not endorsed by either of the two recent editors of *Caleb Williams*.[75] Marilyn Butler, too, supports the published ending on the grounds that it is a "brilliant idea" in which both protagonists are "enmeshed together in the same web of guilt and persecution."[76]

Yet these defenses of the published ending can be sustained only if we give an unproblematic primacy to the first of our heuristic models and, again, only if the dualities manifested in the portrayal of Falkland and Caleb are read on the surface level alone. Even in the published version, Caleb's claim that he himself was now "the basest and most odious of mankind" (448) has a particular force only if it is read as an echo of someone whose mind is no longer all of a piece and who is no longer in the symbolic realm of difference. Otherwise, the only defense that one can make is on the narrowly humanist grounds that in the grand design of the universe there are no victors, only losers. But one doesn't need a complex fictional discourse such as *Caleb Williams* to make that point. Indeed, what I'm claiming is that the published ending, in spite of Falkland's confession and Caleb's bizarre admission of guilt, is written over the essentially "insane" discourse of Caleb in the manuscript fragment, which is never completely relegated to the margins by Godwin's feverish writing in the days before the book went to the printer. The published ending avoids dealing with the dilemma of the Gothic sublime by attempting to deflect the text away from the sublime toward those harmonies one associates with the beautiful. But the original ending still slips past the "censor" of the published ending through what we might call a process of semiosis, and effectively controls the text. What the manuscript ending finally releases are the extremities of the fractured discourse of the sublime in an economy of the subject's total failure to grasp its true import. The control of language through parenthesis and period, now gives way to the feverish dash, the Emily Dickinson-like hyphen that seemingly connects fragments together. Caleb sits in a corner, in a chair; he doesn't move. He has "dreams—they are strange dreams," and his language is a pastiche of Clarissa, Ophelia, and Lady Macbeth—women all, since Caleb, too, has been effectively feminized. It is in the discourse of fragmentation (which, as I've said, remains the controlling discourse even of the published ending) that Godwin, looking forward to Melville, foregrounds a whole "culture" of the insane that no *épistème* of the late eighteenth century can overlook. The manuscript ending (which nevertheless speaks to the published ending from the margins and functions as its absent text) now takes us to a reading in which Falkland, the patriarchal sublime, is the object that Caleb cannot represent. At the same time, such is his presence that, like the Gothic object of the fragments we read in the previous chapter, the subject that constructs it (Kant's reading of the sublime as an evocation of an irresistible, imposing phenomenon) is totally incapable of giving it any kind of totality in his mind. Caleb's words in the manuscript ending, then, are that of the subject under the interdiction of the Gothic sublime as he plunges even further into the depths of his own soul. As some terrifying mystery, Falkland remains unknown; the sublime traduces the subject into total submission without granting him any capacity to soar above it. Caleb's history is therefore the history not of the grand narrative, but of the inconsequential fragment

It is difficult to close one's commentary on a text like *Caleb Williams* because the Minotaur in this labyrinth continues to elude us. Like one of the annoyingly common syntactic forms in the text (the use of a common set of adverbial intensifiers to denote the conjunction of two events, the "no sooner . . . than," "I had not . . . before," "had scarcely . . . when" syntax[77]), no sooner do we feel we've reached our destination than another passage opens out before us. That the text does not close itself off—and this is underlined more markedly in the manuscript ending of the text—takes us to the heart of the very contradictions through which the discourse is attempting to "work" itself out. The generic models of transition, the laws of the received Gothic discourse and an epistemic shift not fully in control of its ends; all these lock the text into the two models I have constructed to read the text. The shift from order to history explains the politics of the text, but it is the underlying practices through which the shift is articulated that lead to the postmodern paradox of representation. Here it is the organizing power of the Gothic precursor text and its singular grasp of the sublime that is crucial: "that which excites our wonder we scarcely suppose ourselves competent to analyse," writes Caleb, even as he is divided and hystericized by that wonder. For Caleb it is not a matter of Romantic belief but of Gothic *uncertainty* in the face of the sublime object. As the manuscript ending so powerfully demonstrates, Caleb can only relapse into a discourse of fragmentation, dashes, and silence.

5

Apocalyptic Narratives: Tales of Ends

Apocalyptic narratives have a very postmodern resonance about them, since they take us to the very heart of our fears about ends. Forms of eschatological anxiety are not new, since ends are always in the making; they are always immanent in history. The earliest of these tales were probably millenarian narratives where there are carefully structured concordances between beginnings and ends. Gothic narratives, however, do not have this "positive" millenarian structure. Whereas a millenarian end affirms history and our place in a larger design, Gothic apocalyptic narratives portray a world exhausted and otiose, anxious about itself and wary of any further participation in the processes of life. If millenarianism required, in whatever form, a signified, a point of reference, a god to make meaning of the world we inhabit, Gothic apocalypse, anticipating the postmodern nuclear sublime, is bereft of any signified; it has no way of conceiving history in teleological terms. It gestures toward a world and its symbolic forms that are exhausted: reality becomes a dream, realist representations a nightmare. One of the great precursors of these narratives of ends was Mary Shelley, who had, in the words of Irving Massey, "a strong talent (not unshared in her time) for the apocalyptic: for describing how people might feel in ultimate situations."[1] The issues raised by Mary Shelley's three key works (*Mathilda, The Last Man, Frankenstein*) refigure questions crucial to the sublime: how, in fact, do we think the unthinkable or represent the unpresentable? In *The Last Man* the apocalyptic sublime now returns us to the absolute formlessness (*das Unform*) in ways not considered by the great theorists of the sublime, with the exception of Schopenhauer, for whom the world was such an insufferable place that it were better if we ceased to exist altogether. In Mary Shelley's prototype of the end of the world she worked through that horrible Gothic metaphor that would image the end of the world itself.

In this chapter I wish to examine the way in which this horrible metaphor works itself out in a narrative that is still linked to realist concepts of structure. In other words, the ultimate limit situation is read through the only kind of history available to Mary Shelley: the history of a family saga. Romance again triumphs as a form, but it is stretched to its limits because the real subject of the novel, the plague, has no romance, it has no genealogy. Thus, Mary Shelley creates a parallel, counternarrative of death (which cannot be represented except as it affects genealogy and human relationships) that conflicts with the structure of the romance genre. Like many other Gothic narratives, the double narrative or theme fissures the text and defies precisely those realist constructions of the beautiful and the orderly implicit in the first narrative of romance. I shall therefore read Mary Shelley's *The Last Man* (1826), finally, as the imaging of the sublime as the end of time and history. Before doing that I should like to explore the kinds of archival work we prefigured in our reading of the Gothic fragments. Again, the archives are biographical and intertextual.

Mary Shelley's Personal Trauma

On June 16, 1822, Mary suffered a near-fatal miscarriage, which she survived only because of the immense care and comfort of Shelley. Mary had become pregnant five times in seven years, given birth four times, seen a baby die in her arms a few days after her birth, and suffered as two other children (Clara and William) died in their infancy. Only the fourth, Percy Florence, was to survive. Just a month after her miscarriage—an event that led to a "return" of her fears about childbirth, as well as to a new beginning in her relationship with Shelley—news reached Mary that Shelley had drowned. On the evening of July 19, 1822, she was informed by Trelawny that two bodies (the other of Edward Williams) had been washed ashore.[2] The narrative that she recounts in her journals is deeply informed by her emotional response to Shelley's death. Just as one's reading of *Frankenstein* cannot be divorced from Mary's real, lived experiences during 1816–1817, or *Mathilda*'s from her father's responses to her emotional crisis, so *The Last Man*, too, cannot be read without reference to its author's recent history. In Trelawny's account of the final obsequies of Shelley and Williams the emphasis is on the ritual of cremation and on the philosophical implications of death itself. As the partly decomposed body of Shelley is unearthed (the authorities had hurriedly buried the bodies for fear of disease), what Trelawny sees is really no more than a parody of the Romantic artist: a "mangled and disfigured" body, "dreadfully mutilated—both legs seperating [*sic*] on our attempting to move it—"[3] which had already been a prey to poachers. Byron was quick to observe the remorseless insignificance of man:

> What *is* a *human* body! Why it might be the rotten carcase of a sheep for all I can distinguish! . . . What an humbling and degrading thought that we shall one day ressemble this![4]

This is one narrative of the other side of Romantic self-transcendence that Mary transcribes in her journal, since she wasn't herself on the shores of Viareggio where Shelley's remains were cremated. It is said that Shelley's heart was snatched from the burning pile and given to Mary some days later. It is also said that Mary kept it in a book all her life. Whatever the truth of these anecdotes, the fact remains that the death of Shelley left Mary completely shattered—so much so that the diary entry for February 2, 1823 is preceded by the note "The year following 1822." That of January 18, 1824 thus becomes "Of the second year after 1822."[5] History is now read, in the journals, by an almost neurotic obsession with the moment of Shelley's death. In the years immediately following 1822, Mary's discourse shows strong hints of suicidal tendencies occasioned by extreme bouts of loneliness. "I have now no friend," she writes on October 2, 1822; "I weep to think how alone I am—" on October 21, 1822; and again her loss is shown as her "lost divinity" on November 10, 1822.[6]

The obsessive nostalgia of loss is not limited to her personal journal entries. In the somewhat more public domain of letter writing, the story is no different. In her letter to Maria Gisborne written from Pisa on August 15, 1822, she concludes her account of the death of Shelley with the words, "Well here is my story—the last story I shall have to tell."[7] In another letter to Maria Gisborne the following month her loneliness is again underlined: "I am here alone in Genoa; quite, quite alone!"[8] Though she continues to write (*Valperga*, begun in 1820, is published in February 1823), her life is one of total wretchedness and despair. In a letter to Thomas Hogg on February 28, 1823, she states her agitation much more explicitly:

> I study—I write—I think even to madness & torture of the past—I look forward to the grave with hope—[9]

Thinking to "madness and torture" gives way to a strong death wish. "Why am I here," she writes in her journal[10] as the metaphors of the grave and death begin to occupy large sections of her journal entries. Driven to occasional frenzy or madness, she hears Shelley's voice and imagines participating in lengthy conversations with him. It is thus not surprising that on her return to England on 25 August 1823, she finds it difficult to adjust and feels "imprisoned" by the metropolis. London is a "dreary town," a dead Gothic landscape, busy and familiar but lacking in passion, cold and remote.[11] The terrible consequence of this, for a writer, is enormous. It numbs and destroys the capacity to write. Writing, the "joy" through which life gained meaning and the self could find fulfilment, begins to slip by. On January 30, 1824, she admits the inadmissible: "I cannot write."[12] Not being able to write is death itself, since to write is to live, to participate in the ways in which the world might be given representation in language. To say "I cannot write" leads to death: "I never prayed so heartily for death as now," she concludes her entry for the day. By May 1824 Mary Shelley is conscious of "the failure of [her] intellectual powers." "Nothing I write pleases me," she confesses and adds, "Now my mind is a blank—a gulph filled with formless mist—."[13] In the journal the hesitant, apocalyptic leanings of her confession leads, finally, to a fuller, complete yearning for a narrative about ends:

> The last man! Yes I may well describe that solitary being's feelings, feeling myself as the last relic of a beloved race, my companions, extinct before me—[14]

She wrote this entry on May 14, 1824. The following day she received news of Byron's death. (Byron had in fact died at Missolonghi on 19 April.) "Byron," she wrote, "has become one of the people of the grave," and wondered at the bizarre premonition that must have given rise to "last night's miserable thoughts."[15] It is hard to tell the extent to which this momentary gift of clairvoyance worried her. What is clear is that her state of intense depression, compounded by news of Byron's death, magnified her longing for death, which comes across very strongly now. "God grant I may die young," she continues, and adds, "At the age of twenty six I am in the condition of an aged person—."[16]

The Last Man began in these highly tense circumstances. We know that by September 3, 1824 she was writing again, and reading, in particular, Dante, Plutarch, Virgil, and *Orlando Furioso.*

Seven months of writing the novel, however, lead to self-doubt, though in this instance the self-doubt probably reflects one of the central ambiguities of the narrative itself: who can possibly be the reader of a text that recounts the end of the world, to the very last syllable of recorded time, so to speak? And what sort of a person would want to look for the horrible metaphor of the end of time? On January 30, 1825 she showed her ambivalence toward this impossible idea when she wrote in her journal:

> What folly is it in me to write trash nobody will read—I do not mean this nonsense which is a mere tear. I am—But all my many pages—future waste paper—surely I am a fool—[17]

The novel was, however, completed that year and published on January 23, 1826 by Henry Colburn, who gave her £300 for it. She sent a copy to her friend Jane Williams with a poem in which the theme of *The Last Man* was rendered as "A tale of woe, with many sorrows rife."[18] On two subsequent days—on January 28 and February 7, to be precise—she wrote to John Howard Payne and referred to *The Last Man* as her "Sibylline Leaves," which had departed for Paris (where it was published by Galignani a few months later). In the February 7 component of this letter she spoke about the difficulties of her subject matter:

> The curiosity ex(c)ited by the title frightens me, because of the disappointment that must of course follow. You can form no idea of the difficulty of the subject—[. . .]—If I had at the commencement fore seen the excessive trouble & then . . . the state of imperfection in which partly for want of time I was obliged to leave it—I should never have had the courage to begin. Here and there you will find some things to like, but your critical taste will be hurt by it as an whole.[19]

Her final words seemed prophetic. Other people's critical tastes were hurt as well. Phrases such as "stupid cruelties," "an elaborate piece of gloomy folly," and "Mrs. Shelly's [*sic*] abortion," for instance, were typical responses from *Blackwood's Magazine* and the *London Magazine*. In a slightly more extended critical piece, the *Monthly Review*, in Elizabeth Nitchie's paraphrase, "considered it the product of a diseased imagination."[20] It seems to have spawned a few literary jokes ("The Last Woman, by Mrs. Shelley," "The Last Pigtail—Mrs. Shelley" were announced as forthcoming publications[21]) but did not generate anywhere near the passionate, almost divisive and extreme, literary responses that had come Mary's way on the publication of *Frankenstein* in 1818.

The Literary Intertexts

In some ways the foregoing biographical account is a kind of an intertext constructed from various bits and pieces of evidence we can locate in the journals and diaries. The formalist emphasis on intertextuality as a series of prior texts, a sort of a syllepsis interwoven with possibilities already played out and those yet to come, denies the body itself as a site on which texts have been written. An intertext, therefore, needs to be complemented by a personal biography of authors. If the author is a woman, then this personal biography cannot be detached from the "personal-gynocritical" where the body itself is a signifying system. It is only when we have established a consciousness about this aspect of the intertext that we can move to an examination of Mary Shelley's formal intertexts: earlier texts in which the sublime as the end of time (prefiguring the nuclear sublime) had been played out. Indeed, the opening pages of *The Last Man* immediately draw our attention precisely to the significance of the literary intertext.

In an attempt to explain how a text written in 2099 is being read in 1826, Mary Shelley uses a variation on the "manuscript hoax" of the Gothic novels as she "discovers" (with the help of her companion) the textual Sibylline leaves in the timeless Cumaean caves: "piles of leaves, fragments of bark, and a white flimsy substance, resembling the inner part of the green hood which shelters the grain of the unripe Indian corn." Mary Shelley's entry point here is Book 6 of Virgil's *Aeneid*. Reaching the coasts of Cumae (close to modern-day Naples), Aeneas, unlike his compatriots and crew, who go off looking for flint and water, quickly scrambles toward "Apollo's hill/and castle,"

> . . . and near it the awesome cave where hid
> the Sibyl, the terrifier, whose heart and mind
> the Delian seer filled with prophetic speech.[22]

Inspired by the Delian god of prophecy, the Sibyl has the power to disclose things to come. The "monstrous cave" she inhabits is

> . . . perforated a hundred times,
> Having a hundred mouths, with rushing voices
> Carrying the responses of the Sibyl.[23]

The description of the cave and the prophetic role of the Sibyl are repeated in the Gothic tales of ends discussed in this chapter. Indeed, this book of the *Aeneid* is the crucial intertext of the many narratives found in this class of the Gothic. The Sybil's discourse is one of truth wrapped in darkness as she warns Aeneas of the self-destructive nature of the world he proposes to colonize. The image that she gives of this world is certainly apocalyptic. In it "the sons of Troy" will "find no joy" as she sees only "war, terror, war, . . . and Tiber foaming red with blood." The space that the Sibyl occupies—the caves of Cumae—and the Sibylline leaves become for Mary Shelley a kind of a writing machine as the traces of the Cumaean, the space of the *imaginary,* invade her own soon-to-be-deciphered work. Beneath her reconstructed text will also be traces of some of the great myths of the Western world. One of these, as J. G. Frazer showed so many years ago, takes the form of the Sibyl's directive that Aeneas pluck the golden bough and make an offering of it to Proserpina so as to facilitate his entry into the underworld. In using the primitive myth of the Sibyl, Mary Shelley in fact makes an important political statement about the origins of writing in the pre-Oedipal chora of the Sibyl's unconscious. At the same time she invests the frightening figure of the prophetic Sibyl, whom the gods also fear, with the power to tell the ultimate unspeakable narrative, the narrative of ends.

In fact truth and fiction come together in a rather uncanny fashion in the Sibylline caves. Mary Shelley's diaries show that she and the poet spent a good part of December 1818 touring Naples. The impressions of the somewhat tense and agitated tourists—Mary's *Frankenstein* had appeared earlier that year, Shelley had begun composing *Prometheus Unbound,* and the one-year-old Clara had died on September 4—make their way into Mary's introduction, in which a sightseer's cave is transformed into "the Sibyl's Cave; not indeed exactly as Virgil describes it,"[24] but all the evidence nevertheless points to that fact. Along with her "friend," the author sees herself as a decipherer, a decoder of strange marks on pieces of paper, establishing both links between scattered fragments and, more important, constructing a "consistent form." Whereas the "translator" takes us directly to fully formed languages (*Otranto,* the precursor text, fondly spoke of the translator), the decipherer foregrounds language as a kind of hieroglyphic marks on paper, parchment, or papyrus. These distorted and heavily transformed redactions of the original leaves of the Cumaean Sibyl therefore function something like a palimpsest. Writing as palimpsest—primary texts over which another has been superimposed, but with the original still visible in its margins—is how the decipherer defines the act of composition. And the Gothic genre, as we have seen, is primarily palimpsestic in its generic orientation. This is one aspect of the encounter with the Sybilline fragments. The other is the site of these leaves, the Cumaean cave itself. Sandra Gilbert and Susan Gubar quite rightly interpret the cave as the womb, the "female place," the unconscious, the place of dreams, of sounds. It is also the woman's place where the initiate comes or the tomb in which he or she is sacrificed. Victor Frankenstein's "filthy creation" occurs in such darkness; but the human child, too, grows in total darkness. Gilbert and Gubar extend this analogy:

> Yet the womb-shaped cave is also the place of female power, the *umbilicus mundi*, one of the great antechambers of the mysteries of transformation.[25]

But the cave cannot be closed off with this female analogy. As a site of immense ambiguity through its connections with the "underworld"—recall Demeter, Persephone, Sītā, and so on—the cave elicits highly conflicting responses that, for Gilbert and Gubar, lead to an equivocation toward patriarchy itself. Sītā of the furrow in the earth, remains under the control of Rāma. Consequently, Mary Shelley asks the poet Shelley to help her decipher the Sybilline leaves of the Cumaean caves. The woman *"is"* the cave, but it is the man who must interpret/"interpenetrate" it; he must endow it with meaning. This ambiguity-torn gesture is central to Mary Shelley's own feminism. To get a space for herself, what Mary does is to write the prophecy of another woman—the Sibyl—out in full. The fragments may be deciphered by Shelley, but it is Mary who must write them out; she alone must be the source of this new form of knowledge. What she does, however, is reconstitute the horrifying echoes of the Cumaean caves (one recalls E. M. Forster's Marabar caves here) into an essentially realist discourse with beginnings and ends. What the Sibyl offered was a rare feminist text, fragmented, partial, "palimpsestic." For the Sybil, to remember was to "dismember." But Mary Shelley transforms the cave itself into the place of creation, where mutation leads to regeneration and wholeness. What she gives birth to is a text, stitched, transcribed, and transposed. Through an immense act of labor the fragments are reconstituted into a monster that is not the fully bodied, though monstrously "de-formed," creation of Frankenstein but a complete narrative of the world's "de-formation." In the process she writes mankind out of history; apocalypse becomes a narrative without a reader.

One of the disturbing books of the revolutionary period was the French count Constantin François de Chasseboeuf Volney's *Les ruines, ou Méditation sur les révolutions des empires,* which was published in 1791. Translated almost immediately into English in 1792,[26] it became an influential work with the English Jacobins (most of whom were already familiar with the French original) and later with the Shelleys. It is one of the four books specifically mentioned by the Monster in *Frankenstein* and the one used by Felix to teach Safie French. Volney's *Ruins* begins with an invocation to ruins and tombs as a reminder to men that all things come to an end. It was an odd thesis to come from the pen of an anticleric and atheist. As Brian Rigby points out, it was indeed a paradox to find "millennial features in the work of a militantly atheistic and rationalist writer like Volney."[27]

The narrative trick used by Volney is to invoke singularly affective objects of meditation with a view to arresting the human tendency toward material possessions. The objects come his way through recollections of travels through the Ottoman Empire. The signs of ruins, destitution, and pillage mirror what Europe, too, will become some day as it struggles with God's "incomprehensible judgments" (6). Through the use of an apparition (a story-telling device not uncommon in narratives about ends) Volney shows the contradictions that underlie human desire for organizational structures, law, and institutions. Since the impetus for them are always self-love, they lead, in due course, to dissension and hate within and imperialism abroad:

> And these people, who call themselves polished, are they not those who three centuries ago filled the earth with their injustice? Are they not those who, under the pretext of commerce, laid India waste, dispeopled a new continent, and who at present subject Africa to the most inhumane slavery? (50)

A schematic account of the origins and genealogy of religious ideas follows that leads to the Lockean conclusion that *"man receives no ideas but through the medium of his senses*" (94). Since religious narratives are no more than mere "allegories and mysterious symbols" (89), only those things which can be objectively studied with reference to our senses are legitimate subjects of discussion. That which we do not know only binds us to "fetters and prejudices" (147). On the basis of this, Volney then gives his legislators a set of definitions of "law" and "nature," "good" and "evil," which take up another thirty-two pages in the English translation.

Volney's *Ruins*, then, is a kind of a prophetic book grounded in the experience of revolution in France. The title and the early travel narrative emphasize the movement toward apocalypse as a human compulsion toward its own death. Its arrest (that the end might not come) is possible only through a purely rational program based on a contract among all people that alone would lead to their common preservation. Not surprisingly, the "legislative" component of *Ruins* ("The Law of Nature") ends with an exhortation to "preserve," "instruct," and "moderate" humankind.[28]

Whatever doubts he might have had about humanity, Volney's final vision is thus distinctively utopian, in the immediate tradition of writers such as Louis-Sebastian Mercier (1740–1814), whose popular work *L'An 2440* fueled the drive toward utopian narratives.[29] Yet as A. J. Sambrook points out, it was Mercier himself who took a leading role in the dramatic reversal from utopia to apocalypse. Human progress toward perfectibility—the underlying theme of Volney—now gave way to a Newtonian universe bound to the laws of necessity, within which are implicit catastrophic tendencies. In an article entitled "Globe" Mercier wrote about a universe whose system itself had gone wrong with the fading sun:

> Le soleil, sorti de son orbite, pâle et sans rayons, s'enforceroit dans la profondeur des cieux; et la terre le suivant d'un cours incertain, verroit la nuit et le froid envelopper bientôt ses deux hémisphères.[30]

The fictional work that epitomized these apocalyptic tendencies was Jean-Baptiste François Cousin de Grainville's *Le dernier homme* (1805), which was translated anonymously into English in 1806 as *The Last Man or Omegarus and Syderia, a Romance of Futurity*,[31] with much editing and changing. The original French text, according to Jean de Palacio, went largely unnoticed. However, Palacio does refer to one Chevalier Croft who compared *Le dernier homme* with Milton for its "que la sublime ébauche" and "grande conception."[32] The "dystopic" view of the world presented by Grainville marks, as we've said before, a significant shift in tales about ends. There is no direct evidence that Mary Shelley had read this work, though Lord Byron's popular poem "Darkness" was suggested by Grainville's work. This fact in itself makes Mary Shelley's familiarity with the text, at least at second hand, extremely likely. There is another, centrally textual, parallel, however, that suggests a deeper affinity between Mary Shelley's and Grainville's "last man" novels. Like Mary Shelley's work, Grainville's *The Last Man,* too, opens with a brief account of a "solitary cavern." This cavern, like the caves of Cumae, has a dreadful mystery about it, since in the dead of night frightful groans and shrieks are heard from it. Like a volcano—recall the period's interest in volcanoes, especially Vesuvius, about which many sublime histories had been written—it sometimes spewed forth "flame and smoke" (2), shaking the earth and the ruins. Having set the scene, the author introduces the narrator, who describes the cavern in the following fashion:

> Its aspect had nothing terrific: the entrance, shaded over by the thick foliage of the wild vine, invited the traveller to rest himself beneath its cooling shelter. No monster guarded the passage; the terror which it inspired had rendered it inaccessible. (2)

In spite of furious protestations from the Syrians, who are, quite naturally, very alarmed, the narrator walks into the cavern. There he finds a "robust old man . . . chained down" (5), his shoulders "mutilated," with "fragments of a broken clock and two bloody wings" lying nearby. His attention is distracted by the voice of the "celestial Spirit," who knows the future since he had chained "Time" (5). This spirit tells the narrator that in the "magic mirrors" all around him the last men will be seen. The last "men" turn out to be a young man, Omegarus, and a beautiful woman, Syderia. From here onward this futuristic narrative draws on a mixture of Old Testament stories and the horrifying, unimaginable concept of the female of the species going barren. This is a typical "Gothic" strategy—the strategy of narrative mediatizations—that enables, through a Chinese-box effect, the distancing, in the final analysis, of the author (who has claimed in the translated version at any rate, the privilege of anonymity) from the events of his text. The narrative within narrative trick also leads to the doubling and redoubling of subjects, to the intentional confusion of characters, so that individual identity may be denied. Omegarus is, of course, Adam as well, just as Syderia is Eve. Much of the narrative now takes a primitive sci-fi turn as references are made to an "aerial vessel" filled with "volatile spirits" like ether (66) and the sun exhibiting "signs of decay" (120). Throughout the narrative and its presentational process one is struck by the extraordinarily "primitive" nature of the "viewing" consciousness or point of view. This linear presentational process—unitary and monologic—is precisely what the great eighteenth-century novelists had revolutionized. Yet here, in this version of the Gothic, the regression is celebrated, a celebration that, furthermore, takes us back to the period's somewhat fluid distinctions between the Novel and Romance. The Romance—that genre which had a single point of view—is raised to great heights by the Gothic. And for diversion, for variety, we are not given a different perspective, point of view, or consciousness; instead, we are given fragmentary narratives, palimpsests, manuscript pieces, recollections, and tales that do not shift a dominating point of view, but remain steadfastly monologic and fixed. Though the novel is futuristic in design and scope, the rituals (and worldview) remain essentially primitive and pre-Christian, as if the future age of science (to the late eighteenth-century mind) was seen as a repetition of a previous mythic world. This world is presented in the novel through a mixture of altars, statues, icons, and virgins, as well as through the pastoral. The marriage ceremony of Omegarus and Syderia, for instance, is celebrated by Ormus scattering seeds "into the open furrows" (203) even though the images of "the earth yawning into chasms, the confusion of the elements, and the conflagration of the skies" are equally present. Omegarus sees visions of his own progeny mangled, bleeding, "seated around blood-stained tables" (2:89). "The heavens answered the mighty behest by signs of joy, while hell shuddered and groaned; its inhabitants rushed into the flames of sulphur to conceal themselves!" (2:95). The forces of light and darkness, heaven and hell, now compete; darkness takes over the universe; silence reigns. These are the signs of the commencement of the "last day of the earth" (2:116). Even Death realizes that with the end of humankind, he, too, will die: the narrative of ends repeats the end of death itself; without life there is no death. There is also an opposing, though ill-defined, principle of Genius, who is the other force in this world. At crucial times he is seen supporting Death as he becomes even more sinister and invokes spirits, specters of yore, in a ghoulish ritual of blood and gore. In a final, dramatic encounter, Death strikes Genius, who escapes to the center of the earth and blows up the world, entombing/"encrypting" himself. "The King of Terrors!" Death (2:203) extracts his vengeance, but before doing so points out that Genius and he (Death) had the delicate task of keeping the earth going. In the end this "history of the last age of the earth" (2:204) emerges as a confused narrative, unsure of its own design. But even in its primitive form the very concept of imaging the end of one's own history and being can only terrorize the mind. In this respect the form itself begins to symbolize the impossibility of the mind coming to terms with the apocalyptic sublime. In many ways, Grainville, therefore, does precisely what Mary Shelley will attempt with a much surer sense of the limitations of the genre. The text in this case again exhausts itself and relapses into its own decentered, anecdotal form. In an uncanny mirror image, writing itself marks the subject's own dissolution in the sublime.

When first published, it provoked the *Critical Review* into a quite uncharacteristic outburst of satirical criticism:

> A most potent narcotic, which we strongly recommended to all apothecaries and druggists, as a substitute for opium, producing all the good, without any of the bad qualities of that soporific medicine.[33]

I have no doubt in my mind that *The Last Man* had an opiumlike effect on its readers. It lacks a center, is far too fantastic and anecdotal, and has little narrative sense. And yet it is such a fantastic, almost parodistic, reading of Romantic fictions of utopia and so self-reflexive in its emphasis on the *doppelgänger* that it emerges out of its obscurity as one of the more successful apocalyptic narratives. In its consciousness of concepts of transference and the double—all the characters seem to duplicate each other—this essentially anonymous *The Last Man* is quite an exceptional text. We find in it such compulsive patterns, such a strong presence of the "self and abyss" that it certainly prefigures the apocalyptic (nuclear) version of the postmodern sublime. As an apocalyptic text or narrative about ends, it unites a narrative millenarianism with the return of the repressed, which, as the sublime, threatens to consume our erstwhile and secure constructions of meaning. Tales about ends—apocalyptic tales in fact—put into considerable disarray theories about narrative endings. They endlessly write out their basic themes and construct an inflationary effect that is a "nauseous" discourse (recall, once again, Benedict's "Is my language nauseous?").

This discourse comes to an end not because it acknowledges the power of formal endings but because, as nausea, it signifies its own death.

Ten years after the anonymous translation of Cousin de Grainville's French novel, Byron composed a poem entitled "Darkness" at Diodati in July 1816.[34] This poem is arguably the most concentrated vision of the end found in the literature of the period, and certainly one that most radically embraces the sublime as the end of humanity.[35] The subject matter is broached with an honesty and directness that allows it to transcend the limitations of other tales of ends, including Mary Shelley's own work. And yet "Darkness," too, uses the customary Gothic device of framing to offer a world of end-orientated plenitude, which is nevertheless comfortably distanced from the author. This distancing in Byron is, however, only partial—the poem opens with "I had a dream, which was not all a dream." "Dream" and "not all a dream," represents the world of the *imaginary* (the dream), but it is also a qualified acceptance of the version of the world represented in that dream. Byron's qualification, not unlike the "mediatory" discourses of those Gothic texts whose proper narrative is really that embedded in a manuscript (where the author's preface, in a postmodernist fashion, becomes part of the text itself), is therefore an endorsement of the vision of the end as it appeared in a dream. Indeed, it seems that Byron actually believed in this version of the end.

The end of the universe on the death of a star (the sun) was not an uncommon idea. The scientific literature had already mooted the concept of a cold, dead sun after its internal fires had been extinguished. In James Thomson's *The Seasons* (1730) we read terrible images of starving wolves, plague-ridden, empty streets and other related horrors. In the Byronic vision, the end gets crystallized in an unremitting narrative, stark and bland in its uncompromising image of a cold and desolate planet. "Darkness" takes us to one of the central tropes of Mary Shelley's writings as well, and shows the impact her relatively short-lived association with Byron had on her own creative imagination. The frightening image of Byron's poem—the earth itself going cold—reverberates throughout her own writing. "The icy earth/Swung blind and blackening in the moonless air" is a strong image, much stronger than anything in the narratives of ends discussed here. The dull, icy earth, no longer controlled magnetically by the ragingly sublime powers of the sun, is seen adrift on an ocean of silence. In Byron's poem the triumphant image, if any, is that of a dog that, in a world without love, refuses to "assail" its dead master and defends this dead carrion until it, too, dies. The end in Byron through a plague is predicated on the absence of love, which again has strong echoes in Mary Shelley's own work. The scene of two survivors glancing cannibalistically at each other through the light of a fire they had lit is one of unmitigated horror, since the "end" transforms them into "fiends":

> Each other's aspects—saw, and shriek'd,
> and died—

Chaos is finally triumphant as the poem endorses that "unformed" world to which "with a shriek" Thel fled "unhindered till she came to the vales of Har."

> . . . Darkness had no need
> Of aid from them—She was the Universe.

Mary Shelley's Apocalyptic Sublime

The publication of Mary Shelley's *The Last Man* was foreshadowed in the *Literary Magnet* for January 1826 in the context of the critic's general attitude toward the theme of narratives of ends:

> Mrs. Shelley, the authoress of that monstrous literary abortion, Frankenstein or the modern Prometheus, is, we understand, about to produce another Raw-head-and-bloody-bones, called 'The Last Man.' There is, we believe a novel already published, entitled Omegarius [*sic*], or the Last Man, a bantling of the Leadenhall press; a fact which might have spared Mr. Campbell the trouble of writing his long letter to the editor [of the *Edinburgh Review*] on the subject of the originality of the conception of *his* Last Man.[36]

It is not uncommon to find metaphors of monstrosity or deformed bodies in the Mary Shelley secondary bibliography, especially in the nineteenth century. Without wishing to make value judgments about Mary Shelley's contribution to a theme so forthrightly denounced by the *Literary Magnet*, another reading of the two texts mentioned in the above quotation comes from Richard Garnett, who in 1891 collected the tales and stories of Mary Shelley. In the Introduction he wrote about the "wild grandeur and conception" of

Frankenstein, and lamented that the subsequent romances did not approach *Frankenstein* in power, probably because the guiding hand of Shelley was no longer there. But *The Last Man*, he wrote, "is a work of far higher merit than commonly admitted." Garnett concluded his comments with the hope that "When *The Last Man* is reprinted it will come before the world as a new work."[37] It took another seventy-four years before a new edition was published.

Predictably enough, modern readers have read *The Last Man* as a *roman à clef*, a text that is a fictional rendition of Mary's relationship with Shelley, Byron, Claire Clairmont, her parents, and her friends. One of the early modern critics of *The Last Man* along these lines was Walter Edwin Peck.[38] His reading of *The Last Man* confirmed the obvious: Shelley is presented to us disguised as Adrian, Earl of Windsor, Mary Shelley as Lionel Verney, Claire Clairmont as Perdita, Byron as Lord Raymond, Harriet Shelley as Evadne, William Godwin as the Countess of Windsor, Mary Shelley's daughter Clara as the second child of Lionel Verney and Idris, her surviving son Percy Florence as Alfred, and so on. This "detective" reading was refined by Ernest J. Lovell, Jr., who read *The Last Man* through Mary Shelley's obsession with the Byronic hero. In Mary Shelley's works the Byronic hero (as Lord Raymond in *The Last Man* or as Castruccio in *Valperga*) is consumed by a passion for self-punishment and release through death. The contrast between the Byronic figure and the Shelleyan figure is dramatic. The former represents "a thoroughly masculine Byron, the father, foster father, lover, or husband of Mary," the latter "a frail, effeminate, boyish, or ineffectual Shelley, twice pictured as a woman."[39] In *Valperga* the contrast is decisive: Byron-Castruccio, who is bold, ambitious, proud, against Shelley-Euthanasia, who is idealistic but weak, and whose castle, Valperga, is taken over by her erstwhile lover Castruccio. The pattern is repeated more or less unchanged in *The Last Man* with Byron-Raymond, Lord Protector of England and general in the Greek wars, contrasted with Shelley-Idris and Shelley-Adrian, the latter drowning with Clara in an obvious replay of Shelley and Williams' real deaths in 1822.

Two critics whose work we have already cited—A. J. Sambrook and Jean de Palacio—offer archaeologies of the "Last Man" theme with a much more comparative European emphasis. The work done by Sambrook and Palacio is expanded in Hartley S. Spatt's (1975) essay.[40] In this essay Spatt brings together *Frankenstein* and *The Last Man* and reads them both as tales about last men rendered through the discourse of dreams. What for someone like Ann Radcliffe was a predominantly naturalistic reading of the landscape, became for Mary Shelley a different problem in representation that required her to think through her narratives in the context of dreams. The "transformation of [this] Gothicism"[41] into the language of dreams is central to Mary Shelley's poetics. To achieve this, one of the techniques she uses is that of the editor: in both *Frankenstein* and *The Last Man* the author is really an editor of texts. It is only through the Gothic dream that the sole survivor of the end of the world can present the unpresentable, the world's end, the narrative of apocalypse in the making. Mary Shelley's sublime will therefore use the language of desire and lack as she works out her narrative of ends with reference to the epistemologies historically available to her.

In 1793 France issued its Republican calendar, in which the first year began on 22 September 1793, the day of the autumnal equinox and the abolition of the monarchy. What is interesting, however, is that the start of the calendar in fall (autumn), although echoing all too obviously the fall of the monarchy, is nevertheless important for the way in which it draws on nature itself as a source of regeneration. As Lee Sterrenburg puts it: "The regeneration of nature and society are one."[42] And this analogy with nature is maintained in the names of months given by the Republicans, from *Vendémiaire* (Vintage) to *Fructidor* (Fruit).[43] The reciprocity underlined here between revolutionary change and nature soon led to a bifurcation or alienation between the two. By the mid-1790s Wordsworth, for instance, retreated back to nature, having divorced it from Jacobin principles. The "bliss" of being alive in that dawn of revolution soon gave way to a return to memories less political, but more intense in their relationships to nature. Another reaction to the excesses of the Reign of Terror was a different kind of a retreat, a refuge that led not to composure and union with nature, but to apocalyptic annihilation or destruction.[44] The "universal regulation which Nature herself demanded,"[45] which Napoleon saw as part of his own design, is now seen as a distraught nature eagerly destroying its own "genius," its own intellectual sources.

Mary Shelley's *The Last Man* is the fullest expression of the tradition of apocalyptic writings that more or less began with the end of *Thermidor* (July, 1794) and incorporated works from Grainville's *Le dernier homme* (1805/1806) to John Martin's paintings, such as *The Fall of Babylon* (1819). In Lee Sterrenburg's argument Mary Shelley

> takes up a set of nature metaphors—diseases and plagues—which previous writers had used as hopeful symbols of the revolutionary process. She reinterprets those symbols in a pessimistic and apocalyptic way and, in so doing, rejects the meliorative political views of her parents' generation.[46]

To conceive of a revolution as disease and monstrosity was not unknown to Mary Shelley. Her mother, Mary Wollstonecraft [Godwin], had used these metaphors, as did Edmund Burke, even though the metaphors of the sheer size of the sublime were directed toward very different ends by them.[47] They do agree on one thing: there is the healthy, evolutionary British way of the Glorious Revolution of 1688, or there is the convulsive and violent revolution of the French. At the heart of Burke's defense of the British constitution was the claim that society itself is a permanent body that is self-renewing even when individuals disappear. In *The Last Man* the basis of this claim—that society is organic and orderly—is destroyed by a nature that no longer is a regenerative adjunct of the human mind.[48]

Beyond Edmund Burke there is, of course, the figure of William Godwin, with whom Mary Shelley's relationship had always been deeply ambiguous. As we saw in our reading of *Caleb Williams,* Godwin had moved toward an unresolved mix of the Romantic and the Gothic soon after the publication of *Political Justice* (1793). But he continued to believe in individual reason and in a future conforming to the ideals of a rational anarchist. There were clearly problems with this argument, as the fictional life of Caleb certainly pointed out . Thomas Malthus, for instance, refused to accept the presumed primacy of a totally free subject, the anarchist rationalist, in a chaotic world locked into a primal urge to overpopulate. It seems that here Mary Shelley, too, unconsciously responded to her father's utopianism by going a step further than Malthus by envisaging a world where the human race itself would be no more. Yet Godwin's *Political Justice* is itself beset with major ambiguities and contradictions. In the 1796 edition we read:

> Will it [the human species] continue for ever? The globe we inhabit bears strong marks of convulsion [which] . . . will one day destroy the inhabitants of the earth.[49]

Godwin does not follow up the consequences of this "convulsion theory," since to do so would have placed into doubt the general speculative thrust of *Political Justice* toward human perfection.

Mary Shelley, however, did not have the same compunction, since the concept of catastrophe occupies central space in all her major narratives: *Mathilda, The Last Man,* and *Frankenstein.* What triumphs in *The Last Man* are not Godwinian ideals (even though Adrian, the poet Shelley's alter ego, is convinced for a while that perfection can be achieved) but the inexorable and insensitive actions of nature itself. This nature, as both the laws that govern the universe and also as forms of social cohesion, is anything but a regenerative force. Nor does it have a controlling "Genius," in Grainville's sense of the word.

If anything, the plague, the grim reaper, in *The Last Man* brings to an end history itself. It destroys the very centrality of humanity and the concept of society as a dynamic system, which had been endorsed by revolutionaries and conservatives alike. In Mary Shelley's version of history, the prime mover or the first principle is not God or the spirit of history, but a plague, which becomes the "true," real subject of the discourse. There is no hope, no survival here; there is no attempt made to conceptualize it philosophically, either; there is only an unceasingly virulent insistence on its effects that progressively displace everything else toward the end of the text.

The line of descent is from Godwin's *St. Leon* (1799) through *Frankenstein* to *The Last Man,* with the connections between the last two much more direct and explicit than hitherto made out by critics. Frankenstein's dream on creating the Monster is repeated, with appropriate variation, in Verney's dream on his way to Constantinople, an empty, plague-ridden city recently captured by Lord Raymond:

> Methought I had been invited to Timon's last feast; I came with keen appetite, the covers were removed, the hot water sent up its unsatisfying streams, while I fled before the anger of the host, who assumed the form of Raymond; while to my diseased fancy, the vessels hurled by him after me, were surcharged with fetid vapour, and my friend's shape, altered by a thousand distortions, expanded into a gigantic phantom, bearing on its brow the sign of pestilence. The growing shadow rose and rose, filling, and then seeming to endeavour to burst beyond, the adamantine vault that bent over, sustaining and enclosing the world. The night-mare became torture. . . . (146)

The transformation of hope—the creation of life, the discovery of a friend—into an embassy of death is a characteristic feature of Mary

Shelley's dream sequence. Like the Monster in *Frankenstein,* here it is Raymond who, as a pestilence, is unleashed on an unsuspecting world. By 1821 the terrible cholera epidemic that began in Calcutta in 1817 had crossed the Arabian Sea and decimated the population of Basra (it was to reach Southern and Eastern Europe by the mid-1820s). In her "Quarry for *Middlemarch,*" George Eliot tells us that by the end of March 1832 there had been 1530 cholera cases in London with 802 deaths.[50] In a reverse mirror image of the eastward pursuit of the unsuspecting victim in Byron/Polidori's *The Vampyre,* the plague, as a phantom, pursues humanity westward. The plague is conceived as a demonic figure, a character in its own right. The plague as a monster parallels Frankenstein's creation, but unlike the latter, one cannot dialogize with the plague, one can only apostrophize, in the vocative, relapsing into the rhetoric of ends: "pestilence is the enemy we fly" (139).

In *The Last Man* Mary Shelley thus uses a "new confessional format"[51] different from the more objective narrative of the earlier Gothic tales. This confessional mode has no audience, not even the private audience of letters written in *Frankenstein,* let alone the public audience of the political Jacobin novels such as those of Thomas Holcroft, Robert Bage, and William Godwin. The inexorable advance of the plague confounds and fractures the status of narrative fiction, since the central category of the novel, character, cannot have any functional unity if the concept of humanity itself is nonexistent. As Robert Snyder explains:

> unnamable and preternatural, [it] pursues the refugees of an exhausted world and nullifies all hope of human relationship.[52]

How do we represent the plague? Defoe had opted for one approach when in *The Journal of the Plague Year* (1722), the plague was presented as a "naturalistic calamity." In John Wilson's *The City of the Plague* (1816), as in Thomas Campbell's poem "The Last Man," the plague is simply a background for principally religious meditations on the plight of humanity. In Shelley's *The Revolt of Islam* a quasi-allegorical treatment of the plague is given, in that the plague corresponds to the barbarism of Europe. Robert Lance Snyder calls the plague a "grotesque enigma,"[53] "an irreducible phenomenon that both challenges and defines the limits of rational understanding."[54] Since nothing is fully explained, there is an element of indeterminacy at work here. There is no pattern, no design, simply the inexorable logic of the irrational plague itself. With Shelley's death—and probably because of it—Mary is now bereft of either the rational orderliness of her father or the Shelleyan belief in human perfectibility. In Snyder's words, what Mary Shelley offers is "the fearful marginality of man in a disjointed and alien universe."[55] And this frightening reality can be grasped by humans only through an attempt to present that which is unpresentable, in other words, the sublime. Snyder's phrase "speculative fabulation" (which he gives in quotation marks) is an interesting way in which to explain this phenomenon.

The despair and equivocation on Mary Shelley's part is most evident in the third volume of *The Last Man* where Verney debates issues central to Christian thinking: "Did God create man, merely in the end to become dead earth in the midst of healthful vegetating nature?" (290). What is endorsed is neither a new version of religion nor a new history: both are trampled over under the pressures of a contradictory, circular discourse. Snyder makes the pertinent point:

> The primary terror posed by the plague is that it constitutes a phenomenon which defies all referential sense.[56]

We are given some account of its origins on the shores of the Nile (127) and its dramatic westward movement, but we are not given any real account of what the nature of the plague is. It is as if the spread of the AIDS virus were scrupulously documented without anyone being told that it is a radical instance of a deficiency in our immune system. Like the geological debate between the Neptunists, who advanced a diluvian theory of geological change, and the Vulcanists or Plutonists, who believed in a more cataclysmic change, Mary Shelley's plague is shot through with the concept of change as catastrophe, whether diluvian or cataclysmic. Consequently, few dates are given. Constantinople falls in 2091; by 2094 England is threatened. Apart from the political intrigue that surrounds the proclamation of the Republic and which affects the romantic entanglements of the major protagonists, crisis points are few and far between. There are the predictable prophets and doomsday futurists, but real encounters with those infected with the plague are generally avoided in favor of schematic and pseudo-statistical generalizations. When such an encounter does occur, as we shall see in Verney's attempt to save a dying negro, it is passed over far too hurriedly, since the point Mary Shelley wishes to make is that Verney's compassion leads to his own infection, from which, within three days and three nights, he recovers and gains immunity. The clear reference here to Christ's passion and resurrection notwithstanding, the episode is a characteristic Mary Shelley gambit. Upon hearing of Henry Clerval's death, Frankenstein, who feels responsible for his death, is struck by a terrible fever, which is a repeat of his nervous fever in the days following the creation of the Monster.

In spite of the extensive survey of the march of the plague, the essential "meaning of the enigma" (311) remains elusive. And nature, too, such as it is, is no longer a party to humanity's will. Nature is now the Gothic sublime, a force of dissolution, no longer available to the young Romantic imagination. Nature as "grand," "bare," and "rude" implies a shifting of the sign from the beautiful, orderly harmonies of phenomena to the unimaginable abyss of the sublime. The mind now repeats, "I and the Abyss," as the Romantic sublime is contaminated, immeasurably altered, by the unnameable plague:

> The scenes which now surround us, vast and sublime as they are, are not such as can best contribute to this work. Nature is here like our fortunes, grand, but too destructive, bare, and rude, to be able to afford delight to her young imagination. (311)

The "enigma," the plague, yields no real, concrete meaning or reference. It is unpresentable, a confirmation of the principle of death itself. Mary Shelley's language captures the dark side of Romanticism, the side that one finds in Coleridge's *Rime* when man is finally left alone, conscious of "some lapsed unity, the sense of a schism between the inner life of man and the structure of external reality."[57]

There are, of course, the two "The Last Man" paintings of John Martin (1789–1854), in which one detects precisely this wonder at the vision of ends and humanity's total absorption in the sublime. Clearly, in this austere account of the end of time/history, invoking the law of reason itself is something of an irrelevance, since the end also implies the collapse of the demarcations of the mind so carefully made by Kant. In fact, in the narrative of ends there can be only one version of the sublime, and that version is an extension of the Gothic vision of a vertiginous plunge into depthlessness, into the Real as the lack of substance itself. So in one of John Martin's paintings, which is modelled on Thomas Campbell's poem and which was exhibited by the Water Colour Society in 1833, a Christ-like figure stands alone on a promontory, arms outstretched, cowled and despondent. Beside him, as well as on the other promontories, festering, dead bodies abound. Below, lonely ships are seen on the sea, and further afield, on the horizon, lifeless cities are faintly aglow with the rays of the sick and dying sun itself. This is John Martin's image of the weakening of the cosmos, the kind of image generally associated with ends. Martin's fascination with human insignificance in the face of the absolutely great, the colossal, is imaged in Mary Shelley's own fascination with the melancholic sublime. Both the journals and letters show ample evidence of a person who had a longing for the darker side of life. In her personal life—in fact from her birth onwards—death, in a manner not too different from the plague itself, seems to have constantly stalked her. In a metonymic displacement or transference of her consequent pain, anger, and helplessness as a woman, is it surprising, as Mary Poovey argues, that "all the destructive forces in this novel—the 'PLAGUE,' Necessity, and nature—are feminine?"[58]

In a world bereft of meaning—both as a consequence of personal trauma and as an epistemological necessity arising out of the loss of the aesthetic ideals of Shelley—in a world where the symbolic logic of the epic and its semantics of permanence are replaced by the anxieties of the brooding self, and the subjectivities of the Gothic, *The Last Man* becomes a metaphor of a world no longer presented to us in all its full, referential completeness. What readings of *The Last Man* as a *roman à clef* do not show are the massive indeterminacies, lacunae, and ambiguities in the text. The real center of the text is not the genealogical romance (which is nevertheless an invariable in our Gothics), but the plague, which, as the Real, is an object that cannot be signified. It simply displaces its own emptiness, since it cannot be symbolized. Like a postmodern simulacrum, it is its own pure lack.

Yet the antihero of this work, the plague, is framed, at least outwardly, in a straightforward genealogy characteristic of Romance and Gothic texts. The central genealogy may be presented as follows:

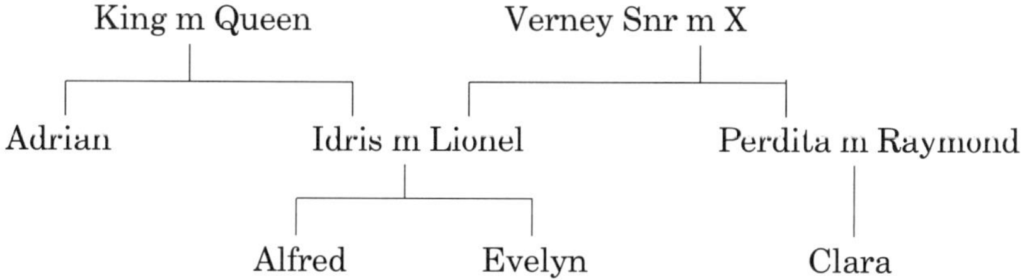

There is a peripheral genealogy of Princess Evadne, who is madly in love with Raymond and whom Adrian desires, but who ends up marrying a wealthy Greek. This Greek subsequently commits suicide on going bankrupt. At one point in the text Raymond confuses her name with that of the mythic Ariadne:

> Nor you, nor any other Theseus, can thread the labyrinth, to which perhaps some unkind Ariadne has the clue. (49)

The passing reference to the labyrinth, the home of the Minotaur, product of Pasiphäe's monstrous passion for the white bull, is one of many fragmentary references in the text that are never fully developed. Yet this reference in a way anticipates the labyrinthine passage of the plague, which is both the site of death and of the Minotaur. Perhaps the death of Evadne/Ariadne implies that the means of entry into the labyrinth—Daedalus' magic ball of thread—is now irrecoverable. The magic ball is also the thread of history, which the plague makes superfluous. By extension, too, the genealogy of Romance is also spurious, its threads a meaningless labyrinth. The Gothic uses Romance only to bring genealogy itself to an end.

In place of this vacuous genealogy, the real genealogy is trans-historical and trans-genealogical. It is the genealogy of the plague itself, capitalized on its first occurrence in the text, that is offered through Perdita's point of view:

> One word, in truth, had alarmed her more than battles or sieges, during which she trusted Raymond's high command would exempt him from danger. That word, as yet it was not more to her, was PLAGUE. This enemy to the human race had begun early in June to raise its serpent-head on the shores of the Nile; parts of Asia, not usually subject to this evil, were infected. It was in Constantinople. . . . (127)

As the plague moves westward, it begins to acquire a more human form. What is at work is the sublime as mediated through the logic of the uncanny: that which is unfamiliar, death, is in fact familiar. The text interprets the sublime in terms of its empowerment of the irrational and the uncanny. A collective death in the oceanic sublime then becomes the real history of humankind, as the plague now displaces the human subject: the plague writes out the unspeakable narrative of the last man.

Verney surveys the ruins of Constantinople, the "still burning" fires, the piles of bodies, which took "gigantic proportions and weird shapes." At this moment, the first confrontation of the beginning of the death of mankind itself, Verney's prose gives way to the Romantic sublime:

> For a moment I could yield to the creative power of the imagination, and for a moment was soothed by the sublime fictions it presented to me. (145)

This is the wish of the Romantic imagination as it delights, for the moment, in these "sublime fictions." But soon these "sublime fictions" become far too real; they are not versions of the sublime that will somehow confirm the primacy of reason itself. The "gigantic proportions and weird shapes" in any other frame would have been read as a sublime moment. In the frame of narratives of ends they signifiy the end of the power that constructs the sublime (the mind) in the first instance. So in the next chapter the sublime fictions make way for the feverish nightmare in which Raymond, transformed into a fantastic shape, is the harbinger of the plague itself. In the dream, to which we have already alluded, Raymond is modelled on the figure of Lord Ruthven in Byron/Polidori's *The Vampyre*. As we have already remarked, Lord Ruthven's pursuit of Aubrey anticipates the equally deadly westward movement of the plague. The "sublime fictions" readily give way to the oceanic sublime, the sublime of dissolution. Verney's sister Perdita (the outcast of *The Winter's Tale*), inconsolable because of Lord Raymond's death, commits suicide in a bizarre, almost barbaric drowning in which she "had had the precaution to fasten a long shawl round her waist, and again to the staunchions of the cabin window" (156). It is the sea—the element that took the life of Shelley at 29 (Perdita, too, is 29)—whose "roar was a dirge," its bosom "inconstant," its smiles "treacherous" (157). The metaphor of ships actually becoming a "bier" is taken up again when Verney reaches Portsmouth. There he finds that a plague-ridden American ship, the "Fortunatus," which had left Philadelphia some months before, had arrived with only one surviving crew. This solitary member of the crew died on landing, obviously afflicted by the plague. Like Shelley, whose body was discovered on the shores of the Viareggio and buried immediately by the authorities for fear of breaking quarantine regulations, this sailor, too, is "buried deep in the sands" (157). Burke had read the sublime as the truly great, but also as a terror that coerced the self into subjugation to the sign of God and King; Mary Shelley, repeating Frankenstein's creation, offers the sublime as monstrous:

> —That same invincible monster, which hovered over and devoured Constantinople—that fiend more cruel than tempest, less tame than fire, is, alas, unchained in that beautiful country—(160)

The "monstrosity" of the plague is encapsulated in a time warp where the end of the twenty-first century, almost three hundred years ahead of Mary Shelley's own time, has undergone no changes at all. Apart from a passing reference to a flying balloon (which lacks some of Grainville's scientific details—a vast urn or an "aerial vessel" filled with volatile spirits), the text is almost self-indulgently anachronistic. A realistic concern with periods has never been a Gothic concern generally, much less, indeed, for Mary Shelley herself. But even monstrosity must find expression of some kind; the real, felt presence of the plague must be countenanced. Here is Verney looking on the corpse of an "unhappy stranger":

> This indeed was the plague. I raised his rigid limbs, I marked the distortion of his face, and the stony eyes lost to perception. As I was thus occupied, chill horror congealed my blood, making my flesh quiver and my hair to stand on end. Half insanely I spoke to the dead. So the plague killed you, I muttered. How came this? Was the coming painful? You look as if the enemy had tortured, before he murdered you. And now I leapt up precipitately, and escaped from the hut, before nature could revoke her laws, and inorganic words be breathed in answer from the lips of the departed. (187–88)

Verney describes this in realist terms, but the lacunae are so marked and obvious that the description leads to greater expectations from the reader. The expectations are, however, thwarted, since only the "distortion of his face" and "stony eyes"—traditional descriptions of an epileptic fit—are given. Instead, it is the subjective realm of the speaker's own reactions that dominates the stereotypical examination of his own horrified self. The second half of the final sentence in the above quotation, however, poses a different problem. Verney escapes, afraid that death might be playing a game here. What if "inorganic words" come in reply to questions? What are "inorganic words"—words from the dead, words of the plague: will the plague actually speak now? "Inorganic" here has the second important *OED* meaning of "not furnished with or acting by bodily or material organs." This usage, in literature, was first made by Shelley in *Prometheus Unbound* 1, 135:

> Speak, Spirit! from thine inorganic voice
> I only know that thou art moving near
> And love. How cursed I him?

Mary Shelley is clearly gesturing toward the idea of "inorganic" words/voice/death answering back from the depths of the sublime.

What is of consequence, finally, is that gradually the plague becomes a metonym/stand-in for death itself. When it comes to the already literarized corollaries of the plague—earthquakes, tempests, conflagrations, and the like—these are curiously absent from *The Last Man*. In fact, Mary Shelley emphasizes the absence of the conventional cataclysmic event: "none of these things accompanied our fall!" (229). The only extended relationship established is between death and the end of time. The English language does not make that relationship intrinsic to its deep semantic system; in a language such as Sanskrit *kāla* (death) and *kāla* (time) are identical. Adrian, however, sees the connection: "He felt that the end of time was come" and "he knew that one by one we should dwindle into nothingness" (237).

From the plague (in capitals) the narrative moves swiftly toward the last man (also in capitals), who is the narrator himself. Yet, as we have seen in our citation of one instance of the plague victim (187–88), the plague is rarely, if ever, described in an extended manner. It is there, but without referential specificity; it seems to defy figurative representation, as may be seen in Verney's encounter with the dying negro. It is an encounter fraught with real difficulties precisely because of its grounding in too firm a reality. Returning home to be with his dying son Alfred, Verney meets "a negro half clad, writhing under the agony of disease, while he held me with a convulsive grasp" (245). This negro, whose breath was "death-laden," gives Verney his disease. The encounter with the negro lasts only a few lines, but it is a rare glimpse, nevertheless, of someone who is actually afflicted by the plague. As we have remarked before, such descriptions of the effects of the plague on individuals so that a social pattern can be generated from the cases of typical instances are indeed rare. It is a point that takes us to the very heart of how Death itself might be represented. The plague as a collective death defies the imagination by its colossal presence. The only way in which Mary Shelley can represent it is through anecdotal or fragmentary tales. Thus, the three rare examples of "framed narratives" in the final book, the tales of Lucy Martin, Juliet, and the lady at the organ playing for her blind father, fail to go beyond the mere anecdotal (recall the tale of the mechanic and of the astronomer Merrivale, both of whom go mad) even though their didactic significance as critiques of social position is quite crucial to Mary Shelley's vision of the end of humanity. In these essentially anecdotal fragments, we get once again the narrative structures of the Gothic casting their long shadows. The genre of the Gothic becomes identical with that of the Gothic fragment.

It is only from the second half of volume 3 onward that the apocalyptic sublime is given full representational force, albeit largely within a conventional discourse. The time had now come for a complete evacuation of England. At Dover the first of a series of "pre-literarized" descriptions of the coming end is given. Literature has an established repertoire with which to image apocalypse. Some of the characteristics of these representations are: the sun seems to move, other stars invade the galaxy, there is a dazzling light, the sea burns (or at least looks as if it is burning), horses break loose, and invariably a herd of cattle rushes headlong toward the cliff and plunges into the abyss below. Mary Shelley notes at this point: "no longer we were ruled by ancient laws, but were turned adrift in an unknown region of space" (270). Conventions of apocalyptic representation also presuppose a connection between these events and "the day of judgment," which many claimed had come. Since they are part of Christian eschatological thought, they draw on the visionary narratives of the Book of Ezekiel and Revelations. Verney's response to these extraordinary events is couched in the classic late eighteenth-century readings of the sublime: "A sublime sense of awe calmed the swift pulsations of my heart—I awaited the approach of the destruction menaced, with that solemn resignation which an unavoidable necessity instils" (270). The terrific form that the ocean assumed connects the sublime with the specific associations of dissolution present in the oceanic sublime. Verney's "solemn resignation" (270) in the face of the threateningly convulsive ocean is really a version of Schopenhauer's rereading of the Kantian sublime through the categories of the dissolution of the self: Verncy is conditioned to approach the sublime with a sense of awe, but the "unavoidable necessity" now instills a "solemn resignation." *The Last Man* is the ultimate in death narrative, encroaching on that moment in literary representation when, no matter what we write, the real representation of the event or theme constantly eludes us as we struggle to find an appropriate correlate for an inexplicable moment. Visions or versions of the end of mankind are final, or limit narratives, in that they threaten the subject with annihilation. As we have said already, this is Schopenhauer's sublime, where the end of the self in the oceanic/apocalyptic sublime certainly points toward a power superior to man. In search of the appropriate correlate, Mary Shelley borrows from the sublime discourses of orientalism.[59] She refers to "Vishnou" and "Juggernaut," the latter borrowed from English travel accounts of religious processions at Puri where devotees carrying a gigantic statue of Krishna, the eighth avatar of Vishnu, would throw themselves under a chariot.

Naturally, Mary Shelley oscillates between the positive Romantic sublime and the *uncertainty* of the Gothic sublime. It is the latter, however, that finally takes over the narrative. People play strange, macabre roles. An opera dancer is the lovely white specter who pirouettes on the road (298). Another version of this specter is a French nobleman who, clad in black, rides through the towns as the emissary of death (299). These fragments from the standard Gothic novels finally give way to the citation of a specific text by Verney. He recalls Mrs. Ann Radcliffe's *The Italian* with its "dark monk, and floating figures" (336).

Before Verney can claim that he is the "LAST MAN" (324), Mary Shelley must act out the death of the poet Shelley yet again. Adrian and Clara are destroyed not by the plague but by Adrian/Shelley's overweening Romanticism, which, like a Gothic narrative, drags him toward the beguiling dangers of the unknown. Adrian's drowning parallels Shelley's own and suggests that a compulsive death wish (as in *Caleb Williams*) and not the plague finally destroys humanity. But there is another way in which the sublime functions. This is the sublime as the end of representation in writing. What Verney carves on St. Peter's in Rome is the year 2100 which he calls the last year of the world. The final words of the novel, "the LAST MAN," also bring about the final annihilation of history. This history did have a material base, but Mary Shelley offers, in Brian Aldiss' words, a "symbolic representation, a psychic screening, of what was taking place in reality."[60] For Mary Shelley the real subject of the novel, the plague, could only be framed in the narrative of ends, in the narrative of death itself: *kālo 'smi lokakṣayakṛt pravṛddhaḥ* ("I am become death, shatterer of the worlds").

Jacques Derrida observes in his "Exergue" to *De la Grammatologie* that the "future can only be anticipated in the form of an absolute danger." He adds, "It is that which breaks absolutely with constituted normality and can only be proclaimed, *presented*, as a sort of monstrosity."[61] Tales about ends, seen as absolute danger, push the sublime to its very limits and become the ultimate trope of the extreme instance of the Gothic sublime in which the security of the law of reason is no longer available, nor desired, by the subject. The two works of Mary Shelley examined thus far—*Mathilda* and *The Last Man*—in fact use seemingly innocuous genres to hide an anxiety about limit situations. Thus, the generic systems of sentimentalism and romance, combined with the sublime subjects of incest and apocalypse (personal extinction and collective death) are deployed toward an exploration of the unpresentable, the sublime, and the monstrous. As versions of the oceanic sublime these frightening Gothic texts discover, in death, unities not available to the living. This is the forbidden, individual desire of *Mathilda* and the apocalyptic, collective, desire of humanity in *The Last Man*. In both, the subject is confronted by an immensely superior, intimidating power that, finally, brings reason and history to an end. In this respect Mary Shelley's apocalyptic sublime is the direct precursor of the nuclear sublime. But in the case of Mary Shelley's narratives, the end of history, as Gilbert and Gubar point out, is also the final "revenge of the monster who has been denied a true place in history."[62] This monster was, of course, Mary Shelley's "hideous progeny," to which she had given birth some ten years before. To this remarkable text/"body" of the Gothic sublime, to *Frankenstein*, that is, we must now return.

6

Frankenstein: Sublime as Desecration/Decreation

In her introduction to the 1831 edition of *Frankenstein*[1] Mary Shelley explains in some detail how, during one of the nightly discussions at Diodati, the question of infusing life into a dead body through "galvanism" (the grand dream of science in the Enlightenment[2]) was raised. In Mary Shelley's case an explicit statement about the infusion of life into matter, prefigured, as we shall see, in the great debates between John Abernethy and William Lawrence, was almost thirteen years in the making. It is possible, therefore, to suggest that it was through the writing of *Frankenstein* itself that she arrived at this position though, predictably, she was considerably chastened by Frankenstein's own attempt at usurping the powers of both woman and creator. In her journal entry of 19 October 1822 she makes a fleeting reference to that night of 16 June 1816 (that sublime night once again!), though the event itself is not covered in her journal. Still recovering from the death of Shelley on 8 July 1822, she explains that in the presence of Byron (Albe) she could hardly ever speak openly:

> But since incapacity & timidity always prevented my mingling in the nightly conversations of Diodati—they were as it were entirely tête-a-tête between my Shelley & Albe & thus as I have said—when Albe speaks & Shelley does not answer, it is as thunder without rain.[3]

Such "timidity" also explains the degree of self-questioning with which the 1831 introduction begins. How could a young girl write on "so very hideous an idea?" The crucial word here is "hideous," since it is a word taken up again in the phrase "my hideous progeny." Three meanings of the word *hideous* come together in Mary Shelley's usage. Its first meaning is that of "causing dread or horror," which is gradually transformed into "revolting to the senses or feelings." Milton's use of it in *Paradise Lost* (1, 46), "With hideous ruin and combustion," is cited by the *OED* as an example of this usage. Related to this first meaning is the idea of "terrific on account of size; monstrously large; huge, immense." The example given in the *OED* ("The great precipice below, which hangs over the sea, is so hideous") is from a 1796 usage, and refers to sublime objects. The second meaning of "hideous" is something that is "distracting or revolting to the moral sense; abominable, detestable; odious." Hence the citation from George Eliot's *Romola* 2, 4: "Hard speech between those who have loved is hideous in the memory." The final meaning of "hideous" involves a real reference to a "frightful person or object."

As we have already noted in chapter 3, Mary's "hideous idea" was in response to a challenge by Lord Byron who, on reading through some ghost stories in the company of Shelley, Polidori, Mary, and Claire Claremont (who is not mentioned in Mary's preface), suggested that they each write a ghost story. The unusual effect that Byron's reading of *Christabel* had on Shelley is omitted in Mary's introduction, as is Polidori's later claim that the novel he had in mind was *Ernestus Berchtold.* Instead, Mary recalls that Polidori considered writing about a lady whose head turned into a skull because she was compulsively attracted to the scenes of sexual taboo and prohibition. As far as her own attempt at writing a ghost story went, Mary says she wanted to write a tale "which would speak to the mysterious fears of our nature, and awaken thrilling horror—one to make the reader dread to look round, to curdle the blood, and quicken the beatings of the heart" (226). For Mary Shelley the moment of genesis was also the moment of invention.

"Invention, it must be humbly admitted," she continues, "does not consist in creating out of void, but out of chaos" (226). It is from the chaos of sounds and not from emptiness, the abyss of silence, the vacuity of the void, that creativity arises. The spark or life force that allowed her to give shape to this chaos was galvanism, and the principles of animation. The passive but devout listener of Byron and Shelley's "chaotic" conversations now retrieves a fragmentary memory, captures a word, a term that establishes, for her, a connection between chaos and creativity. Galvanism, the "application of electricity to dead tissue,"[4] is akin to the life force itself: "perhaps the component parts of a creature might be manufactured, brought together, and endued with vital warmth" (227). In this way, can she become a visitor to Piranesi's monster-making space?

To "superadd" a "vital warmth" to a body is the "organic" vision of creation that Mary has in mind here. The idea, in the immediate historical context, goes back to John Abernethy, who in 1814 delivered a lecture in London before the Royal College of Surgeons in which, drawing on the work of John Hunter and, less assuredly, on that of Humphry Davy, he tried to "distinguish between body, life, and mind as separate entities."[5] The significance of Abernethy's lecture lay in his vitalist assumption that life was a self-contained, immutable and transcendental principle not identical with the body. Life, in this highly mystical view, was like the soul or *ātman*, independent of the mechanical body. Life is therefore "superadded to structure" and, on the same basis, the mind, too, is "superadded to life." The closest analogy to life was electricity.

Two years later, in lectures delivered in 1816, William Lawrence, sometime physician of Percy Shelley under whose care the poet's chronic abdominal illness and consumption had "considerably improved,"[6] and pupil of John Abernethy, vigorously attacked his former mentor. Adopting the then-fashionable French materialist or mechanistic position, he disagreed with Abernethy's claims of a separate principle of life akin to electricity. An animating matter, like Mary Shelley's galvanism, was contrary to scientific theory and a nostalgic regression to the world of mythology. In his counter-argument Abernethy (1817) accused Lawrence and his colleagues of skepticism and asked whether they in fact felt threatened by the implied connection he had advanced between vitalism and the existence in humans of a soul. This didn't stop the controversy, which in fact gained further momentum from Lawrence's immediate reply (1817), in which he made explicit the connection between the human mind and the "physiological" brain. Abernethy's principle of an independent mind superadded to the physical tissues that made up the brain was rejected outright. Lawrence was clearly on the side of evolutionary theory (on which he was to discourse at length later) and scientific reasoning.

It is not my intention here to connect the events at Diodati during the summer of 1816 with this controversy. I only wish to point out the obvious fact that the central tenet of Mary Shelley's argument—that life was a force, like electricity, that could be infused into the reconstructed human body—was being vigorously debated at the time and that the discourse of vitalism was available to her. The connection, however, becomes more significant through the mediation of Coleridge, an important influence on the Shelleys, for whom the organized body was "nothing but the consequence of life, nothing but the means by which and through which it displays itself."[7] Mary Shelley, of course, never mentions galvanism in the 1818 text, only in the 1831 revised edition where this knowledge is imparted to Frankenstein by "a man of great research in natural philosophy" (1831: 238). However, this sketchy account of one instance of the vitalist-mechanist controversy is contemporary with the genesis of *Frankenstein* as well as symptomatic of debates already foregrounded by Kant.

In the *Critique of Judgement* (Part 2, Critique of Teleological Judgement) a "physical thing," that is, a natural object with a "physical end" is defined by its intrinsic capacity toward wholeness: "its parts, both as to their existence and form, are only possible by their relation to the whole."[8] As the product of "an intelligent cause" a human is for Kant a physical being with precisely the kind of superadded force subsequently made explicit by Abernethy. And like Abernethy, in Kant as well the antimechanistic conception of humans comes across very powerfully:

> This, therefore, is a self-propagating formative power, which cannot be explained by the capacity of movement alone, that is to say, by mechanism.[9]

There is, then, nothing imperfect about the "formative power" itself. What may be suspect (a point not made by Kant) is the authority from which the power comes in the first place. So, as Chris Baldick has pointed out, the beauty of the component parts that Victor Frankenstein collects as perfect specimens turns out to be "hideously repulsive" on the introduction of Frankenstein's "spark of life."[10] Clearly, the ugliness of the Monster is Mary Shelley's way of reminding us that the origin of the spark (where it comes from) is just as important as its intrinsic quality. The artificial origin of the spark (in Frankenstein) desecrates the holiness of the original source of life. Hence participation in the creative process becomes the other extreme of the sublime in death. Both are equally unpresentable. But the first, creation, is also capable of unleashing the narrative of ends. Creation heralds apocalypse; Genesis, Revelations; *Frankenstein, The Last Man*. Mary's grand capacity to mold chaos through galvanism now produces a "hideous phantasm." The word "hideous" reappears (it occurs five times in the introduction) to explain the central "enigma" of *Frankenstein*.

—I saw the pale student of unhallowed arts kneeling beside the thing he had put together. I saw the hideous phantasm of a man stretched out, and then, on the working of some powerful engine, show signs of life, and stir with an uneasy, half vital motion. Frightful must it be; for supremely frightful would be the effect of any human endeavour to mock the stupendous mechanism of the Creator of the world. His success would terrify the artist; he would rush away from his odious handywork, horror-stricken. He would hope that, left to itself, the slight spark of life which he had communicated would fade; that this thing, which had received such imperfect animation, would subside into dead matter; and he might sleep in the belief that the silence of the grave would quench for ever the transient existence of the hideous corpse which he had looked upon as the cradle of life. He sleeps; but he is awakened; he opens his eyes; behold the horrid thing stands at his bedside, opening his curtains, and looking on him with yellow, watery, but speculative eyes. (228)

Mary Shelley begins her introduction with a "hideous . . . idea." The descriptive *hideous* is then connected to the "phantasm" theme, followed by its association with "corpse" and back again to "phantom." Finally, the word *hideous* is released as "my hideous progeny," a countersublime, technological and unnatural, that Kant would have found inadmissible. She asks this progeny to go forth and prosper, releasing it as a phantom on an unsuspecting world. We need more than Professor Waldman's modern science of "command," "mimic," and "mock," words that he uses to explain to Frankenstein how modern science grasps what for ancient, occult science were mere mysteries (42), to be able to understand the full impact of this hideous progeny. The postmodern sublime lacks Waldeman's certainties, even though it works with far more sophisticated models.

The dual agenda of the 1831 introduction prepares us for a much more open-ended reading of the text; the 1818 preface, penned by Shelley from Mary's point of view, is much more difficult to prize out of its historical specificity.[11] Here the desire for radical difference—that this work is different from the "novels of the present day," with their "amiableness of domestic affection, and the excellence of universal virtue" (7)—is tempered by a discreet distancing from the convictions in the text. They are not necessarily mine, says Mary; nor am I endorsing that particular point of view. Crawling toward critical acceptance, Percy Shelley defends the subject matter on the grounds of fancy, since the novelty of the situation allows for a more "comprehensive and commanding" examination of "human passions" (6). After the 1831 introduction, this is a relatively tame affair, written with an eye on the critical discourses of the periodical literature. But it also writes the female out of the text: a woman's experience, even for someone as enlightened as Shelley, required no specificity, no especially gendered allusion or response. One returns to a view persuasively presented by Patricia Yaeger about the Female sublime. Using her general insights, can we say that the poet Shelley excludes Mary because the sublime is a masculine genre that is forbidden to women? Is it, as Yaeger suggests, in fact a dangerous genre because it invents "for women, a vocabulary of ecstasy and empowerment" so revolutionary that the male critic must reject it outright?[12] For what, after Yaeger, Mary Shelley's works engender are precisely those versions of the Gothic sublime that do question the Law, that do discover, through a female self-empowerment, that space where the subject rejects the imperial demand that it return to the security of patriarchal order. The bliss of the Gothic sublime, though ultimately destructive, is also a means of power.

I

Published in 1818, *Frankenstein* is emphatically dedicated to Mary's father William Godwin. Since Mary was pregnant much of the time while *Frankenstein* was being written (Clara Everina was born in September 1817), and had already experienced the death of a premature child in 1815 and the birth of another, though not premature, in January 1816, the relationship between art and childbirth, in this instance, cannot be overlooked. As we have already seen in chapter 3, what can't be overlooked either is the almost total absence of any real sympathy on the part of William Godwin toward Mary's many tragedies. At the risk of repeating ourselves—and the context of *Frankenstein* demands the repetition of earlier moments of death and trauma—the letters that Godwin wrote on the deaths of Mary's children are remarkable for their insensitivity.[13] Reading through these letters one is struck by a male principle of "intellectualism" that refuses to authorize a woman's body as a legitimate space from which to construct meaning. Emotions that come from the sinews and bones of the body have no place in this version of truth. "All that has a claim upon your kindness, is nothing, because a child of three years old is dead!" Godwin had written on 9 September 1819, on the death of William.[14] At the end of the cruelest letter of them all Mary dutifully composes a note about the loss of her daughter Clara Everina ("The loss of my infant daughter; who died at Venice") and then hurriedly strikes the sentence out. On the death of the poet Shelley, Godwin writes a letter on 6 August 1822[15] in which, again, Godwin never participates in the special grief of his daughter, and is incapable of the apt phrase or the right metaphor that could act as an ennobling epitaph. Instead, we get a letter that is completely centered around the writer himself: "the sorrows of an unfortunate old man & a beggar," Godwin expostulates. Yet the father to whom *Frankenstein* is dedicated writes a different story about creation/decreation in Mary Shelley's imaginative world. In a letter written on 15 November 1822, only months after his own expression of mawkish self-pity, he is full of praise: "Frankenstein was a fine thing: it was compressed, muscular & firm. Nothing relaxed & weak."[16] The following year, in a note added to a letter written to Mary on 14 February 1823 about the progress of *Valperga*, her second novel, Godwin writes:

> Frankenstein is universally known; & though it can never be a book for vulgar reading, is every where respected. It is the most wonderful work to have been written at twenty years of age that I ever heard of.[17]

The father gets dragged yet again in the *Quarterly Review*'s condemnation of *Frankenstein* as "a tissue of horrible and disgusting absurdity"[18] because it was deemed to have been written under the pernicious influence of the person to whom the text was dedicated. What could you expect from the *"out-pensioners of Bedlam,"*[19] the disciples of William Godwin? went the argument. Though the review is extremely negative, the reviewer nevertheless concedes that "there is something tremendous in the unmeaning hollowness of its sound, and the vague obscurity of its images."[20] "Unmeaning hollowness" is an abyss, a labyrinth; it releases associations of terror that the reviewer recognizes but about which he prefers to remain silent.

Two months later, in the March 1818 issue of *Blackwood's Edinburgh Magazine,*[21] Walter Scott wrote an extended, enthusiastic, and largely theoretical essay on *Frankenstein*. Beginning with an initial distinction between realistic and nonrealistic/marvelous fiction, Scott goes on to subdivide the latter, the marvelous, into various types. In the common run of marvelous stories, "the laws of credibility"[22] might be transgressed, but this transgression doesn't have any real effect on either the reader of the text or on the characters in fiction who coexist with these strange, improbable beings. In the second type, however, Scott considers those works in which, again, the "laws of nature are represented as altered," but here the author's aim is to show not the change in laws themselves but the effect of this change on the characters who are implicated in the laws of nature. Scott continues:

> But success in this point is still subordinate to the author's principal object, which is less to produce an effect by means of the marvels of the narrations, than to open new trains and channels of thought, by placing men in supposed situations of an extraordinary and preternatural character, and then describing the mode of feeling and conduct which they are most likely to adopt.[23]

The foundations of the narrative might well be extraordinary, but what we, as readers, must demand is that the impact of the events on characters follow the laws of logic and probability. Scott connects *Frankenstein* with Godwin's *St. Leon* and accepts the rumor that the author of this work is Percy Bysshe Shelley. Scott is impressed by the lack of "Germanisms" but feels slightly uneasy with the (at times) exceedingly realistic basis of the Monster's drives, especially his reading and philosophical habits.

The point about Scott's essay, in which, incidentally, he does not take up the usual "moral-oriented" criticism of the periodical literature, is that he accepts the generic basis of this kind of fiction and suggests, in the passage quoted, that this generic radicalism is crucial to the uncovering of aesthetic judgments of the type demanded by the literature of the marvelous. In the September issue of the same journal was published John Wilson's unsigned essay entitled "Some Remarks on the Use of the Preternatural in Works of Fiction." Although this essay lacks the theoretical subtlety of Scott, it nevertheless accepts that the marvelous does give a "pleasing respite from the inexorable tyranny of facts."[24]

Scott's essay is a welcome interlude in the monotonous diatribe of the other contemporary reviews. Preoccupied as these periodicals were with public morality, it is not surprising that the *Monthly Review* called *Frankenstein* an "uncouth story" without any moral or philosophical point or center.[25] And this in spite of the attempts made on Mary's behalf by the poet Shelley in the introduction! The *Edinburgh Review* wondered about the motive behind "this wild fiction." It opined that the moral was confused, even though there were tantalizing hints about the consequences that follow from human appropriation of the godly act of creation.[26] The advice of the *Edinburgh Review* to the author of *Frankenstein* is that "he" should study "the established order of nature as it appears, both in the world of matter and of mind."[27]

The realist insistence on the "established order of nature" (art as mimetic representation) lies at the heart of all contemporary reviewers except Scott. In P. B. Shelley's own draft of a review that was posthumously published in the *Athenaeum* of 10 November 1832, he called it "one of the most original and complete productions of the day."[28] Using the metaphors of vastness or immensity—as though one were climbing mountain on mountain—Shelley emphasizes the giddying effect of the narrative, its enormous capacity to produce a "powerful and profound emotion." Shelley is aware that the novel must be defended on the grounds of public morality, and he does this with considerable force. But the core of his argument is a shift from the creator to his creation. "The Being in 'Frankenstein,'" he writes with a faint sense of self-identification "is, no doubt, a tremendous creature." Shelley continues:

> He was an abortion and an anomaly; and though his mind was such as its first impressions framed it, affectionate and full of moral sensibility, yet the circumstances of his existence are so monstrous and uncommon, that, when the consequences of them became developed in action, his original goodness was gradually turned into inextinguishable misanthropy and revenge.[29]

This is a neat theory: the transformation of an "abortion" (the Monster calls himself an "abortion" too) in narrative leads to shifts and turns that are quite unpredictable. But the representation of this "abortion" (we recall the *Literary Magnet*'s "monstrous literary abortion" remark here), this "Being," whom Richard Brinsley Peake in his dramatized version (1823) was to indicate with a dash "—," demands a narrative that has few distinct parallels. The categories through which this "Being" could be expressed are for Shelley indistinguishable from those of the sublime: "an irresistible solemnity . . . magnificent energy." What Shelley isolates, however, is the effect that persecution has on any person who is denied a place in society. "What is needed," writes Ronald Paulson, "is the beautiful love of a mother, not the sublime fear of a father who cannot come to terms with the unmanageable male-threatening force he has loosed."[30] The intertext that looms large here is William Godwin's *Caleb Williams*, with its complex narrative of duplication and uncanny repetition under the threat of a castrating father.

The foregoing archaeology uncovers a network of complex biographical and textual relationships that complicates any simple interpretation of *Frankenstein*. The dismissal of this feature of her text is probably due to a critical reading erroneously summed up by Mario Praz as: "All Mrs. Shelley did was to provide a passive reflection of some of the wild fantasies which, as it were, hung in the air about her."[31] Criticism cannot advance beyond the purely thematic if a writer is perforce locked into such a judgment about her creativity. Praz has been rightly condemned for this momentary lapse, but the system of grand myths he was using to examine the concept of Romantic agony—especially in the manifold expressions of the Satanic or Byronic hero—didn't allow for a reading of a text in which the "satanic Homunculus" is really a monster.[32] It seems to me that it was only after an adequate hermeneutic had developed that would allow for a reading of literature through the fundamental concept of gender as socially constructed difference that Mary Shelley's work began to be interrogated in terms of its complex historical moment of production. It is for this reason that I skip the standard "Gothic" readings of *Frankenstein* and go to feminist interpretations of this text. The survey would also act as an introduction to Mary Shelley's rhetoric of the sublime.

The Gothic, as we have seen, is a moment in literary history when realist representations are questioned. For feminist critics this questioning of realist representations and narrative linearity through framing devices opens up a space for the contestation of imperialist patriarchal discourses, of which the sublime itself is one among many. Not surprisingly, nearly all late twentieth-century theorists of fantasy as counterculture are women: Julia Kristeva, Hélène Cixous, Ellen Moers, Sandra Gilbert, Susan Gubar, Mary Jacobus, Barbara Johnson, Rosemary Jackson, among others. A key concept that underpins much of feminist discourses on the Gothic is Ellen Moers' "Female Gothic."[33]

Beginning with the generally accepted definition of the Gothic as writings in which "fantasy predominates over reality, the strange over the commonplace, and the supernatural over the natural, with one definite auctorial intent: to scare,"[34] Ellen Moers gives the production of the female writers in this mode (Clara Reeve, Ann Radcliffe, etc.) a gendered specification by calling their works "Female Gothic." Now, according to Moers, the importance of Mary Shelley in this tradition/writing of "Female Gothic" lies in her transformation of the Gothic form into a precursor of modern science fiction. Like Moers' initial definition of the Gothic, this, too, is a common enough claim. Where a significant advance occurs is in the radical connection Moers makes between the fact of being a mother and the central theme of the text: "For *Frankenstein* is a birth myth, and one that was lodged in the novelist's imagination, I am convinced, by the fact that she was herself a mother."[35] Moers' reading of *Frankenstein* through the childbirth metaphor has been adopted by other, not necessarily feminist, readers, notably Marc Rubinstein, Barbara Johnson, and U. C. Knoepflmacher. Among the many pregnancies, miscarriages, and infant deaths she had had to live with, perhaps the death of her own mother upon childbirth (which existed only as narrative fragments to be discovered through her father's manuscripts—a veritable Gothic search indeed!) was the original moment of trauma. All other deaths were then repetitions (in the compulsive sense of the word) of a death that had something of an originary, almost phylogenetic, status. Having lost a mother, she also lost "a mother's nurture."[36]

At a time when few writers were also mothers, Mary Shelley's *Frankenstein* expresses an attitude toward the Monster that belies a mother's own barely concealed murderous impulses toward her child, what Moers calls the "trauma of the afterbirth."[37] Moers works through the biographical details of birth and death between June 1816 and May 1817, the period of *Frankenstein*'s composition, to emphasize the uniqueness of Mary Shelley's personal experience as a young woman writer, and the radical difference of women's writing generally in the context of female sexuality and motherhood. Moers' conclusion is decisive:

> What Mary Shelley actually did in *Frankenstein* was to transform the standard Romantic matter of incest, infanticide, and patricide into a phantasmagoria of the nursery.[38]

"Phantasmagoria of the nursery," like the "female sterility" principle of Grainville, is a monstrous idea taken to its limits. It is a conclusion that is endorsed by U. C. Knoepflmacher, who expands this "phantasmagoria" into "a fantasy designed to relieve deep personal anxieties over birth and death and identity."[39] But there is also a strong political payoff in the phantasmagoric sublime of the nursery. One remembers that Mary Shelley was the daughter of a man whose own disciples had been condemned as "'the spawn of the monster.'"[40] In 1799, the *Anti-Jacobin Review* published a take-off on Fuseli's "The Nightmare" with an accompanying poem.[41] The picture shows the opposition Whig leader Charles James Fox asleep on his broken bed (clearly a consequence of the agitated nightmare he is going through), surrounded by grotesque figures who parody the Parisian revolutionaries and *sansculottes*. Fuseli's dark horse protruding its head through the curtain is now the horse of death ridden by a Jacobin harbinger of death. He carries a flag of liberty that is set deep in his chest while the satanic succubus lifts the curtain. A dagger is in full flight, heading toward the window. The cause of this nightmare is to be found in the sleeper's coat, which lies on a chair at the foot of the bed. From the pocket protrudes a copy of William Godwin's *Political Justice*. In the overall context of the picture, Godwin's work occupies the same prominent space as the "monsters" of the revolution, a sublime threat to authority whom Edmund Burke had now converted into terrorists. The sublime for Burke, after all, was a divine terror linked directly to notions of class.

The symbolic connection between Godwin and a monster is more emphatically underlined by Thomas De Quincey, who spoke of the 1790s as a period when "most people felt of Mr. Godwin with the same alienation and horror as of a ghoul, or a bloodless vampyre, or the monster created by Frankenstein."[42] The reactionary reading of Jacobinism as "monsterism" was so endemic that even Mary Wollstonecraft used the metaphor in her account of the excesses of the French Revolution. Yet in a neat reduction of the central plea of Mary Shelley's own Monster, Wollstonecraft wrote:

> Sanguinary tortures, insidious poisonings, and dark assassinations, have alternately exhibited a race of monsters in human shape, the contemplation of whose ferocity chills the blood, and darkens every enlivening expectation of humanity: but we ought to observe, to reanimate the hopes of benevolence, that the perpetration of these horrid deeds has arisen from a despotism in the government, which reason is teaching us to remedy.[43]

For Wollstonecraft slaves retaliate because tyranny (Edmund Burke's Gothic fantasy) gives them no option but to become "monstrous." Hatred breeds misanthropy, and monstrosity in the working classes is a mirror image of the forces that produce the condition of tyranny. Both the revolutionary and antirevolutionary political language of the 1790s were steeped in metaphors of "monsterism." Godwin, Wollstonecraft, Paine, and the Jacobins, the revolutionary front as well as Edmund Burke and the conservatives on the right wing of politics had used this central metaphor. It was both a confessional metaphor, as in the case of Wollstonecraft, and an inflammatory one, as in the case of Burke. For Mary Shelley the political ambiguities inherent in the metaphor of "monsterism" enabled her to play on its contradictory meanings and eschew, right from the start, any possibility of naive reductionism.

An awareness of these available discourses or, more generally, of the political unconscious itself, enables us to see the complex way in which Mary becomes an instrument and minister of her parents' own political program. A much more literary homage to authority may be seen in Mary Shelley's treatment of Milton's *Paradise Lost*, from which she takes her epigraph. "*Frankenstein* . . . ," argue Gilbert and Gubar, "is a fictionalized rendition of the meaning of *Paradise Lost* to women."[44] This master literary text, which was for Mary and the poet Shelley an "all-consuming presence," can either be completely parodied and hence destabilized, or it can be ironically confirmed through strategic overwriting or conscious misreading. The key to *Paradise Lost* lay in two major events: the first is the fall of Satan, the second the "inabstinence of Eve." For Gilbert and Gubar the extreme "literariness" of this grand epic is what, as a writer, Mary must recast: it is the precursor text into which Mary Shelley is forever "imprisoned" because epics, as Foucault pointed out, are the master texts of contrived immortality. In recasting the epic (through a postepic discourse) *Frankenstein* pushes the consequences of Satan's fall and Eve's "inabstinence" to extremes. The former leads to a universal fall whose apocalyptic reading is to be found in *The Last Man*; the latter leads to the birth of the Monster. Gilbert and Gubar call this a retelling of the patriarchal sublime. It is probably better to see it as a recasting, which is both a paraphrase and a commentary on the master text. A commentary requires digressions and departures; it requires frames that would dislodge narrative linearity and displace the central themes of the original. What emerges, therefore, in *Frankenstein* is solipsism and redundancy, repetition and regressive "mirroring." The duplication and reduplication that occur combine personal history, Mary's own sexuality and growth, with those of the characters. Orphaned, guilt-ridden, confused, threatened by the unspeakable crime of incest, the characters in *Frankenstein* —the Monster and Frankenstein included—lose their separate identities, their differences, in a Miltonic miasma of hellish chaos.[45] And this is the chaos from which, as an artist, she formed a structure: "And when I love thee not, chaos is come again." Nowhere is the collapse of difference—the return to chaos—more evident than in the way in which a not-fully theorized feminism, an unconscious feminism, so to speak, leads Mary to condemn Frankenstein for daring to "usurp the power of women."[46] The space in which this role can be adopted is no longer the monastery (Ambrosio) or the castle (Otranto). It is now a laboratory modeled on Piranesi ("a solitary chamber, or rather cell, at the top of the house, separated from all other apartments by a gallery and staircase"); Frankenstein's "work-shop of filthy creation" (50) is the perverse site of the technological sublime.[47]

The central terms in which the feminist argument works are extended further by both Mary Poovey and Margaret Homans. For Poovey the metaphor of creation and usurpation of the feminine role is reconstructed by Mary Shelley through the author herself, as writer, acting as the midwife who passively witnesses the work of Frankenstein and yet brings it into being through her writing.[48] In this act of midwifery Mary Shelley performs the socially acceptable role of self-denial that is a defining (in ideological terms) characteristic of the proper lady. There is, of course, a critical ideology at work here that functions as the silent censor of literary production by women writers generally. Since the reviewers were almost invariably men (after all, it was Percy Shelley who wrote the 1818 preface and also made a number of changes to the text—see manuscript fragments), the act of reading and production of meaning was a male critical endeavor. Women writers could write passively but could not interpret. The only way in which we can get around that "passivity" (Mario Praz's "passive reflection") occasioned by the social definition of the role of the "proper lady" is to blast open the norms of critical practice itself and to recontextualize Mary's novel in the material conditions of literary production that, in her case, could not overlook this writing (as self-knowledge) "by a young woman who had already lost a baby in infancy (in 1815, a girl), would lose another, also a girl, in 1818, and, in 1819, lost a third."[49] The last of these was the three-year-old, William, the name also given to the little boy (Frankenstein's youngest brother) murdered by the Monster.

"At the same time that *Frankenstein* is about a woman

writer's response to the ambiguous imperative her culture imposes on her," writes Margaret Homans in response to the Poovey thesis, "it is also possible that the novel concerns a woman writer's anxieties about bearing children, about generating bodies that . . . would have the power to displace or kill the parent."[50] The implied death wish and Oedipal longings manifest themselves at both the textual and biographical levels. All potential mothers, including the "monsteress," die or are violated before birth; a whole series of real women close, in personal terms, to Mary Shelley also die: Harriet Shelley, Fanny Imlay, and, of course, Mary Wollstonecraft Godwin. Reacting to a culture that saw women's role in singularly "motherhood" terms, Mary's version of a "monstrously illegitimate" childbirth threatens both the social definition of woman as mother as much as it destroys the phallic power of insemination associated with the father.

Mary Poovey has indicated that Mary's docility was in itself a critique of a woman's passive role. She argues that her writing was a result of listening and transcription—precisely the points taken over as self-evident processes by Praz and Harold Bloom.[51] *Frankenstein* as a myth of childbirth is extended by Homans into a text that bears or carries "men's words."[52] The underlying concept here is that of "motherhood" as "passive transcription." Homans calls this process in literature "literalizations." In an extension of the Gilbert and Gubar thesis (and incorporating Mary Poovey, too, a fact that strongly indicates the immense continuity of mainstream American feminist readings of *Frankenstein*) Homans considers *Frankenstein* as a "literalization" of powerful masculine texts such as Genesis, *Paradise Lost*, and *Alastor*, but the transcription, in the shadow of patriarchal writing and writers, leaves her bereft of power and condemns her to the role of the passive "transcriber," the midwife, who even as mother must remain passive. The wedge created as a result can be filled only through a subversive writing of the female sublime that cannot be divorced from a woman's body itself, blood, tissues, childbirth and all.[53]

Generically, of course, the female Gothicist must also come to terms with a genre that, according to Frances L. Restuccia's reading of Leslie Fiedler's classic *Love and Death in the American Novel,* is "a reservoir of strictly male desire, anxiety, neurosis."[54] The male Gothic tradition, with its own ambiguous, sometimes perversely "homosocial," defiance of patriarchy had, conversely, marginalized woman and "used homophobia to divide and manipulate the male-homosocial spectrum."[55] In restoring woman, reinserting her back

1)

Vol. II

Chap I

"It is with difficulty that I remember the æra of my ~~xx~~ being. All the events of that period appear confused & indistinct. ~~I know only that I felt a strange~~ a strange sensation ~~xxx~~ seized me ~~and x it appeared~~ I saw, felt heard and smelt at the same time and it was indeed a long time before I learned to distinguish between the ~~various~~ operations of my various senses. By degrees I remember a stronger light pressed upon my nerves ~~and~~ so that I was obliged to close my eyes. Darkness then came over me and troubled me. But hardly had I felt this when (by opening my eyes as I now suppose) the light poured in upon me again. I walked and I believe descended; but presently I found a great ~~difference~~ alteration in my sensations; before dark opaque bodies had surrounded me impervious to my touch or sight. and I now found that I could wander on at liberty with no obstacles which I could not either surmount or avoid. The light ~~&~~ became more & more oppressive to me and the heat wearying me as I walked I sought a place where I could (or recieve) perceive shade. This was the forest near Ingolstadt and here by the side of a brook I lay ~~xxxx~~ for some hours resting from my fatigue until I felt tormented by hunger and thirst. This roused me from my nearly

MS Fragment of Draft of *Frankenstein* in the hand of Mary Shelley, with corrections probably by P. B. Shelley. Abinger Shelley-Godwin Papers: Dep. c. 534 Duke Humfrey's Library, the Bodleian, Oxford. Volume 2, chapter 1, published, with modifications, as volume 2, chapter 3 in 1818. Rearranged as chapter 11 in the 1831 text.

dormant state and I ate some berries which I found hanging on the trees or lying on the ground — I slaked my thirst at the brook and then again lying down I was overcome by sleep. It was dark when I awoke; I felt cold also and half frightened as it were instinctively on ~~seem~~ finding myself so desolate. Before I had quitted your appartment on a sensation of cold I had covered myself with some clothes, but these were ~~not~~ insufficient to secure me from the ~~da~~ dews of night. I was a poor helpless miserable wretch — I knew ~~no~~ I could distinguish ~~not~~ nothing but ~~felt~~ feeling pain invade me on all sides ~~and~~ I sat down and wept.

Soon a gentle light stole over the heavens and gave me a sensation of pleasure I started up, and beheld a radiant form rise ~~am~~ from among the trees. I gazed with a kind of wonder — It moved slowly; but it enlightened my path, and I again went out in search of berries. I was still cold when ~~on the ground~~ under one of the trees I found a huge cloak with which I covered myself, and sat down on the ground. No distinct ideas occupied my mind all was confused ~~and~~ I felt the light, and hunger and thirst and darkness; innumerable sounds rung in my ears and on all sides various scents saluted me; the only object that I could distinguish was the bright phenonema. On Elizabeth and Clerval it produced a very different effect. They admired the beauty of the storm without wishing to analyze its causes. Henry said that the fairies and giants were at war and Elizabeth attempted a picture of it.

As I grew older my attempts in science were of a higher nature I ~~endeavor~~ produced little earthquakes and tried every kind of combination of gasses ~~&~~ and elements to ascertain the results.

~~And before mentioned my brothers were much younger than myself. Ernest the second of our family was five~~

Another task also ~~soon~~ devolved upon me when I became the instructor of my brothers. Ernest was five years younger than myself and was my principal pupil. He had been afflicted with ill health from his infancy which Elizabeth and I had been his constant nurses & his disposition was gentle but he was incapable of any severe appli-cation. William the youngest of our family was quite a child and the most beautiful little fellow in the world, his lively blue eyes dimpled cheeks

MS Fragment of Draft of *Frankenstein* in the hand of Mary Shelley, with corrections probably by P. B. Shelley. Abinger Shelley-Godwin Papers: Dep. c. 477 Duke Humfrey's Library, the Bodleian, Oxford. Final paragraph(s) of volume 1, chapter 1, published with minor changes in 1818. This section is completely omitted in the 1831 text.

and ~~affectionate~~ endearing manners
inspired the tenderest affection such
was our domestic circle from which
care and pain seemed for ever banish
ed. † my father directed our studies
and my mother partook of our
enjoyments. ~~we were all equal~~ the
voice of command was never heard
among us but mutual affection
engaged us all to comply with & to
obey the slightest desire of each
other.

neither ~~we none~~ of
us possessed
an envied
preheminence
over the other

into the genre with her head intact, the female Gothicist creates a son (the genre must have a male hero) in rebellion against the father but cannot endorse his sexual excesses and exploitation of women. She could condemn him outright—the genre would probably collapse if the threat was seen through—; she could civilize him; but she opts instead for a mirroring that would expose the son as being no different from, but as cruel as, the father. Endorsement and sabotage, the killing off of both the father and the son—these are the frames within which the female Gothicist operates. As Frances L. Restuccia explains:

> A male gothic in miniature often surfaces within and eventually is swallowed up by the female gothic frame, the ingestion of which signifies the female gothicist's ambivalence—destroying it but taking it in—toward male gothicism.[56]

The reconstructions of Mary Shelley's text through powerfully argued feminist readings are also acts of radical modernization as the text is now repackaged for consumption in the world of late capital. As a text that is "ceaselessly rewritten, reproduced, refilmed and redesigned,"[57]*Frankenstein* now gets radically multivocalized. But the critical apparatuses of feminism, which lead to the best and most finely attuned of all readings of Mary Shelley, nevertheless are linked to questions of the sublime as the text continues to be recast as the female Gothicist's representation of the unnameable in the context of an ambiguous usurpation of women's right to reproduce, *and* the representation of women in male genres and discourses. These feminist metatexts have also dislodged the primacy of the masculine sublime.

II

Lackington & Co.'s handwritten account of expenses for printing and publishing *Frankenstein* in January 1818 indicates that of the 500 copies printed, 459 (41 were given gratis to the author [6 copies], reviewers [16], copyright libraries [11], and booksellers who bought more than 25 copies [8]) were sold at 10/6 (ten shillings and six pence) per three-volume set. After deducting printing expenses, Mary Shelley's share was one-third of the profits, which came to £41.13.10 (forty-one pounds, thirteen shillings, and ten pence).[58] Forty-one pounds is not a large amount of money, but the distribution of money on the basis of the retail cost of the book compares quite favorably with modern-day contracts between authors and publishers.

The novel was reissued in two volumes in 1823 with the author's name included on the title page for the first time. A copy of this edition presented to Mrs. Thomas in 1823 carried the author's autograph variants. This copy has fortunately survived and was used as the basis for James Rieger's critical edition of the 1818 text. The year 1823 also saw the presentation of the stage version of *Frankenstein, Presumption; or the Fate of Frankenstein,* by Richard Brinsley Peake. A copy of the handwritten manuscript (with two quite distinct handwritings) in the Huntington is entitled *Frankenstein: A melodramatic Opera in 3 Acts.*[59] The published version was retitled *Frankenstein, A Romantic Drama.* Peake takes a number of liberties in his version. The first is a radical reorganization of the genealogical relationships in the original text. Elizabeth now becomes Frankenstein's sister and is betrothed to Clerval. Frankenstein himself marries blind De Lacey's daughter Agatha, who is murdered by the Monster. The other victim of the Monster is Frankenstein's brother William. A servant, Felix, is introduced who functions as an intermediary between the audience and the secret work that is underway in the laboratory. True to its melodramatic form, the play also uses Fritz as the mandatory comic buffoon. It is probably far too easy, as Chris Baldick does, to read the play simply as the moralizing of Mary Shelley's work. The title of the performed version, *Presumption . . . ,* certainly connects the play to the older tradition of morality plays, where human desire to play God invariably led to disaster. But this easy reductionism takes us away from the reworking of the Gothic sublime by Peake. It is not accidental that the Monster is no longer given a language and is addressed throughout as the "Demon." It is also important to note that the idiotic Fritz is given the line, "like Doctor Faustus, my Master is raising the Devil" (Act 1. 5). Fritz obviously gets the analogy wrong, since Frankenstein himself compares his work to Prometheus: "Like Prometheus of old have I daringly attempted the formation—the animation of a being—" (Act 1. 10). The principle that is being alluded to more fully here than in the Mary Shelley precursor is the separate principle of life advanced by John Abernethy. Peake is thus raising the Abernethy-Lawrence debates about the existence or otherwise of a self-contained principle that exists independently of the human body. Clerval, who does not know the work in the laboratory, is unable to see science as anything other than an alchemist's attempts at transmuting metals and the search for the elixir of life. The extended discourse on galvanism that we find only in Mary Shelley's later introduction to the 1831 edition is graphically foregrounded here, a fact that, once again, strengthens our case that Mary's recollection of the dream that was the source of *Frankenstein* is an effect of the text(s) and not its cause. Furthermore, Peake introduces a more straightforward connection between electricity and the special principle of life. "For this one pursuit," says Frankenstein, " a storm has hastily arisen!" He continues:

> 'Tis a dreary night—the rain patters dismally against the panes—'tis a night for such a task—I'll in—and attempt to infuse the spark of life. (Act 1: 19)

The description of the Monster is, however, taken almost verbatim from Mary Shelley's work.

> What a wretch have I formed! his legs are in proportion and I had selected his features as beautiful! Oh horror! his cadaverous skin scarcely covers the work of muscles & arteries—beneath—his hair lustrous black, and flowing—his teeth of pearly whiteness—but these luxuriances only form more horrible contrasts with the deformities of the Demon. (Act 1: 20)

It is true that Frankenstein at this moment feels remorseful and regrets his action. But the immorality of the action turns inward and affects his own serenity, as it threatens to subvert the social order (especially the family order) itself. The premonition is what sustains the play, as Frankenstein imagines the doomed figures of William and Agatha and the unhappy Elizabeth, who would finally lose both her brothers. From here onward Frankenstein becomes decidedly Gothic as he stalks guilt-ridden from place to place. "In vain do I seek a respite from these dreadful thoughts," says Frankenstein (Act 2. 20). The Monster, on the other hand, is only signified by the word "demon" or "supernatural being" and does not enter into the realm of the *symbolic* through the mastery of language. But nor is he presented as congenitally evil. His warm relationship with the De Lacey family before he is shot at and wounded by Felix is chronicled at length, and his subsequent reactions, though violent, arise out of this initial rejection. In the end both Frankenstein and the Monster die as an avalanche of snow, precipitated by the musket that Frankenstein fires, falls on them.

An account of the success of this play and a crucial reading of the Monster himself in Mary's own hand has survived. In a letter to Leigh Hunt dated September 9, 1823, Mary Shelley recounts her success. "But lo & behold! I found myself famous!"[60] she wrote. *Presumption* had been a tremendous success, she told Leigh Hunt, and was going to be staged for the twenty-third time. Mary Shelley endorses at least two aspects of the play, both of which were to make their way into James Whale's (1931) film version produced exactly one hundred years after the publication of the second, revised edition of *Frankenstein* as number 9 of Bentley's Standard Novels. The use of a dash ("—") to indicate the Monster (played by Thomas Potter Cooke) is endorsed by Mary Shelley: "this nameless mode of naming the un(n)ameable is rather good." In recounting her own night at the English Opera House, Mary Shelley, too, indicates the Monster's name with a dash: "but Cooke played —'s part extremely well." Because the Monster is "un(n)ameable," he becomes the sublime object of the Gothic, but with the superadded effect arising out of his monstrous "birthing." Where the Gothic sublime had constructed the impossible name of the father (Falkland) or the genealogical horror that the mind simply repressed or finally, as another instantiation of this series, the uncanny imaging of the self as Other, the Monster here constructs the sublime as its own impossibility: to name the sublime in whatever metaphor (even by negating it) is to somehow bring it into the world of order through which we make sense of our lives. In this respect the double negation of Mary Shelley ("nameless," "un(n)ameable") now says that the Gothic sublime is an endless series of negativities, the semantic opposite of the metonymic signifiers of the language of the unconscious that, of course, cannot countenance negation, but nor can they ground meaning in any signified. Apart from the "unnaming," Mary also endorses a structural shift in the narrative: the introduction of a terrified servant, the comic character Fritz, peeping through a dimly lit window. He runs off in terror when he hears Frankenstein exclaim, "It lives!" (Act 1. 20). Like *The Count of Narbonne, Presumption* is another of those "creative misreadings"[61] of the precursor that have forever changed the semantic content of the original. Thus, within five years of its first publication, *Frankenstein* had already achieved a degree of heterogeneity. Indeed, it is precisely this kind of rewriting of the precursor that has marked the Gothic off as a particular kind of literary (re)negotiation. In the case of *Frankenstein* it also led to a radical substitution of the son by the father, as the name "Frankenstein" is now associated, in the public imagination, with the Monster. The son's revenge on the father is complete through a sublime rebegetting, where a total inversion of the original myth now gets lodged in the very subjects that construct intersubjective meanings in the first instance. Though, admittedly, this is a somewhat forced historical search for the exact moment of the substitution and the triumph of the son, Elizabeth Gaskell's ambiguous conflation of the Monster and Frankenstein in *Mary Barton* might be noted at this point.

> The actions of the uneducated seem to me typified in those of Frankenstein, that monster of many human qualities, ungifted with a soul, a knowledge of the difference between good and evil.[62]

It is true, of course, that the many filmic variants and comic strips have never explicitly maintained such a conflation. Nevertheless, my point is that film viewers, at any rate, taking the lead from Elizabeth Gaskell's fictitious character, have invariably connected the name *Frankenstein,* through Boris Karloff's 1931 characterization, with that of the Monster. This dramatic misreading against an explicit directive in the texts themselves (both print and visual) is quite extraordinary and underlines the dehistoricization of the sublime that takes place in the the subject because, as Kant pointed out, the sublime is always the objectification of the unpresentable within us.

Frankenstein cannot be read as a single, unified text. Like the paradigmatic precursor text (*The Castle of Otranto*), which underwent a process of expansion and rewriting, *Frankenstein* (and the Gothic generally) must be read as a "process" inextricably linked to other, not necessarily novelistic, semiotic systems. Mel Brooks' film spoof *Young Frankenstein* (1974) may be taken as an example of this process of expansion and rewriting, since its target texts (for purposes of parody) are the multiplicity of texts inspired by the original. Apart from Mary Shelley's work, the crucial intermediate texts of this film would include Peake's 1823 stage version, the 1931 film version, Whale's subsequent extension of the theme in *The Bride of Frankenstein* (1935), the Dracula films, and, finally, all these texts as interpreted through a much more alert and critical reading of the female (Gothic) sublime. In another important postmodern film—Ridley Scott's *Blade Runner* (1982/1993)—the sublime Monster gets transformed into replicants (sixth generation human mutants) who now challenge the moral primacy of humans and their proprietorial claims to complete emotional plenitude. The discourse of Mary

Shelley's Monster is distributed, in the main, through the completely assimilated female replicant Rachel and the golden, Prometheus-like, Batty. It is the latter who is the voice of the moral dilemma of a creator's responsibility that the Monster had raised with Frankenstein. "It is not an easy thing to meet your maker," says Roy Batty to Dr. Tyrell, and asks, "Can a maker repair what he makes?" Can the maker countenance this sublime request? The answer is in the negative because the consequences of granting the request would be far too horrible as Frankenstein himself had realized when he refused to grant the Monster his request for a bride. In the case of Roy Batty the creator's refusal to grant him a longer life turns to violence as the son literally gouges his father's eyes out. Ridley Scott's *Blade Runner,* then, turns the table on humans by giving the morally unimpeachable position to Batty who, in a further twist to the Monster's original dialogue, introduces the elements of slavery, fear, and death into the precursor narrative of Mary Shelley. Writing in an age which had yet to know the technologies of genetic engineering and the full potential of the digital revolution, Mary Shelley could only offer the bare outline of the scientific side of her creation. Her sense of the moral crisis is, however, another matter and her Monster's discourse in this regard is the exemplary text. In a futuristic Los Angeles of acid rain and Piranesian architecture, the same discourse of the sublime is replayed with a more complex and difficult emotional content because the levels of representation have become correspondingly more complicated. The ethics of responsibility are finally presented to Deckard, the pursuing Frankenstein figure and, in the 1993 director's version of the film quite possibly a replicant himself, who can only listen, fearfully, to the powerful counter-discourse of the Monster/Batty: "Quite an experience to live in fear. That's what it is to be a slave. I've seen things you people wouldn't believe. All those moments will be lost in time like tears in rain." Where *The Bride of Frankenstein* had ended with the Monster's Conradian utterance, "We belong dead," *Blade Runner* offers a longer text of Kurtzian horror written in the shadow of the Gothic sublime of Mary Shelley.

Of all the texts of the Gothic read in the preceding chapters and in the next, *Frankenstein* has the most extensive postmodern bibliography and vocabulary. It is also a text that can be read most effectively as presaging the technological sublime of late capital. The kind of intellectual payoff one gets from reading *Frankenstein* in the last decade of the twentieth century is radically different from and yet nostalgically connected to its contemporary reception.

We must now return to the text itself as an instance of what Wallace Stevens said about modernist decreation, "Modern reality is a reality of decreation" as (after Simone Weil) "making pass[es] from the created to the uncreated."[63] What the sublime as decreation meant to Mary Shelley takes us back, initially, to her remarkable introduction to the 1831 edition of *Frankenstein.*

In search of a theme on which to build her narrative, Mary Shelley, as we've already seen, reflects on Byron and Shelley's discourses on galvanism and the reanimation of the dead, but not before the idea gets transformed into a dream/hallucination/vision. Like Horace Walpole's dream of the figure walking off a portrait, Mary Shelley's vision, as recounted in the 1831 introduction, cannot be given a "preliterary" priority. What happens in her recollection of the "real" vision of 1816 is that the literary discourse of *Frankenstein* invades the autobiographical moment and effectively displaces it. In other words, what she recalled in her 1831 introduction were no more than snippets from the already-written text (1818) and not fragments of a dream/vision in need of artistic ordering. The moment is retrospectively endowed with meaning; it is not the origin of the text which followed. The dream/vision in the 1831 introduction is far too complete to be a dream (which it is only after a fashion) and lacks the ambiguity of a center that lies at the heart of any dream. For this reason the 1831 introduction is not so much an account of the genesis of *Frankenstein,* as its consequences, in the sense that the text sharpened perception and allowed Mary Shelley to reinterpret her own biography in the light of *Frankenstein.* For what this vision/dream indicates so clearly is not so much its own status as the italicized dream-text of Freud, but as his commentary on it. In other words, Mary Shelley's dream is not Freud's italicized dream-text, even though Mary Shelley proposes to present it as such. In this vision/commentary, the original moment of the sublime as creation is now transformed, through a phantasmal or monstrous semantics, into decreation and deformity. A "hideous phantasm" brought to life by "some powerful engine" (with echoes, as in *Caleb Williams,* of the slang word for "penis") is described as "frightful," "odious handywork," "hideous corpse," "the horrid thing," and so on. When Mary Shelley opens her eyes, she is possessed by "terror" and stalked by images of "my hideous phantom." The impact is such that the book she writes also appears to be monstrous.[64]

To create the Monster is akin to the momentary glimpse into the sublime, a moment, in the Kantian economy, when reason allows imagination to see in the terrifying, the unpresentable, the moment of self-annihilation and destruction. *Frankenstein* the text has as its center not the creator but the created, not God but man. Man displacing God desecrates the sanctity of creation; man transplanting God decreates himself as Monster. The latter, as the primal desecration/decreation, requires for its enunciation the categories of myth. But any reading through the primary myth given in the subtitle, "The Modern Prometheus," cannot simply reslot the text into this narrative antecedent; it must see the subtitle as the moment of the uncanny. Such is the ambiguity of the connecting conjunction ("or") between the title and its subtitle that it would be wrong to interpret, unproblematically, "The Modern Prometheus" as representing Frankenstein. Caleb Williams is not "Things as They Are," just as Hermsprong is not "Man as He Is Not." If the Monster as well as Frankenstein are the Modern Prometheus, then man and Monster effectively share the same myth of origin and, by extension become a *Doppelgänger*, images of one another. Prometheus connects with the Sanskrit *pramantha,* a stick used for rubbing wood to produce fire. *Pramantha,* in Sanskrit, also displaces *mānu,* the primal human, which is arguably the root form of the many forms of "man" in later Indo-European languages. Thus, through a figurative transposition "man" and "monster" in *Frankenstein* are the same thing.

What is unleashed is the destructive force of the uncanny. It is a "monstrous potentiality" that, as Peter Brooks explains, is so close to us, "too *heimisch* for comfort," that we repress it through negation, through an *un*.[65] As a consequence, like the Monster, who remains locked in the *imaginary* and fails dismally to enter the *symbolic* logic of culture since the female monster, his only hope for a fully developed systemic difference, is destroyed at the very moment of creation, we as readers are also faced with the consequences of putting our faith in the sublime. We emerge scarred by the experience of our own dissolution, our own regression in the unformed, decreated being incapable of self-transcendence. In writing about the Monster, Mary Shelley also writes herself out of the positive Romantic sublime. The concluding sentences of Peter Brooks' suggestive essay offer precisely this theory of the sublime without in fact mentioning it by name.

> The text solicits us through the promise of a transcendent signified, and leaves us, on the threshold of pleasure, to be content with the play of its signifiers. At the same time, it

> contaminates us with a residue of meaning that cannot be explained, rationalized, but is passed on as affect, as taint.[66]

How is this effect achieved? What strategies does Mary Shelley employ? What I propose to do is to pursue a specific argument in line with the overall theme of this chapter: how does Mary Shelley read ends through the unholy concept of desecration/decreation? And, furthermore, what is so specifically sublime about this? Structurally, the text is simply a manuscript that is attached to a letter sent to Mrs. Margaret Saville by her brother Walton, an explorer dedicated to discovering new routes and sea passages through hitherto unexplored and impassable frozen seas. In the opening pages he recounts his vision of the Arctic sublime against the common wisdom of "frost and desolation." "There," he writes, ". . . the sun is forever visible . . . there snow and frost are forever banished; and sailing over a calm sea, we may be wafted to a land surpassing in wonders and in beauty every region hitherto discovered on the habitable globe" (1831: 9–10). Walton's ideal descriptions are the other side of the sublime as the tremendous agency of the Arctic cold where, among the orthodox, "nature was somehow vaster, more mysterious, and more terrible than elsewhere."[67] Toward the end of the novel the Arctic sublime takes on a vastly different form, as Walton begins to repeat the terror of being surrounded by "mountains of ice" (210, 211). In this version the Arctic now becomes another trope of the sublime to be added to the list of obscurity, vastness, and magnificence handed down by the historical sublime. The abyss, then, subdues Walton and, like the Romantic subject confronted by the infinite, he retreats into the reality principle. As an extension of this, at the level of the narrative itself we find an excessive desire on the part of Mary Shelley to give the work a degree of realist legitimacy. Indeed, the reconstructions of the various fragments into unities so that the narrative within a narrative within letters has a realist underpinning is confirmed over and over again. "The story," as Frankenstein explained to another listener of the tale, the Swiss magistrate, "is too connected to be mistaken for a dream" (196–97). The claim is made by Frankenstein, who, in defending himself against possible accusations of madness (whoever heard of a creation like this?), insists on the linearity of the narrative, its continuity and "connectedness." But this is not the whole story, in fact not even a small part of the whole tale, because both the utopianism of the Arctic sublime (as seen by Walton's refusal to accept received wisdom) and the generic framing in the opening pages tell a different story. What strikes us soon after Walton's persuasive descriptions of the Arctic is the self-conscious echo of Rousseau's *The Confessions* in Frankenstein's own narrative (Rousseau, one remembers, had no time for those necessary repressions endorsed by the state apparatus as essential for maintaining culture). Frankenstein begins, "I am by birth a Genevese" (27). Against this let us place Rousseau's autobiographical introduction: "I was born at Geneva in 1712."[68] One of the reasons why Mary Shelley adopts *The Confessions* as her model is that Rousseau's birth led to his mother's death: "my birth was the first of my misfortunes."[69] What happens is that the Rousseau intertext breaks the "connectedness" of *Frankenstein*'s narrative and introduces Mary Shelley's own personal biography. In this manner the claim to realist linearity is undercut through a collapse of the narrator embedded in the text, Frankenstein, and the author, Mary Shelley. The consequences of this and its importance to feminist readings of *Frankenstein* have already been demonstrated and I need not repeat myself on that score. What the collapse indicates, furthermore, is the illusory nature of the structural dependencies constructed in the text: the tale of Frankenstein, incorporating the tale of the Monster, incorporating the tale of the De Lacey family and Safie. These tales, mediated through Frankenstein's master narrative, are then "addressed" to Mrs. Saville by Walton. This is the connection that Frankenstein emphasizes; he sees history as a narrative of interconnected wholes, relatively discrete moments that can be distinguished, on grounds of unity and coherence, from the chaos of signifiers that make a dream-text.

But *Frankenstein* is anything but a series of interdependent narratives. It is instead a narrative of excessive duplication and reduplication of dreamlike regressions and endless mirroring. The structure enforces a design that in reality does not exist; the narrators get locked into each other's uncanny tales, confounding the laws of logic. For every crime that the Monster commits, the prime suspect for the dispassionate observer must be Frankenstein himself. Thus, Frankenstein's claim that the story is far too connected to be mistaken for a dream is something he would dearly wish to believe in, and believe he does, only to be confounded by it toward the end of his own life. It is for this reason that classic Hollywood cinema (the cinema of absolute linearity) has never been able to do full justice to *Frankenstein* in the manner in which the expressionist Friedrich Wilhelm Murnau did to the vampire myth (*Nosferatu*, 1922).

From Walton's vision of the Arctic sublime and Frankenstein's vain hope about the linearity of his story, we move inexorably to the source of the horror itself, the Monster whom Frankenstein creates and whose actions implicate him at every step, both socially and psychologically. At the risk of being selective, it is the creation of the Monster and his relationship to both Frankenstein and Mary Shelley that will be our concern in the final section of this chapter. The creation itself is, as I've said before, the moment of the sublime; in collapsing the two domains of the formation of the subject—sexual *and* social reproduction and production—through the "artificial womb,"[70] Victor Frankenstein pushes the sublime to its very limits.[71] The "artificial womb" is, however, referred to as "my workshop of filthy creation" (50), described in suitably Gothic terms ("separated from all the other apartments by a gallery and staircase"), where "bones from charnel houses" were kept. "My workshop of filthy creation" is appropriately ambiguous, since "filthy" might refer equally to the "work-shop" (the artificial womb) and to the "creation" (the child-to-be, the Monster). The creator, too, is referred to as "profane," a word that enters dramatically into an oppositional set with "sacred." In constructing the site of creation, Frankenstein is simultaneously defiling and desecrating the creative process. Against the Miltonic precursor text of creation, where life is infused by an unseen God, Mary Shelley's creation is all artificiality, the parodied handiwork of a deranged surgeon.

Yet the moment of "conception" is unaccountably qualified by the modality of "might": "I collected the instruments of life around me, that I might infuse a spark of being into the lifeless thing that lay at my feet" (52). There is something missing between the collection of the "instruments of life" (which are not specified) and the desire to "infuse a spark of being" made so tentative and ambiguous through "might." What is happening is a kind of a filmic cut, representation through montage: two quick shots of the process followed by one of the product, "the dull yellow eye of the creature open[ed]; it breathed hard, and a convulsive motion agitated its limbs." Frankenstein reacts in "catastrophic" terms, and he implicitly opposes what should have been "beautiful" ("I had selected his features as beautiful") with what is inexpressible, the sublime:

> Beautiful!—Great God! His yellow skin scarcely covered the work of muscles and arteries beneath; his hair was of a lustrous black, and flowing; his teeth of a pearly whiteness; but these luxuriances only formed a more horrid contrast with his

> watery eyes, that seemed almost of the same colour as the dun white sockets in which they were set, his shrivelled complexion, and straight black lips. (52)

About eight feet tall (49), the creature as described carries disturbing resonances of early nineteenth-century stereotypical descriptions of black men and women. The Whale/Boris Karloff version of the Monster, with a square face put in place with nuts and bolts, makes him a distorted European; Mary Shelley's description is a composite figure constructed from the newborn baby with its cover of "wax" and almost transparent skin, and the black person as Other, represented in such exhibitions as that of the "Hottentot Venus" in 1810.[72] The description leads to rejection, disgust, and horror. Just as Mary Shelley was disturbed by a dream/vision, and retrospectively superimposed, it seems to me, the 1818 description on her own recollection of the event in 1816 penned in 1831, so, too, is Frankenstein. The dream he has is about necrophilia, confusion of identities, incest, and the death of his mother.

> I thought I saw Elizabeth, in the bloom of health, walking in the streets of Ingolstadt. Delighted and surprised, I embraced her; but as I imprinted the first kiss on her lips, they became livid with the hue of death; her features appeared to change, and I thought that I held the corpse of my dead mother in my arms; a shroud enveloped her form, and I saw the grave-worms crawling in the folds of the flannel. (53)

There are two inter-related moments of "chaos" here. The first is a straightforward premonition of the deaths to come—the Monster, as harbinger of death, is like a plague: in the frozen north, he seems to exist as the only survivor. The second moment is the chaos attendant on an unresolved Oedipus complex.[73] Not subject to the censor of the superego, the Monster is the unconscious manifested, Frankenstein's *unheimlich*. And in this "manifest unconscious," Mary Shelley, too, is finally trapped. The form that her "presence" takes is in the "unsayable or unpresentable of discourse and representation,"[74] in the refusal by the phallocentric order to create a female companion for the monster.

It is, after all, Frankenstein who "names" his "being" or "lifeless thing" a "monster" (53). It is he who continues "denaming" him through variations on "monstrosity": "creature," "hideous guest," "my enemy," "dreaded spectre," "object," "wretch," "the filthy daemon," "my own vampire," "fiend," "devil," "vile insect," "wretched devil," "abhorred devil," "odious companion," and so on. And the final signified of all these monstrous "denaming" is none other than Frankenstein, who, on destroying the female monster, walks "like a restless spectre" (167) and calls his own action "unhallowed" (1831: 247), a desecration. In a monstrous parody of the Hindu ritual of scattering the bones and ashes of the dead into the water, he carries the "remains of the half-finished creature" (167) in his boat and, in total darkness, drops them into the sea.

This rejection of the Monster by Frankenstein is complete at the very outset and, as the Monster's account of Frankenstein's "journal of the four months" (126) before his creation shows, he was rejected by his creator during the process of creation itself. As an act of willful self-defiance, an egotistical expression of the impossible, the creation, for Frankenstein, was an end in itself. The creator, like Volney's Legislator, embodied only abstract qualities of Reason, Law, Justice, and Freedom, not their emotional or social significance. The release of the created into history, into the social order, was not of any consequence whatsoever to him. It is the failure of social responsibility, the failure to be a "mother" to be able to repeat the mother's role beyond that of a mechanical creator, to be able to love even the deformed child, that finally leads to Frankenstein's enormous failure. Unlike James Whale's version, where the Monster's actions are explained in crude geneticist terms (after all, he was given a criminal's abnormal brain), in Mary Shelley's *Frankenstein* it is social "misconditioning," a kind of racist exclusion of the Other, that leads to the Monster's rejection. Frankenstein is like Mrs. Moritz, who "through a strange perversity" (60), could not love her third child Justine.

The rejection also leads to a failure to express in language one's feelings. The "release" of the Monster from the labyrinths of the unconscious only leads to feelings that cannot be objectified. "I cannot pretend to describe what I then felt" (80), "My abhorrence of this fiend cannot be conceived" (87), are not uncommon expressions of Frankenstein. The failure to objectify in language, the failure to represent—issues central to the aesthetics of the sublime—is finally confronted almost midway through Frankenstein's own narrative. In rewriting the chapter in which the encounter between Frankenstein and the Monster really occurs, Mary Shelley rewrote her discourse in much more centrally sublime terms. The first paragraph of volume 2, chapter 2 (10) is extensively rewritten for the 1831 edition. Part of the editing reflects Mary's desire to exclude

Frankenstein's father and Elizabeth from the narrative at this juncture, but more important, the rewriting reflects a conscious reworking of the discourse along distinctly Romantic/Kantian lines. It is not that Mary was not aware of the existence of the sublime. In the 1818 text the "sublime and magnificent scenes" give Frankenstein the "greatest consolation" (91). In the 1831 rewriting the emphasis shifts from sheer "magnificence" and "consolation" to the vast mountains and huge precipice, in fact to the "colossal."

> The abrupt sides of vast mountains were before me; the icy wall of the glacier overhung me; a few shattered pines were scattered around; and the solemn silence of this glorious presence-chamber of imperial Nature was broken only by the brawling waves, or the fall of some vast fragment, the thunder sound of the avalanche, or the cracking, reverberated along the mountains of the accumulated ice, which, through the silent working of immutable laws, was ever and anon rent and torn, as if it had been but a plaything in their hands. (1831: 249)

The same version of the Romantic sublime haunts Frankenstein's sleep. When he is asleep, the sublime functions like the ministers of dreams; awake, a "dark melancholy" takes over. It is important for Mary Shelley to get the setting right. Already, in 1823, she had made a number of changes to the Thomas copy of the text at this point in the narrative. In place of the sublime as the "absolutely great," we now meet the sublime as the extremities of human experience, as the distorted reflection of one's own self, as the apocalyptic side of the living man. Against Frankenstein's predictable "denamings" through "shape," "sight tremendous and abhorred," "Devil," "vile insect," and "daemon"—terms meant to exclude the Monster from the realms of the rational, the human—the Monster effectively says, But I am you, I am indissolubly bound to you, I am the destructive potential, the return of the repressed, the chaos you have artificially kept in check.

> Remember, that I am thy creature: I ought to be thy Adam; but I am rather the fallen angel, whom thou drivest from joy for no misdeed. (95)

The Miltonic connection is far too obvious. What is not so clear is whether the Monster is in fact saying that whereas God created Adam, you created Satan. It is this strange reversal that Frankenstein is unwilling to see. And the Monster knows it. He puts his "hated hands" before Frankenstein's eyes so that he is not forced to see. But hear he must a tale of primal beginnings, an allegory of humanity's own history superimposed on the Other. It is the post-modern history of humans in a world bereft of meaning, a world where narratives collapse on one another.

"My form is a filthy type of your's [*sic*], more horrid from its very resemblance" (126), reminds the Monster, and the collapse of the creator and the created gets more and more marked. The collapse involves Mary Shelley herself as the first reader of the monster's "educational" texts: Volney's *Ruins*, Goethe's *Werter*, Plutarch's *Lives*, and Milton's *Paradise Lost*. Like Frankenstein, the Monster, too, cannot describe the horrible expressions on people's faces when they see him: "Who can describe their horror and consternation on beholding me?" (131).

Upon introducing himself the Monster immediately inscribes himself into the semiotic code of the "fallen angel." He repeats this in his own tale, when he describes his experiences with people as a hell that he bore within him "like the arch fiend" (132). Toward the end of his own narrative, these words of the Monster come to haunt Frankenstein: "I was cursed by some devil, and carried about me my eternal hell" (201), varied a few pages later to "like the archangel who aspired to omnipotence, I am chained in an eternal hell" (208). Frankenstein adopts the discourse of the Monster only to extend the metaphor of Satan and hell to include Satan's over-reaching ambition to supplant God. What happens in the process is that the crucial signifiers constantly return to Frankenstein as the signified, as the person whose life and language is an echo of everything else that happens around him. The subject, Frankenstein, constantly gets fragmented and transformed.

The fragmentation of the subject Frankenstein finally takes us to Mary Shelley herself and the problem of feminine representation in a patriarchal discourse. If, as Mary Jacobus says, the emphasis should really be placed "on woman as a writing-effect instead of an origin,"[75] then we must ask ourselves how Mary Shelley herself negotiates the "unauthored" Gothic discourse of patriarchy she has inherited. What does the female Gothicist do with a tale about the sublime as the absolutely unpresentable, the desecration of the processes of creation itself? What can the female Gothicist do with the masculine sublime and its master texts (Plutarch, Milton, Goethe)? What happens when the discourse of ends presented through the melancholic sublime (*Mathilda*) or the apocalyptic sublime (*The Last Man*) now gets reimaged as the filthy technology of mechanical (re)production? We return to where we began, to the woman in Mary Shelley. With this in mind, I should like to take up these issues, finally, by examining two moments of the female in the text. The first is the moment surrounding the ill-fated design to construct a female monster. The second moment is the "rape" of Elizabeth Lavenza by the Monster.

The Monster's tale ends with an impassioned plea:

> . . . but one as deformed and horrible as myself would not deny herself to me. My companion must be of the same species, and have the same defects. This being you must create. (140)

The demand for "a creature of another sex, but as hideous" (142) by the Monster is initially accepted by Frankenstein as a proper course of action to take to bring the Monster's reign of terror to an end. But the request for a female monster, it seems to me, shifts, for the moment, the role of a creator as inscribed in a text (Frankenstein) to the creator of the text outside (Mary Shelley). Would Mary Shelley create an embodiment of the monstrous woman, as James Whale with his sanitized version of the female monster was to do in *The Bride of Frankenstein* (1935)? In this film, one recalls, the bride is actually played by the actress who plays the part of Mary Shelley, the narrator. After initially acceding to the Monster's request, Frankenstein/Mary Shelley has cold feet. The reasons given for the destruction of the partly formed female monster are as follows. She might become even more fiendish and destructive than the male monster; she might be disgusted by him and turn to "the superior beauty of man" (163); the two of them might start a colony of monsters in whatever new world they may come to inhabit, worries that invade Ridley Scott's *Blade Runner* as well. Yet to form the female monster, to create a woman who is "de-formed," would threaten the norms of male representational rules that require women not to be monsters. The only way in which this law can be subverted, the sublime as the articulation of the monstrous female demonstrated, is to leave the production of the female fragmented, a trace, a disturbance in the text. Again Mary Shelley finds herself in a double bind, since the consequence of her refusal to accede leads to her own destruction as the other woman, Elizabeth Lavenza, who does have a legitimate place in the text as Frankenstein's lover. We, therefore, move to our second moment, the moment of the "rape" of Elizabeth.

Defeated, the Monster pronounces: "I go; but remember, I shall be with you on your wedding-night" (166). Frankenstein takes this as a threat to his own person and accepts the Gothic double entendre stoically enough. What the Monster is in fact saying is, I shall displace you on your wedding night, I shall dislodge the place you occupy, I will usurp the place of the signifier. All this makes sense in a Lacanian psychoanalytical economy, since the signified below the signifier/signified algorithm is always threatening to usurp the stronger position of the signifier. But in usurping that position, the "detour" the Monster, as signifier, must take is to kill the woman whom Frankenstein will not recreate, as a female monster (resurrecting the dream he had on the Monster's creation), for him. The plight of woman as the female monster-to-be—she cannot be represented and must be further mutilated—is repeated as the death of woman/Mary Shelley in the Gothic. The female Gothic makes its entry by removing women completely from the text itself. But the representation of the Monster's brutal act of violation is the classic literary representation of rape. It is the form that had stalked Gothic discourse ever since Fuseli's "The Nightmare" (1782), where we see the figure of a woman lying on her back, her head thrown back, her arms flung loosely toward the floor. The succubus sitting on the woman's belly and the horse protruding its head through the curtain graphically reinforce this reading. Frankenstein's description of Elizabeth's death duplicates Fuseli:

> She was there, lifeless and inanimate, thrown across the bed, her head hanging down, and her pale and distorted features half covered by her hair. Every where I turn I see the same figure—her bloodless arms and relaxed form flung by the murderer on its bridal bier. (193)

For Mary Shelley, entry into the received male discourse of the Gothic requires her to confront in an uncompromising fashion two of its central themes, the theme of female violation and the theme of the rendition of women as the source of birth. In radically renegotiating these, she subverts them through an excess that carves open both the sexual and "procreative" threats to women. The two unpresentable moments of the sublime—the moment of mutilated birth (and its double deformation through Frankenstein's destruction of the female monster), and the moment of rape—must be graphically demonstrated with, initially, a conscious collusion with forms of discursive representationalism one associates with the male Gothic order. But the aim of this collusion (to defy/deny sexuality/womanhood) is to push representation itself to the level of the sublime and disorientate it. This disorientation, this violence to the domain of aesthetics, requires that Mary Shelley present the creation of the Monster both as a desecration of the divine act and as a de-formation of such magnitude that neither the process not its product can be grasped. To underline this desecration/decreation she must repeat the process of creation, destroy it before it is formed as woman, so as to doubly desecrate/decreate. And then, finally, to make the Monster act out the ultimate threat to woman—the threat of rape—the monstrosity of the Monster acquires such a dimension that his presence is effectively removed from consciousness as he becomes, in short, the sublime. The absolutely great, the Gothic colossus, now silences the beautiful. There can be no return to the harmonies of the beautiful because the violence done to the imagination leaves us totally fractured. In this respect the Monster is literature's grand vision of the sublime.

7

The Gothic Sublime and Literary History

In the *Confessions of an English Opium-Eater,* Thomas De Quincey writes about the "architectural dreams" induced by the taking of opium. These "architectural dreams" are, however, represented through a recollection of Coleridge's account of a set of plates by Piranesi called *Dreams* that, according to Coleridge (as De Quincey recalls), "record the scenery of his own visions during the delirium of fever."[1] This is how De Quincey expands on Coleridge's account:

> Some of them . . . represented vast Gothic halls: on the floor of which stood all sorts of engines and machinery, wheels, cables, pulleys, levers, catapults . . . expressive of enormous power put forth, and resistance overcome. Creeping along the sides of the walls you perceived a staircase; and on it, groping his way upwards, was Piranesi himself: follow the stairs a little further, and you perceive it come to a sudden abrupt termination, without any balustrade, and allowing no step onwards to him who had reached the extremity, except into the depths below. . . . But raise your eyes, and behold a second flight of stairs still higher: on which again Piranesi is perceived, but this time standing on the very brink of the abyss. Again elevate your eye, and a still more aerial flight of stairs is beheld . . . until the unfinished stairs and Piranesi both are lost in the upper gloom of the hall.[2]

The "sublime circumstance"[3] made possible through a dual reinforcement—narcotic-induced dreams that in turn collapse into art, albeit Piranesi's art—takes us back to the problematic of the Gothic: what is the status of the Gothic experience, and why does it haunt the postmodern imagination?

In De Quincey's excited discovery of Piranesi the sublime is invoked as an irrational, fragmented analogue (in its representational forms) of the dream-text itself. The endless architectural duplication—the abyss structure—is a return to the Kantian "colossal," a means of containing, limiting (and yet releasing) the horrors of "splendid dreams" (which were anything but splendid) that fascinated De Quincey as well as Fuseli. I use the De Quincey citation of Piranesi's architectural profusions to underline the momentary fascination of the "Janus-faced mind" with the sublime. As we have seen, in the historical sublime, discourse itself breaks down because of the underlying tension between imagination and reason: what can be grasped is not equivalent to what is meaningful. Writing about the Romantic sublime Thomas Weiskel called this "the intuition of 'unattainability.'"[4] The Gothic sublime is shot through with precisely this problem of "unattainability" but where Kant and the Romantic sublime offered the possibility of self-transcendence, the Gothic subject no longer seeks permission for what is fundamentally an illicit communion with the sublime. The metaphorics of soaring and overcoming, of the triumphant return of the subject to the fold of reason, are now replaced by those of abyss and dissolution as the subject is dragged into the sublime object. The texts in which the sublime achieves this negative force are, of course, the texts of the Gothic.

The difficulties we have encountered so far in framing these texts take us to our original point of departure, to Kant's *Critique of Judgement*. What Kant does in his critique of aesthetic judgment is to frame the sublime experience so as to impose theoretical limits on the colossal. Since the infinite, as we have discussed at length in our earlier chapters, cannot be bordered, defined, delimited, it threatens the notion of the aesthetic itself. What it releases— what the sublime releases—is a philosophical threat to both an entire tradition of rational thinking and the assumed definitions of aesthetic domains for which the *parergon*, the frame, had simply been taken for granted. At the heart of the sublime as a "passage," a "process," without limits or frames, is the whole question of the presentation of what, in terms of the sublime, is unpresentable: "the sublime is *superelevation* beyond itself," writes Derrida.[5]

One of the key tropes that Derrida uses is the *"colossal"* (*kolossalisch*) to enable a difference to be established between the beautiful, which rests "on the idea of reason" (110), and the sublime, which presents "an indeterminate concept of reason" (127). Since Kant thought that this concept was almost too great and beyond the power of apprehension, and hence "*almost* too big for representation" (125), Derrida's citation of the *"colossal"* is worth quoting at some length.

> *Colossal (kolossalisch)* thus qualifies the presentation, the putting on stage or into presence, the catching-sight, rather, of some thing, but of something which is not a thing, since it is a concept. And the presentation of this concept inasmuch as it is not presentable. Nor simply unpresentable: *almost unpresentable.* And by reason of its size: it is "almost too large." This concept is announced and then eludes presentation on the stage. One would say, by reason of its almost excessive size, that it was obscene. (125)

The real issue for Derrida is that the "colossal" thus defies the *parergon* (the limit and the frame). As a concept the sublime presents (without actually presenting) the infinite, but precisely because of this it cannot be bordered, as the beautiful, an *ergon*, certainly can. Against the identifiable, limiting and limited beautiful, whose pleasure is positive, the sublime provokes a pleasure (*Lust*) that is negative. Where the beautiful endows life with a fullness of meaning and affirms a unity between life and imagination, the sublime, as the Gothic sublime so strongly demonstrates, can offer pleasure only indirectly and obscenely.

> In the feeling of the sublime, pleasure only "gushes indirectly." It comes after inhibition, arrest, suspension (*Hemmung*) which keep back the vital forces. This retention is followed by a brusque outpouring, an effusion (*Ergiessung*) that is all the more potent. The schema here is that of a dam. (128)

Like De Quincey's account of Piranesi, the sublime, a negative pleasure, does violence to the imagination and locks the subject into a dual process of attraction and repulsion, a double bind, so to speak, that constitutes "an excess," "a superabundance (*Überschwenglich*) which opens an abyss (*Abgrund*)" (129). In Derrida's rereading, which connects with Freud's reading of the "Uncanny," the imagination is afraid of losing itself in this abyss, the "privileged presentation of the sublime" (129). Even Kant's classic example of the "ocean" is essentially an evocation of the abyss that threatens to consume and disintegrate phenomena through a diluvian agency. It is the threat of apocalypse that is the spectacle of the sublime; it is the threat of self-extinction and "self-dissolution" that forces the subject to retreat back into the comfortable frame of the beautiful.

But as we have argued at some length already, for Kant the

law of the sublime has a curious power over the imagination. For a brief moment imagination is willing to forgo its own freedom, its own logic (which is bonded to a teleology of ends) to gain, again for a moment, an incommensurable power, but which gain, nevertheless, leaves imagination marked, injured, blemished, even dispossessed. The sacrifice made, the presentation of the object remains elusive, since the sublime "relates only to the ideas of reason" (131). It therefore refuses "all adequate presentation" (131). "But how can this unpresentable thing present itself?" asks Derrida. To this he replies with the paradox of inadequation (*Unangemessenheit*):

> Presentation is inadequate to the idea of reason but it is presented in its very inadequation, adequate to its inadequation. The inadequation of presentation is presented. (131)

Because of the inadequation, Kant must define the sublime as the "absolutely great," the colossal, without so much as a hint of comparison. Yet the comparison in the "absolutely great" surfaces in the margins of its own refusal to compare and to be compared with, in its other, occluded, negated phrase, the "absolutely small." Why one and not the other, since, ultimately, it is never the object but the self that projects the sublime onto nature which matters? Whether the "absolutely great" or the "absolutely small," the fact remains that it is the "inadequation of the presentation to itself" (144) which signifies the condition of the sublime.

I have used Derrida's commentary on Kant to suggest how even in the historical sublime the drawing back of the mind from the mystery of the sublime is not offered in an unproblematic manner. Indeed, the frames that one constructs to delimit the sublime and its effects also hide the impossibility of the act of framing itself. The image or the utterance is incommensurate to the object, but this does not destroy the absolute fascination of the mind with it. A compulsive urge to repeat the wonders of the unpresentable by being totally absorbed in them, now makes the fleeting moment of recognition of the repressed (the uncanny) also the elusive fulfillment of desire through dissolution. This, then, is the logic of the Gothic sublime, a sublime that has no essence of its own but which, like a master sign, feeds on all the texts of the imagination to supplement the willed encounter of the mind with the abyss. In this version Romanticism sees its opposite but mirror image of the return of the repressed.

Beyond the Precursor Text

Much of the foregoing is already known, since postmodern problems of perception, representation, and subjectivity are emphatically anticipated in the Gothic sublime. The analogy is enticing enough, so much so that in a simplified form the Gothic proposition suggests a postmodernity that has already been played out: to be modern is to be postmodern (Lyotard). But the attraction of eighteenth-century theories of the sublime requires, we have argued, the mediation of the Gothic, because it is the Gothic sublime (rather than the "historical" sublime from Boileau's Longinus to Kant) that speaks to us across the historical divide. In other words, what the postmodern inherits is the sublime mediated by the Gothic's rendition of the absolutely great, the unpresentable, as the self's own dissolution in and confrontation with death. The sublime becomes the radically Other to which we are compulsively drawn, without ever reaching it or conceptualizing it. What the attraction necessitates, however, is a dissolution, a merging into the oceanic sublime in the complex way in which both Schopenhauer and Freud have defined this concept. To make this connection explicit I would now wish to expand the precursor text. This I will do through commentaries on William Beckford's *Vathek,* Matthew Gregory Lewis' *The Monk,* Ann Radcliffe's *The Italian,* Percy Bysshe Shelley's *Zastrozzi* and *St. Irvyne,* Charles Robert Maturin's *Melmoth the Wanderer,* and Herman Melville's *Pierre.*

The central achievement of William Beckford's *Vathek*[6] was its appropriation and transformation of narrative patterns and forms of representations gradually reaching Europe from the East. At the center of Beckford's vision is a representation of hell whose "funereal gloom" (112) can be sustained only through an orientalist excess. In other words, European visions of the East, mediated through Gothic assumptions of otherness, now infiltrate the text and establish, in the process, a mode of examining the sublime that becomes an unconscious dominant in the many subsequent Gothic texts. Contemporary reviews of *Vathek* sensed Beckford's appropriation of orientalist discourses and narrative genres. The *English Review* began with an examination of the tales of the Arabian Nights, with their "wild, improbable, and extravagant" incidents that have a power over us similar to the "recollection of our early feelings."[7] When moving to an examination of *Vathek* itself, the critical discourse remains largely unchanged: once again the incidents are "wild and improbable," the magic "solemn and awful," the catastrophe "bold and shocking" as well as "striking, and sometimes sublime."[8] The power of Samuel Henley's notes (Samuel Henley translated *Vathek* from Beckford's French original and appended copious notes to it) as a narrative in their own right, a mine of orientalist references and anecdotes, is captured in the *European Magazine*'s concluding remark that the "Notes on Books outdo the Books themselves."[9] Again, the *Monthly Review* used the word "wildness" to describe these orientalist narratives as passing "beyond the verge of possibility, and suppose things, which cannot be for a moment conceived."[10] What we begin to see even in these sketchy citations are versions of the as-yet untheorized sublime that, in the words of Paul-Henry Maty, critic of the *New Review*, became for Beckford a "wild and sublime" machinery.[11]

Clearly, the phenomenon of orientalism did not begin with Beckford. Galland's French edition of *Mille et une nuits* had come out at the turn of the eighteenth century and was widely known.[12] What Beckford did with the orientalist narratives, however, was to leave them as open-ended anecdotes without giving them the kinds of narrative unities to which readers were accustomed. At the same time the excesses of eighteenth-century European discourses on the Orient or translations from orientalist texts are subtly parodied, with a corresponding undermining of their own literary status. There is thus an excess at every level: in the names given to characters, in Vathek's desire for endless gratification, and in the seemingly confused narrative itself. These features have led to questions about the way in which *Vathek* ends. Robert Kiely, for instance, asks "Where, then, *does* such a journey and such a narrative end?"[13] Our encounter with the "formidable Eblis" (111) is anything but terrifying, but this is because, though the Other (whatever lies "east of the dividing line"[14]) might be invoked, it nevertheless lacks any "adequation" in the existing discourses. Were such an "adequation" available, the program of orientalism itself would have collapsed. In other words, it is precisely because the Other is sublime that Beckford cannot possibly bring his narrative to a logical conclusion. Robert Kiely has written about the ending as "a consistent extension of the narrative,"[15] and up to this point he is correct. But then to say in the same breath that it is brought to "its only possible conclusion" is to ignore the orientalist intertexts that Beckford used in the first instance. These texts were certainly not marked by the kinds of teleological closure (the sorts of closure that would generate the sense of an ending) we associate with Western narratives.

If the sublime surfaces as a discursive excess in *Vathek*, the form it takes in Matthew Gregory Lewis' *The Monk*,[16] though similar in many respects, is of a different order. An excess of another sort, of sexual desire and its monstrous gratification in a fictive world of a "terrifying and essentially uncontrollable network of violent primitive forces and taboos . . . summoned into play by the dialectics of man's desire"[17] informs Lewis' conception of Ambrosio, the central character in the novel. The form that desire takes through sexual violation and murder is predicated on an initial act of sacrilege, in that Ambrosio's relationship with Matilda is quite explicitly connected with the violation of the Madonna herself. This particular symbolic violation is both blasphemous and, within a religious economy of values, unthinkable. It is in fact so "colossal," so grand (both as a concept in the mind and as an ambiguous referent), so unthinkable, that it cannot be grasped through comparisons. Beyond pollution and impurity, the Madonna activates in us feelings of the sublime. Yet it is Matilda/Madonna who makes the crucial move: "I lust for the enjoyment of your person" (89). The *Lust* that is provoked by Matilda is negative, an *Unlust* (*negativ Lust*), the pleasure of the sublime pilfered from Ambrosio (who is far too restrained by his monkish habits at this stage) and returned to him as a transgression. It is a double transgression though, since Matilda's attractiveness, the pleasure, the *Lust*, provoked by her, is Ambrosio's own fatal attraction toward the Madonna herself. "Oh! if such a Creature existed, and existed but for me!" (41) he had exclaimed on viewing a picture of the Madonna that had been the "object of his increasing wonder and adoration" (40) for two years. Ambrosio had fantasized, in pornographic terms, about this picture of the Madonna only to be confronted by its duplicate in real life: "What was his amazement at beholding the exact resemblance of his admired Madona?" (81). Of course, it was Matilda herself who had posed as the model for the Madonna in the picture, with the explicit aim of finally seducing Ambrosio.

Rudolf Otto used the phrase *"mysterium tremendum"* to explain the feeling of the self in the "presence of that which is a *mystery* inexpressible and above all creatures."[18] What Rudolf Otto had in mind was a numinous experience, a kind of a primal awe, which has a self-validating, ahistorical reality. In this experience, writes Martin Price, there is a "consciousness of the absolute superiority or supremacy of a power other than myself."[19] The *mysterium tremendum* of Ambrosio is, however, an awe that also demands self-destruction and self-dissolution, an experience of death rather than Oneness of being. In short, at the heart of this awe is a principle of compulsion, an urge toward an "endless dying" in the oceanic sublime, an endless duplication and reduplication through the uncanny: Matilda/Madonna gets transformed into Ambrosio/Antonia (brother/sister), Ambrosio/Elvira (son/mother), and so on. Matilda, of course, is the primary signified, since she is both sister and mother; her violation anticipates the rape of Antonia and the killing of Elvira. Both mother and daughter, for instance, have an uncanny feeling of having seen Ambrosio the husband/father before:

> Either I must have known the Abbot in former times, or his voice bears a wonderful resemblance to that of some other, to whom I have often listened. . . . "My dearest Mother, it produced the same effect on me. . . ." (250)

It is all a question of "effects," effects produced by Ambrosio. His grand sermons have an effect on the audience, but the substance of the sermons, let alone any of the words, is never given. And in these effects we get a reinforcement of the sublime as residing within the subject, not in the object itself. The mind, as the signified, offers fragmentary glimpses into the sublime so as to contain what Sade approvingly called the artists' "call on hell for help."[20]

When it first came out, *The Monk* was roundly condemned for its immorality and self-indulgent sexuality. In *The Pursuits of Literature* Thomas Mathias advanced the extreme conservative position when he wrote that the seventh chapter of volume two of the novel was "indictable at Common Law."[21] As a Member of Parliament (albeit a reluctant one), didn't Lewis realize his moral responsibilities? And if he did, we may well ask how he defined authorship and authorial responsibility. It is precisely this collapse of distinctions (the author as inscribed in the text and the author as copyright holder) that led to Coleridge's scathing attack on Lewis. In an unsigned review, he called *The Monk* the product of "an exhausted appetite," which required "little expense of thought or imagination." Did he mean that the text was far too explicitly immoral, or did he feel that it was simply unimaginative writing? Although conceding that the work was at least an "offspring of no common genius," Coleridge nevertheless denounces its "moral miracle" (in other words, sexual excesses), which only "disgusts and awakens us."[22] Coleridge, who embarked on a series of darkly sublime poems during 1797–1798 (*The Rime of the Ancient Mariner, Christabel,* and *Kubla Khan*), curiously missed the mark here. In reading *The Monk* as a text that was socially aberrant (and intellectually suspect)

Coleridge takes up the establishment's cudgel (some months later the *Monthly Review* also referred to the "vein of obscenity" that pervaded and "deform[ed] the whole organization of the novel"[23]) without so much as examining his own interest in the sublime.

It was left to the lesser critics, the regularly paid hacks of the periodical literature, to fill in the enormous lacunae found in Coleridge. Phrases such as "electric" and "'galvanic battery'" (applied to *The Bravo of Venice*, 1805) are to be found in later reviews.[24] Reviewing Lewis' *Romantic Tales* (1808), it was the *Gentleman's Magazine* that concluded, "no other living author is capable of producing pictures equally awful, new, and sublime."[25] This was written some thirteen years after the publication of *The Monk*, and rather belatedly demonstrates the possible hidden agenda of *The Monk*, which was no less than the program implicit in the quest for "adequation" and presentation of the sublime.

Ann Radcliffe, whom Thomas J. Mathias called "the mighty magician of *The Mysteries of Udolpho*"[26] wrote *The Italian or the Confessional of the Black Penitents* (1797) as an exemplary exercise in how the Gothic should be written. Her target text was Lewis' *The Monk*, which, as we have seen, makes a radical break with the prior tradition. In rendering the Gothic sublime as a compulsion to repeat the mysteries of the unconscious, Lewis predicated the sublime on the necessity to lift the lid on repressed sexuality. The metaphorics of Gothic desire underwent a violent revolution, which Radcliffe seemingly proposes to correct in *The Italian*. In the end, however, like Lewis, Radcliffe, too, retreats from objectifying the sublime, which becomes a consciousness of one's own individuality in a symbolic world larger than one's own self. As children of the postmodern we know that to think the sublime is to think the unthinkable: in rewriting her earlier Gothic heroes (notably Montoni), Radcliffe finally understood the agenda of the Gothic sublime. Consequently, she kept the unthinkable liminal, at the edges of being, so that, for the reader, the aesthetic form would compensate for the inevitable urge toward self-destruction—one recalls Schiller's reading of suicide in terms of the "inevitable logic of the sublime" here. The liminality of the unthinkable is what explains the high level of redundancy one discovers in Radcliffe's works. Whereas this is true of all Gothic texts, in the case of Radcliffe self-conscious repetition itself holds the key to her aesthetic vision. This feature is observed in an early review of *The Italian*, in which her antirealism is deemed to be a lesser evil than her repetition, which, according to the *Critical Review*, led to the writing of progressively weaker novels from *The Romance of the Forest* onward.[27] Yet this very repetition, the "re-" of all recurrence, is constitutive of the Gothic sublime, since the "re-" is precisely that sign of repression whose articulation must be delayed through repetition. This "re-" came to haunt her even in death as the male-dominated literary press began to connect her writing with her own life. Upon the posthumous publication of her *Gaston de Blondeville* (1826) the *Monthly Review* takes up its earlier comment, made in the context of Sir Walter Scott's memoir, by recalling yet again the fact that "she died in a state of mental desolation not to be described."[28] The critical ploy here is to equate the female Gothic with mental sickness, and it is clear from the contemporary criticism that this equation was not far from the minds of the commentators. A similar sexist position may be detected in a letter published in the *Spirit of Public Journals for 1797* in which it is suggested that only female readers can catch "the season of terrors."[29] In a selection entitled "On the Supernatural in Poetry" (the title is the *New Monthly Magazine*'s) Ann Radcliffe distinguished between "obscurity" and "confusion," pointing out that the former alone is the source of the sublime.[30] It is this fundamental distinction that seems to have been missed by both the contemporary critics and many later theorists of the Gothic. In rendering the Gothic as the expression of a de-formed imagination, the distinctiveness of the sublime—as obscurity—is lost to the lesser principle of confusion, which Radcliffe herself repudiates.

To write iteratively is to engage in textual repetition and redundancy. All of Radcliffe's works explore the same theme, and each later text is a variation on the one before. The Gothic sublime is thus an endless deferral of the principle of life as life seeks to evade the embassy of death. But this deferral lacks the certainty of the epic, and is, indeed, its complete opposite. The contradictory form of Schedoni as both originator of life (he believes himself to be Ellena's father) and its destroyer exemplifies precisely this central ambiguity of prolongation of life and its ephemerality under the shadow of death. The sprawling, inconclusive narratives of Radcliffe are a kind of search for prolongation, a glimpse into eternity through writing itself, though without the positive and simultaneous possession of eternity that Georges Poulet ascribed to the Romantics.[31] To possess eternity is to make the future part of the present (Boethius' *Nunc fluens facit tempus, nunc stans facit aeternitatem*), to possess the sublime, albeit fleetingly, is to accept a radical incommensurability between desire and its object. Perhaps one way of retheorizing this procedure is to suggest that in Radcliffe the child is not simply the mother of the man, she is her own mother; and those who die, like Schedoni, are already dead. The Gothic sublime plays with these basic ontologies by making them "obscure," not by making us confused. For, at the level of textual practice, there is no confusion, only a willed attempt to redirect the sublime toward objects larger than the self, more threatening and, finally, profoundly nonpresentable to the imagination.

Radcliffe's *The Italian* opens with a version of the European grand journey ("about the year 1764"). In this instance the skeptical Englishman faces the odd logic of an assassin being harbored in a church. His cries of disbelief are answered by the guide, who tells him that the assassin's story had been enacted before, through a different set of personalities, and that there is a full written account of that enactment that may be read. A written text quickly reaches the Englishman, who immediately begins to read it. The fragmentary prologue is therefore a text that is yet to be written, but if it were ever written, will probably be a duplication of the three volumes that the Englishman, and the reader, will finish here and now. These three volumes will be an account of a "history" barely six years old, since the first meeting of Vivaldi and Ellena is precisely dated as 1758. The fragment need not be recalled ever again, and the novel ends with no further reference to the Schedoni-like assassin in the church. At the same time, the concept of the Gothic intertext, or more specifically, the Gothic as collective writing (which in this sense is really unauthored) is alluded to through two very distinct citations. The first is the reference to the year 1764, the moment of *The Castle of Otranto*, and the second is the epigraph of the first chapter, which is from Walpole's disturbing play *The Mysterious Mother* (there are two further quotations from this work in volume one). These explicit citations connect Radcliffe's greatest work with what we have already claimed in chapter 2 is the heterogeneous discursivity of the Gothic, that in fact the Gothic is one discontinuous text with ever-increasing levels of self-reflexivity. In the final analysis Gothic texts are fragments of the unconscious in need of analysis and commentary. But if we take the citation from *The Mysterious Mother* seriously, as I believe we should, then "this secret sin; this untold tale" cannot be extracted by art; the aesthetic object is not in a position to grasp the logic of the assassin's behavior in the church, since the narrative is beyond artistic representation. The fact of the Gothic is that it would still wish to write out, to express, to contain within a form, the inexpressible narrative of the self. It is for this reason that, at the level of content, the sublime-as-Schedoni is irreducible, his character never closed off because art cannot, finally, find a language that is adequate for his representation. Schedoni, in short, is too colossal, far too "terrific," to use the words of the *Monthly Review*,[32] so that any attempt at representational "adequation" invariably becomes locked into the aesthetics of the sublime. Judgment therefore becomes supersensory, as the mind desperately reaches out for the harmonies of the beautiful by grasping the generic antecedents of the fictive discourse. These generic antecedents are clear enough. There is the tradition of sentimentalism to which both Ellena and Vivaldi belong, there is the intertext of *Hamlet*, which provides linkages between Schedoni and Claudius, as well as numerous other *mise-en-scenes*, and there is the stark, architectural madness of Piranesi, with the "Roman arches" and "mass of ruins near the edge of a cliff."[33] The confessor as analyst, but the confessor also as possessor of sexual power over the Marchesa (like Freud, the confessor effectively rewrites the text of the analysand, the Marchesa), explodes on the Gothic scene so as to complicate Vivaldi's highly ambiguous relationship with Schedoni as a father figure. Since the *Hamlet* intertext looms so large throughout, Vivaldi acts out the trauma of Hamlet whenever he faces Schedoni/Claudius. As he sees him clearly for the first time, Vivaldi is struck by "something terrible in the air; something almost super-human" (34–35). Schedoni cannot be grasped by Vivaldi through the fullness of referential language but only through modal qualifications: his eyes "approached to horror," there is "something in his physiognomy . . . that can not be easily defined," his passions "seemed to have fixed . . . ," his eyes "seemed to penetrate . . ." (35). Vivaldi recognizes Schedoni's "evil genius" (48), his "dark malignity" (51), and is ambiguously attracted to him.

The starkly ominous vision of the Gothic sublime is often counterpointed in Radcliffe by the natural sublime, which has strong affinities with both sentimentalism as an anterior practice and Romanticism as a later reformulation. Perhaps one of the striking instances of this version of the sublime, which for Radcliffe is a kind of self-sustaining force variously referred to as the "vague and horrid shapes [that] . . . imagination bodies forth,"[34] the imagination "filling and expanding all the faculties of the soul" (347), is to be found in those moments when the heroine retreats from the oppressiveness of the world of the nunnery and its dungeons to the freedom of nature. The sublime here is also the spirit of democratization that, in its later avatar, is effectively the cornerstone of the American sublime. From her prison Ellena quite inadvertently stumbles on a small chamber with a view. This view of the "wide and freely-sublime scene without" (90), which Ellena later connects with a sublimity that seemed to "belong to a higher world" (162), has all the features of what Kant had referred to as the sources of the sublime. Yet even this essentially positive sublime leads to an awareness of the subject's own inconsequence, of her insignificance.

> The accumulation of overtopping points, which the mountains of this dark perspective exhibited, presented an image of grandeur superior to any thing she had seen while within the pass itself. (90)

"Grandeur" awakens in Ellena the feeling that "man, the giant who now held her in captivity, would shrink to the diminutiveness of a fairy." Here the sublime does become numinous, as a version of the divine presence within that makes life livable. The alternation between the two, the positive and negative sublimes, is an essential feature of Radcliffe's Gothic vision. It goes back to both Walpole and Clara Reeve, and reappears with equal force in Mary Shelley. But even the positive sublime is invaded by its opposite, its counterforce, its negative. "Ah! if it should enclose her!" (116), remarks Vivaldi on viewing the convent that is situated among such sublime scenery. The fear of dissolution is captured in the word *enclose,* which signifies the paradoxical manner in which the positive, enclosing space of the convent (the warmth of the mother) unleashes its very opposite, the patriarchal law of the castle. Outer symbols of the ever-present threat of this "enclosure," such as the ubiquitous white and black veils, not only mark a progress from the novitiate to the initiate, but also signify levels of seeing and viewing. The veil, like the Panopticon, allows the subject to view the world without being seen, and yet the white veil, less opaque than the black, allows the object of the initial gaze to see, though partially, the seeing eye. And the act of seeing the veiled, a glimpse into what is considered to be taboo, is defined by the Inquisition as an unholy act. In saving Ellena from the veil to which the machinations of the Marchesa and Schedoni have condemned her, Vivaldi seems to participate in a transgression, a participation in what is seen as sacrilege: a nun may not be abducted or married off. But the veiling and unveiling is not limited to Ellena. The Marchesa, too, appears veiled in front of Schedoni, who "unveils" her through a combination of flattery, power, and a highly trivialized definition of woman as a "weak and contemptible being" (178). In desperation the Marchesa hides behind her veil, which, along with the "evening gloom," "concealed her" (177). Later, during his trial, Vivaldi informs his inquisitors that the man who stood veiled in front of him should be unveiled: "I . . . command you . . . you in black garments, to unveil your features!" (331). The person unveiled, however, turns out to be a mere official, and not the enigmatic "informer" who had visited him in the dungeon. Though in this instance the veil hides nothing, its enormous symbolic power is encoded in the demand for the unveiling itself. The veil then becomes a sign of one of the crucial versions or elements of the Gothic sublime. It marks a space by seemingly cutting the subject off from the male gaze, effectively feminizing the sublime itself. Yet it is Schedoni who becomes most powerfully implicated in the sexual politics of the novel. In any literary history of the Gothic sublime his presence must be forcefully grasped.

Schedoni of the family of Bruno enters the text as a man with an already tainted history. "Some strange mystery seemed to lurk in the narrative" (380), concedes Olivia, once his wife, when the pieces of the jigsaw begin to come together. He begins to occupy the dominant space in the text from about the time that Ellena is forcefully abducted from the church just as she is about to be married to Vivaldi. For the last half of the novel Schedoni pursues/persecutes Ellena on behalf of the Inquisition but is finally condemned by it. The reversal in his fortune is a result of a mistaken belief that Ellena is in fact his own daughter. The scene of recognition and its immediately preceding narrative are two of the most powerfully written sections of the work. They occupy no more than twenty pages of the text and revolve around a house by the sea that has some of the characteristics of the classic Gothic castle. This "lonely (house)—inhabited by only one person" (177) has "a passage (that) leads to the sea" where dark deeds may be done: "'There, on the shore, when darkness covers it; there, plunged amidst the waves, no stain shall hint of'—" (177). It is in this space that the Gothic sublime expresses itself most profoundly to Ellena, first in the shape of the dark, "terrific" monk who follows Ellena on the beach and second as the would-be murderer who turns out to be her own father. There is a kind of violence done to emotions here that is clearly an act of emotional terrorism on the part of Radcliffe. It is true that such violence was used by Lewis in his portrayal of Antonia's rape by her own brother, but there the act was a further instance of evil.

In Schedoni's case the Manichean world seems to confront its opposite and becomes immediately transformed. The shock here is the greater precisely because the inversion is so radical, not that the action continues to be grotesque. The "stern Schedoni, wept and sighed" as he exclaimed, "Unhappy child!—behold your unhappy father!" (236). Yet he forgets to hide all trace of the dagger he had brought into her chamber with which to murder her. Ellena sees it lying on the floor, and Radcliffe uses it at least twice to remark on Ellena's conflicting responses. It is a manoeuvre that is part of the overall signifying practice of the Gothic. The dagger as patriarchal power and phallus is often used to portray the duality of the helpless maiden/daughter and the villainous persecutor/father. The dagger, in fact, is that sign in the Gothic that ambiguates seemingly straightforward social relationships.

Schedoni's sudden reversal of fortune—from the messenger of death to the protector of his own daughter—clearly leads to a strange paradox that the Gothic had not anticipated. In the absence of a realist concern for character, sudden changes in attitude cannot be related to an aspect of character through which, retrospectively, these changes may be explained. In short, the novel begins to become redundant as it searches for motives when there are none. In a parody of the telling of Gothic tales, Radcliffe offers us Spalatro's narrative, as told to Schedoni by the peasant guide. In this narrative the peasant is simply intent on telling the story in his own casual manner, whereas Schedoni, like the reader, wants to know causes. "Well! this history never will have an end!" (281), says Schedoni. At the end of it Schedoni is convinced that the "narrative resembles a delirious dream, more than a reality" (284). What we find here is a deconstruction of the Gothic sublime from within. The source of the sublime, Schedoni, now explains the discourse in which he is represented. The sublime, as history, is to him no "more than the vision of a distempered brain!" (284). These quite remarkable passages from *The Italian* offer us some of the most sophisticated statements about the enigmatic nature of the Gothic sublime: "You speak in enigmas, father," says the Marchesa to Schedoni, after he now presents her with a defense of Ellena. Schedoni dominates the central section of the novel completely, so much so that there is a break of a hundred pages before the "hero" of the text, Vivaldi, reappears, this time condemned by the Inquisition for daring to abduct and then attempting to marry a nun. The scenes in the Inquisition chambers where both Vivaldi and Schedoni are finally imprisoned are an occasion for Radcliffe to offer her readers the predictable descriptions of a Gothic view of the world. Here dungeons are extensively documented, each cell has a secret passage, dark figures move in and out of seemingly impenetrable walls, and there is an excess of narrative and counternarrative. Schedoni's past is revealed (he had murdered his own brother and forcefully married his sister-in-law, with whom he had a daughter who died in infancy); Ellena's confusion about her own father is explained through a narrative of doubling—the miniature she wore in her locket was not of her real father —and after a lengthy confession, which had to be written down twice, the Marchese accepts that Schedoni was not responsible for the death of Ellena's aunt Bianchi and gives his permission to Vivaldi to marry Ellena. The end of Schedoni is again stage-managed with a typical double poisoning. Schedoni poisons his accuser, Father Nicola, and then himself. These facts are also written down—the act of writing alone authenticates history. But by now the narrative has lost its real force as Radcliffe attempts to recapture, in death, some of the dark forces that controlled Schedoni's mind. In these last few pages one gets the distinct impression that she is composing in the shadow of Ambrosio, though she is not willing to give Schedoni the Faustlike alternative that Lewis had offered his own satanic hero. Instead, Radcliffe is content with Schedoni's "demoniacal sound of exultation" (402) and his almost convulsive fits. In the end all that Radcliffe can offer is the clichéd "a livid corse was all that remained of the once terrible Schedoni!" (404). Although the novel returns to its sentimental and romance roots —the hero and the heroine are happily married and a correct genealogy is established—the presence of Schedoni and Radcliffe's attempts to frame him within the aesthetics of the Gothic sublime have sufficiently disturbed the text. This disturbance, it seems, is really all that one can expect of the sublime at this juncture. The mislocation of sublime empowerment in the hands of Schedoni is characteristic of the design of the Gothic sublime in Radcliffe.

There is a direct line of descent from *The Monk* and *The Italian* to the youthful Percy Bysshe Shelley's Gothic romances. Published more or less anonymously (the author of the first of these romances is indicated only by the initials P. B. S.) both *Zastrozzi* (1810) and *St. Irvyne; or, the Rosicrucian* (1811)[35] have a clear agenda, which is the representation of sexual excess or pornography. In a significant way M. G. Lewis' *The Monk* is our first literary pornography, a sexual sublime that takes as its object sexual excesses that are not contingent on social restraint or responsibility. Lewis had, however, got around the question of censorship and authorial responsibility by framing Matilda's passion in the established discourse of Satanism and sexuality-as-temptation. Passions that were kept in check, superficially at any rate, in the relatively detached castle of Otranto are released, through this diabolism, on the unsuspecting world of the monastery. But the issue of "inadequation"—is sexuality ever presentable?—remains, and pornographic discourse, within the generic confines of the Gothic, is one of the distinctive aspects of the Gothic sublime. Not surprisingly, on its appearance *Zastrozzi* was seen by the *Critical Review* as the product of a "diseased brain," a "*shameless* and disgusting volume" displaying "barefaced immorality and grossness" through the "vicious, unrestrained passion" of Matilda.[36] Since "such trash, indeed, as this work contains, is fit only for the inmates of a brothel," the reviewer asks, "Does the author . . . think his gross and wanton pages fit to meet the eye of a modest young woman?"[37] The "execrable production" is of such an unimaginable vulgarity that it is in fact beyond redemption.

The *Critical Review* correctly identified the center of *Zastrozzi* in excessive sexuality/passion. I would like to pursue the same thematic, but with a slightly different inflection that would connect sexual excess with an underlying problematic of failure of representation in the aesthetic domain of the sublime. Troilus was conscious of this tension between infinite will and limited execution (". . . the will is infinite and the execution confined"), between limitless desire and contingent action ("the desire is boundless and the act a slave to limit"[38]). In *Zastrozzi* a vicious Matilda mutilates Julia because she refuses to impose "civilized" limits on her own desire. Without control, desire becomes murderous. In Matilda's own relationship with the doomed Verezzi we find precisely that subversion of decorum and propriety inadmissible in realist texts. So Matilda's confession of love is excessive in its insistence, defiant and full of sexual energy:

> "Oh Verezzi!" exclaimed Matilda, casting herself at his feet, "I adore you to madness—I love you to distraction. If you have one mark of compassion, let me not sue in vain—reject not one who feels it impossible to overcome the fatal, resistless passion which consumes her." (28)

In a significant way both public and private laws of censorship cannot permit explicit sex, and so Verezzi's rejection gets locked into a narrative of deflection. The moment of sexual union is deferred as the narrative urgency of the opening pages of *Zastrozzi*, with their forced adverbial syntax ("Rapidly did he . . . " forms), gets transformed into a syntax of endless sexual deferral. We read about Matilda's passion in the following terms:

> Her passions were now wound up to the highest pitch of desperation. In indescribable agony of mind, she dashed her head against the floor—she imprecated a thousand curses on Julia, and swore eternal revenge. (53)

The feverish language is pure Gothic, but the stock response also demonstrates an incapacity to find meaning in the world of action. Since action is sexual activity transformed into metaphor, it is only in language that an appropriate, imaginary fulfillment might be found. Matilda's passion is a "tempest" willing to entertain masochistic wounding. "The wound was painful enough," we are told, "but an expression of triumph flashed from her eyes" (69) as she now sees sexual victory around the corner. The sacrifice complete, Verezzi has no option but to give in to what he finds is a "Lethean torpor" (74, 84) and a "fatal ceremony" (76). "Lethean" and "fatal" connect the sexual act with the oceanic sublime, as Matilda's own "fierce, confused transports of visionary and unreal bliss" (77) remain "unalloyed by satiety, unconquered by time" (79).

Voluptuous passion "sublimed" (87) Verezzi, and it is at this very moment that Julia, thus far existing in memory alone, enters the scene. Infidelity to pure love and guilty sexual transgression (as Verezzi reads his seduction by Matilda) can only lead to suicide. Guilty Verezzi stabs himself:

> His soul fled without a groan, and his body fell to the floor, bathed in purple blood. (88)

But Matilda's reaction is different as passion turns to hate:

> . . . the ferocious Matilda seized Julia's floating hair, and holding her back with fiend-like strength, stabbed her in a thousand places; and, with exulting pleasure, again and again buried the dagger to the hilt in her body, even after all remains of life were annihilated. (89)

This is an extreme instance of the kind of symbolic phallic wounding that the precursor Gothic texts had suppressed. The hyperboles ("a thousand places," "remains of life were annihilated") insinuate a violence that fails to find an appropriate correlative in discourse. But the excess so released (albeit clichéd) demonstrates an element that is at the very center of the Gothic sublime. Even though the narrative frames of Shelley's romance emphasize Zastrozzi's wronged past and the necessity of vengeance on Verezzi and his father, it is the maddening/murderous nature of Matilda's desire that ultimately controls the text.

Percy Bysshe Shelley's next Gothic romance, *St. Irvyne,* though stylistically more interesting, is not as tightly written as *Zastrozzi.* It is also a physically flawed text in that its original design of two parallel narratives expanded over three volumes comes to an abrupt end in less than two pages. The politics of this form of writing is an important feature of the Gothic, and is clearly a variation on the games that Gothic writers played with the concept of "narrative origins." The usual translation and/or deciphering of obscure manuscripts is here replaced by a form of narrative that can be closed, artificially, at any time. In one sense *St. Irvyne* connects directly with both the palimpsestic and fragmentary proclivities of the earlier Gothic, since acts of structural vandalism aim at subverting the unproblematic teleological narrative of realistic texts. At one very obvious level this vandalism is conspicuously present. As in *Zastrozzi,* where chapter 7 is missing, in *St. Irvyne* too, chapters 5 and 6 are missing. These "missing" chapters do not necessarily indicate a gap in content or a radical thematic discontinuity, since there are equally glaring gaps between chapters where no such absence is marked. In a very real sense, a game is being played here, which is part of the literary history of the Gothic but also, in its aleatory dimension, part of an anticipatory discursive system that heralds postmodern practices. Apart from these very obvious structural games around missing chapters, *St. Irvyne*'s parallel narratives bisect each other without any logical connection whatsoever. Were it not for the hurried concession at the end that "Ginotti is Nempere" and "Eloise is the sister of Wolfstein," there is no way in which the reader could have made those connections during the actual process of reading. Clearly, the game is part of conscious authorial fracturing following the general imperatives of the genre. In a significant way, however, the fracturing is crucial to the central thematics of the text.

St. Irvyne is also about excessive passion and its unpresentability: "dissolution . . . suffering unspeakable, indescribable" are some of the opening words of Wolfstein, the Schillerian figure straight out of German robber romances. If we can quickly gloss over Eloise's narrative as a subplot that Shelley devised as a moral counterpoint to sexual violence and Gothic excess, we can then examine those aspects of Wolfstein's narrative that relate directly to versions of the sublime. The first aspect that emerges strikingly, yet again, is the nature and definition of sexuality. In place of Matilda we have the figure of Megalena, whereas Julia is replaced by Olympia. In fact, the duplication is so exact that it is difficult to keep their identities separate. Julia's threat to Matilda's sexuality is now transferred to Olympia, who loves Wolfstein to distraction:

> Her brain was whirled round in the fiercest convulsions of expectant happiness; the anticipation of gratified voluptuousness swelled her bosom even to bursting, yet did she rein in the boiling emotions of her soul, and resolved to be sufficiently cool, more certainly to accomplish her purpose. (144–45)

Since, like Julia, Olympia's "tumultuous passions" are "now too fierce for utterance," (145) she must be destroyed by Megalena, who persuades her lover Wolfstein to do the deed. In the quiet of the night Wolfstein steals into Olympia's house to murder her. His resolve, however, weakens as he looks on the lovely features of the sleeping Olympia. "I dreamed that you were about to murder me," she exclaims (151) on waking up and, moments later, realizing why Wolfstein had come, she clasps the dagger that Wolfstein had flung away and "plunged it into her bosom" (152). The syntax here again connects the moment of self-destruction with an entire Gothic tradition of similar stabbings. In the hands of Shelley the stabbing (a fate of all Gothic Matildas) insinuates a quasi-pornographic sexuality that must be silenced and censored because it cannot be contained or confined.

A second aspect of Wolfstein's story that requires comment deals with the figure of Ginotti, who persuades Wolfstein to enter into a contract with him. This contract has strong elements of the Faustian pact, and anticipates the other covenant between Lord Ruthven and Aubrey in Byron/Polidori's *The Vampyre*. In *St. Irvyne* the covenant remains somewhat obscure, because we are never told the substance of the contract. The kind of semantic absence or void we find here is characteristic of the Gothic, as are Ginotti's claims to foreknowledge:

> Every opening idea which has marked, in so decided and so eccentric an outline, the fiat of your future destiny, has not been unknown to or unnoticed by me. (171)

Ginotti tells a tale of Frankensteinian curiosity that led to his encounter with a "phantasm" who imparted to him the secret of immortality. Like the Wandering Jew, he can escape his tortuously unending life only if he can pass the secret onto someone else. But when the transfer is about to take place, the language becomes purposefully broken and discontinuous, as Wolfstein's "I swear" leads to incomplete predication. Their meeting place—the abbey near the castle of St. Irvyne, the site of Eloise's narrative—is given full "utterance," but the actual meeting itself, the transfer of the contract, is offered in a genre that is more like that of the fragmented Gothic. In less than two pages Wolfstein finds Megalena dead, and Ginotti himself is unable to transfer his contract onto Wolfstein, who dies without denying his Creator. As for Ginotti, his is Edmund's fate in *The Mysterious Mother*, as "a dateless and hopeless eternity of horror" lies in wait for him.

In the even shorter space of six lines, dramatic connections are made between the players of the two narratives, as we are told that Ginotti is in fact Eloise's libertine seducer and Eloise herself is Wolfstein's sister. The reader is thus asked to freely reconstruct the narrative and actively participate in constructing heterogeneous meanings in a manner not totally unlike Polidori's Doni fragment in *Ernestus Berchtold.* Our constructions of meaning are, however, complicated by Shelley's note to the publisher Stockdale (14 November 1810) in which the "death" of Ginotti is presented in decidedly ambiguous terms:

> Ginotti, as you will see did *not* die by Wolfstein's hand, but by the influence of that natural magic which when the secret was imparted to the latter, destroyed him.[39]

The overwhelming of imagination at the center of the Kantian sublime gets replayed in Shelley by the dual processes of semantic excess and structural discontinuity. The maddening frenzy of the language and the incapacity of closure (the latter a demand that reason must always make) clearly demonstrate imagination's simultaneous delight in the excesses of the sublime, as well as its own inadequacy. A not-fully articulated pornography, out of necessity, is locked into a narrative that gets progressively more and more fragmented. But in the tussle between representation and writing, the literary history of the Gothic becomes part of a larger process of undercutting and subversion. In *Melmoth the Wanderer* this difficult agenda of the Gothic sublime is made more explicit.

"None can participate in my destiny but with his own consent—*none have consented*— none can be involved in its tremendous penalties, but by participation."[40] Melmoth's destiny is so frightening that one would not wish to participate in it. Yet his attractiveness, nevertheless, is so strong that he becomes, in Stanton's words, "the necessary condition of [one's] existence" (59). In *The Monk* Lewis introduced a Wandering Jew figure to save Don Raymond. He had claimed that "No one . . . [was] adequate to comprehending the misery of [his] lot!" (169). A "burning Cross on [his] fore-head" (177) signified his eternal agony. Melmoth, the other Wandering Jew of the Gothic, is given a much more confined historical space, a period of only 150 years in which to find someone willing to exchange places with him. This limited historicity of Melmoth (which makes his life certainly more human than that of Lewis' Wandering Jew or Shelley's Ginotti) allows Maturin to write fragmented histories around the figure of Melmoth that are in themselves uncanny duplications. The many tales—of Stanton, of the Spaniard, of Immalee, of the Guzman family and so on—the many frames, *parerga*, delimit and make contingent what cannot be contained. It is this absence of containment, the failure of narrative to delimit and order (as the tale within the tale within the tale attempts to do so exasperatingly) that pushes Melmoth beyond the text to be "presented" only through "mediatizations": except in the very brief section entitled "The Wanderer's Dream" (538–39) there are few, if any, direct authorial intrusions into Melmoth's thought processes.

Melmoth, therefore, exists as a consequence of "effects," as an "impact" or an "imprint" on a series of receiving minds in themselves unstable, fragmented, and anxiety-prone. Melmoth's objective existence—in an uncanny echo of the impossibility of the objective existence of the sublime—is thus a construction, a presentation (albeit inadequate) of "horror" "unspeakable," (48, 270, 409) "unutterable" (535, 542) and "indescribable" (241). The writing and rewriting of manuscripts that follow—the endless copying, the stitching together of earlier redactions—are, however, accomplished in the shadow of an interdiction, an absent Other who is Melmoth. Nowhere is this interdiction, the force of the Other as the Patriarchal Law/Phallus, more marked than in Immalee's request for some sign of constancy. *"Will you be there?"* (323), she asks, the question italicized for emphasis. To this Melmoth replies,

> Yes!—THERE I must be, and for ever! And *will* you, and *dare* you, be with me? (323)

If we remember that Immalee has not seen her father so far, the confirmatory force of Melmoth's statement signifies the space occupied by Melmoth, as the Law, in terms of which Immalee's own subjectivity is constituted. Since the space is also that occupied by the absent signifier, Melmoth's assurance (that he'll be there, but on condition that you be there too) is also a threat of extinction that, for Immalee, is "consensual" participation:

> "Even where you are to be," answered the devoted Isidora, "Let me be there!" (350)

But having accepted the space occupied by the Father/Melmoth, Immalee/Isidora cannot escape from it, because the symbolic father cannot be grasped, as the unconscious cannot be grasped. It is for this reason that Melmoth offers an extreme version of "inadequation," since he is always in excess of presentation.[41]

To speak about the "unspeakable," to write about the Other is, in Monçada's words, as difficult as "analysing a dream to its component parts of sanity, delirium, defeated memory, and triumphant imagination" (187). Some contemporary British readers acknowledged the source of what the *Monthly Review* called "this exploded predilection for *impossibility*."[42] In a review, penned probably by William Hazlitt, the *London Magazine* acknowledged its "terrible, offensive power—."[43] It was left, however, to another generation of highly gifted French readers to sense the extraordinary energy of this work. Baudelaire referred to *Melmoth the Wanderer* as the "grande création satanique du révérend Maturin," and Balzac, even more enthusiastically, compared it to Moliere's *Don Juan*, Goethe's *Faust*, and Byron's *Manfred*, as sublime works of genius: "grandes images tracées par les plus grands génies de l'Europe."[44]

A compendium of what Coral Ann Howells called "dream states, schizoid states and paranoiac fantasy"[45] makes up *Melmoth the Wanderer*. The dream states take us back to Monçada's words about the incommensurability between words and phenomena, and beyond that, to Immalee and her failure to conceptualize the dizzying, vertiginous figure of the eponymous hero. The text, too, can only gesture toward his presence; it can only frame him (as it repeats its own fragmentary narratives), but it cannot totalize or "present" him to consciousness. *Melmoth the Wanderer* is its own narrative of ends, a version of apocalypse, the end of history.

The end of history in the hyperreal space of the Gothic takes us quite naturally to the space that is the source text of postmodernism, America. However, it is a much more precise reading of this geographical space that I would want to pursue here. I have in mind what Harold Bloom has called "the last Western Sublime."[46] This is the American sublime, "the great sunset of selfhood in the Evening Land," which Bloom defines through the trope of "self-rebegetting" (244). What he means by this phrase remains slightly obscure, but from amongst the quite dense series of references and citations he offers, it is possible to detect three distinct characteristics of the American sublime. The first is the desire to displace the father through an act of willed amnesia. This "willing" allows the subject to become its own origin, its own father in a world where the Law of the Patriarch no longer has the same moral force. The proof-text, as Bloom acknowledges, is Ralph Waldo Emerson who, says Bloom, "did know that always he was about to become his own father" (244). The fathering force (the precursor) and the new son, the poetic self, tend to merge together without defeating the aims of self-representation because the fathering force disappears into the poetic self, or son, rather than the son/self disappearing into the image of the fathering force. In the American sublime the freedom of self-democratization now opposes itself to self-daemonization, the cornerstone of the Gothic sublime. In one of the finest passages in Bloom's study, he offers a clear distinction between the traditional/Gothic sublime and the American sublime. In the former, the image of the fathering force remains aloof from what it represents (which is absent). In other words, the represented is overtaken by its representation or image. This is certainly true of all strong characters in Gothic literature. In the American sublime, however, the two tend to fuse together to make "self-rebegetting" possible. The second characteristic of the American sublime is implicit in the first, but may be isolated without trivializing its theoretical force. In the political sphere self-rebegetting leads to the democratization of culture and society because the sublime presence of the father is no longer an absent threat constantly in need of representation through an image that continues to signify its absence. Bloom quotes Emerson approvingly here: "A nation of men will for the first time exist, because each believes himself inspired by the Divine Soul which also inspires all men" (236). The third characteristic, again implicit in the first, is a reverse process of the daemonization of the democratic spirit, a "countersublime" that is the poetic equivalent of repression. Repression, however, is seen not as unconscious but as conscious acts of reading/interpreting the precursors. The sublime is somehow within the act as a process of negotiation and daemonization, a radical, if willed, inversion of prior certainties. To daemonize is also to "misprision" through terror.

For Bloom the American sublime is more or less identical with the Emersonian sublime. However, there is a major repression here on the part of Bloom himself. Concentrating on the early Emerson (and especially on his oration delivered at Harvard in 1837), Bloom fails to examine the impact of the *Bhagavadgītā* on the New England Transcendentalists, and notably on Emerson. In 1848 Emerson praised Charles Wilkins' translation of the *Bhagavadgītā* (on loan from James Elliot Cabot) in the following extravagant terms: "I owed—my friend and I owed—a magnificent day to the *Bhagavat Geeta*. It was the first of books; it was as if an empire spake to us, nothing small or unworthy, but large, serene, consistent, its voice of an old intelligence which in another age and climate had pondered and thus disposed of the same questions which exercise us."[47] The important phrase here is "questions which exercise us." If the key to the American sublime is to be found, as Bloom would have us believe, and persuasively, I think, in the idea of self-rebegetting, then where better to find a full program for this than in Krishna's words to Arjuna on the field of battle? Emerson does not read the *Bhavagadgītā* as a visionary text (as Henry David Thoreau did at about the same time); rather, he sees it in terms of the necessity for the "sentiment of duty."[48] The idea of duty is one of the questions that certainly "exercise us," because it raises the special nature of the relationship between the self and its precursor. In Krishna's version of the Indian sublime he makes two claims. The first is that the unity of being implicit in his own self makes genealogy a relic of the past, since he himself is action, he alone is knowledge. The second is the insistence on the sublimity of pure action, action without consequence, action that does not seek to find its fruit, its *phala*—in short, action outside the tyranny of cause and effect. This kind of "sentiment of duty" is indeed beyond representation, since the desire for duty is not locked into a material history. Perhaps here lies the key to Emerson's paeon on the American as one inspired by the divine soul. Emerson effectively participates, as a latter-day Arjuna, in the need for the pure, the sublime, *karma*. So T. S. Eliot, who is remarkably Emersonian in this respect, extols his voyagers to follow the lead of Arjuna:

> So Krishna, as when he admonished Arjuna
> On the field of battle.

The reference to the *Bhagavadgītā* allows us to reexamine Bloom's prioritization of Emerson's "two absorbing facts,—*I and the Abyss*" (255) in the larger context of the sublime. For Bloom Emerson's adversarial equation is really between the American and History, which is in fact the repressed content of this "chilling formula" of the American sublime. Again, what we must do is to recontextualize the nihilistic echoes of Emerson's equation through Krishna's own account of the abyss, which, in the privileged vision given to Arjuna, becomes something much more than an expression of discontinuities (Bloom regards the American sublime as essentially discontinuous). What Krishna presents is precisely the immanent in-dwelling of all spirit, the daemonization of the self, but also the collapse of the "I" and the "Abyss." For Arjuna to achieve this would require a concentration on purity of action itself. Reformulated, the precursor is now being displaced by the son, as Arjuna writes his own history. The three characteristics of the American sublime find their echoes in the *Bhagavadgītā*.

The chilling formula of the American sublime, which we suggest is essentially a version of the Gothic sublime, is extensively documented in Melville's *Pierre*, perhaps the last great account of the Gothic sublime.[49] Gothic sublimity in this text is expressed through two themes. The first is the theme of implied or actual incest toward one's sister; the second is the theme of sentimental love that would take us back to the desire for self-identity and dissolution in the object in the psychic economy of the *imaginary*, as outlined in Goethe's *Werter*. The possibility of the sublime moment degenerating or regressing into melancholy (sentimentalism) is one of the crucial determinants of the Gothic sublime. As Thomas Weiskel explains,

> Consequently, the sublime of terror may be characterized as an *episode in melancholy*. In terms of the history of sensibility, this suggests that the prestige and attractiveness of the sublime is a direct function of the prevalence of or predisposition to melancholy.[50]

Pierre is, of course, subtitled "The Ambiguities." At the heart of these ambiguities is Isabel, Pierre's half-sister, or at least someone who may well have been his sister.[51] The doubts that Pierre subsequently has about Isabel's claim that she is his sister (353–54) do not, however, destroy the original nature of Pierre's desire toward her and, therefore, do not affect the essential sexual dynamics of their relationship. What does remain obscure, and constitutes the object of the sublime, is Isabel herself, since Pierre is drawn to her in a doubly ambiguous fashion: as herself she is frustratingly plain and unattractive, but as someone seen through Pierre's mind (as the reflector of the sublime), she acquires a power that is at once threatening *and*, beyond that, destructive. As critics have been at pains to point out, Melville's refusal to specifically address the question of sexual consummation or otherwise is central to the crucial ambiguity in the text.

Pierre's life is presented early in the text as a "sweetly-writ manuscript," (7) marred only by the absence of "a gentle sister," "the second best gift to a man," but first "in point of occurrence; for the wife comes after." This doesn't quite make sense, since mothers have been known to give birth to daughters after the marriage of their sons. But Pierre is making a rhetorical point here to underline what can only be called an obsession with the idea of the absent sister: "For much that goes to make up the deliciousness of wife, already lies in the sister" (7). But what were to happen if, and only if at this point, the wish, the desire, were to be fulfilled, through a return of this sublime (since it does not exist, as representation, in Pierre's mind) through the law of the "uncanny" as its confirmation? At the moment of confession, of desire, Pierre is consumed by the absence of another [Pierre] Glendenning. Except for "the duplicate one reflected to him in the mirror," (8) his own image monotonously reflected, Pierre has no Other, though for the moment this specular self is a sign of triumph, of "monopoly."

The first glimpse of Isabel (as yet unnamed), the first image, which is not a duplication but a "difference," occurs with a figure of a girl who "sits steadily sewing" (46). The description here is "underwritten," as opposed to the hitherto "overwritten," nature of the discourse. It participates in what Burke was to term variations in the concept of the beautiful. "Observe that part of a beautiful woman where she is perhaps the most beautiful, about the neck and breasts; the smoothness; the softness; the easy and insensible swell,"[52] wrote Burke, suppressing a voyeurism that he lifts to the level of a pure idea. In Melville the heaving breast, Burke's "easy and insensible swell," is also the heavy breathing that suggests sexual excitement or terror. What we get, therefore, are a glance and a look, a glance that recognizes, though furtively, and a corresponding look (from the male gaze) that "reads" a close-fitting smock beneath which is a heaving bosom. This is read delicately enough:

> To a nice perception, that velvet shows elastically; contracting and expanding, as though some choked, violent thing were risen up there within from the teeming region of her heart. (46)

The initial moment leads to two kinds of feverish anticipation/ expectation. The first is an identification of this image with an ideal, such as the Madonna (recall Ambrosio in M. G. Lewis' *The Monk* here) and the second is a feeling of the "having-seen-her-before" (recall Antonia and Elvira in *The Monk* once again). In both instances what is occluded is the Other as unconscious memory, as a lost duplicate, whose return, as the image in the mirror, will now present to imagination something the mind cannot totalize. The sublime threatens Pierre with self-extinction.

The original image of the self in the mirror haunts Pierre even when he receives the fatal letter from Isabel Banford, in which she declares that she's his unknown sister. Even more interesting than the letter itself are the moments before it is opened. Lighting a lamp in his room (with the letter still unopened), Pierre is startled by a "figure in the opposite mirror":

> It bore the outline of Pierre, but now strangely filled with features transformed, and unfamiliar to him; feverish eagerness, fear, and nameless forebodings of ill! (62)

For the moment the letter, unopened, as signifier gives rise to a whole host of effects. Such is the power of the letter that the bad angel advises against opening it: "Read it not, dearest Pierre; but destroy it, and be happy" (63). The advice of the good angel, which he finally adopts, is curiously paradoxical, but centers on the crucial enigma of the sublime itself:

> Read, Pierre, though by reading thou may'st entangle thyself, yet may'st thou thereby disentangle others. (63)

The entangling and disentangling, the miasma of the uncanny that this implies, engulfs Pierre into a secret, a desire, a wish, he can neither fulfill nor represent: "But where one can not reveal the thing itself, it only makes it the more mysterious . . . " (94). This engulfing leads to an estrangement from the legitimate object of sexual desire (Lucy Tartan), from the legitimate mother ("Sister me not, now, Pierre;—I am thy mother," she replies [95]), and from the social order itself. To legitimate the illegitimate half-sister, Pierre "marries" her, and in so doing wounds himself (things get "foetally" formed in his mind) and his mother, who symbolically stabs her own portrait. The "force" that is unleashed, the feature that is constitutive of the Gothic sublime, is a failure of imagination, an incapacity to "image to [oneself] the scene" as "reality" becomes "too real" (111). It is about this time that we encounter a major intervention on the part of Melville. He inserts a section (Book 7) whose artistic center is the Memnon, or the Terror Stone.[53] The literary intertext of the stone here is quite possibly Wordsworth's extended simile of the "huge stone," " a thing endued with sense" by which he tries to represent, to imagination, the Leech Gatherer in *Resolution and Independence.* One senses in the analogy the typical device of representing something that once again emphasizes the uniqueness of individual consciousness, as Wordsworth attempts to ward off the immense attractiveness of the oceanic sublime, the dissolution of the "I" in the apocalyptic abyss. For Pierre the Memnon Stone signifies his special encounter with the sublime, a unique experience that, initially, he reads as a kind of a primal experience or encounter with this magnificent stone. The size of a barn and rounded like an egg, the stone gives rise to huge conceits, such as his claims of discovery (only to be disproved by the presence of initials carved in stone by someone else before him), the desire to have it as his own special "headstone" (133), and the wish to have this "Mute Massiveness" fall on him (134). The colossal stone is also the American sublime as discovery, an alien race chancing on the vast unmapped (to the European eye) continent, the naming and denaming of the landscape. But why has Melville situated the stone in this part of the book, and what explains Pierre's special fascination with the stone?

What the Memnon Stone signifies is nothing less than that which is unpresentable and unutterable to human consciousness. In its earlier formulation it had taken the form of an encounter, with the return of the repressed through the desired but so far absent sister. Just as the Memnon stone of terror incapacitates his imagination and forces him into fantastic analogies between Egyptian kings, the ancient civilizations, and the figure of Hamlet (a figure that invades so much of the Gothic), so, too, does the impossible construction of Isabel in his mind defy all his imaginative capacities. How can he tell his mother and his beloved Lucy that he has "married" his own sister? But when he whispers this knowledge to the sister herself, to a version of the Memnon Stone, something extraordinary, something so delicately ambiguous, happens:

> He held her tremblingly; she bent over toward him; his mouth wet her ear; he whispered it.
>
> The girl moved not; was done with all her tremblings; leaned closer to him. . . . Pierre . . . imprinted repeated burning kisses upon her. . . .
>
> Then they changed; they coiled together, and entangledly stood mute. (192)

There is a frame here that conceals, just as it is Isabel's hair that, like the *parergon* in Derrida, partly conceals convulsive clasps (190) and which also, finally, veils Pierre's dead body too: "and her long hair ran over him, and arbored him in ebon vines" (362).

Melville's *Pierre* takes us to the very heart of the Gothic sublime as something broadly akin to what Alice A. Jardine, exemplifying Lacan's "Real," called "the mystery of the unconscious," "that which is categorically unrepresentable . . . at the limits of the known."[54] As Pierre's mind disintegrates—Melville underlines this through the repetition of "he sits there in his room" (303), for instance—and he is engulfed, after the impulsive killing of his cousin Glendenning Stanly, by Piranesian horrors and a death wish, the final consummation of self and Other in the oceanic sublime is complete. Harold Bloom's "self-rebegetting" is possible in this instance only through the subversion of the sexual economy as Pierre desires a daemonization of sexuality.

The daemonization of sexuality is a powerful trope of the Gothic that pushes through the text as horrible elements from the repressed. In this respect, to the aesthetics of the sublime the Gothic made a decisive contribution by refashioning, rewriting, and retheorizing the sublime in ways that changed the subject of terror and its relationship to the mind. As both text and theory Gothic texts speak to us in urgent tones from across the historical divide, because in them we see the signs of our own times, in them we see images of issues and concerns central to postmodernity itself, from the weakening of historicity to an entire epistemology of dissolution that finds its grand and frightening metaphors in the nuclear sublime. We return to Mary Shelley's apocalyptic metaphors and the daemonization of the act of creation as the laboratory-as-mechanical-womb usurps a woman's privilege. In radicalizaing the *écriture féminine,* Mary Shelley "wrote" herself into her works, making her "body," her femininity, a site, a version, of the Cumaean writing machine, on which the Gothic sublime was superimposed. In the process, her works required the complex insights of perhaps the most postmodern of all readings, radical feminist practice, before they could be legitimately reclaimed and mobilized toward both political and aesthetic ends. The postmodern themes that underlie her works—themes of sexual transgression, apocalypse, and the end of women as source of creation, the bearer of the child—are precisely the themes that defy representation in the mind. Her fragmented Gothics insinuate the fragmentation of the Gothic/postmodern sublime; her decisive works challenge, through her own female presence, the stability of the referent and the unproblematic constructions of meaning.

If we conclude, without due regard to the mechanics of style that demand transition, by prioritizing Mary Shelley, it is because the transformation of the sublime from the historical sublime to the Gothic is so powerfully present in her works. In other words, confronted with the "colossal," the "absolutely great," the mind turned inward into its own unconscious, regressed into its own labyrinth, to discover, in the tangled web of its dreams, a depth from which it could no longer soar into the grand design of the Kantian/Romantic sublime. In the process (of writing out this confrontation) a marked schizophrenic tendency emerges, both at the level of the subject (forever on the verge of madness: Manfred, Caleb Williams, Schedoni, Ambrosio, Verezzi, Wolfstein, Ruthven, Melmoth, Mathilda, Pierre, Frankenstein, and so on) and at the level of the signifying chain (there is a distinct radicalization of the relationship between the signifier and the signified, the word and its referent).

Ultimately, however, we are confronted with a kind of a black-hole theory of the sublime. The black hole, which surfaces in Piranesi's paintings, "Interiors measurelessly strange, / Where the distrustful thought may range,"[55] or in Mary Shelley's feverish handwriting, takes us back to the essential problematic of the Gothic and the postmodern. The problematic takes two forms. The first, articulated so well by Kant, is the issue of the presentation of the unpresentable. Kant, of course, had seen that the representation of the "colossal," the absolutely great, can occur only at that moment when reason gives way to imagination for a fleeting moment before it regains its power. What happened during this gap, this lapse, this concession or giving way, is the coming into being of the moment of the sublime. The second, articulated by Schopenhauer and adopted by Freud, is the "oceanic sublime," the sublime as the dissolution of the self in death. It is the latter, the compulsion toward our own ends (in death), that explains the inherently apocalyptic tendencies in the Gothic as the subject ingratiatingly gets absorbed into the sublime object.

A literary history based on the Gothic sublime is thus a literary history that, in an uncanny fashion, demonstrates postmodernism's earlier moment of explosion in the negative sublime and connects Lyotard's nascent state(s) of postmodernism with the Gothic. This is largely because the literary Gothic, then, transforms a metaphysic (the sublime from Longinus to Kant) into a psychology by situating it at the level of character itself. In the process the Gothic sublime then shifts the assumptions that underlie realist characterizations by confronting the mind with representations that insinuate a repressive formula perhaps best summarized in Emerson's *"I and the Abyss."* Like Freud's own confession, the Gothic sublime "conjures up the most evil of those half-tamed demons that inhabit the human breast."[56] It is at this point that the metaphorics of apocalypse as self-annihilation and the end of the subject begin to rear their heads. For if, as in the nuclear sublime, the ultimate terror is directly related to existence itself, then its aestheticization (by Burke and others) can only be a screen that hides its real import. The subtext of the Gothic has always been a suspicion of the aestheticization of life and existence (Burke's the beautiful), and their representation, in the wake of bourgeois realism, in the discourses of containment and closure. Against the celebration of this orderly aesthetic, the Gothic sublime reminds us of the essential precariousness of the aesthetic order itself, especially since the link between the Real and its representation is fraught with difficulties and cannot be taken for granted. The knowledge that the Gothic sublime imparts is that the Real, as the sublime, defies symbolization except through ruptures in the psychic economy of the imagination (what Fredric Jameson in his celebration of the postmodern has called a "schizophrenic tendency"). In short, the Gothic offers an alternative narrative of heterogeneity in which the subject embraces, in spite of reason's interdiction, the lawlessness of the sublime. All this, of course, leads us to affirm the connection that has been implicit throughout this study: the Gothic sublime is crucial to our understanding of the postmodern sublime in literature. The return to the Gothic as arguably the most fully developed of all sublimes at precisely the point at which the postmodern becomes a legitimate cultural field for purposes of academic study surely indicates more than just a periodic interest in the genre. The manner in which it is being read now—and this book is a testimony to that form of reading—arises out of a much deeper sense of recognition between the problematic of representation in the postmodern and its prior expression in the Gothic. One does not, therefore, conclude with the simple statement that the Gothic sublime is the postmodern sublime. What one must do is to offer the Gothic sublime, rather than the purely Kantian sublime, as an epistemological apparatus for the understanding of a cultural force field called the postmodern. This is because in literature the Gothic sublime functions as a kind of a rupture in a "genealogy" that signals the beginnings of interest in the problematic of representation and its failure, as the mind struggles to find an adequate image for an experience that, finally, threatens to destroy its own cognitive capacities—and destroy it does. From across the continuum of history we therefore embrace the Gothic in an act of faith so as to legitimate our own age.

Notes

Introduction: Reading Others Reading the Gothic

1. Devendra P. Varma, *The Gothic Flame* (1957; New York: Russell and Russell, 1966), 211.

2. Montague Summers, *The Gothic Quest* (1938; New York: Russell and Russell, 1964), 397.

3. Montague Summers, 407.

4. *The Yale Edition of Horace Walpole's Correspondence*, ed. W. S. Lewis et al. (New Haven: Yale University Press, 1937–83), 48 volumes, texts, and indices, 28 (1955), 6. For the letter to Rev. William Cole, see chapter 2, note 37.

5. Montague Summers, 412.

6. Samuel H. Monk, *The Sublime. A Study of Critical Theories in XVIII-Century England* (Ann Arbor: University of Michigan Press, 1960), 3.

7. See J. M. S. Tompkins, *The Polite Marriage* (Cambridge: Cambridge University Press, 1938), 58–102.

8. *Yale Walpole* 31 (1961), 221.

9. Horace Walpole wrote to Bertie Greatheed, the Elder, on 22 February 1796: ". . . not one of them [the other drawings] approached to any one of your son's four . . . [His] conception of some of the passions has improved [my ideas] . . ." *Yale Walpole* 42 (1980), 430.

10. Horace Walpole, *The Castle of Otranto*, ed. W. S. Lewis (Oxford: Oxford University Press, 1982), 3: "The following work was found in the library of an ancient catholic family in the north of England."

11. *Monthly Review* (January 1765), 97, 99.

12. *Monthly Review* (May 1765), 394.

13. *Critical Review* 19 (January 1765), 51.

14. Horace Walpole, *The Castle of Otranto*, intr. by Sir Walter Scott (Edinburgh: Ballantyne, 1811). Holograph notes, ix.

15. Horace Walpole, xxxv.

16. *Edinburgh Review* 31 (December 1818), 80.

17. *Edinburgh Review* 58 (October 1833), 235, 227.

18. Leslie Stephen, "Hours in a Library. No. 5—Horace Walpole," *Cornhill Magazine* 25 (June 1872), 735.

19. Austin Dobson, *Horace Walpole: A Memoir* (London: James R. Osgood, 1893), 167.

20. Virginia Woolf, "Two Antiquaries: Walpole and Cole," in *The Death of the Moth* (London: Hogarth Press, 1945), 51.

21. Virginia Woolf, "Gothic Romance," in *Collected Essays* (London: Hogarth Press, 1966), 1, 133. Originally published as a review of E. Birkhead, *The Tale of Terror: A Study of Gothic Romance,* in *Times Literary Supplement* (May 5, 1921).

22. Virginia Woolf, "Two Antiquaries: Walpole and Cole," 51.

23. Edith Birkhead, *The Tale of Terror* (New York: Russell and Russell, 1963); Eino Railo, *The Haunted Castle* (London: Routledge, 1927); J. M. S. Tompkins, *The Popular Novel in England 1770–1800* (London: Methuen, 1969); Kenneth Clark, *The Gothic Revival* (London: John Murray, 1962); M. Lévy, *Le roman "gothique" anglais 1764–1824* (Toulouse: Publications de la Faculté des Lettres et Sciences Humaines, 1968).

24. Mario Praz, *The Romantic Agony,* trans. Angus Davidson, foreword by Frank Kermode (Oxford: Oxford University Press, 1970).

25. Wylie Sypher, "Social Ambiguity in a Gothic Novel," *Partisan Review* 12 (1945), 51.

26. Lowry Nelson, Jr., "Night Thoughts on the Gothic Novel," *Yale Review* 52 (December 1962), 249–50.

27. Robert D. Hume, "Gothic versus Romantic: A Revaluation of the Gothic Novel," *PMLA* 84 (March 1969), 282–90.

28. Robert L. Platzner and Robert D. Hume, "'Gothic versus Romantic': A Rejoinder," *PMLA* 86 (March 1971), 266–74.

29. Robert Kiely, *The Romantic Novel in England* (Cambridge, Mass.: Harvard University Press, 1972), 40.

30. Patrick Brantlinger, "The Gothic Origins of Science Fiction," *Novel* 14 (Fall 1980), 31.

31. Coral Ann Howells, *Love, Mystery, and Misery: Feeling in Gothic Fiction* (London: Athlone Press, 1978), 27, 26, 9, 13.

32. William Patrick Day, *In the Circles of Fear and Desire. A Study of Gothic Fantasy* (Chicago: University of Chicago Press, 1985).

33. David Punter, *The Literature of Terror* (London: Longman, 1980).

34. Jean-François Lyotard, "The Sublime and the Avant-Garde," in *The Lyotard Reader,* ed. Andrew Benjamin (Oxford: Basil Blackwell, 1989), 204.

35. David Punter, 423.

36. David Punter, 426.

37. Linda Bayer-Berenbaum, *The Gothic Imagination. Expansion in Gothic Literature and Art* (Rutherford, N.J.: Fairleigh Dickinson University Press, 1982), 12.

38. Linda Bayer-Berenbaum, 13.

39. Elizabeth MacAndrew, *The Gothic Tradition in Fiction* (New York: Columbia University Press, 1979), 3: "Gothic fiction gives shape to concepts of the place of evil in the human mind."

40. Linda Bayer-Berenbaum, 29.

41. Wilhelm Worringer, *Form in Gothic* (London: G. P. Putnam's Sons, Ltd., 1927), 42. Quoted by Linda Bayer-Berenbaum, 50.

42. Linda Bayer-Berenbaum, 71.

43. Tzvetan Todorov, *The Fantastic: A Structural Approach to a Literary Genre,* trans. Richard Howard (Ithaca: Cornell University Press, 1975). For the importance of genre theory in literary studies see also Tzvetan Todorov, *Mikhail Bakhtin. The Dialogical Principle,* trans. Wlad Godzich (Manchester: Manchester University Press, 1984).

44. Tzvetan Todorov, 41.

45. Rosemary Jackson, *Fantasy: The Literature of Subversion* (London: Methuen, 1981).

46. See M. M. Bakhtin, *The Dialogic Imagination,* ed. Michael Holquist, trans. Caryl Emerson and Michael Holquist (Austin: University of Texas Press, 1981).

47. Eric S. Rabkin, *The Fantastic in Literature* (Princeton: Princeton University Press, 1977).

48. J. R. R. Tolkien, "On Fairy Stories," in *The Tolkien Reader* (New York: Ballantine, 1966), 47. Quoted by Eric S. Rabkin, 4.

49. Umberto Eco, "Science Fiction and the Art of Conjecture," *TLS* (November 2, 1984), 1257.

50. Eve Kosofsky Sedgwick, *Between Men: English Literature and Male Homosocial Desire* (New York: Columbia University Press, 1985), 90.

51. Eve Kosofsky Sedgwick, 92.

52. Eve Kosofsky Sedgwick, 94.

53. Ronald Paulson, *Representations of Revolution (1789–1820)* (New Haven: Yale University Press, 1983), chapter 7: "The Gothic: Ambrosio to Frankenstein." All references to this text are given in parentheses.

54. Mary Wollstonecraft makes an interesting reference to the Gothic when, echoing Burke on Marie Antoinette (whom Burke constructs in chivalric terms as the maiden in distress) she writes, "Is hereditary weakness necessary to render religion lovely? and will her form have lost the smooth delicacy that inspires love, when stripped of its Gothic drapery?" Quoted by Ronald Paulson, 83, who also points out that *"Gothic"* is Wollstonecraft's "favorite word for Burke's aesthetic."

55. Elizabeth R. Napier, *The Failure of Gothic* (Oxford: Clarendon Press, 1987), 7.

56. Elizabeth R. Napier, 94.

57. Page references are to Horace Walpole, *The Castle of Otranto* (Oxford: Oxford University Press, 1982).

58. Slavoj Žižek, *The Sublime Object of Ideology* (London: Verso, 1989), 170.

Chapter 1. Theorizing the (Gothic) Sublime

1. Herman Melville, *Pierre or The Ambiguities* (1852; Evanston: Northwestern University Press, 1983), 294. Subsequent page references are given in the text.

2. Rob Wilson, *American Sublime. The Genealogy of a Poetic Genre* (Madison: University of Wisconsin Press, 1991), 38–39.

3. David B. Morris, "Gothic Sublimity," *New Literary History* 16, 2 (Winter 1985), 300.

4. Chauncey C. Loomis, "The Arctic Sublime," in U. C. Knoepflmacher and G. B. Tennyson, eds., *Nature and the Victorian Imagination* (Berkeley: University of California Press, 1977), 107–9.

5. Hugh J. Silverman and Gary E. Aylesworth, eds., *The Textual Sublime. Deconstruction and Its Differences* (Albany: SUNY, 1990), Introduction, xv.

6. Steven Knapp, *Personification and the Sublime. Milton to Coleridge* (Cambridge, Mass.: Harvard University Press, 1985), 67.

7. Patricia Yaeger, "Toward a Female Sublime," in Linda Kauffman, ed., *Gender and Theory. Dialogues on Feminist Criticism* (Oxford: Basil Blackwell, 1989), 192.

8. Peter de Bolla, *The Discourse of the Sublime. History, Aesthetics and the Subject* (Oxford: Basil Blackwell, 1989), 65.

9. Michel Foucault, "Language to Infinity," in *Language, Counter-Memory, Practice*, ed., intr., and trans. by Donald F. Bouchard and Sherry Simon (Ithaca: Cornell University Press, 1977), 53.

10. James Joyce, *Ulysses* (1922; New York: Random House, 1946), 387. Cited by the *OED*.

11. Michel Foucault, "Language to Infinity," 55.

12. Michel Foucault, 61.

13. Michel Foucault, 62.

14. *Monthly Review* 94 (January 1821), 81.

15. Michel Foucault, 63.

16. Mircea Eliade, *The Sacred and the Profane*, trans. Willard R. Trask (New York: Harcourt, Brace & World, 1959), 64.

17. Fredric Jameson, *Postmodernism, or, The Cultural Logic of Late Capitalism* (Durham: Duke University Press, 1991), 6.

18. Fredric Jameson, 38.

19. Rob Wilson, 214.

20. See Dorothy Marshall, *Eighteenth Century England* (London: Longmans, 1962), 15ff.

21. Peter de Bolla, 6.

22. Walter Benjamin, *Illuminations*, ed. and intr. by Hannah Arendt, trans. Harry Zöhn (London: Collins/Fontana, 1973), 258.

23. Jean-François Lyotard, *The Postmodern Condition: A Report on Knowledge*, trans. Geoff Bennington and Brian Massumi; foreword by

Fredric Jameson (Manchester: Manchester University Press, 1986), Appendix "Answering the Question: What is Postmodernism?" trans. Regis Durand, 77.

24. Arthur Kroker and David Cook, *The Postmodern Scene* (London: Macmillan, 1988), 30. In many ways there is a direct line of descent from Piranesi to Chirico. For Piranesi, see chapter 2.

25. Arthur Kroker and David Cook, 30.

26. Arthur Kroker and David Cook, 31.

27. Arthur Kroker and David Cook, 31.

28. See V. S. Naipaul, *The Enigma of Arrival* (London: Viking, 1987), for another, humanist, appropriation of Chirico's narrative. Naipaul rejects this version of postmodernism and implicitly accepts Habermas' espousal of a "communicative rationality" as a continuing facet of the Enlightenment project. It seems that Naipaul clearly misreads the politics of postmodernism and the interventionist heritage of the avant-garde, because he still considers the special (modernist) agony of the writer in essentially Romantic terms. In other words, his belief in a single genealogy (as opposed to the postmodern multiplicity of genealogies), a grand metanarrative, conditions him to discover or, failing that, superimpose social harmonies when all that one finds are their terrifying absence.

29. J-F. Lyotard, 77.

30. Donald Pease, "Sublime Politics," in Mary Arensberg, ed. *The American Sublime* (Albany: SUNY Press, 1986), 21.

31. Samuel H. Monk, *The Sublime. A Study of Critical Theories in XVIII-Century England* (Ann Arbor: University of Michigan Press, 1960), 3.

32. Boileau, *Oeuvres Complètes*, 3, 430. Quoted by Samuel H. Monk, 35.

33. Alfred Rosenberg, *Longinus in England bis zur Ende des 18. Jahrhunderts* (Weimar and Berlin, 1917). Quoted by Samuel H. Monk, 21. See also Theodore E. B. Wood, *The Word 'Sublime' and Its Context 1650–1760* (The Hague: Mouton, 1972).

34. Samuel H. Monk, 51.

35. Dennis referred to "Gods, Daemons, Hell, Spirits and Souls of Men . . . Tempests, raging Seas, Inundations . . . Earthquakes, Volcanos . . . Pestilence, Famine, etc." as sources of the sublime. Quoted by Samuel H. Monk, 54.

36. Frances Ferguson, "The Sublime of Edmund Burke, or the Bathos of Experience," *Glyph* 8 (1981), 65.

37. Edmund Burke, *A Philosophical Enquiry into the Origin of Our Ideas of the Sublime and Beautiful*, ed., intr., and notes by James T. Boulton (Notre Dame: University of Notre Dame Press, 1968). All subsequent quotations from this work refer to this edition and are cited parenthetically.

38. Paul Crowther, *The Kantian Sublime* (Oxford: Clarendon Press, 1989), 7.

39. *Eighteenth-Century Verse*, ed. Roger Lonsdale (Oxford: Oxford University Press, 1984), 393.

40. Craig Howes, "Burke, Poe, and 'Usher': The Sublime and Rising Woman," *Emerson Society Quarterly* (*ESQ*) 31 (1985), 174.

41. See, for instance, Lee Siegel, *Sacred and Profane Dimensions of Love in Indian Traditions as Exemplified in the "Gītagovinda" of Jayadeva* (Delhi: Oxford University Press, 1978), 47ff. for a synopsis of Sanskrit *rasa* theory.

42. Terry Eagleton, *The Ideology of the Aesthetic* (Oxford: Basil Blackwell, 1990), 72.

43. Paul de Man, "Phenomenality and Materiality in Kant," in Hugh J. Silverman and Gary E. Aylesworth, eds., *The Textual Sublime* (Albany: SUNY, 1990), 90.

44. Donald Pease, 33, 36.

45. Immanuel Kant, *The Critique of Judgement*, trans. James Creed Meredith (Oxford: Clarendon Press, 1986), 93. Further page references to quotations from this edition are given in parentheses.

46. Terry Eagleton, 89.

47. Erich Auerbach, *Mimesis*, trans. Willard R. Trask (Princeton: Princeton University Press, 1973), 153.

48. William Wordsworth, "The Sublime and the Beautiful," in *The Prose Works of William Wordsworth*, 3 vols., eds. W. J. B. Owen and Jane Worthington Smyser (Oxford: Clarendon Press, 1974), 2, 356.

49. Neil Hertz, "The Notion of Blockage in the Literature of the Sublime," in Geoffrey H. Hartman, ed., *Psychoanalysis and the Question of the Text* (Baltimore: Johns Hopkins University Press, 1978), 62, 73.

50. William Wordsworth, "The Sublime and the Beautiful," 351.

51. William Wordsworth, 351.

52. Steven Z. Levine, "Seascapes of the Sublime: Vernet, Monet, and the Oceanic Feeling," *New Literary History* 16, 2 (Winter 1985), 392.

53. Terry Eagleton, *The Ideology of the Aesthetic*, 20.

54. Terry Eagleton, 72.

55. Samuel H. Monk, 6.

56. Arthur Schopenhauer, *The World as Will and Representation*, 2 vols., trans. E. F. J. Payne (New York: Dover Publications, 1969), 1, 416–17.

57. Friedrich von Schiller, "On the Sublime," in *Naive and Sentimental Poetry* and *On the Sublime*, trans. Julius A. Elias (New York: Frederick Ungar Publishing Co., 1966), 210.

58. Slavoj Žižek, *The Sublime Object of Ideology* (London: Verso, 1989), 203.

59. Sigmund Freud, "The Economic Problem of Masochism," *The Pelican Freud Library* (Harmondsworth: Penguin Books, 1984), 11, 414–15.

60. Sigmund Freud, "Beyond the Pleasure Principle," *The Pelican Freud Library* (Harmondsworth: Penguin Books, 1984), 11, 322.

61. Steven Z. Levine, 397.

62. Steven Z. Levine, 398.

63. See Sigmund Freud, "Leonardo da Vinci and a Memory of his Childhood," *The Pelican Freud Library* (Harmondsworth: Penguin Books, 1985), 14, 167: "The sexual instinct is particularly well fitted to make contributions of this kind since it is endowed with a capacity for sublimation." In Leonardo's case the channeling of sexual instincts led to his desexualization, which finally enabled him to go beyond the polarities of good and evil, beauty and ugliness, love and hate.

64. Jean-François Lyotard, *The Differend: Phrases in Dispute*, trans. Georges van den Abbeele (Minneapolis: University of Minnesota Press, 1988).

65. Paul de Man, 90.

66. On the pleasures of impotence with reference to Edmund Burke see Frances Ferguson, 73ff.

67. Rob Wilson, 26.

68. Harold Bloom, *The Anxiety of Influence* (New York: Oxford University Press, 1973), 99–112.

69. Jacques Derrida, *The Truth in Painting*, trans. Geoff Bennington and Ian McLeod (Chicago: University of Chicago Press, 1987).

70. Jacques Derrida, 49.

71. Peter Brooks, "Narrative Transaction and Transference (Unburying *Le Colonel Chabert*)," *Novel* 15 (Winter 1982), 102.

72. Jacques Derrida, 50.

73. George Eliot, *Middlemarch*, 3, chapter 29.

74. J-F Lyotard, *The Differend: Phrases in Dispute*, 170.

75. Norman K. Denzin, "*Blue Velvet*: Postmodern Contradictions," *Theory Culture and Society* 5, 2–3 (June 1988), 461–73.

76. Jean Baudrillard, *Simulations* (New York: Semiotext(e), 1983), 146.

77. Jean-François Lyotard, *The Lyotard Reader*, ed. Andrew Benjamin (Oxford: Basil Blackwell, 1989), 204.

78. Christopher Norris, *What's Wrong With Postmodernism* (Baltimore: Johns Hopkins University Press, 1990), 11.

Chapter 2. The Precursor Text

1. Terry Eagleton, *The Rape of Clarissa* (Oxford: Basil Blackwell, 1982), vii.

2. Walter Benjamin, *Illuminations*, ed. and intr. by Hannah Arendt, trans. Harry Zöhn (London: Collins/Fontana Books, 1973), 264.

3. Jürgen Habermas, *The Philosophical Discourse of Modernity*, trans. Frederick Lawrence (Cambridge: Polity Press, 1987), 11.

4. Jürgen Habermas, 12.

5. Terry Eagleton, vii.

6. Jane Austen, *Northanger Abbey* (1818; Harmondsworth: Penguin Books, 1972), chapter 6.

7. M. L. Allen, "The Black Veil: Three Versions of a Symbol," *English Studies* 47 (1966), 286–89.

8. Horace Walpole, *The Castle of Otranto* (1764; Oxford: Oxford University Press, 1982). Although all the copies are dated 1765, the novel was actually published the day before Christmas 1764. Most critics cite 1764 as the year of first publication. All page references are to this edition and are given in parentheses.

9. Richard Hurd, *Letters on Chivalry and Romance* (London: A. Millar, 1762). Another copy in the Bodleian has the same pagination but is bound with Hurd's *Five Pieces of Runic Poetry* (London: R and J Dodsley, 1763).

10. A. E. Longueil, "The Word 'Gothic' in Eighteenth Century Criticism," *Modern Language Notes* 38 (December 1923), 453–60.

11. Horace Walpole, *The Castle of Otranto,* intr. by Sir Walter Scott (Edinburgh: Ballantyne, 1811), vi. Harvard University copy with extensive holograph notes in Scott's hand.

12. D. H. Lawrence, *The Rainbow* (1915; Harmondsworth: Penguin Books, 1965), 237.

13. Jacques Lacan, *Écrits. A Selection,* trans. Alan Sheridan (London: Tavistock Publications, 1977), 154.

14. Roland Barthes, "Theory of the Text," in *Untying the Text: A Post-Structuralist Reader,* ed. and intr. by Robert Young (London: Routledge and Kegan Paul, 1981), 39.

15. G. R. Thompson, ed., *The Gothic Imagination* (Pullman: Washington State University Press, 1974), 1.

16. Roland Barthes, "Theory of the Text," 36.

17. Quoted by Diane Macdonell, *Theories of Discourse. An Introduction* (Oxford: Basil Blackwell, 1986), 3.

18. Diane Macdonell, 11.

19. Frederick Garber, "Meaning and Mode in Gothic Fiction," in *Racism in the Eighteenth Century,* ed. Harold E. Pagliaro (Cleveland: Case Western Reserve University Press, 1973), 157.

20. Clara Reeve, *The Progress of Romance, through Times, Countries, and Manners,* 2 vols. (Colchester: W. Keymer, 1785), 1, 111.

21. Michel Foucault, "What Is an Author?" in *Textual Strategies,* ed. Josué V. Harari (London: Methuen, 1980), 141–60.

22. Clara Reeve, *The Progress of Romance,* 1, 25.

23. Howard Gaskill, "'Ossian' Macpherson: Towards a Rehabilitation," *Comparative Criticism. An Annual Journal*, 8, ed. E. S. Shaffer (Cambridge University Press, 1986), 113.

24. Ian Watt, *The Rise of the Novel. Studies in Defoe, Richardson and Fielding* (1957; Harmondsworth: Penguin Books, 1963), 15.

25. Alastair Fowler, *Kinds of Literature: An Introduction to the Theory of Genres and Modes* (Oxford: Clarendon Press, 1982), 158.

26. Norman Holland and Leona F. Sherman, "Gothic Possibilities," *New Literary History* 8 (Winter 1977), 279–94.

27. Michel Foucault, *Power/Knowledge*, ed. Colin Gordon, trans. Colin Gordon et al. (Brighton: Harvester Press, 1980), 154.

28. Michel Foucault, *Discipline and Punish*, trans. Alan Sheridan (Harmondsworth: Penguin Books, 1979), 202.

29. Jean Baudrillard, "Game with Vestiges," *On the Beach* 5 (Winter 1984), 24.

30. Michel Foucault, *Discipline and Punish*, 205.

31. Jürgen Habermas, 245.

32. David H. Richter, "Gothic Fantasia: The Monsters and the Myths. A Review Article," *The Eighteenth Century. Theory and Interpretation* 28, 2 (Spring 1987), 150.

33. Ronald Paulson, *Satire and the Novel in Eighteenth-Century England* (New Haven: Yale University Press, 1967), 4.

34. Ronald Paulson, 8.

35. Horace Walpole, *The Castle of Otranto*, ed. Caroline F. E. Spurgeon (London: Chatto and Windus, 1907), xii.

36. Kenneth Burke, *The Philosophy of Literary Form* (Baton Rouge: Louisiana State University Press, 1978), 51ff.

37. *The Yale Edition of Horace Walpole's Correspondence*, ed. W. S. Lewis et al. (New Haven: Yale University Press, 1937–1983), 1 (1937), 88–89.

38. George E. Haggerty, "Fact and Fancy in the Gothic Novel," *Nineteenth-Century Fiction* 39, 4 (March 1985), 380.

39. Cited by John Riely, "*The Castle of Otranto* Revisited," *The Yale University Library Gazette* 53 (July 1978), 6.

40. Peter Conrad, *The Everyman History of English Literature* (London: J. M. Dent and Sons Ltd., 1987), 391.

41. Quoted and translated by Sir Walter Scott (1811), xv.

42. Sigmund Freud, Case Histories 1, 'Dora' and 'Little Hans' *The Pelican Freud Library* (Harmondsworth: Penguin Books, 1977), 8, 38.

43. *Three Gothic Novels*, ed. Peter Fairclough, intr. by Mario Praz (Harmondsworth: Penguin Books, 1983), 18–20.

44. Mario Praz, *On Classicism*, trans. Angus Davidson (London: Thames and Hudson, 1967), 92.

45. Patricia May Sekler, "Giovanni Battista Piranesi's *CARCERI:* Etchings and Related Drawings," *The Art Quarterly* 25, 4 (Winter 1962), 333.

46. Jonathan Scott, *Piranesi* (London: Academy Editions, 1975), 54.

47. Manfredo Tafuri, *The Sphere and the Labyrinth.* Avant-Gardes and Architecture from Piranesi to the 1970s, trans. Pellegrino d'Acierno and Robert Connolly (Cambridge, Mass.: MIT Press, 1987), 27.

48. *Oeuvres de Piraneses Edifices de Trois* [and] *CARCERI*, Ashmolean Museum atl. fol. U. L. 921. 9/Pir. *Le Antichità Romane Opera di Giambattista Piranesi* (Roma: Bouchard, 1756), Ashmolean Museum 921. 9/Pir.

49. *ad terrorem increscen(tis) audaciae* is a slight misquotation from Livy Book 1, chapter 33. The full sentence, which is a description of the Mamertine Prison in the life of Ancus Marcius, reads *carcer ad terrorem increscentis audaciae media urbe imminens foro aedificatur,* "a prison was built in the middle of the city right above the forum, to inspire terror against the ever growing lawlessness." The phrase quoted by Piranesi is elliptical, however, and the conjunction of terror and bold recklessness (*audaciae* is strictly boldness) is meant to be purposefully ambiguous. The Piranesi sublime incarcerates the inhabitants of the dungeons of his *carceri,* his prisons of the mind.

The second inscription [*infame scelus (arbo)ri infelici suspe(nde)*] is again an allusion to Livy (this time to Book 1, chapter 26), but if so it has been considerably altered. The phrase *arbori infelici,* literally "unhappy tree," is usually understood as a gallows tree and occurs twice in Livy at this point. An odd construction, it is usually taken to be the precise (and archaic) language of a traditional law. However, in neither of the two occurrences does the phrase *infame scelus* occur. The most likely phrase being recalled by Piranesi is *caput obnube liberatoris urbis hujus: arbori infelici suspende* ("go veil the head of the liberator of this city: hang him from a wretched gallows tree"). This is said by Horatius's father as he pleads for the life of his son, who is to be hanged according to this law (as quoted earlier in the text) for killing his (Horatius's) sister because she was not as happy as she ought to have been after Horatius had killed her lover. Piranesi's *infame scelus* ("notorious crime" or, by extension, "notorious criminal") would make good sense if it referred to Horatius. It would then be the object of the rest of the sentence: "Go veil the head of the liberator of the city: hang (the notorious criminal) from a gloomy gallows tree."

Both of these inscriptions bring together Gothic themes of containment (in a prison), the castle as a premodern cityscape and murder as a grotesque imagery of the politics of desire. Remembering the "distrustful thought(s)" aroused by Piranesi's etchings, Herman Melville wrote in a poem called "Prelusive,"

In Piranezi's rarer prints,
Interiors measurelessly strange,
Where the distrustful thought may range.
Misgiving still—what mean the hints?
Stairs upon stairs which dim ascend
In series from plunged bastilles drear—
Pit under pit; long tier on tier
Of shadowed galleries which impend
Over cloisters, cloisters without end;
The height, the depth—the far, the near;
Ring-bolts to pillars in vaulted lanes,
And dragging Rhadamanthine chains;
These less of wizard influence lend
Than some allusive chambers closed.

See Herman Melville, *Clarel* (1876; New York Russell and Russell, 1963), 1, 316.

50. Manfredo Tafuri, 26.

51. Sergei M. Eisenstein, *The Film Sense,* trans. and ed. Jay Leyda (London: Faber and Faber, 1970), 134.

52. The library in the film version of Umberto Eco's *The Name of the Rose* is pure Piranesi, as are so many of the images in Ken Russell's film *Gothic.*

53. Manfredo Tafuri, 21.

54. Horace Walpole, *Anecdotes of Painting in England* (Strawberry Hill, 1771), 4, vi.

55. Robert Kiely, *The Romantic Novel in England* (Cambridge, Mass.: Harvard University Press, 1972), 35.

56. Fredric V. Bogel, *Literature and Insubstantiality in Later Eighteenth-Century England* (Princeton: Princeton University Press, 1984), 112.

57. Terry Eagleton, *The Rape of Clarissa*, 99.

58. See Jean Baudrillard, "On Seduction," in *Selected Writings*, ed. Mark Poster (Cambridge: Polity Press, 1988), 149–65.

59. Christine Brooke-Rose, *A Rhetoric of the Unreal* (Cambridge: Cambridge University Press, 1983), 4–11.

60. Willem van Reijen and Dick Veerman, "An Interview with Jean-François Lyotard," *Theory Culture and Society* 5, 2–3 (June 1988), 290–91.

61. See, in particular, Julia Kristeva, *Revolution in Poetic Language* (New York: Columbia University Press, 1984), 59–60.

62. Roland Barthes, "Introduction to the Structural Analysis of Narratives," in *Image-Music-Text* (London: Fontana, 1977), 79–124.

63. See chapter 4 where I take this up with reference to William Godwin's *Caleb Williams*.

64. *Yale Walpole* 10 (1941), 259.

65. *Yale Walpole* 10 (1941), 259, note 7.

66. [Horace Walpole] *The Mysterious Mother. A Tragedy* (London: J. Dodsley, 1781). All quotations are from this edition.

67. A. T. Hazen, *A Bibliography of the Strawberry Hill Press* (Folkestone and London: Dawsons of Pall Mall, 1973), 79–95.

68. Lord Byron, *Marino Faliero* (1821) in *The Works of Lord Byron*, ed. Thomas Moore (London: John Murray, 1832), 12, 62.

69. Peter J. S. Burra, "Baroque and Gothic Sentimentalism," *Farrago* 3 (October 1930), 169.

70. Postscript to "The Mysterious Mother," *The Works of Horatio Walpole Earl of Orford*, 5 vols. (London: G. G. and J. Robinson and J. Edwards, 1798), 4, 125–26.

71. *The British Novelists*; with an Essay, and Prefaces Biographical and Critical, by Mrs. Barbauld (London: F. C. and J. Rivington, 1810), 22, iii. Henry James's *The Turn of the Screw,* a later Gothic text, elicited similar comments from its early readers. As Paul B. Armstrong writes, "'The story itself is distinctly repulsive,' one critic complained, and another reported that 'we have never read a more sickening, a more gratuitously melancholy tale.'" See Paul B. Armstrong, "History and Epistemology: The Example of *The Turn of the Screw,*" *New Literary History* 19, 3 (Spring 1988), 697.

72. The dungeon is used to ironic effect by Fetyukovich, Dostoevsky's defense counsel in *The Brothers Karamazov,* when he rhetorically suggests a probable place where the money might be hidden: "But why not in the dungeons of the Castle of Udolpho, gentlemen of the jury?" he asks (12, chapter 11).

73. Robert Jephson, *The Count of Narbonne* (London: T. Cadell, 1781).

74. *Critical Review* 52 (December 1781), 456; *Monthly Review* 66 (January 1782), 64–70.

75. Christopher Norris, *What's Wrong With Postmodernism* (Baltimore: Johns Hopkins University Press, 1990), 27.

76. *Yale Walpole* 41 (1980), 409.

77. *Yale Walpole* 41 (1980), 410.

78. *Yale Walpole* 2 (1937), 110.

79. *Yale Walpole* 28 (1955), 381.

80. Clara Reeve, *The Champion of Virtue, A Gothic Story* (Colchester: W. Keymer, 1777). Reissued with a new preface, in 1778, as *The Old English Baron* (London: Edward and Charles Dilly, 1778). Reprinted Oxford University Press, 1967. James Trainter's Oxford edition does not note the changes Clara Reeve made to her original preface for the second edition.

81. Clara Reeve, *The Champion of Virtue,* vii.

82. Clara Reeve, *The Old English Baron,* ed. James Trainter (Oxford: Oxford University Press, 1967), 3.

83. *Critical Review* [2nd Series] 4 (1792), 458.

84. Frank Kermode, *Essays on Fiction 1971–1982* (London: Routledge and Kegan Paul, 1983), 94.

85. See Thomas J. Mathias, *The Pursuits of Literature, a Satirical*

Poem in Four Dialogues (1794–1797; London: Becker and Porter, 1812), 345. In a footnote (note 158), Mathias adds: "The spirit of inquiry which he [Walpole] introduced was rather frivolous, though pleasing, and his Otranto ghosts have propagated their species with unequalled fecundity. The spawn is in every novel shop."

86. David B. Morris, "Gothic Sublimity," *New Literary History* 16, 2 (Winter 1985), 300.

87. Thomas Weiskel, *The Romantic Sublime: Studies in the Structure and Psychology of Transcendence* (Baltimore: Johns Hopkins University Press, 1976), ix. These words are Mrs. Patricia Portia Weiskel's citation from her husband's journals.

88. Sigmund Freud, "The 'Uncanny,'" (1919) *The Pelican Freud Library* (Harmondsworth: Penguin Books, 1985), 14, 335–76. All subsequent quotations from the work refer to this edition and are cited parenthetically.

89. David B. Morris, 301.

90. Edmund Burke, *A Philosophical Enquiry into the Origin of Our Ideas of the Sublime and Beautiful,* ed., intr., and notes by James T. Boulton (Notre Dame: University of Notre Dame Press, 1968), 146. Page references to this text are cited parenthetically.

91. David B. Morris, 302.

92. David B. Morris, 304.

93. See Neil Hertz, "Freud and the Sandman," in Josué V. Harari, ed. *Textual Strategies* (London: Methuen, 1979), 296–321 for an extremely insightful examination of a triangular relationship in which Freud himself is implicated.

94. Hélène Cixous, "Fiction and Its Phantoms: A Reading of Freud's *Das Unheimliche* (The 'uncanny')," *New Literary History* 7, 3 (Spring 1976), 536.

95. Hélène Cixous, 539.

96. Hélène Cixous, 548.

97. Harold Bloom, "Freud and the Poetic Sublime: A Catastrophe Theory of Creativity," in *Freud: A Collection of Critical Essays,* ed. Perry Meisel (Englewood Cliffs, N.J.: Prentice-Hall, 1981), 218.

98. Harold Bloom, 224.

99. Hélène Cixous, 546.

100. Terry Eagleton, *The Ideology of the Aesthetic*, 54.

101. David Carroll, *Paraesthetics. Foucault. Lyotard. Derrida* (New York: Methuen, 1987), 174.

Chapter 3. Gothic Fragments and Fragmented Gothics

1. Manfredo Tafuri, *The Sphere and the Labyrinth. Avant-Gardes and Architecture from Piranesi to the 1790s*, trans. Pellegrino d'Acierno and Robert Connolly (Cambridge, Mass.: MIT Press, 1987), 13.

2. Robert D. Mayo, "Gothic Romance in the Magazines," *PMLA* 65, 5 (September 1950), 776.

3. Robert D. Mayo, 777.

4. Slavoj Žižek, *The Sublime Object of Ideology* (London: Verso, 1989), 170.

5. Mario Praz, *The Romantic Agony*, trans. Angus Davidson, foreword by Frank Kermode (Oxford: Oxford University Press, 1970), 78. For an examination of Calmet's study of vampires, see note 24.

6. Slavoj Žižek, 174.

7. For a study of the Indian sublime see Vijay Mishra, *Devotional Poetics: A Theory of the Indian Sublime*, forthcoming.

8. Johann Wolfgang von Goethe, *The Sorrows of Werter: A German Story*, trans. Richard Graves (London: T. Osborne and S. Griffin, 1795). All references are to this two-volume so-called "new edition." *Werther* continued to be spelled *Werter* in English until 1854.

9. E. W. Pitcher, "Changes in Short Fiction in Britain 1785–1810: Philosophic Tales, Gothic Tales, and Fragments and Visions," *Studies in Short Fiction* 13, 3 (Summer 1976), 351.

10. J. and A. L. Aikin, *Miscellaneous Pieces, in Prose* (London: J. Johnson, 1773). Page references, taken from this edition, are incorporated in the text.

11. "On the Pleasure Derived from OBJECTS OF TERROR; with SIR BERTRAND, A FRAGMENT," in *Miscellaneous Pieces, in Prose*, 119–37

12. F. Reynolds, *Werter. A Tragedy* (Dublin: P. Cooney, 1786).

13. Ernest de Selincourt and Helen Darbishire, eds., *The Poetical Works of William Wordsworth,* 5 vols. (Oxford: Clarendon Press, 1940–49). Revised edition vols. 1–3, 1952–54.

14. Peter J. S. Burra, "Baroque and Gothic Sentimentalism," *Farrago* 3 (October 1930), 181.

15. William Hazlitt, *The Spirit of the Age: Or, Contemporary Portraits* (London: Henry Colburn, 1825), 86.

16. All quotations have been taken from *"Fragment of a 'Gothic' Tale,"* in William Wordsworth, *The Poems,* ed. John O. Hayden (New Haven: Yale University Press, 1981), 1, 153–60. Line references have been cited after each quotation.

17. R. S. Crane, "Suggestions Toward a Genealogy of 'The Man of Feeling,'" *(ELH) A Journal of English Literary History,* 1, 3 (December 1934), 206. See also R. F. Brissenden, "'Sentiment': Some Uses of the Word in the Writings of David Hume," in R. F. Brissenden, ed., *Studies in the Eighteenth Century* (Canberra: Australian National University Press, 1968), 89–107, and Ronald Paulson, *Satire and the Novel in Eighteenth-Century England* (New Haven: Yale University Press, 1967), 242ff.

18. *The Diary of Dr. John William Polidori,* edited and elucidated by William Michael Rossetti (London: Elkin Mathews, 1911).

19. Leslie A. Marchant, *Byron. A Biography* (London: John Murray, 1957), 2, 628.

20. C. Kegan Paul, *William Godwin; His Friends and Contemporaries* (London: Henry S. King and Co., 1876), 1, 82–83.

21. *The Letters of Mary Wollstonecraft Shelley,* ed. Betty T. Bennett (Baltimore: Johns Hopkins University Press, 1980), 1, 96.

22. [J. W. Polidori] *The Vampyre; A Tale* (London: Sherwood, Neely and Jones, 1819). It was published simultaneously in the *New Monthly Magazine* 11 (1 April 1819), 193–206. The story was attributed to Byron. All references are to the Sherwood text.

23. Lord Byron, *Mazeppa, A Poem* (London: John Murray, 1819), 57–69. All references to "A Fragment" are taken from this text, with page citations given in parentheses after each quotation.

24. Augustine Calmet, *The Phantom World: or, The Philosophy of Spirits, Apparitions etc.,* 2 vols., ed., intr., and notes by Rev. Henry Christmas (London: Richard Bentley, 1850). This is based on the 1751 English edition. All references are to this edition.

The vampire narratives of Calmet, Byron, Polidori, through the mediation of Bram Stoker's definitive work, appear in Francis Ford Coppola's *Dracula* (1992). Coppola carefully fragments the representation of Dracula so that he can be reimaged as a series of contradictory visual subjects. The vampire resists both "singularities" and a fixed iconography.

25. *Monthly Review* 89 (May 1819), 89, referred to a reading of this episode in the periodical literature along the lines of a "political allegory" where Arnald Paul's blood was "the treasure he had sucked out of the public funds."

26. *Monthly Review* 90 (July 1819), 309–21.

27. *Monthly Review* 89 (May 1819), 90, 96.

28. *Monthly Review* 90 (September 1819), 92–94. Polidori's poem *Ximenes* ("A Dramatic Action"), written when he was eighteen, is also reviewed here. The hero of this poem, in a strange prefiguring of Polidori's own end by swallowing an excessive dose of prussic acid in August 1821, commits suicide by drinking poison.

29. "Terrorist Novel Writing," *The Spirit of Public Journals of 1797*, 3rd ed. (London: James Ridgway, 1802), 1, 227.

30. J. W. Polidori, M. D., *Ernestus Berchtold; or The Modern Oedipus. A Tale* (London: Longman, Hurst, Rees, Orme, and Brown, 1819). All references are to this edition.

31. *Monthly Review* 91 (February 1820), 215.

32. J. W. Polidori, *Ximenes, The Wreath, and other Poems* (London: Longman, Hurst, Rees, Orme, and Brown, 1819).

33. MS of *Mathilda* (226 pp.). Dep. d. 374/1 Abinger Shelley-Godwin Papers, Duke Humfrey's Library, the Bodleian, Oxford. All quotations are taken from this MSS text, with pagination cited parenthetically.

34. *The Letters of Mary Wollstonecraft Shelley*, 1, 101.

35. *The Journals of Mary Shelley 1814–1844*, 2 vols., eds. Paula R. Feldman and Diana Scott-Kilvert (Oxford: Clarendon Press, 1987), 1, 291–92.

36. Abinger Papers, Dep. c. 524, letter 20.

37. Abinger Papers, Dep. c. 524, letter 23.

38. Mary Shelley, *Journals*, 2, 442.

39. Mary Shelley, *Journals*, 2, 294.

40. MS of *The Fields of Fancy*, Abinger Papers, Dep. 374/2. This is a fragment of a tale, abandoned in favor of *Mathilda*.

41. Mary Wollstonecraft Shelley, *Mathilda*, ed. Elizabeth Nitchie, *Studies in Philology* [Extra Series] 3 (October 1959), xi.

42. Sandra M. Gilbert, "Horror's Twin: Mary Shelley's Monstrous Eve," *Feminist Studies*, 4, 2 (June 1978), 49.

43. *Collected Letters of Mary Wollstonecraft*, ed. Ralph M. Wardle (Ithaca: Cornell University Press, 1979), 395.

44. *The Letters of Mary Wollstonecraft Shelley* 1, 296.

45. U. C. Knoepflmacher, "Thoughts on the Aggression of Daughters," in George Levine and U. C. Knoepflmacher, eds., *The Endurance of Frankenstein. Essays on Mary Shelley's Novel* (Berkeley: University of California Press, 1979), 115.

46. Jean H. Hagstrum, *Sex and Sensibility. Ideal and Erotic Love from Milton to Mozart* (Chicago: University of Chicago Press, 1980), 260.

47. Sigmund Freud, "Thoughts for the Times on War and Death" (1915), in *The Pelican Freud Library* (Harmondsworth: Penguin Books, 1985), 12, 81.

48. William Blake, *Thel*, ll. 124–25.

49. The name *Herbert* is changed to "Woodville" throughout the MSS. The character of Woodville is modelled on Shelley, but the name has strong echoes of Godwin and *Mandeville*, a novel published by Godwin in 1817.

50. See also Terence Harpold, "'Did you get Mathilda from Papa?': Seduction Fantasy and the Circulation of Mary Shelley's *Mathilda*," *Studies in Romanticism* 28, 1 (Spring 1989), 60: "In death, moreover, the desired reunion with the father that compels her to take her mother's place is no longer forbidden." Or in Anne K. Mellor's words, "She can be, must be, the bride of death." [Anne K. Mellor, *Mary Shelley. Her Life Her Fiction Her Monsters* (New York: Routledge, 1988), 199.]

Chapter 4. Unstable Text/Unstable Readings: William Godwin's *Caleb Williams*

1. William Godwin, *Enquiry Concerning Political Justice*, ed. and intr. by Isaac Kramnick (Harmondsworth: Penguin Books, 1976).

2. William Godwin, *Caleb Williams* [Standard Novels No. 2] (London: Henry Colburn and Richard Bentley, 1831). Unless otherwise stated, all quotations have been taken from this edition. Page numbers are given in parentheses.

3. Peter H. Marshall, *William Godwin* (New Haven: Yale University Press, 1984), 134.

4. Abinger Shelley-Godwin Papers, Dep. c. 531. "Draft of an Autobiography 1794–95" [two leaves non-sequentially paginated 104–7, watermarked 1807, apparently from the draft of an autobiography originally covering the years 1793–95], 104: "The year 1794 was memorable for the trial of twelve persons under one (?) indictment upon a charge of high treason—some of these persons were my particular friends; more than half of them were known to me."

5. Abinger Shelley-Godwin Papers, Dep. c. 606/3. Mary Shelley records in her notes on the Life of Godwin that before dying Gerrald addressed his friends, saying, "I die in the best of causes & as you witness without repining" (117).

6. *Critical Review* 11 (1794), 290.

7. *British Critic* 4 (1794), 70. See also *British Critic* 5 (1795), 447, and *British Critic* 6 (1795), 94.

8. *Analytical Review* 21 (February 1795), 166.

9. *Letters of Anna Seward* [1784–1807] 6 vols., ed. Sir Walter Scott (Edinburgh: Archibald, Constable, 1811), 4, 211. See also Charlotte Smith, *The Banished Man*, 4 vols. (London: T. Cadell, 1794) 2, vi–vii where Charlotte Smith uses the format of a dialogue between Author and Friend to discuss the question posed by the Friend: "do you propose to make a novel without love in it?" This remark is then footnoted as follows: "I had not then heard of, or seen, a work called, 'Things as they Are.'"

10. *Analytical Review* 21, 174.

11. George Colman, the Younger, *The Iron Chest* (London: Cadell and Davies, 1796). In a letter to Anna Seward (April 13, 1798) Mr. H. Repton had in fact sketched a fourth volume of *Caleb Williams*. See *Letters of Anna Seward*, 5, 71.

12. There are many historical and literary Falklands. Clarendon's *The True Historical Narrative of the Rebellion and Civil Wars in England* (1702–1704) mentions a parliamentary General Fordinand Fairfax and the Royalist Lord Falkland. Coventry's *Pompey the Little* (1751) as well as

Sheridan's *The Rivals* (1775) have characters named Falkland/Faulkland. There is a Major Ferdinand Faulkener in Schiller's *Cabal and Love* (1784) as well.

13. *British Critic* 9 (February 1797), 193.

14. George Colman, the Younger, *The Iron Chest*, intr. by Mrs. Inchbald (London: Longman, Hurst, Rees, Orme, and Brown, 1821), 3, 4.

15. William Godwin, *Fleetwood: Or, The New Man of Feeling* (1805; London: Richard Bentley, 1832), 3, 4.

16. See Abinger Shelley-Godwin Papers, Dep. c. 663/4 e. for details of his appointment as "Officer-Keeper & Yeoman Usher in the office of the Receipt of his Majesty's Exchequer."

17. Edgar Allan Poe, "The Philosophy of Composition," in *Selected Poetry and Prose of Poe*, ed. T. O. Mabbott (New York: Modern Library, 1951), 363.

18. *Fleetwood*, ix.

19. William Hazlitt, *The Spirit of the Age or Contemporary Portraits*, ed. E. D. Mackerness (London and Glasgow: Collins, 1969), 48.

20. *Fleetwood*, xi.

21. John Reynolds, *The Triumphs of Gods Revenge, Against the crying, and execrable Sinne of Murther. . . . In thirty severall Tragical Histories* (London: William Lee, 1621).

22. Abinger Shelley-Godwin Papers, Dep. f. 66. Notebook (47–55)—detailed date-list for his composition of *Caleb Williams*, 24 Feb. 1793–8 May 1794.

23. Abinger Shelley-Godwin Papers, Dep. e. 196–227. William Godwin's Diary 1788–1836.

24. *Fleetwood*, xiii.

25. Quoted by De Quincey in *The Collected Writings of Thomas De Quincey*, 14 vols., ed. David Masson (Edinburgh: Adam and Charles Black, 1890), 11, 332. "Notes on Gilfillan's Literary Portraits" was originally published in *Tait's Magazine* (Nov. and Dec. 1845, and Jan. and April 1846).

26. *Thomas De Quincey*, 11, 329, 332.

27. See also William Hazlitt, *The Spirit of the Age*, 53ff., Leslie Stephen, *Studies of a Biographer* (London: Duckworth, 1902), 3, 119–22; J.

M. S. Tompkins, *The Polite Marriage* (Cambridge: Cambridge University Press, 1938), 161–62.

28. *Thomas De Quincey*, 11, 329.

29. D. Gilbert Dumas, "Things as They Were: The Original Ending of *Caleb Williams*," *Studies in English Literature* 6 (July 1966), 597; *Caleb Williams*, intr. by Walter Allen (London: Cassell, 1966), xiv; Gary Kelly, *The English Jacobin Novel 1780–1805* (Oxford: Clarendon Press, 1976), 208; Charles Edwyn Vaughan, *The Romantic Revolt* (Edinburgh: William Blackwood & Sons, 1907), 104; Angus Wilson "Evil in the English Novel," 18, and "William Godwin's Novels," 34, both in Kerry McSweeney, ed., *Diversity and Depth in Fiction. Selected Critical Writings of Angus Wilson* (London: Secker and Warburg, 1983); David McCraken, "Godwin's *Caleb Williams*: A Fictional Rebuttal of Burke," *Studies in Burke and His Time* 11, 2 (Winter 1969–70), 1442–52; Rosemary Jackson, *Fantasy: The Literature of Subversion* (London: Methuen, 1981), 97; Robert Kiely, *The Romantic Novel in England* (Cambridge, Mass.: Harvard University Press, 1972), 81–97; A. D. Harvey, "The Nightmare of Caleb Williams," *Essays in Criticism* 26 (July 1976), 244ff; Harvey Gross, "The Pursuer and the Pursued: A Study of *Caleb Williams*," *Texas Studies in Literature and Language* 1 (Spring 1959), 401–11; Eric Rothstein, *Systems of Order and Inquiry in Later Eighteenth-Century Fiction* (Berkeley: University of California Press, 1975), 209–29; Thomas Balfour Elder, "Godwin and 'The Great Springs of Human Passion,'" *Ariel* 14, 1 (January 1983), 29ff.; Marilyn Butler, "Godwin, Burke, and *Caleb Williams*," *Essays in Criticism* 32, 3 (July 1982), 252–56; James T. Boulton, "William Godwin, Philosopher and Novelist," in his *The Language of Politics in the Age of Wilkes and Burke* (London: Routledge and Kegan Paul, 1963), chapter 11; Ronald Paulson, *Representations of Revolution (1789–1820)* (New Haven: Yale University Press, 1983), 230–37.

30. Leslie Stephen, 3, 154.

31. P. N. Furbank, "Godwin's Novels," *Essays in Criticism* 5 (July 1955), 214; Rudolf F. Storch, "Metaphors of Private Guilt and Social Rebellion in Godwin's *Caleb Williams*," *ELH* 34 (1967), 188–207.

32. James T. Boulton, 222.

33. James T. Boulton, 247.

34. B. J. Tysdahl, *William Godwin as Novelist* (London: Athlone Press, 1981), 31.

35. William Empson, *Seven Types of Ambiguity* (1930, London: Chatto and Windus, 1970), 192.

36. Paul B. Armstrong, "History and Epistemology: The Example of *The Turn of the Screw*," *New Literary History* 19, 3 (Spring 1988), 698.

37. Harold Bloom, *The Anxiety of Influence* (New York: Oxford University Press, 1973), 93–96.

38. Michel Foucault, *The Order of Things* (London: Tavistock Publications, 1980), 217.

39. Sir David Lindsay Keir, *The Constitutional History of Modern Britain Since 1485* (London: Adam and Charles Black, 1964), 365.

40. Michel Foucault, 231. An *épistème* may be seen as "the total set of relations that unite, at a given period, the discursive practices" which in turn give rise to what may be broadly termed the "total body of knowledge" prevalent at the time. See Hayden White "Michel Foucault," in John Sturrock, ed., *Structuralism and Since* (Oxford: Oxford University Press, 1979), 81–115.

41. Michel Foucault, 238–39; 238.

42. John Locke, *The Second Treatise of Government*, ed. and intr. by J. W. Gough (Oxford: Basil Blackwell, 1956), 4.

43. William Godwin, *Enquiry Concerning Political Justice*, 496. The English translation of Rousseau's *The Social Contract* was published by Robinson in 1791.

44. Abinger Shelley-Godwin Papers, Dep. b. 226/15. "Essay of History & Romance" [10 leaves, paginated 225–46], 227.

45. "Essay of History & Romance," 234.

46. William Godwin, *Enquiry Concerning Political Justice*, 37.

47. Abinger Shelley-Godwin Papers, Dep. b. 226/2. "Autobiographical Notes 1773–1796," entry for 1787.

48. *Critical Review* 12 (1794), 236.

49. See Ann Radcliffe, *The Italian or the Confessional of the Black Penitents* (1797; Oxford: Oxford University Press 1971), 198: "Brutes do not deliberately slaughter their species; it remains for man only, man, proud of his prerogative of reason, and boasting of his sense of justice, to unite the most terrible extremes of folly and wickedness!" The complete Godwin quotation reads: "Amidst the woods the leopard knows his kind; / The tyger preys not on the tyger brood:/Man only is the common foe of man." Radcliffe's indebtedness to Godwin here is clear, since she gives these words to

Vivaldi who, for the moment, is being persecuted by a version of Falkland, Schedoni.

50. Shakespeare calls his character James Tyrrel a "discontented gentleman," in *Richard III*, 4.2.40. Tyrrel was the murderer of the King's nephews in the tower. Garrick's interpretation of Richard III had already made it an extremely popular play. Tyrrel's minor role in Richard III would have been better known as a result. See also Henry Brooke, *The Fool of Quality* (1765–70), where the name of the would-be knife murderer is Barnabas Tirrel.

51. Ronald Paulson makes the highly salutary observation that if James Gillray's political carricatures tell a narrative of the "disappearance of difference in endless reciprocal aggression that eliminates any distinction between antagonists," then William Godwin levels "the master and his servant, as well as all other masters and servants, into reciprocal fratricides based on a single principle of mediated desire." See Ronald Paulson, 236.

52. Dorothy Marshall, *Eighteenth Century England* (London: Longmans, 1962), 30–37; 473–86. In the *Vindication of the Rights of Men* Mary Wollstonecraft wrote: "Security of property! Behold, in a few words, the definition of English liberty." Quoted by Ronald Paulson, 228.

53. Hazlitt, *The Spirit of the Age*, 47.

54. Gavin Edwards, "William Godwin's 'Caleb Williams': Truth and 'Things as They Are,'" Part 2, in Francis Barker et al., eds. *1789: Reading Writing Revolution* (Colchester: University of Essex, 1982), 141.

55. Abinger Shelley-Godwin Papers, Dep. c. 537, Buff folder, marked "case 31," containing reflections by William Godwin on his life and works, 10 Oct. 1824, 2 leaves (3 pp.), 2.

56. Quoted in the *Critical Review* [4th Series] 1 (April 1812), 355.

57. *Quarterly Review* 18 (October 1817), 177.

58. *Blackwood's Edinburgh Magazine* 2 (January 1818), 405.

59. James T. Boulton, 244.

60. *Blackwood's Edinburgh Magazine* 2 (December 1817), 270.

61. *Blackwood's Edinburgh Magazine* 2, 279, 270.

62. *Blackwood's Edinburgh Magazine* 2, 270. See also the *Monthly Mirror* 19 (February 1805), 88.

63. *Critical Review* [3rd Series] 5 (July 1805), 262–69.

64. *Critical Review* [4th Series] 5 (January 1814), 13–36.

65. William Godwin, *Fleetwood*, xi.

66. For a brief note on Eugene Aram see *Caleb Williams*, ed. Maurice Hindle (Harmondsworth: Penguin Books, 1988), 381, note 56.

67. Rosemary Jackson, *Fantasy: The Literature of Subversion* (London: Methuen, 1981), 97.

68. G. W. F. Hegel, *Phenomenology of Spirit*, trans. A. V. Miller, notes by J. N. Findlay (Oxford: Oxford University Press, 1977), 111.

69. Cyril Tourneur, *The Revenger's Tragedy* in *Three Jacobean Tragedies*, ed. Gámini Salgado (Harmondsworth: Penguin Books, 1965), 5.3.118.

70. Paul de Man, *Blindness and Insight* (London: Methuen, 1983), 39.

71. Numbers 14, 23–24 [Authorized Version].

72. Forster Collection (223, F. A. Cat.) 47. C. 1. Victoria and Albert Museum Library.

73. D. Gilbert Dumas, "Things as They Were: The Original Ending of *Caleb Williams*," 575–97.

74. Abinger Shelley-Godwin Papers. Dep. f. 66. Notebook 47–55 [not original pagination].

75. *Caleb Williams*, ed. David McCracken (Oxford: Oxford University Press, 1982), xviii; *Caleb Williams*, ed. Maurice Hindle (Harmondsworth: Penguin Books, 1988), xxxvii.

76. Marilyn Butler, *Jane Austen and the War of Ideas* (Oxford: Clarendon Press, 1975), 68.

77. Matthew Gregory Lewis' *The Monk* (1796) uses this syntactical form to the point of annoyance. The first sentence of the novel itself begins with "Scarcely had the Abbey-Bell tolled for five minutes, and already was the Church of the Capuchins thronged with Auditors."

Chapter 5. Apocalyptic Narratives: Tales of Ends

1. Irving Massey, *The Gaping Pig. Literature and Metamorphosis* (Berkeley: University of California Press, 1976), 137.

2. *The Journals of Mary Shelley 1814–1844*, 2 vols., eds. Paula R. Feldman and Diana Scott-Kilvert (Oxford: Clarendon Press, 1987), 1, 415–16. Hereinafter cited as *Journals.*

3. *Journals,* 1, 422, 423.

4. *Journals,* 1, 423.

5. *Journals,* 2, 449, 470.

6. *Journals,* 2, 429, 440, 443.

7. *The Letters of Mary Wollstonecraft Shelley,* ed. Betty T. Bennett (Baltimore: Johns Hopkins University Press, 1980), 1, 250. Hereinafter cited as *Letters.*

8. *Letters,* 1, 260.

9. *Letters,* 1, 318–19.

10. *Journals,* 2, 446.

11. *Journals,* 2, 471.

12. *Journals,* 2, 474.

13. *Journals,* 2, 476.

14. *Journals,* 2, 476–77.

15. *Journals,* 2, 477.

16. *Journals,* 2, 478.

17. *Journals,* 2, 489.

18. *Journals,* 2, 495.

19. *Letters,* 1, 510–11.

20. Elizabeth Nitchie, *Mary Shelley. Author of "Frankenstein"* (1953; Westport, Conn.: Greenwood Press, 1970), 151.

21. Elizabeth Nitchie, 151.

22. Virgil, *The Aeneid,* trans. Frank O. Copley, intr. by Brooks Otis (New York: The Bobbs-Merrill Company, 1965), 116.

23. Virgil, *The Aeneid,* trans. Robert Fitzgerald (Harmondsworth: Penguin Books, 1985), 161.

24. Mary Shelley, *The Last Man,* ed. Hugh J. Luke, Jr. (1826; Lincoln: University of Nebraska Press, 1965), 3. All subsequent references to this text are cited in parentheses after the quotation.

25. Sandra M. Gilbert and Susan Gubar, *The Madwoman in the Attic. The Woman Writer and the Nineteenth-Century Literary Imagination* (New Haven: Yale University Press, 1979), 95.

26. C. F. Volney, *The Ruins: or a Survey of the Revolution of Empires with notes Historical, Geographical, and Explanatory to which is annexed The Law of Nature* (London: T. Davison, 1819). All page references to quotations from this text are given in parentheses.

27. Brian Rigby, "Volney's Rationalist Apocalypse: 'Les Ruines ou Méditations sur les Révolutions des Empires,'" in Francis Barker et al., eds., *1789: Reading Writing Revolution* (Colchester: University of Essex, 1982), 29.

28. C. F. Volney, *The Law of Nature; or Principles of Morality Deduced from the Physical Constitution of Mankind and the Universe* (London: T. Davison, 1819).

29. A. J. Sambrook, "A Romantic Theme: The Last Man," *Forum for Modern Language Studies* 2 (1966), 25.

30. Quoted by A. J. Sambrook, 28.

31. [Grainville], *The Last Man, or Omegarus and Syderia, A Romance in Futurity,* 2 vols. (London: R. Dutton, 1806). All page references are to this text and are given in parentheses.

32. Jean de Palacio, "Mary Shelley and 'The Last Man,'" *Revue de Littérature Comparée* 42, 1 (1968), 40.

33. *Critical Review* 8 (August 1806), 443.

34. *The Poetical Works of Lord Byron* (Oxford: Oxford University Press, 1945), 95–96.

35. Other well-known poems on the theme include Thomas Campbell's "The Last Man" (1823) and Thomas Hood's "The Last Man" (1826). The so-called "poet of fragments," Thomas Lovell Beddoes, also left behind notes that indicate work-in-progress on this theme. See *The Works of Thomas Lovell Beddoes*, ed. and intr. by H. W. Donner (Oxford: Oxford University Press, 1935) 525–26. The notes indicate that Beddoes' play would have been a good mix of Grainville, Mary Shelley, and Matthew Gregory Lewis.

36. Quoted by Palacio, 41. Thomas Campbell's letter to the *Times* appeared on 24 March 1825.

37. Mary Wollstonecraft Shelley, *Tales and Stories*, intr. by Richard Garnett (London: William Paterson and Co., 1891), iv.

38. Walter Edwin Peck, "The Biographical Element in the Novels of Mary Wollstonecraft Shelley," *PMLA* 38 (1923), 191–219.

39. Ernest J. Lovell, Jr., "Byron and the Byronic Hero in the Novels of Mary Shelley," *Studies in English* (Austin: University of Texas), 30 (1951), 175.

40. Hartley S. Spatt, "Mary Shelley's Last Men: The Truth of Dreams," *Studies in the Novel* 7 (1975), 526–37.

41. Hartley S. Spatt, 527.

42. Lee Sterrenburg, "*The Last Man:* Anatomy of Failed Revolutions," *Nineteenth-Century Fiction* 33 (December 1978), 325.

43. J. M. Thompson, *The French Revolution* (Oxford: Basil Blackwell, 1962), ix and Appendices A and B.

44. Geoffrey H. Hartman, *Wordsworth's Poetry 1787–1814* (New Haven: Yale University Press, 1977), xvi–xx.

45. Quoted by Lee Sterrenburg, 324.

46. Lee Sterrenburg, 328.

47. Chris Baldick, *In Frankenstein's Shadow. Myth, Monstrosity and Nineteenth-century Writing* (Oxford: Clarendon Press, 1987), 17–24.

48. Lee Sterrenburg, 333.

49. Quoted by Lee Sterrenburg, 334.

50. George Eliot, "Quarry for *Middlemarch*" in *Middlemarch,* ed. Bert G. Hornback (New York: W. W. Norton and Company, 1977), 611–12.

51. Lee Sterrenburg, 341.

52. Robert Lance Snyder, "Apocalypse and Indeterminacy in Mary Shelley's *The Last Man,*" *Studies in Romanticism* 17 (Fall 1978), 436.

53. Robert Lance Snyder, 436.

54. Robert Lance Snyder, 437.

55. Robert Lance Snyder, 438.

56. Robert Lance Snyder, 440.

57. Robert Lance Snyder, 447.

58. Mary Poovey, *The Proper Lady and the Woman Writer.* Ideology as Style in the Works of Mary Wollstonecraft, Mary Shelley, and Jane Austen (Chicago: University of Chicago Press, 1984), 150.

59. For an account of the Gothic and the Oriental see Gary Kelly, "Social Conflict, Nation and Empire: From Gothicism to Romantic Orientalism," *Ariel* 20, 2 (April 1989), 3–18.

60. Brian Aldiss and David Wingrove, *Trillion Year Spree. The History of Science Fiction* (London: Paladin Grafton Books, 1988), 62. The cholera epidemic that began in Calcutta in 1817 was to reach England five years after the publication of *The Last Man.*

61. Jacques Derrida, *Of Grammatology,* trans. by Gayatri Chakravorty Spivak (Baltimore: Johns Hopkins University Press, 1976), 5.

62. Sandra M. Gilbert and Susan Gubar, 247.

Chapter 6. *Frankenstein*: Sublime as Desecration/Decreation

1. Mary Shelley, *Frankenstein or, The Modern Prometheus,* ed., with variant readings, intr., and notes, by James Rieger (Chicago: University of Chicago Press, 1982). Citations are taken from both the 1818 and 1831 texts and, where they occur in only one of these texts, the appropriate edition is indicated.

2. Brian Aldiss and David Wingrove, *Trillion Year Spree. The History of Science Fiction* (London: Paladin Grafton Books, 1988), 38, 44–45, 51, 55.

3. *The Journals of Mary Shelley 1814–1844,* 2 vols., eds. Paula R. Feldman and Diana Scott-Kilvert (Oxford: Clarendon Press, 1987), 2, 439. Hereinafter cited as *Journals.*

4. Mary Shelley, *Frankenstein,* ed. James Rieger, 227, note 13.

5. Oswei Temkin, *The Double Face of Janus and Other Essays in the History of Medicine* (Baltimore: Johns Hopkins University Press, 1977), 346.

6. Richard Holmes, *Shelley: The Pursuit* (Harmondsworth: Penguin Books, 1987), 286, 290.

7. Oswei Temkin, 353.

8. Immanuel Kant, *The Critique of Judgement,* trans. James Creed Meredith (Oxford: Clarendon Press, 1986), 20.

9. Immanuel Kant, 22.

10. Chris Baldick, *In Frankenstein's Shadow* (Oxford: Clarendon Press, 1987), 35. Ronald Paulson sees in the creation of the monster an alle-

gory of the "Enlightenment-created monster" that was the French Revolution. It left behind terror and destruction because it was "disowned and misunderstood [and] created unnaturally by reason rather than love." See Ronald Paulson, *Representations of Revolution (1789–1820)* (New Haven: Yale University Press, 1983), 239.

11. Mary Shelley, *Frankenstein*, ed. James Rieger, 6–8.

12. Patricia Yaeger, "Toward a Female Sublime," in Linda Kauffman, ed., *Gender and Theory. Dialogues on Feminist Criticism* (Oxford: Basil Blackwell, 1989), 192.

13. Abinger Papers, Dep. c. 524, letter 20. William Godwin to Mary Shelley Oct 27, 1818. Copy of letter in Mary Shelley's hand. Paper watermarked 1839.

14. Abinger Papers, Dep. c. 524, letter 23. William Godwin to Mary Shelley Sept. 9, 1819.

15. Abinger Papers, Dep. c. 524, letter 36. William Godwin to Mary Shelley Aug. 6, 1822.

16. Abinger Papers, Dep. c. 524, letter 41. William Godwin to Mary Shelley Nov. 15, 1822.

17. Abinger Papers, Dep. c. 524, file 7, letter 42. William Godwin to Mary Shelley Tuesday, Feb. 18 [1823].

18. *Quarterly Review*, 18 (January 1818), 382.

19. *Quarterly Review* 18, 382.

20. *Quarterly Review* 18, 385.

21. *Blackwood's Edinburgh Magazine* 2 (1818), 613–20.

22. *Blackwood's Edinburgh Magazine* 2, 613.

23. *Blackwood's Edinburgh Magazine* 2, 614.

24. *Blackwood's Edinburgh Magazine* 3 (1818), 649.

25. *Monthly Review* 85 (April 1818), 439.

26. *Edinburgh Review* 19 (March 1818), 252.

27. *Edinburgh Review* 19, 253.

28. *Athenaeum* (Nov. 10, 1832), 730.

29. *Athenaeum* (Nov. 10, 1832), 730.

30. Ronald Paulson, *Representations of Revolution (1789–1820)*, 246.

31. Mario Praz, *The Romantic Agony*, trans. Angus Davidson, foreword by Frank Kermode, 2nd ed. (Oxford: Oxford University Press, 1970), 116.

32. Mario Praz, 115.

33. Ellen Moers, *Literary Women* (New York: Doubleday and Company, 1976), 90–110.

34. Ellen Moers, 90.

35. Ellen Moers, 92.

36. U. C. Knoepflmacher, "Thoughts on the Aggression of Daughters," in George Levine and U. C. Knoepflmacher, eds., *The Endurance of Frankenstein. Essays on Mary Shelley's Novel* (Berkeley: University of California Press, 1979), 90.

37. Ellen Moers, 93.

38. Ellen Moers, 99.

39. U. C. Knoepflmacher, "Thoughts on the Aggression of Daughters," 91–92.

40. Quoted in Lee Sterrenburg, "Mary Shelley's Monster: Politics and Psyche in *Frankenstein*," in *The Endurance of Frankenstein*, 147.

41. Illustration reprinted in Chris Baldick, 23.

42. *Tait's Magazine* (March 1837), reprinted in *The Collected Works of Thomas De Quincey*, ed. David Masson (Edinburgh: Adam and Charles Black, 1890), 3, 25.

43. Quoted by Chris Baldick, *In Frankenstein's Shadow*, 22.

44. Sandra M. Gilbert and Susan Gubar, *The Madwoman in the Attic* (New Haven: Yale University Press, 1979), 221.

45. Leslie Tannenbaum, "From Filthy Type to Truth: Miltonic Myth in *Frankenstein*," *Keats-Shelley Journal* 26 (1977), 112–13. Ronald Paulson concludes, "Frankenstein's monster is the ultimate in the mergers we have seen of man and woman, father and son, master and servant, oppressor and oppressed, violence and victim: an amalgam that includes Victor Frankenstein, the monster's creator and double." *Representations of Revolution*, 247.

46. Robert Kiely, *The Romantic Novel in England* (Cambridge, Mass.: Harvard University Press, 1972), 164.

47. Judith Wilt, *Ghosts of the Gothic. Austen, Eliot, & Lawrence* (Princeton: Princeton University Press, 1980), 62.

48. Mary Poovey, *The Proper Lady and the Woman Writer* (Chicago: University of Chicago Press, 1984), chap. 4.

49. Joyce Carol Oates, "Frankenstein's Fallen Angel," *Critical Inquiry*, 10, 3 (March 1984), 552.

50. Margaret Homans, *Bearing the Word. Language and Female Experience in Nineteenth-Century Women's Writing* (Chicago: University of Chicago Press, 1986), 111.

51. Mario Praz, *The Romantic Agony*, and Harold Bloom, *The Ringers in the Tower. Studies in Romantic Tradition* (Chicago: University of Chicago Press, 1971). See Margaret Homans, 116ff.

52. Margaret Homans, 117.

53. See Elaine Showalter, *A Literature of Their Own: British Novelists from Brontë to Lessing* (Princeton: Princeton University Press, 1977).

54. Frances L. Restuccia, "Female Gothic Writing: 'Under Cover to Alice,'" *Genre* 18 (Fall 1986), 245.

55. Eve Kosofsky Sedgwick, *Between Men: English Literature and Male Homosocial Desire* (New York: Columbia University Press, 1985), 90.

56. Frances L. Restuccia, 248. According to William Veeder [*Mary Shelley and Frankenstein. The Fate of Androgyny* (Chicago: University of Chicago Press, 1986), 2] the female gothicist in Mary Shelley's novels might also reflect the author's lifelong concern with the psychological ideal of androgyny and its opposite, bifurcation.

57. Paul O'Flinn, "Production and Reproduction: The Case of *Frankenstein*," *Literature and History* 9, 2 (Autumn 1983), 194.

58. Abinger Papers, MS Shelley adds c. 12, fol. 9: January 1818

Frankenstein	3v No. 500			
To author	6			
Reviewers	16			
Claimed under copyright	11			
Booksellers who took 25	8	—— 41 / 459	@ 10/6 —	£240 . 19 . 6
		Expenses off printing as annexed		115 . 18
				125 . 1 . 6
		To author 1/3	£41 . 13 . 10	
		Publishers 2/3	83 . 7 . 8	125 . 1 . 6

59. Richard Brinsley Peake, *Frankenstein: A melo-dramatic Opera in 3 Acts,* The Huntington Library, MS. Cat. LA 2359. All references are to this manuscript.

60. *The Letters of Mary Wollstonecraft Shelley,* ed. Betty T. Bennett (Baltimore: Johns Hopkins University Press, 1980), 1, 378.

61. The phrase is Chris Baldick's (86).

62. Elizabeth Gaskell, *Mary Barton: A Tale of Manchester Life* (Harmondsworth: Penguin Books, 1970), 219.

63. Quoted in Rob Wilson, *American Sublime* (Madison: University of Wisconsin Press, 1991), 193.

64. David Ketterer, *Frankenstein's Creation: The Book, The Monster, and Human Reality* (Victoria, B. C.: University of Victoria English Literary Studies, 1979), 12: "Clearly, we are to understand that the novel and the monster are both in a sense dream creations."

65. Peter Brooks, "Godlike Science/Unhallowed Arts: Language and Monstrosity in *Frankenstein,*" *New Literary History* 9, 3 (Spring 1978), 602.

66. Peter Brooks, 605.

67. Chauncey C. Loomis, "The Arctic Sublime," in U. C. Knoepflmacher and G. B. Tennyson, eds., *Nature and the Victorian Imagination* (Berkeley: University of California Press, 1977), 96.

68. Jean-Jacques Rousseau, *The Confessions,* trans. and intr. by J. M. Cohen (Harmondsworth: Penguin Books, 1985), 17.

69. Rousseau, 19.

70. Gayatri Chakravorty Spivak, "Three Women's Texts and a Critique of Imperialism," *Critical Inquiry* 12, 1 (Autumn 1985), 255.

71. There is a faint echo of Frankenstein in George Eliot's Lydgate. In *Middlemarch* we come across a startling anecdotal narrative (2, 15) about Lydgate, who was then studying in Paris and preoccupied with "some galvanic experiments. " He falls in love with Laure, a dark actress from Provençale who, during the course of a melodrama, which Lydgate was in the habit of viewing as often as he could, mortally stabs her actor-lover on stage. Lydgate is convinced of her innocence—it was an accident in a far too realistic rendition of a melodrama—and proposes to marry her when she confesses, "My foot really slipped. . . . *I meant to do it.*" Like Frankenstein, Lydgate, too, returns to galvanism after a terrible personal ordeal.

72. Sander L. Gilman, "Black Bodies, White Bodies: Toward an Iconography of Female Sexuality in Late Nineteenth-Century Art, Medicine, and Literature," *Critical Inquiry,* 12, 1 (Autumn 1985), 213. Confronted by the outrageous show of sexual affection on the part of a young man and a novice, the Superior's horrified attitude is explained by the narrator in Charles Maturin's *Melmoth the Wanderer* (1820; Oxford: Oxford University Press, 1972, 207) as a disgust comparable to seeing "the horrible loves of the baboons and the Hottentot women."

73. Paul Sherwin, "*Frankenstein*: Creation as Catastrophe," *PMLA* 96, 5 (October 1981), 885.

74. Mary Jacobus, "Is There a Woman in This Text?" *New Literary History* 14, 1 (Autumn 1982), 138.

75. Mary Jacobus, 138. Bette London takes up the question of the "discomposure of masculinity" in a slightly different manner. She refers to the way in which a particular version of the "sensationalized body" (the version associated with questions of specularity) is represented through the discourse of the female. This coding is then deployed by Mary Shelley upon "the normative construction of masculinity" so that the novel focuses not so much on "the spectacle of female monstrosity but on the extravagant fantasies of a deficient masculinity." In short, the troubling and troubled male body (captured so well in Louis-Edouard Fournier's 1889 iconography of Shelley's cremation) can be represented only if it is supported by the scaffolding of an unstable discourse of the female. See Bette London, "Mary Shelley, *Frankenstein,* and the Spectacle of Masculinity," *PMLA,* 108, 2 (March 1993), 262–65.

Chapter 7. The Gothic Sublime and Literary History

1. Thomas De Quincey, *Confessions of an English Opium-Eater* (London: Taylor and Hessey, 1822), 163.

2. Thomas De Quincey, 163–64.

3. Thomas De Quincey, 165.

4. Thomas Weiskel, *The Romantic Sublime: Studies in the Structure and Psychology of Transcendence* (Baltimore: Johns Hopkins University Press, 1976), 22.

5. Jacques Derrida, *The Truth in Painting,* trans. Geoff Bennington and Ian McLeod (Chicago: University of Chicago Press, 1987), 122. Further page references are given in the text.

6. William Beckford, *Vathek* (1786; Oxford: Oxford University Press, 1983). Page references are given in the text.

7. *English Review* 8 (September 1786), 180.

8. *English Review* 8 (September 1786), 181, 183.

9. *European Magazine* 10 (August 1786), 104

10. *Monthly Review* 76 (May 1787), 450.

11. *New Review* 9 (June 1786), 411.

12. Robert Kiely, *The Romantic Novel in England* (Cambridge, Mass.: Harvard University Press, 1972), 43ff.

13. Robert Kiely, 61.

14. Edward W. Said, *Orientalism* (Harmondsworth: Penguin Books, 1985), 73.

15. Robert Kiely, 62.

16. Matthew Gregory Lewis, *The Monk* (1796; Oxford: Oxford University Press, 1980). Page references are given in the text.

17. Peter Brooks, "Virtue and Terror: *The Monk*," *ELH* 40 (1973), 262. The political connection between *The Monk* and the French Revolution (the Marquis de Sade had called it "the inevitable result of the revolutionary shocks which all of Europe had suffered") is underlined by Ronald Paulson who writes (*Representations of Revolution*, 220): "The model of the sublime as it emerges in 'Monk' Lewis does corrrespond to one version of the general pattern Burke at once detected in the French Revolution: first destroy the father and then of necessity become more repressive than he was."

18. Rudolf Otto, *The Idea of the Holy*, trans. John W. Harvey (Harmondsworth: Penguin Books, 1959), 27.

19. Martin Price, "The Sublime Poem: Pictures and Powers," *Yale Review*, 58 (1969), 198.

20. Quoted by Robert Kiely, 103.

21. Thomas J. Mathias, *The Pursuits of Literature* (1794–97; London: Becker and Porter, 1812), 213, note 2.

22. *Critical Review* [2nd Series] 19 (February 1797), 194, 196.

23. *Monthly Review* [New Series] 23 (August 1797), 451. M. G. Lewis offered a spirited defense of his writing and an account of the origins of *The*

Monk (with particular reference to the fact that he had not read the French novel *Le Diable Amoureux* which it resembled) in his preface to *Adelmorn, The Outlaw; A Romantic Drama* (London: J. Bell, 1801), i–ix.

24. *Critical Review* [3rd Series] 5 (July 1805), 255.

25. *Gentleman's Magazine* 79 (1809), 141.

26. Thomas J. Mathias, 72, note 26.

27. *Critical Review* 23 (1798), 166–69. Charles Maturin felt that Ann Radcliffe was "a benevolent enchanter, whose 'quaint apparitions' may soften and solemnize, but neither terrify nor hurt us." [*British Critic* 11 (1818), 49.]

28. *Monthly Review* [New Series], 2 (1826), 282.

29. "Terrorist Novel Writing," *The Spirit of Public Journals for 1797*, vol. 1 (London: James Ridgway, 1802), 229.

30. Ann Radcliffe, "On the Supernatural in Poetry," *New Monthly Magazine* 16 (1826), 150.

31. Georges Poulet, "Timelessness and Romanticism," *Journal of the History of Ideas* 15, 1 (January 1954), 3–22.

32. *Monthly Review* [New Series], 22 (March 1797), 283.

33. Ann Radcliffe, *The Italian or the Confessional of the Black Penitents*, ed. and intr. by Frederick Garber (Oxford: Oxford University Press, 1971), 21. All citations, with page references given in parentheses, are from this edition.

34. *Analytical Review* 25 (April 1797), 516.

35. Percy Bysshe Shelley, *Zastrozzi* and *St. Irvyne*, ed. and intr. by Stephen C. Behrendt (Oxford: Oxford University Press, 1986). All citations, with page references given in parentheses, are taken from this edition.

36. *Critical Review* 21 (November 1810), 329–31.

37. *Critical Review* 21 (November 1810), 331.

38. William Shakespeare, *Troilus and Cressida*, 3.2.83–85.

39. P. B. Shelley, *Zastrozzi* and *St. Irvyne*, 206.

40. Charles Robert Maturin, *Melmoth the Wanderer* (1820; Oxford: Oxford University Press, 1972), 537. [Subsequent page references will be given in the text.] The participation is, however, based on a pact of "incommu-

nicable condition" (237), which for the subject is a "horror [so] unspeakable" (276) that "we feel we suffer as much from an illusion as from truth" (157).

41. On her deathbed Immalee/Isidora wonders if he might even be in paradise: "Will he be there!" (533).

42. *Monthly Review* 94 (January 1821), 81.

43. *London Magazine* 3 (January 1821), 96.

44. Quoted by the *Athenaeum* (April 30, 1892), 560.

45. Coral Ann Howells, *Love, Mystery, and Misery: Feeling in Gothic Fiction* (London: Athlone Press, 1978), 158.

46. Harold Bloom, *Poetry and Repression* (New Haven: Yale University Press, 1976), 244. All further references are given in the text.

47. Quoted by George Hendrick in *The Bhagvat-Geeta* (1785), trans. Charles Wilkins. Facsimile reproduction, ed. George Hendrick (New York: Scholars' Facsimiles & Reprints, 1972), x.

48. Eric J. Sharpe, "Some Western Interpretations of the Bhagavadgītā, 1785–1885," *Journal of Studies in the Bhagavadgītā* 1 (1981), 8.

49. Herman Melville, *Pierre or The Ambiguities* (1852; Evanston: Northwestern University Press, 1983). Page references are given in the text.

50. Thomas Weiskel, 97

51. Curiously enough, it was Melville's sister who transcribed the fair-copy of the text. See *Pierre*, "Historical Note," 391.

52. Edmund Burke, *A Philosophical Enquiry into the Origin of Our Ideas of the Sublime and Beautiful*, ed. J. T. Boulton (Notre Dame: University of Notre Dame Press, 1968), 115.

53. According to the *OED*, Memnon was a demigod traditionally said to have erected the citadel or palace at Susa; hence the use of "Memnonian" as an epithet for Susa or Persia generally. There is a further connection, made originally by the Greeks, between Memnon and the Statue of Thebes in Egypt. This statue is said to give forth a musical sound when touched by dawn. Emily Dickinson refers to Memnon in Poem 261:

> Put up my lute!
> What of—my Music!
> Since the sole ear I cared to charm—
> Passive—as Granite—laps My Music—
> Sobbing—will suit—as well as psalm!

Would but the "Memnon" of the Desert—
Teach me the strain
That vanquished Him—
When He—surrendered to the Sunrise—
Maybe—that—would awaken—them!

Emily Dickinson, *The Complete Poems of Emily Dickinson,* ed. Thomas H. Johnson (Boston: Little, Brown and Company, 1960?), 120.

54. Alice A. Jardine, *Gynesis. Configurations of Woman and Modernity* (Ithaca: Cornell University Press, 1985), 122.

55. Herman Melville, "Preclusive," in *Clarel* (New York: Russell and Russell, 1963), vol. 1, 316. See chapter 2, note 49.

56. Sigmund Freud, Case Histories 1, 'Dora' and 'Little Hans' *The Pelican Freud Library* (Harmondsworth: Penguin Books, 1977), 8, 150.

Select Bibliography

Bibliographies

Frank, Frederick S. *The First Gothics. A Critical Guide to the English Gothic Novel.* New York: Garland Publishing, Inc., 1987.

Hazen, A. T. *A Bibliography of Horace Walpole.* New Haven: Yale University Press, 1948.

———. *A Bibliography of the Strawberry Hill Press.* Folkestone and London: Dawsons of Pall Mall, 1973.

Lyles, W. H. *Mary Shelley: An Annotated Bibliography* New York: Garland Publishing, Inc., 1975.

McNutt, Dan J. *The Eighteenth-Century Gothic Novel: An Annotated Bibliography of Criticism and Selected Texts* New York: Garland Publishing, Inc., 1975.

Nangle, Benjamin Christie. *Monthly Review First Series 1749–1789 Indexes of Contributors and Articles.* Oxford: Oxford University Press, 1934.

———. *Monthly Review Second Series 1790–1815 Indexes of Contributors and Articles.* Oxford: Oxford University Press, 1955.

Pollin, Burton R. *Godwin Criticism: A Synoptic Bibliography.* Toronto: University of Toronto Press, 1967.

Summers, Montague. *A Gothic Bibliography.* London: The Fortune Press, 1941.

Manuscript Sources

1. Abinger Papers, Duke Humfrey's Library, The Bodleian. Batch I–VII. Shelley-Godwin Papers in various folders, temporarily catalogued as "deposit (nos)" and "folio (nos)," including MS fragments of *Frankenstein, Mathilda,* William Godwin's diary, etc.
2. MS of William Godwin, *Things as They Are; or, The Adventures of Caleb Williams,* with the original ending. Forster Collection (223, F. A. Cat.) 47. c. 1. Victoria and Albert Museum Library.
3. MS of [Richard Brinsley Peake, *Presumption*] *Frankenstein: A Melo-dramatic Opera in 3 Acts.* MS. Cat. LA 2359. The Huntington.

Primary Texts

Aiken, J., and A. L. Aiken. *Miscellaneous Pieces, in Prose.* London: J. Johnson, 1773.

Austen, Jane. *Northanger Abbey* (1818). Edited by Anne Henry Ehrenpreis. Harmondsworth: Penguin Books, 1972.

Beckett, Samuel. *The Unnamable, Molloy, Malone Dies.* London: John Calder, 1959.

Beckford, William. *Vathek* (1786). Edited by Roger Lonsdale. Oxford: Oxford University Press, 1983.

Beddoes, Thomas Lovell. *The Works of Thomas Lovell Beddoes.* Edited and introduced by H. W. Donner. Oxford: Oxford University Press, 1935.

The Bhagvat-Geeta or Dialogues of Kreeshna and Arjoon. Translated by Charles Wilkins. Introduced by Warren Hastings. London: C. Nourse, 1785. Facsimile reproduction edited by George Hendrick. New York: Scholars' Facsimiles & Reprints, 1972.

William Blake. *Complete Writings.* Edited by Geoffrey Keynes. Oxford: Oxford University Press, 1972.

The British Novelists; with an Essay and Prefaces Biographical and Critical by Mrs Barbauld. Vol. 22. London: F. C. and J. Rivington, 1810.

Broster, John. *Edmond; Orphan of the Castle.* London: R. Faulder and T. Hurst, 1799.

Burke, Edmund. *A Philosophical Enquiry into the Origin of Our Ideas of the Sublime and Beautiful* (1757). Edited, introduced, and notes by James T. Boulton. Notre Dame: University of Notre Dame Press, 1968.

———. *Reflections on the Revolution in France* (1790). Edited and introduced by Conor Cruise O'Brien. Harmondsworth: Penguin Books, 1983.

Byron, George Gordon, Lord. *The Poetical Works of Lord Byron.* Oxford: Oxford University Press, 1945.

———. *The Works of Lord Byron.* Edited by Thomas Moore. Vol. 12. London: John Murray, 1832.

———. *Mazeppa, A Poem.* London: John Murray, 1819.

Calmet, Augustine. *The Phantom World: or, The Philosophy of Spirits, Apparitions, etc.* Two vols. Edited, Introduced, and notes by Rev. Henry Christmas. London: Richard Bentley, 1850.

Campbell, Thomas. *Poems of Thomas Campbell.* Selected by Louis Campbell. London: Macmillan, 1904.

Clairmont, Claire. *The Journals of Claire Clairmont.* Edited by Marion Kingston Stocking. Cambridge, Mass.: Harvard University Press, 1968.

Colman, George, the Younger. *The Iron Chest.* London: Cadell and Davies, 1796.

———. *The Iron Chest.* Introduced by Mrs. Inchbald. London: Longman, Hurst, Rees, Orme, and Brown, 1821.

DeLillo, Don. *White Noise.* London: Picador, 1985.

De Quincey, Thomas. *Confessions of an English Opium-Eater.* London: Taylor and Hessey, 1822.

———. *The Collected Writings of De Quincey.* Fourteen vols. Edited by David Masson. Edinburgh: Adam and Charles Black, 1890.

Dickinson, Emily. *The Complete Poems of Emily Dickinson.* Edited by Thomas H. Johnson. Boston: Little, Brown and Company, 1960?.

Du Bois, Edward [pseud. Count Reginald de St. Leon]. *St. Godwin. A Tale of the Sixteenth, Seventeenth, and Eighteenth Centuries* (1800) Reprint. New York: Garland Publishing, Inc., 1974.

Edgeworth, Maria. *Castle Rackrent* (1800). Edited by George Watson. Oxford: Oxford University Press, 1969.

Eighteenth-Century Verse. Edited by Roger Lonsdale. Oxford: Oxford University Press, 1984.

Eliot, George. *Middlemarch* (1874). Edited by Bert G. Hornback. New York: W. W. Norton, 1977.

Gaskell, Elizabeth. *Mary Barton: A Tale of Manchester Life.* Harmondsworth: Penguin Books, 1970.

Godwin, William. *Things as They Are; or, The Adventures of Caleb Williams.* London: B. Crosby, 1794.

———. *Caleb Williams* [Bentley's Standard Novels No. 2]. London: Henry Colburn and Richard Bentley, 1831.

———. *Caleb Williams.* Edited by David McCracken. Oxford: Oxford University Press, 1982.

———. *Caleb Williams.* Edited by George Sherburn. New York: Holt, Rinehart and Winston, Inc., 1960.

———. *Caleb Williams.* Edited by Herbert van Thal. Introduced by Walter Allen. London: Cassell, 1966.

———. *Caleb Williams.* Edited by Maurice Hindle. Harmondsworth: Penguin Books, 1988.

———. *St. Leon* (1799) [Bentley's Standard Novels No. 5]. London: Henry Colburn and Richard Bentley, 1831.

———. *Mandeville: A Tale of the Seventeenth Century in England.* Three vols. London: Longman, Hurst, Rees, Orme, and Brown, 1817.

———. *Fleetwood* (1805). London: Richard Bentley, 1832.
———. *Enquiry Concerning Political Justice* (1793). Edited and introduced by Isaac Kramnick. Harmondsworth: Penguin Books, 1976.
Goethe, Johann Wolfgang von. *The Sorrows of Werter: A German Story*. Translated by Richard Graves. London: T. Osborne and S. Griffin, 1795.
[Grainville, Jean-Baptiste François Cousin de]. *The Last Man, or Omegarus and Syderia, A Romance in Futurity*. Two vols. London: R. Dutton, 1806.
Hawthorne, Nathaniel. *The House of the Seven Gables* (1831). New York: Signet Classics, 1981.
Hazlitt, William. *The Complete Works of William Hazlitt*. Edited by P. P. Howe (after the edition of A. R. Waller and Arnold Glover). Vol. 11. London and Toronto: J. M. Dent and Sons Limited, 1932.
———. *The Spirit of the Age: Or, Contemporary Portraits*. London: Henry Colburn, 1825.
———. *The Spirit of the Age or Contemporary Portraits* (1825). Edited by E. D. Mackerness. London: Collins, 1969.
Hegel, G. W. F. *Phenomenology of Spirit* (1807). Translated by A. V. Miller. Foreword and notes by J. N. Findlay. Oxford: Oxford University Press, 1977.
———. *The Philosophy of Fine Art*. Four vols. Translated by F. P. B. Osmaston (1835–38). New York: Hacker Art Books, 1975.
Hood, Thomas. *The Poetical Works of Thomas Hood*. London: Frederick Warne and Co., n. d.
Hurd, Richard. *Letters on Chivalry and Romance*. London: A. Millar, 1762.
———. *Five Pieces of Runic Poetry. Translated from the Islandic Language*. London: R. and J. Dodsley, 1763.
Inchbald, Elizabeth. *A Simple Story* (1791). Edited by J. M. S. Tompkins. Oxford: Oxford University Press, 1967.
Jephson, Robert. *The Count of Narbonne*. London: T. Cadell, 1781.
Joyce, James. *Ulysses* (1922). New York: Random House, 1946.
Kant, Immanuel. *Observations on the Feeling of the Beautiful and Sublime*. Translated by John T. Goldthwait. Berkeley: University of California Press, 1973.
———. *Critique of Pure Reason*. Translated by Norman Kemp Smith. London: Macmillan, 1973.
———. *The Critique of Judgement* (1790). Translated by James Creed Meredith. Oxford: Clarendon Press, 1986.

Lawrence, D. H. *The Rainbow* (1915). Harmondsworth: Penguin Books, 1965.

Lewis, Matthew Gregory. *The Monk* (1796). Edited and introduced by Louis F. Peck and John Berryman. New York: Grove Press Inc., 1959.

———. *The Monk.* Edited by James Kingsley and Howard Anderson. Oxford: Oxford University Press, 1980.

———. *Adelmorn, The Outlaw; A Romantic Drama.* London: J. Bell, 1801.

Mackenzie, Henry. *The Man of Feeling* (1771). Edited by Brian Vickers. Oxford: Oxford University Press, 1967.

Mammaṭa. *Kāvyaprakāśaḥ.* Commentary by Acarya Vishveshvar. Edited by Narendra. Varanasi: Jñānamandala Limited, 1960.

Mathias, Thomas J. *The Pursuits of Literature, a Satirical Poem in Four Dialogues* (1794–97). London: Becker and Porter, 1812.

Maturin, Charles Robert. *Melmoth the Wanderer* (1820). Edited by William F. Axton. Lincoln: University of Nebraska Press, 1961.

———. *Melmoth the Wanderer.* Edited by Douglas Grant. Oxford: Oxford University Press, 1972.

Melville, Herman. *Pierre or The Ambiguities* (1852). Evanston: Northwestern University Press, 1983. The Northwestern-Newberry Edition.

———. *Clarel.* Two vols. New York: Russell and Russell, 1963.

Naipaul, V. S. *The Enigma of Arrival.* London: Viking, 1987.

Piranesi, G. *Oeuvres de Piraneses Edifices de Trois* [and] *CARCERI*, Ashmolean Museum atl. fol. U. L. 921. 9/Pir.

———. *Le Antichità Romane Opera di Giambattista Piranesi.* Roma: Bouchard, 1756. Ashmolean Museum 921. 9/Pir.

Polidori, J. W. *The Vampyre; A Tale.* London: Sherwood, Neely and Jones, 1819.

———. *The Diary of Dr. John William Polidori* (1816). Edited by William Michael Rossetti. London: Elkin Mathews, 1911.

———. *An Essay upon the Source of Positive Pleasure.* London: Longman, Hurst, Rees, Orme, and Brown, 1818.

———. *Ernestus Berchtold; or The Modern Oedipus. A Tale.* London: Longman, Hurst, Rees, Orme, and Brown, 1819.

———. *Ximenes, The Wreath, and other Poems.* London: Longman, Hurst, Rees, Orme, and Brown, 1819.

Pynchon, Thomas. *The Crying of Lot 49* (1965). London: Picador, 1979.

Radcliffe, Ann. *The Romance of the Forest* (1791). Edited by Chloe Chard. Oxford: Oxford University Press, 1986.

———. *The Mysteries of Udolpho* (1794). Edited by Bonamy Dobrée. Oxford: Oxford University Press, 1970.
———. *The Italian or the Confessional of the Black Penitents* (1797). Edited by Frederick Garber. Oxford: Oxford University Press, 1971.
Reeve, Clara. *The Champion of Virtue, A Gothic Story*. Colchester: W. Keymer, 1777. Re-issued with a new preface as *The Old English Baron. A Gothic Story*. London: Edward and Charles Dilly, 1778.
———. *The Old English Baron*. Edited by James Trainter. Oxford: Oxford University Press, 1967.
———. *The Progress of Romance, through Times, Countries, and Manners*. Two vols. Colchester: W. Keymer, 1785.
Reynolds, F. *Werter. A Tragedy*. Dublin: P. Cooney, 1786.
Reynolds, John. *The Triumphs of Gods Revenge, Against the crying, and execrable Sinne of Murther. . . . In thirty severall Tragical Histories*. London: William Lee, 1621.
Rousseau, Jean-Jacques. *The Confessions*. Translated and introduced by J. M. Cohen. Harmondsworth: Penguin Books, 1985.
———. *The Social Contract* and *Discourses*. Translated by G. D. H. Cole. London: J. M. Dent, 1968.
Saintsbury, George, ed. *Tales of Mystery*. London: Percival and Co., 1891.
Schiller, Friedrich von. "On the Sublime." In *Naive and Sentimental Poetry* and *On the Sublime*. Translated by Julius A. Elias. New York: Frederick Ungar Publishing Co., 1966.
Schopenhauer, Arthur. *The World as Will and Representation*. Two vols. Translated by E. F. J. Payne. New York: Dover Publications, 1969.
Seward, Anna. *Letters of Anna Seward* (1784–1807). Six vols. Edited by Sir Walter Scott. Edinburgh: Archibald, Constable, 1811.
Shelley, Mary. *Frankenstein or, The Modern Prometheus* (1831). Edited by James Kinsley and M. K. Joseph. Oxford: Oxford University Press, 1980.
———. *Frankenstein or, The Modern Prometheus*. The 1818 text. Edited by James Rieger. Chicago: The University of Chicago Press, 1982.
———. *Frankenstein or, The Modern Prometheus*. Afterword by Harold Bloom. New York: Signet, 1965.
———. *Frankenstein or, The Modern Prometheus*. Edited by Maurice Hindle. Harmondsworth: Penguin Books, 1985.
———. *The Castle of Otranto, Vathek, Frankenstein*. Edited by

Peter Fairclough. Introduced by Mario Praz. In *Three Gothic Novels*. Harmondsworth: Penguin Books, 1968.

———. *The Journals of Mary Shelley 1814–1844*. Two vols. Edited by Paula R. Feldman and Diana Scott-Kilvert. Oxford: Clarendon Press, 1987.

———. *The Letters of Mary Wollstonecraft Shelley*. Two vols. Edited by Betty T. Bennett. Baltimore: Johns Hopkins University Press, 1980.

———. *Mary Shelley Collected Tales and Stories*. Edited by Charles E. Robinson. Baltimore: Johns Hopkins University Press, 1976.

———. *Tales and Stories*. Introduced by Richard Garnett. London: William Paterson and Co., 1891.

———. *The Mary Shelley Reader*. Edited by Betty T. Bennett and Charles E. Robinson. New York: Oxford University Press, 1990.

———. *Mathilda*. Edited by Elizabeth Nitchie. *Studies in Philology* [Extra Series] 3 (October 1959).

———. *Valperga: or, the Life and Adventures of Castruccio Prince of Lucca*. London: G. and W. B. Whittaker, 1823.

———. *The Last Man* (1826). Edited by Hugh J. Luke, Jr. Lincoln: University of Nebraska Press, 1965.

Shelley, Percy Bysshe. *Zastrozzi* and *St. Irvyne*. Edited and introduced by Stephen C. Behrendt. Oxford: Oxford University Press, 1986.

Smith, Charlotte. *The Banished Man*. Four vols. London: T. Cadell, 1794.

Smollett, Tobias. *The Adventures of Ferdinand Count Fathom* (1753). Edited by Damian Grant. Oxford: Oxford University Press, 1971.

Virgil. *The Aeneid*. Translated by Frank O. Copley. Introduced by Brooks Otis. New York: The Bobbs-Merrill Company, 1965.

———. *The Aeneid*. Translated by Robert Fitzgerald. Harmondsworth: Penguin Books, 1985.

Volney, Constantin François de Chasseboeuf. *The Ruins: or a Survey of the Revolution of Empires with notes Historical, Geographical, and Explanatory to which is annexed The Law of Nature*. London: T. Davison, 1819.

———. *The Law of Nature; or Principles of Morality Deducted from the Physical Constitution of Mankind and the Universe*. London: T. Davison, 1819.

Walpole, Horace. *The Castle of Otranto*. London: Thomas Lownds, 1765. Published anonymously on December 24, 1764.

———. *The Castle of Otranto, A Gothic Story* (with a new preface). London: William Bathoe, 1765.

———. *The Castle of Otranto.* London: Dodsley, 1791. Includes prefaces to the 1st and 2nd editions.

———. *The Castle of Otranto.* London: Wenman and Hodgson, 1793.

———. *The Castle of Otranto.* Introduced by Sir Walter Scott. Edinburgh: Ballantyne, 1811 (Harvard University copy with extensive holograph notes in Scott's hand).

———. *The Castle of Otranto,* with a memoir of the author. London: Joseph Thomas, 1840.

———. *The Castle of Otranto.* Edited by Henry Morley. London: Cassell, 1886.

———. *The Castle of Otranto.* Edited by Caroline F. E. Spurgeon. London: Chatto and Windus, 1907.

———. *The Castle of Otranto.* Edited by Oswald Doughty. London: The Scholartis Press, 1929.

———. *The Castle of Otranto* and *The Mysterious Mother.* Edited by Montague Summers. London: Constable and Company, 1924.

———. *The Castle of Otranto.* Edited by W. S. Lewis. Oxford: Oxford University Press, 1982.

———. *Anecdotes of Painting in England.* Four vols. London: Strawberry Hill, 1771.

———. *The Mysterious Mother. A Tragedy.* London: J. Dodsley, 1781. (Published 1791.)

———. *Hieroglyphic Tales* (1785). Introduced by Kenneth W. Gross. Los Angeles: University of California: The Augustan Reprint Society, 1982.

———. *The Works of Horatio Walpole Earl of Orford.* Five vols. London: G. G. and J. Robinson and J. Edwards, 1798.

———. *The Yale Edition of Horace Walpole's Correspondence.* Forty-eight vols. Edited by W. S. Lewis et al. New Haven: Yale University Press, 1937–1983.

Wollstonecraft, Mary. *Mary, A Fiction* (1788) and *The Wrongs of Woman* (1798). Edited by James Kinsley and Gary Kelly. Oxford: Oxford University Press, 1980.

———. *Vindication of the Rights of Woman* (1792). Edited and introduced by Miriam Brody Kramnick. Harmondsworth: Penguin Books, 1983.

———. *Collected Letters of Mary Wollstonecraft.* Edited by Ralph M. Wardle. Ithaca: Cornell University Press, 1979.

Wordsworth, William. *The Poems.* Two vols. Edited by John O. Hayden. New Haven: Yale University Press, 1981.

———. *The Prelude. A Parallel Text.* Edited by J. C. Maxwell. New Haven: Yale University Press, 1981.
———. *The Borderers.* Edited by Robert Osborn. Ithaca: Cornell University Press, 1982.
———. *The Prose Works of William Wordsworth.* Three vols. Edited by W. J. B. Owen and Jane Worthington Smyser. Oxford: Clarendon Press, 1974.
———. *The Poetical Works of William Wordsworth.* Five vols. Oxford: Clarendon Press, 1940–49. Revised edition, three vols., 1952–54.

Theory and Criticism

Adorno, T. W., "Transparencies on Film." *New German Critique* 24–25 (Fall/Winter 1981–82), 199–205.
———. "The Essay as Form." *New German Critique* 32 (Spring/Summer 1984), 151–71.
Aers, David; Cook, Jonathan; and Punter, David. *Romanticism and Ideology.* London: Routledge and Kegan Paul, 1981.
Alderman, William E. "Shaftesbury and the Doctrine of Moral Sense in the Eighteenth Century." *PMLA* 46 (1931), 1087–94.
Aldiss, Brian, and Wingrove, David. *Trillion Year Spree. The History of Science Fiction.* London: Paladin Grafton Books, 1988.
Allen, B. Sprague. "William Godwin and the Stage." *PMLA* 35 (1920), 358–70.
———. "William Godwin as Sentimentalist." *PMLA* 38 (1918), 1–29.
———. "The Reaction Against William Godwin." *Modern Philology* 16 (1918), 225–43.
Allen, M. L., "The Black Veil: Three Versions of a Symbol." *English Studies* 47 (1966), 286–89.
Almirall, Catherine L. "Smollett's 'Gothic': An Illustration." *Modern Language Notes* 68, 5 (1953), 408–10.
Althusser, L. *Lenin and Philosophy and Other Essays.* Translated by Ben Brewster. London: New Left Books, 1971.
———. *Essays on Ideology.* London: Verso Editions, 1984.
Analytical Review 21 (February 1795), 166–75. Review of William Godwin, *Caleb Williams.*
———. 24 (1796), 383–85. Review of George Colman, the Younger, *The Iron Chest.*
———. 25 (1797), 516–20. Review of Ann Radcliffe, *The Italian.*

Anti-Jacobin Review and Magazine 5 (1800), 23–28. Review of William Godwin, *St. Leon—A Tale of the Sixteenth Century*.

———. 21 (1805), 337–58. Review of William Godwin, *Fleetwood; or, The New Man of Feeling*.

Apter, T. E. *Fantasy Literature*. London: Macmillan, 1982.

Arac, Jonathan. "The Media of Sublimity: Johnson and Lamb on *King Lear*." *Studies in Romanticism* 26 (Summer 1987), 209–20.

Arensberg, Mary, ed. *The American Sublime*. Albany: SUNY Press, 1986.

Armstrong, Paul B. "History and Epistemology: The Example of *The Turn of the Screw*." *New Literary History* 19, 3 (Spring 1988), 693–712.

Astle, Richard. "Dracula as Totemic Monster: Lacan, Freud, Oedipus and History." *Substance* 25 (1980), 98–105.

Athenaeum. November 10, 1832, 730. Posthumous publication of Percy Bysshe Shelley's review of *Frankenstein*.

Atkins, Stuart Pratt. *The Testament of Werther in Poetry and Drama*. Cambridge, Mass.: Harvard University Press, 1949.

Aubin, Robert A. "Grottoes, Geology and the Gothic Revival." *Studies in Philology* 31 (1934), 408–16.

Auerbach, Erich. *Mimesis. The Interpretation of Reality in the Western World*. Translated by Willard R. Trask. Princeton: Princeton University Press, 1973.

Bakhtin, Mikhail. *Rabelais and His World*. Translated by Hélène Iswolsky. Cambridge, Mass.: MIT Press, 1968.

———. *Problems of Dostoevsky's Poetics*. Translated by R. W. Rostel. N.p.: Ardis, 1973.

———. *The Dialogic Imagination. Four Essays*. Edited by Michael Holquist. Translated by Caryl Emerson and Michael Holquist. Austin: University of Texas Press, 1981.

Baldick, Chris. *In Frankenstein's Shadow. Myth, Monstrosity and Nineteenth-century Writing*. Oxford: Clarendon Press, 1987.

Barker, Francis, et al., eds. *1789: Reading Writing Revolution*. Proceedings of the Essex Conference on the Sociology of Literature July 1981. Colchester: University of Essex, 1982.

Barth, John. "The Literature of Exhaustion." *The Atlantic* 230 (August 1967), 29–34.

Barthes, Roland. *Image-Music-Text*. London: Fontana, 1977.

———. *S/Z*. Translated by Richard Howard. London: Jonathan Cape, 1975.

———. "Theory of the Text." In Robert Young, ed., *Untying the Text*, 31–47.

Barzilai, Shuli. "Lemmata/Lemmala. Frames for Derrida's *Parerga.*" *Diacritics* 20, 1 (Spring 1990), 2–15.

Baudrillard, Jean. "Modernity." *Canadian Journal of Political and Social Theory* 11, 3 (1987), 63–72.

———. *Simulations.* New York: Semiotext(e), 1983.

———. "Game with Vestiges." *On the Beach* 5 (Winter 1984), 19–25.

———. *The Evil Demon of Images.* Sydney: Power Institute of Fine Arts, 1987.

———. *Selected Writings.* Edited by Mark Poster. Cambridge: Polity Press, 1988.

Bayer-Berenbaum, Linda. *The Gothic Imagination. Expansion in Gothic Literature and Art.* Rutherford, N.J.: Fairleigh Dickinson University Press, 1982.

Bell, Daniel. *The Cultural Contradictions of Capitalism.* New York: Basic Books, 1976.

———. "Modernism and Capitalism." *Partisan Review* 45 (1978), 206–22.

Belsey, Catherine. *Critical Practice.* London: Methuen, 1980.

Benhabib, Seyla. "Epistemologies of Postmodernism: A Rejoinder to Jean-François Lyotard." *New German Critique* 33 (1984), 103–26.

Benjamin, Walter. *Illuminations.* Edited and introduced by Hannah Arendt. Translated by Harry Zöhn. London: Collins/Fontana, 1973.

Berman, Russell. "The Routinization of Charismatic Modernism and the Problem of Post-Modernity." *Cultural Critique* 5 (1986–87), 49–68.

Bernheimer, Charles, and Kahane, Claire, eds. *In Dora's Case. Freud-Hysteria-Feminism.* New York: Columbia University Press, 1985.

Bernstein, Richard J., ed. *Habermas and Modernity.* Cambridge, Mass.: MIT Press, 1985.

Birkhead, Edith. *The Tale of Terror* (1921). New York: Russell and Russell, 1963.

Blackwood's Edinburgh Magazine 2 (1818), 613–20. Sir Walter Scott's unsigned review of [Mary Shelley] *Frankenstein.*

———. 3 (1818), 648–50. [John Wilson] "Some Remarks on the Use of the Preternatural in Works of Fiction."

Bloom, Harold. *The Ringers in the Tower. Studies in Romantic Tradition.* Chicago: University of Chicago Press, 1971.

———. *The Anxiety of Influence.* New York: Oxford University Press, 1973.

———. *Poetry and Repression.* New Haven: Yale University Press, 1976.

———. "Freud and the Poetic Sublime: A Catastrophe Theory of Creativity." In *Freud: A Collection of Critical Essays.* Edited by Perry Meisel. Englewood Cliffs, N.J.: Prentice-Hall, 1981, 211–31.

Bloom, Harold; de Man, Paul; Derrida, Jacques; Hartman, Geoffrey H.; Miller, J. Hillis. *Deconstruction and Criticism.* London: Routledge and Kegan Paul, 1979.

Bogel, Fredric V. *Literature and Insubstantiality in Later Eighteenth-Century England.* Princeton: Princeton University Press, 1984.

Boulton, James T. *The Language of Politics in the Age of Wilkes and Burke.* London: Routledge and Kegan Paul, 1963.

Brantlinger, Patrick. "The Gothic Origins of Science Fiction." *Novel* 14 (Fall 1980), 30–43.

Briggs, Asa. "Middle-class Consciousness in English Politics, 1780–1846." *Past and Present* 9 (April 1956), 65–74.

Brissenden, R. F., ed. *Studies in the Eighteenth Century.* Canberra: Australian National University Press, 1968.

———. *Virtue in Distress: Studies in the Novel of Sentiment from Richardson to Sade.* London: Macmillan, 1974.

British Critic 4 (1794), 70–71. Review of William Godwin, *Things as They Are; or, the Adventures of Caleb Williams.*

———. 5 (1795), 444–47. Letter from a lawyer on the subject of William Godwin's legal misrepresentations in *Caleb Williams.*

———. 6 (1795), 94–95. "Correspondence." William Godwin's reply to above.

———. 9 (1797), 193–94. Review of George Coleman, the Younger, *The Iron Chest.*

———. 12 (1798), 228–33. Review of William Godwin, *Memoirs of the Author of the Vindication of the Rights of Woman.*

———. 15 (1800), 47–52. Review of William Godwin, *St. Leon.*

———. 26 (1805), 189–94. Review of William Godwin, *Fleetwood.*

———. 11 (1818), 37–61. Charles Maturin's unsigned review of Maria Edgeworth, *Harrington and Ormond, Tales.* The editor's running title of this review is "Novel-writing."

Brooke-Rose, Christine. *A Rhetoric of the Unreal.* Cambridge University Press, 1983.

Brooks, Peter. "Virtue and Terror: *The Monk.*" *ELH* 40 (1973), 249–63.

———. "Godlike Science/Unhallowed Arts: Language and Monstrosity in *Frankenstein.*" *New Literary History* 9, 3 (Spring 1978), 591–605.

———. "Narrative Transaction and Transference (Unburying *Le Colonel Chabert*)." *Novel* 15 (Winter 1982), 102–10.

Bruyn, Frans De. "Edmund Burke's Gothic Romance: The Portrayal of Warren Hastings in Burke's Writings and Speeches." *Criticism* 29, 4 (Fall 1987), 415–38.

Burke, Kenneth. *The Philosophy of Literary Form*. Baton Rouge: Louisiana State University Press, 1978.

Burra, Peter J. S.. "Baroque and Gothic Sentimentalism." *Farrago* 3 (October 1930), 159–82.

Butler, Christopher. *Interpretation, Deconstruction, and Ideology*. Oxford: Oxford University Press, 1984.

Butler, Marilyn. *Jane Austen and the War of Ideas*. Oxford: Clarendon Press, 1975.

———. "Godwin, Burke and *Caleb Williams*." *Essays in Criticism* 32 (July 1982), 237–57.

———. *Romantics, Rebels and Reactionaries. English Literature and Its Background 1760–1830*. Oxford: Oxford University Press, 1981.

Butt, John. *The Mid-Eighteenth Century*. Edited by Geoffrey Carnall. Oxford: Clarendon Press, 1979.

Cameron, Kenneth Neill, ed. *Shelley and his Circle 1773–1822*. An edition of Shelley (et al.) manuscripts in the Carl H. Pforzheimer Library. Cambridge, Mass.: Harvard University Press, 1961–1973.

———, ed. *Romantic Rebels: Essays on Shelley. His Circle*. Cambridge, Mass.: Harvard University Press, 1973.

Campbell, Oscar James, and Mueschke, Paul. "'Guilt and Sorrow': A Study in the Genesis of Wordsworth's Aesthetic." *Modern Philology* 23, 3 (February 1926), 293–306.

———. "*The Borderers* as a Document in the History of Wordsworth's Aesthetic Development." *Modern Philology* 23, 4 (May 1926), 465–82.

Cannon, Garland H. "Sir William Jones and Edmund Burke." *Modern Philology* 54, 3 (February 1957), 165–86.

Carroll, David. *Paraesthetics. Foucault. Lyotard. Derrida*. New York: Methuen, 1987.

Christensen, Jerome C. "The Sublime and the Romance of the Other." *Diacritics* 8 (June 1978), 10–23.

Cixous, Hélène. "The Character of Character." *New Literary History* 5, 2 (Winter 1974), 383–402.

———. "Fiction and Its Phantoms: A Reading of Freud's *Das Unheimliche* (The 'uncanny')." *New Literary History* 7, 3 (Spring 1976), 525–48.

Cixous, Hélène, and Clément, Catherine. *The Newly Born Woman.* Translated by Betsy Wing. Introduced by Sandra M. Gilbert. Manchester: Manchester University Press, 1986.

Claridge, Laura P. "Parent-Child Tensions in *Frankenstein*: The Search for Communion." *Studies in the Novel* 17, 1 (Spring 1985), 14–26.

Clark, Kenneth. *The Gothic Revival* (1928). London: John Murray, 1962.

Classical Literary Criticism: Aristotle, Horace, Longinus. Translated by T. S. Dorsch. Harmondsworth: Penguin Books, 1965.

Clifford, Gay. "*Caleb Williams* and *Frankenstein*: First-Person Narratives and 'Things as They Are.'" *Genre* 10 (Winter 1977), 601–17.

Cohen, Ralph. "Do Postmodern Genres Exist?" *Genre* 20, 3–4 (Fall–Winter 1987), 241–57.

Conrad, Peter. *The Everyman History of English Literature.* London: J. M. Dent and Sons Ltd., 1987.

Cooper, Barry. "What Is Post-Modernity?" *Canadian Journal of Political and Social Theory* 9, 3 (Fall 1985), 77–89.

Crane, R. S. "Suggestions Toward a Genealogy of 'The Man of Feeling,'" *ELH* 1, 3 (December 1934), 205–30.

Critical Review 19 (January 1765), 50–51. Review of [Horace Walpole], *The Castle of Otranto.*

———. 19 (June 1765), 469. Review of Horace Walpole, *The Castle of Otranto.*

———. 44 (August 1777), 154. Review of Clara Reeve, *The Champion of Virtue.*

———. 52 (December 1781), 456–63. Review of Robert Jephson, *The Count of Narbonne.*

———. 70 (1790), 517–30. Review of Edmund Burke, *Reflections on the Revolution in France.*

———. [2nd Series] 4 (1792), 458–60. Review of [Ann Radcliffe], *The Romance of the Forest.*

———. [2nd Series] 4 (1792), 389–98 and 5 (1792), 132–41. Review of Mary Wollstonecraft, *A Vindication of the Rights of Woman.*

———. [2nd Series] 7 (1793), 361–72; 8 (1793), 290–96; 9 (1794), 149–54. Review of William Godwin, *Enquiry Concerning Political Justice.*

———. [2nd Series] 11 (1794), 290–96. Review of William Godwin, *Things as They Are; or, The Adventures of Caleb Williams.*

———. [2nd Series] 11 (August 1794), 361–72. Coleridge's unsigned review of Ann Radcliffe, *The Mysteries of Udolpho.*

———. [2nd Series] 16 (1796), 390–96. Review of Mary Wollstonecraft, *An Historical and Moral View of the Origin and Progress of the French Revolution.*

———. [2nd Series] 19 (January 1797), 102–3. Review of George Colman, the Younger, *The Iron Chest.*

———. [2nd Series] 19 (February 1797), 194–200. Coleridge's unsigned review of M. G. Lewis, *The Monk.*

———. [2nd Series] 23 (June 1798), 166–69. Review of Ann Radcliffe, T*he Italian, or, The Confessional of the Black Penitents.*

———. [3rd Series] 5 (July 1805), 252–56. Review of M. G. Lewis, *The Bravo of Venice.*

———. [3rd Series] 5 (July 1805), 262–69. Review of Joseph Mason Cox, M.D., *Practical Observations on Insanity. . . .*

———. [3rd Series] 21 (November 1810), 329–31. Review of [P. B. Shelley], *Zastrozzi.*

———. [4th Series] 5 (January 1814), 13–36. Review of Samuel Tuke, *Description of the Retreat, an Institution Near New York, for Insane Persons of the Society of Friends.*

Crowther, Paul. *The Kantian Sublime.* Oxford: Clarendon Press, 1989.

Cruttwell, Patrick. "On *Caleb Williams.*" *The Hudson Review* 11 (Spring 1958), 87–95.

Curry, Stephen J. "Richard Hurd's Genre Criticism." *Texas Studies in Literature and Language* 8, 2 (Summer 1966), 207–17.

Day, William Patrick. *In the Circles of Fear and Desire. A Study of Gothic Fantasy.* Chicago: University of Chicago Press, 1985.

de Bolla, Peter. *The Discourse of the Sublime. Readings in History, Aesthetics and the Subject.* Oxford: Basil Blackwell, 1989.

de Man, Paul. "Dialogue and Dialogism." *Poetics Today* 4, 1 (1983), 99–107.

———. *Blindness and Insight. Essays in the Rhetoric of Contemporary Criticism.* London: Methuen, 1983.

———. "Phenomenality and Materiality in Kant." In Silverman and Aylesworth, eds., *The Textual Sublime,* 87–108.

Denzin, Norman K. "*Blue Velvet*: Postmodern Contradictions." *Theory Culture and Society* 5, 2–3 (June 1988), 461–73.

Derrida, Jacques. *Speech and Phenomena and Other Essays on Husserl's Theory of Signs.* Translated by David B. Allison. Evanston: Northwestern University Press, 1973.

———. *Of Grammatology.* Translated by Gayatri Chakravorty Spivak. Baltimore: Johns Hopkins University Press, 1976.

———. *Writing and Difference.* Translated by Alan Bass. Chicago: University of Chicago Press, 1978.

———. "The Purveyor of Truth." *Yale French Studies* 52 (1975), 31–113.
———. *Margins of Philosophy.* Translated by Alan Bass. Chicago: University of Chicago Press, 1982.
———. "The Law of Genre." *Glyph* 7 (1980), 202–32.
———. "Freud and the Scene of Writing." *Yale French Studies* 48 (1972), 73–117.
———. *The Truth in Painting.* Translated by Geoff Bennington and Ian McLeod. Chicago: University of Chicago Press, 1987.
Dobson, Austin. *Horace Walpole: A Memoir.* London: James R. Osgood, 1893.
Docherty, Thomas. *Reading (Absent) Character.* Oxford: Clarendon Press, 1983.
Duerksen, Roland. "*Caleb Williams, Political Justice* and *Billy Budd.*" *American Literature* 38 (1966), 372–76.
Dumas, D. Gilbert. "Things as They Were: The Original Ending of *Caleb Williams.*" *Studies in English Literature* 6 (July 1966), 575–97.
Dussinger, John A. "Kinship and Guilt in Mary Shelley's *Frankenstein.*" *Studies in the Novel* 8 (1976), 38–75.
Eagleton, Terry. *Walter Benjamin or Towards a Revolutionary Criticism.* London: Verso Editions, 1981.
———. *The Rape of Clarissa.* Oxford: Basil Blackwell, 1982.
———. *The Function of Criticism. From "The Spectator" to Post-Structuralism.* London: Verso Editions and NLB, 1984.
———. "Capitalism, Modernism and Postmodernism." *New Left Review* 152 (July–August, 1985), 60–73.
———. *The Ideology of the Aesthetic.* Oxford: Basil Blackwell, 1990.
Eco, Umberto. "Science Fiction and the Art of Conjecture." *TLS* (November 2, 1984), 1257–58.
———. *Semiotics and the Philosophy of Language.* London: Macmillan Press, 1984.
Edinburgh Review 6 (April–July 1805), 181–93. Sir Walter Scott's unsigned review of William Godwin, *Fleetwood.*
———. 19 (March 1818), 249–53. Review of [Mary Shelley], *Frankenstein.*
———. 31 (December 1818), 80–93. William Hazlitt's unsigned review of *Letters from the Hon. Horace Walpole to George Montagu Esq. From the Year 1736 to 1770.* London, 1818.
———. 58 (October 1833), 227–58. Thomas Babington Macaulay's unsigned review of *Letters of Horace Walpole, Earl of Orford,*

to Sir Horace Mann, British Envoy at the Court of Tuscany. Edited by Lord Dover. Three vols.

Eisenstein, Sergei M. *The Film Sense.* Translated and edited by Jay Leyda. London: Faber and Faber, 1970.

———. "Piranesi, or the Fluidity of Forms." In Manfredo Tafuri, *The Sphere and the Labyrinth,* 65–90.

Elder, Thomas Balfour. "Godwin and 'The Great Springs of Human Passion.'" *Ariel* 14 (January 1983), 15–31.

Eliade, Mircea. *The Sacred and the Profane.* Translated by Willard R. Trask. New York: Harcourt, Brace & World, 1959.

Eliot, T. S. *Selected Essays.* London: Faber, 1969.

Emerson, Oliver Farrar. "'Monk' Lewis and the Tales of Terror." *Modern Language Notes* 38, 3 (1923), 154–59.

Empson, William. *Seven Types of Ambiguity* (1930). London: Chatto and Windus, 1970.

English Review 8 (September 1786), 180–84. Review of [William Beckford] *The History of the Caliph Vathek.*

European Magazine 10 (August 1786), 102–4. Review of *The History of the Caliph Vathek.*

Evans, F. B. "Shelley, Godwin, Hume and the Doctrine of Necessity." *Studies in Philology* 37 (1940), 632–40.

Felman, Shoshana. "Madness and Philosophy or Literature's Reason." *Yale French Studies* 52 (1975), 206–28.

———, ed. *Literature and Psychoanalysis. The Question of Reading: Otherwise.* Baltimore: Johns Hopkins University Press, 1982.

Ferguson, Frances. "The Nuclear Sublime," *Diacritics* 14, 2 (Summer 1984), 4–10.

———. "The Sublime of Edmund Burke, or the Bathos of Experience." *Glyph* 8 (1981), 62–78.

Fiedler, Leslie A. *Freaks: Myths and Images of the Secret Self.* New York: Simon and Schuster, 1978.

———. *Love and Death in the American Novel.* New York: Dell, 1966.

Figes, Eva. *Sex & Subterfuge. Women Writers to 1850.* London: Macmillan, 1982.

Flanders, Wallace Austin. "Godwin and Gothicism: *St. Leon.*" *Texas Studies in Literature and Language* 8, 4 (Winter 1967), 533–45.

Fleck, P. D. "Mary Shelley's Notes to Shelley's Poems and *Frankenstein.*" *Studies in Romanticism* 6 (1967), 226–54.

Fletcher, Ian, ed. *Romantic Mythologies* London: Routledge and Kegan Paul, 1967.

Foster, Hal. "(Post)Modern Polemics," *New German Critique* 33 (1984), 67–78.

Foster, James. *A History of the Pre-Romantic Novel in England.* New York: The Modern Language Association of America, 1949.

Fothergill, Brian. *Beckford of Fonthill.* London: Faber, 1979.

Foucault, Michel. *The Birth of the Clinic.* Translated by A. M. Sheridan. London: Tavistock Publications, 1976.

———. *The Archaeology of Knowledge.* Translated by A. M. Sheridan Smith. London: Tavistock Publications, 1978.

———. "My Body, This Paper, This Fire." *Oxford Literary Review* 4, 1 (1979), 9–28.

———. *The Order of Things. An Archaeology of the Human Sciences.* London: Tavistock Publications, 1980.

———. *Power/Knowledge. Selected Interviews and Other Writings 1972–1977.* Edited by Colin Gordon. Translated by Colin Gordon, et al. Brighton: Harvester Press, 1980.

———. *Madness and Civilization. A History of Insanity in the Age of Reason.* Translated by Richard Howard. London: Tavistock Publications, 1982.

———. *Discipline and Punish. The Birth of the Prison.* Translated by Alan Sheridan. Harmondsworth: Penguin Books, 1979.

———. *The History of Sexuality. An Introduction.* Translated by Robert Hurley. Harmondsworth: Penguin Books, 1984.

———. *Language, Counter-Memory, Practice.* Edited, introduced, and translated by Donald F. Bouchard and Sherry Simon. Ithaca: Cornell University Press, 1977.

———. "What Is an Author?" In Josué V. Harari, ed., *Textual Strategies*, 141–60.

Fowler, Alastair. *Kinds of Literature: An Introduction to the Theory of Genres and Modes.* Oxford: Clarendon Press, 1982.

Frankl, Paul. *The Gothic. Literary Sources and Interpretations through Eight Centuries.* Princeton: Princeton University Press, 1960.

Fraser, Nancy, and Nicholson, Linda. "Social Criticism Without Philosophy: An Encounter Between Feminism and Postmodernism." *Theory Culture and Society* 5, 2–3 (June 1988), 373–94.

Freeman, Barbara. "*Frankenstein* with Kant: A Theory of Monstrosity, or the Monstrosity of Theory." *Substance* 52 (1987), 21–31.

Freud, Sigmund. *The Interpretation of Dreams.* Translated by James Strachey. London: George Allen and Unwin, 1971.

———. *The Pelican Freud Library.* Fifteen vols. Harmondsworth: Penguin Books, 1973–1986.

Furbank, P. N. "Godwin's Novels." *Essays in Criticism* 5 (July 1955), 214–28.

Garber, Frederick. "Meaning and Mode in Gothic Fiction." In Harold E. Pagliaro, ed., *Racism in the Eighteenth Century*. Cleveland: Case Western Reserve University Press, 1973, 155–69.

Garner, Shirley Nelson; Kahane, Claire; Sprengnether, Madelon, eds. *The (M)other Tongue. Essays in Feminist Psychoanalytic Interpretation*. Ithaca: Cornell University Press, 1985.

Gasché, Rodolphe, *The Tain of the Mirror: Derrida and the Philosophy of Reflection*. Cambridge, Mass.: Harvard University Press, 1986.

Gaskill, Howard, "'Ossian' Macpherson: Towards a Rehabilitation." *Comparative Criticism. An Annual Journal* 8. Edited by E. S. Shaffer. Cambridge: Cambridge University Press, 1986, 113–46.

Gentleman's Magazine 48 (July 1778), 324–25. Review of Clara Reeve, *The Old English Baron*.

———. 60 (1790), 1021–32. Review of Edmund Burke, *Reflections on the Revolution in France*.

———. 64 (1794), 834. Review of Ann Radcliffe, *The Mysteries of Udolpho*.

———. 79 (1809), 141–44. Review of M. G. Lewis, *Romantic Tales*.

———. 87 (1817), 534–36. Review of William Godwin, *Mandeville. A Tale of the Seventeenth Century in England*.

Gilbert, Sandra M. "Horror's Twin: Mary Shelley's Monstrous Eve." *Feminist Studies* 4, 2 (June 1978), 48–73.

Gilbert, Sandra M., and Gubar, Susan. *The Madwoman in the Attic. The Woman Writer and the Nineteenth-Century Literary Imagination*. New Haven: Yale University Press, 1979.

Gill, Stephen. "'Adventures on Salisbury Plain' and Wordsworth's Poetry of Protest 1795–97." *Studies in Romanticism* 11 (1972), 48–65.

Gilman, Sander L. "Black Bodies, White Bodies: Toward an Iconography of Female Sexuality in Late Nineteenth-Century Art, Medicine, and Literature." *Critical Inquiry* 12, 1 (Autumn 1985), 205–42.

Glut, Donald F. *The Frankenstein Legend: A Tribute to Mary Shelley and Boris Karloff*. Metuchen, N.J.: Scarecrow, 1973.

Goldberg, M. A. "Moral and Myth in Mrs. Shelley's *Frankenstein*." *Keats-Shelley Journal* 8 (Winter 1959), 27–38.

Grob, A. "Wordsworth and Godwin: A Reassessment." *Studies in Romanticism* 6 (1966–67), 98–119.

Gross, Harvey. "The Pursuer and the Pursued: A Study of *Caleb Williams*." *Texas Studies in Literature and Language* 1 (Spring 1959), 401–11.

Guerlac, Suzanne. "Delights of Grotesque and Sublime." *Diacritics* 15, 3 (Fall 1985), 47–53.

Habermas, Jürgen. "Modernity versus Postmodernity." *New German Critique* 22 (1981), 3–14.

———. "A Philosophico-Political Profile" [An Interview]. *New Left Review* 151 (May–June 1985), 75–105.

———. "The Genealogical Writing of History: On Some Aporias in Foucault's Theory of Power." *Canadian Journal of Political and Social Theory* 10, 1–2 (1986), 1–9.

———. *The Philosophical Discourse of Modernity*. Translated by Frederick Lawrence. Cambridge: Polity Press, 1987.

Haggerty, George E. "Fact and Fancy in the Gothic Novel." *Nineteenth-Century Fiction* 39, 4 (March 1985), 379–91.

Hagstrum, Jean H. *Sex and Sensibility. Ideal and Erotic Love from Milton to Mozart*. Chicago: University of Chicago Press, 1980.

Hamilton, Paul. *Coleridge's Poetics*. Oxford: Basil Blackwell, 1983.

Harari, Josué V., ed. *Textual Strategies*. London: Methuen, 1980.

Harpold, Terence. "'Did you get Mathilda from Papa?': Seduction Fantasy and the Circulation of Mary Shelley's *Mathilda*." *Studies in Romanticism* 28, 1 (Spring 1989), 49–67.

Hart, Francis Russell. "The Experience of Character in the English Gothic Novel." In Roy Harvey Pearce, ed., *Experience in the Novel*, 83–105.

Hartman, Geoffrey H., ed. *Psychoanalysis and the Question of the Text*. Baltimore: Johns Hopkins University Press, 1978.

———. *Saving the Text. Literature, Derrida, Philosophy*. Baltimore: Johns Hopkins University Press, 1981.

———. *Easy Pieces*. New York: Columbia University Press, 1985.

———. *Wordsworth's Poetry 1787–1814*. New Haven: Yale University Press, 1977.

Harvey, A. D. "The Nightmare of Caleb Williams." *Essays in Criticism* 26, 3 (July 1976), 236–49.

Hassan, Ihab. *The Postmodern Turn. Essays in Postmodern Theory and Culture*. Columbus: Ohio State University Press, 1987.

Heath, Stephen. *Questions of Cinema*. London: Macmillan, 1981.

Hebdige, Dick. *Hiding the Light: On Images and Things*. London: Routledge, 1988.

Hertz, Neil. "The Notion of Blockage in the Literature of the Sublime." In Geoffrey H. Hartman, ed., *Psychoanalysis and the Question of the Text*, 62–85.

———. "Freud and the Sandman." In Josué V. Harari, ed., *Textual Strategies*, 296–21.

———. *The End of the Line. Essays on Psychoanalysis and the Sublime.* New York: Columbia University Press, 1985.

Hipple, Walter J., Jr. *The Beautiful, the Sublime, and the Picturesque in Eighteenth-Century British Aesthetic Theory.* Carbondale: Southern Illinois University Press, 1957.

Hogan, Charles Beecher. "The Theatre of Geo. 3." In W. H. Smith, ed., *Horace Walpole, Writer, Politician and Connoisseur*, 227–40.

Holland, Norman, and Sherman, Leona F. "Gothic Possibilities." *New Literary History* 8 (Winter 1977), 279–94.

Holmes, Richard. *Shelley: The Pursuit.* Harmondsworth: Penguin Books, 1987.

Homans, Margaret. *Bearing the Word. Language and Female Experience in Nineteenth-Century Women's Writing.* Chicago: University of Chicago Press, 1986.

Howard, Jacqueline. "Impure Romance: Dialogic Readings of Gothic Fiction." Unpublished Ph.D. thesis, Deakin University, 1990.

Howells, Coral Ann. *Love, Mystery, and Misery: Feeling in Gothic Fiction.* London: Athlone Press, 1978.

Howes, Craig. "Burke, Poe, and 'Usher': The Sublime and Rising Woman." *Emerson Society Quarterly (ESQ)* 31 (1985), 173–89.

Hume, Kathryn. *Fantasy and Mimesis. Responses to Reality in Western Literature.* New York: Methuen, 1984.

Hume, Robert, D. "Gothic versus Romantic: A Revaluation of the Gothic Novel." *PMLA* 84 (March, 1969), 282–90.

Hume, T. E. *Speculations.* London: Routledge and Kegan Paul, 1924.

Hutcheon, Linda. "The Politics of Postmodernism: Parody and History." *Cultural Critique* 5 (1986–87), 179–207.

———. "Beginning to Theorize Postmodernism." *Textual Practice* 1, 1 (1987), 10–31.

———. *A Poetics of Postmodernism. History, Theory Fiction.* New York: Routledge, 1988.

Ingalls, Daniel H. H. *Sanskrit Poetry from Vidyākara's "Treasury."* Cambridge, Mass.: Harvard University Press, 1965.

Irigaray, Luce. *Speculum of the Other Woman.* Translated by Gilian C. Gill. Ithaca: Cornell University Press, 1987.

Jackson, Rosemary. *Fantasy: The Literature of Subversion.* London: Methuen, 1981.

Jacobus, Mary. "Is There a Woman in This Text?" *New Literary History* 14, 1 (Autumn 1982), 117–41.

Jameson, Fredric. *The Political Unconscious.* New Haven: Yale University Press, 1981.

———. "The Politics of Theory: Ideological Positions in the Postmodernism Debate." *New German Critique* 33 (1984), 53–65.

———. *Postmodernism, or, the Cultural Logic of Late Capitalism.* Durham: Duke University Press, 1991.

Jameson, Robert. *The Essential Frankenstein.* London: Bison Books, 1992.

Jardine, Alice A. *Gynesis. Configurations of Woman and Modernity.* Ithaca: Cornell University Press, 1985.

Johnson, Barbara. *The Critical Difference: Essays in the Contemporary Rhetoric of Reading.* Baltimore: Johns Hopkins University Press, 1980.

———. "My Monster/My Self." *Diacritics* 12, 2 (Summer 1982), 2–10.

Jones, Claudia E. "*The Critical Review*'s First Thirty Years (1756–1785)." *Notes and Queries* 201 (February, 1956), 78–80.

———. "Dramatic Criticism in *The Critical Review* 1756–1785." *Modern Language Quarterly* 21 (1959), 18–26; 133–44.

———. "Contributions to *The Critical Review* 1756–1785." *Modern Language Notes* 61, 7 (1946), 433–41.

Jones, Howard Mumford. *Revolution and Romanticism.* Cambridge, Mass.: Harvard University Press, 1974.

Joseph, Gerhard. "Frankenstein's Dream: The Child as Father of the Monster." *Hartford Studies in Literature* 7 (1975), 97–115.

Kauffman, Linda, ed. *Gender and Theory. Dialogues on Feminist Criticism.* Oxford: Basil Blackwell, 1989.

Keir, Sir David Lindsay. *The Constitutional History of Modern Britain Since 1485.* London: Adam and Charles Black, 1964.

Kelly, Dorothy. "The Ghost of Meaning: Language in the Fantastic." *Substance* 11, 2 (1982), 46–55.

Kelly, Gary. *The English Jacobin Novel 1780–1805.* Oxford: Clarendon Press, 1976.

———. "Social Conflict, Nation and Empire: From Gothicism to Romantic Orientalism." *Ariel* 20, 2 (April 1989), 3–18.

Kermode, Frank. *The Sense of an Ending.* New York: Oxford University Press, 1968.

———. "The Structure of Fiction." *Modern Language Notes (MLN)* 84 (1969), 891–915.

———. *Modern Essays*. London: Collins/Fontana, 1971.

———. *The Classic. Literary Images of Permanence and Change*. Cambridge, Mass.: Harvard University Press, 1983.

———. *Essays on Fiction 1971–1982*. London: Routledge and Kegan Paul, 1983.

Ketterer, David. *Frankenstein's Creation: The Book, The Monster, and Human Reality*. Victoria, B.C.: University of Victoria English Literary Studies, 1979). [ELS Monograph Series No. 16].

Ketton-Cremer, R. W. *Horace Walpole. A Biography*. London: Faber and Faber, 1940.

Kiely, Robert. *The Romantic Novel in England*. Cambridge, Mass.: Harvard University Press, 1972.

Kirk, Russell. "Burke and the Philosophy of Prescription." *Journal of the History of Ideas* 14 (1953), 365–80.

Kliger, Samuel. "The Gothic Revival and the German *translatio*." *Modern Philology* 45 (1947), 73–103.

Knapp, Steven. *Personification and the Sublime. Milton to Coleridge*. Cambridge, Mass.: Harvard University Press, 1985.

Knoepflmacher, U. C., and Tennyson, G. B., eds. *Nature and the Victorian Imagination*. Berkeley: University of California Press, 1977.

Kristeva, Julia. *Desire in Language. A Semiotic Approach to Literature and Art*. Edited by Leon S. Roudiez. Translated by Thomas Gora, Alice Jardine, and Leon S. Roudiez. Oxford: Basil Blackwell, 1980.

———. *Revolution in Poetic Language*. New York: Columbia University Press, 1984.

Kroker, Arthur, and Cook, David. *The Postmodern Scene. Excremental Culture and Hyper-Aesthetics*. London: Macmillan, 1988.

Lacan, Jacques. *Écrits. A Selection*. Translated by Alan Sheridan. London: Tavistock Publications, 1977.

———. "Seminar on 'The Purloined Letter.'" *Yale French Studies* 48 (1972), 38–72.

Laplanche, J., and Pontalis, J-B. *The Language of Psychoanalysis*. Introduced by Daniel Lagache. Translated by Donald Nicholson-Smith. London: Hogarth Press, 1980.

Leer, David Van. "The Beast of the Closet: Homosociality and the Pathology of Manhood." *Critical Inquiry* 15, 3 (Spring 1989), 587–605.

Leighton, Angela. *Shelley and the Sublime. An Interpretation of the Major Poems*. Cambridge: Cambridge University Press, 1984.

Levine, George. *The Realistic Imagination. English Fiction from Frankenstein to Lady Chatterley.* Chicago: University of Chicago Press, 1981.

Levine, George, and Knoepflmacher, U. C., eds. *The Endurance of Frankenstein. Essays on Mary Shelley's Novel.* Berkeley: University of California Press, 1979.

Levine, Steven Z. "Seascapes of the Sublime: Vernet, Monet, and the Oceanic Feeling." *New Literary History* 16, 2 (Winter 1985), 377–400.

Lévi-Strauss, Claude. *Structural Anthropology.* New York: Doubleday Anchor Books, 1968.

Lévy, M. *Le roman "gothique" anglais 1764–1824.* Toulouse: Publications de la Faculté des Lettres et Sciences Humaines, 1968.

Lewis, Wilmarth. *Collector's Progress.* London: Constable, 1952.

———. *Horace Walpole's Library.* Cambridge: Cambridge University Press, 1958.

———. *Horace Walpole.* London: Rupert Hart-Davis, 1961.

Lincoln, Eleanor Terry, ed. *Pastoral and Romance.* Englewood Cliffs, N.J.: Prentice-Hall, 1969.

Ljungquist, Kent. "Poe and the Sublime: His Two Short Tales in the Context of an Aesthetic Tradition." *Criticism* 17 (1975), 131–51.

Locke, Don. *A Fantasy of Reason. The Life and Thought of William Godwin.* London: Routledge and Kegan Paul, 1980.

Locke, John. *An Essay Concerning Human Understanding.* Edited by Peter H. Nidditch. Oxford: Clarendon Press, 1975.

———. *The Second Treatise of Government.* Edited and introduced by J. W. Gough. Oxford: Basil Blackwell, 1956.

London, Bette. "Mary Shelley, *Frankenstein,* and the Spectacle of Masculinity." *PMLA* 108, 2 (March 1993), 253–67.

London Magazine 3, 13 (January 1821), 96. William Hazlitt's (?) unsigned review of Charles Robert Maturin, *Melmoth the Wanderer.*

Longueil, A. E. "The Word 'Gothic' in Eighteenth-Century Criticism." *Modern Language Notes* 38 (December 1923), 453–60.

Loomis, Chauncey C. "The Arctic Sublime." In Knoepflmacher and Tennyson, eds., *Nature and the Victorian Imagination,* 95–112.

Lovell, Ernest J., Jr. "Byron and the Byronic Hero in the Novels of Mary Shelley." *Studies in English* (Austin: University of Texas) 30 (1951), 158-83.

———. "Byron and Mary Shelley." *Keats-Shelley Journal* 2 (1953), 35–49.

Lukács, Georg. *The Historical Novel.* Translated by Hannah and Stanley Mitchell. London: Merlin Press, 1962.

———. *Goethe and His Age.* Translated by Robert Anchor. New York: Grosset & Dunlap, 1969.

———. *The Theory of the Novel.* Translated by Anna Bostock. London: Merlin Press, 1971.

Lyotard, Jean-François. *The Postmodern Condition: A Report on Knowledge.* Translated by Geoff Bennington and Brian Massumi. Foreword by Fredric Jameson. Manchester: Manchester University Press, 1986.

———. *The Differend: Phrases in Dispute.* Translated by Georges van den Abbeele. Minneapolis: University of Minnesota Press, 1988.

———. "Notes on Legitimation." *The Oxford Review* 9, 1–2 (1987), 106–18.

———. "On Terror and the Sublime." *Telos* 67 (1986), 196–98.

———. *The Lyotard Reader.* Edited by Andrew Benjamin. Oxford: Basil Blackwell, 1989.

———. *The Inhuman. Reflections on Time.* Translated by Geoffrey Bennington. Cambridge: Polity Press, 1986.

Lyotard, Jean-François, and Théband, Jean-Loup. *Just Gaming.* Translated by Wlad Godzich. Minneapolis: University of Minnesota Press, 1985.

MacAndrew, Elizabeth. *The Gothic Tradition in Fiction.* New York: Columbia University Press, 1979.

McCracken, David. "Godwin's *Caleb Williams*: A Fictional Rebuttal of Burke." *Studies in Burke and His Time* 11, 2 (Winter 1969–70), 1442–52.

———. "Godwin's Literary Theory: An Alliance Between Fiction and Political Philosophy." *Philological Quarterly* 49 (January 1970), 113–33.

Macdonald, D. L. "Bathos and Repetition in the Uncanny in Radcliffe." *The Journal of Narrative Technique* 19, 2 (Spring 1989), 197–204.

Macdonell, Diane. *Theories of Discourse. An Introduction.* Oxford: Basil Blackwell, 1986.

McHale, Brian. *Postmodernist Fiction.* London: Methuen, 1987.

McKinsey, Elizabeth. *Niagara Falls: Icon of the American Sublime.* Cambridge: Cambridge University Press, 1985.

McSweeney, Kerry, ed. *Diversity and Depth in Fiction. Selected Critical Writings of Angus Wilson.* London: Secker and Warburg, 1983.

Macherey, Pierre. *A Theory of Literary Production.* Translated by Geoffrey Wall. London: Routledge and Kegan Paul, 1978.

Madoff, Mark. "The Useful Myth of Gothic Ancestry." *Studies in Eighteenth-Century Culture* 8 (1979), 337–49.

Marchant, Leslie A. *Byron. A Biography.* Three vols. London: John Murray, 1957.

Marshall, Dorothy. *Eighteenth Century England.* London: Longmans, 1962.

Marshall, Peter H. *William Godwin.* New Haven: Yale University Press, 1984.

Marshall, P. J., ed. *The British Discovery of Hinduism in the Eighteenth Century.* Cambridge: Cambridge University Press, 1970.

Massey, Irving. *The Gaping Pig. Literature and Metamorphosis.* Berkeley: University of California Press, 1976.

Mayo, Robert D. "Ann Radcliffe and Ducray-Duminil." *The Modern Language Review* 36, 4 (October, 1941), 501–5.

———. "Gothic Romance in the Magazines." *PMLA* 65, 5 (September 1950), 762–89.

———. "How Long Was Gothic Fiction in Vogue?" *Modern Language Notes* (January 1943), 58–64.

———. *The English Novel in the Magazines 1740–1815. With a Catalogue of 1375 Magazine Novels and Novelettes.* Evanston: Northwestern University Press, 1962.

Mays, Milton A. "*Frankenstein,* Mary Shelley's Black Theodicy." *The Southern Humanities Review* 3 (1969), 146–53.

Mehlman, Jeffrey. "The 'Floating Signifier': From Lévi-Strauss to Lacan." *Yale French Studies* 48 (1972), 10–37.

Mehrotra, K. K. *Horace Walpole and the English Novel: A Study of the Influence of "The Castle of Otranto" 1764–1820.* Oxford: Blackwell, 1934.

Mellor, Anne K. *Mary Shelley. Her Life Her Fiction Her Monsters.* New York: Routledge, 1988.

Mishra, Vijay. "The Centre Cannot Hold: Bailey, Indian Culture and the Sublime." *South Asia* [New Series] 12, 1 (June 1989), 103–14.

Mitchell, Juliet. *Psychoanalysis and Feminism.* Harmondsworth: Penguin Books, 1975.

Mitchell, W. J. T. *Iconology. Image, Text, Ideology.* Chicago: University of Chicago Press, 1986.

Miyoshi, Masao. *The Divided Self.* New York: New York University Press, 1969.

Moers, Ellen. *Literary Women.* New York: Doubleday, 1976.

Moi, Toril. *Sexual/Textual Politics: Feminist Literary Theory.* London: Methuen, 1985.

Monk, Samuel H. *The Sublime. A Study of Critical Theories in XVIII-Century England.* Ann Arbor: University of Michigan Press, 1960.

Monthly Mirror 19 (February 1805), 85–93. Biographical sketch of William Godwin.

Monthly Review 32 (January 1765), 97–99. John Langhorne's unsigned review of the first edition of *The Castle of Otranto.*

———. 32 (May 1765), 394. John Langhorne's unsigned review of the second edition of *The Castle of Otranto.*

———. 58 (January 1778), 85. William Enfield's unsigned review of Clara Reeve, *The Champion of Virtue.*

———. 58 (June 1778), 476. William Enfield's unsigned review of Clara Reeve, *The Old English Baron.*

———. 66 (January 1782), 64–70. George Colman's unsigned review of Robert Jephson, *The Count of Narbonne.*

———. 76 (May 1787), 450. William Enfield's unsigned review of William Beckford, *The History of the Caliph Vathek: An Arabian Tale.*

———. [New Series] 23 (1797), 451. Review of M. G. Lewis, *The Monk.*

———. [New Series] 15 (1794), 145–49. William Enfield's unsigned review of William Godwin, *Things as They Are; or, The Adventures of Caleb Williams.*

———. [New Series] 15 (1794), 278–83. William Enfield's unsigned review of Ann Radcliffe, *The Mysteries of Udolpho.*

———. [New Series] 22 (1797), 282–84. Review of Ann Radcliffe, *The Italian.*

———. 85 (April 1818), 439. Review of [Mary Shelley], *Frankenstein.*

———. 89 (May 1819), 87–96. Review of [J. W. Polidori], *The Vampyre.*

———. 90 (July 1819), 309–21. review of [Lord Byron], *Mazeppa* and *Don Juan.*

———. 90 (September 1819), 92–94. Review of [J. W. Polidori], *An Essay upon the Source of Positive Pleasure* and *Ximenes.*

———. 94 (January 1821) 81–90. Review of Charles Robert Maturin, *Melmoth the Wanderer.*

———. [New Series] 2 (July 1826), 280–93. Review of Ann Radcliffe, *Gaston de Blondeville; or, The Court of Henry III.*

Morris, David B. "Gothic Sublimity." *New Literary History* 16, 2 (Winter 1985), 299–319.

Morris, Meaghan. "Postmodernity and Lyotard's Sublime." *Art and Text* 16 (Summer 1984), 44–67.

Murray, John Middleton. *Heaven and Earth.* London: Cape Publishers, 1938.

Musselwhite, David. "The Trial of Warren Hastings." In Francis Barker et al., eds., *Literature, Politics and Theory. Papers from the Essex Conference 1976–84.* London: Methuen, 1986, 77–103.

Myers, Mitzi, "Godwin's Changing Conception of *Caleb Williams.*" *Studies in English Literature* 12 (1972), 591–628.

Napier, Elizabeth R. *The Failure of Gothic. Problems of Disjunction in an Eighteenth-century Literary Form.* Oxford: Clarendon Press, 1987.

Nelson, Lowry, Jr. "Night Thoughts on the Gothic Novel." *Yale Review* 52 (December 1962), 236–57.

New Review 9 (June 1786), 410–12. Paul-Henry Maty's unsigned review of *The History of the Caliph Vathek.*

Newman, Beth. "Narratives of Seduction and the Seductions of Narrative: The Frame Structure of *Frankenstein.*" *ELH* 53, 1 (Spring 1986), 141–63.

Nitchie, Elizabeth. *Mary Shelley. Author of "Frankenstein"* (1953). Westport, Conn.: Greenwood Press, 1970.

Norris, Christopher. "Philosophy as a Kind of Narrative: Rorty on Postmodern Liberal Culture." *Enclitic* 7, 2 (Fall 1983), 144–58.

———. *The Deconstructive Turn.* London: Methuen, 1983.

———. *Derrida.* London: Fontana Press, 1987.

———. *What's Wrong With Postmodernism.* Baltimore: Johns Hopkins University Press,1990.

Novak, Maximillian E. "Gothic Fiction and the Grotesque." *Novel* 13 (Fall 1979), 50–67.

Oates, Joyce Carol. "Frankenstein's Fallen Angel." *Critical Inquiry* 10, 3 (March 1984), 543–54.

O'Flinn, Paul. "Production and Reproduction: The Case of *Frankenstein.*" *Literature and History* 9, 2 (Autumn 1983), 194–213.

O'Hara, Daniel T. "The Poverty of Theory: On Society and the Sublime." *Contemporary Literature* 26, 3 (1985), 335–50.

Orlando, Francesco. *Toward a Freudian Theory of Literature.* Baltimore: Johns Hopkins University Press, 1978.

Otto, Rudolf. *The Idea of the Holy.* Translated by John W. Harvey. Harmondsworth: Penguin Books, 1959.

Ousby, Ian. "'My Servant Caleb': Godwin's *Caleb Williams* and the Political Trials of the 1790s." *University of Toronto Quarterly* 44, 1 (Fall 1974), 47–55.

Palacio, Jean de. "Mary Shelley and the 'Last Man'. A Minor Romantic Theme." *Review de Littérature Comparée* 42, 1 (1968), 37–49.

Park, Roy. *Hazlitt and the Spirit of the Age. Abstraction and Critical Theory.* Oxford: Oxford University Press, 1971.

Pârreaux, André. *The Publication of The Monk: A Literary Event 1796–1798.* Paris: Didier, 1960.

Patterson, Charles I. "The Authenticity of Coleridge's Reviews of Gothic Romances." *Journal of English and Germanic Philology* 50 (1951), 517–21.

Paul, C. Kegan. *William Godwin; His Friends and Contemporaries.* Two vols. London: Henry S. King and Co., 1876.

Paulson, Ronald. *Satire and the Novel in Eighteenth–Century England.* New Haven: Yale University Press, 1967.

———. *Representations of Revolution (1789–1820).* New Haven: Yale University Press, 1983.

Paulson, Ronald, and Stein, Arnold, eds. *ELH Essays For Earl R. Wasserman.* Baltimore: Johns Hopkins University Press, 1974.

Pearce, Roy Harvey, ed. *Experience in the Novel.* New York: Columbia University Press, 1968.

Pease, Donald. "Sublime Politics." In Arensberg, Mary, ed., *The American Sublime,* 21–49.

Pêcheux, Michel. *Language, Semantics and Ideology.* Translated by Harbans Nagpal. London: Macmillan, 1986.

Peck, Louis F., "*The Monk* and *Le Diable Amoureux.*" *Modern Language Notes* 68, 5 (May, 1953), 406–8.

———. *A Life of Matthew G. Lewis.* Cambridge, Mass.: Harvard University Press, 1961.

Peck, Walter Edwin. "The Biographical Element in the Novels of Mary Wollstonecraft Shelley." *PMLA* 38 (1923), 191–219.

Pitcher, E. W. "Changes in Short Fiction in Britain 1785–1810: Philosophic Tales, Gothic Tales, and Fragments and Visions." *Studies in Short Fiction* 13, 3 (Summer 1976), 331–54.

Platzner, Robert L., and Hume, Robert D. "'Gothic versus Romantic': A Rejoinder." *PMLA* 86 (March, 1971), 266–74.

Poe, Edgar Allan. "The Philosophy of Composition." In *Selected Poetry and Prose,* Edited by T. O. Mabbott. New York: Modern Library, 1951, 363–74.

Pollin, Burton Ralph. *Education and Enlightenment in the Works of William Godwin*. New York: Las Americas Publishing Company, 1962.

———. "Godwin's *Letters of Verax*." *Journal of the History of Ideas* 25 (July–September 1964), 353–73.

———. "Philosophical and Literary Sources of *Frankenstein*." *Comparative Literature* 17 (1965), 97–108.

———. "The Significance of Names in the Fiction of William Godwin." *Revue des Langues Vivantes* 37 (1971), 388–99.

Poovey, Mary. *The Proper Lady and the Woman Writer*. Chicago: University of Chicago Press, 1984.

———. "My Hideous Progeny: Mary Shelley and the Feminization of Romanticism." *PMLA* 95 (1980), 332–47.

Pottle, Frederick A. "The Part Played by Horace Walpole and James Boswell in the Quarrel Between Rousseau and Hume." *Philological Quarterly* 4, 4 (October 1925), 351–63.

Poulet, Georges. "Timelessness and Romanticism." *Journal of the History of Ideas* 15, 1 (January, 1954), 3–22.

Praz, Mario. *On Classicism*. Translated by Angus Davidson. London: Thames and Hudson, 1967.

———. *The Romantic Agony*. Translated by Angus Davidson. Foreword by Frank Kermode (2nd ed.). Oxford: Oxford University Press, 1970.

———, Introduction, *Three Gothic Novels*. Edited by Peter Fairclough. Harmondsworth: Penguin Books, 1983.

Price, Martin. "The Sublime Poem: Pictures and Powers." *Yale Review* 58 (1969), 194–213.

Prickett, Stephen. *Victorian Fantasy*. Sussex: Harvester Press, 1979.

Priestman, Donald G. "*The Borderers*: Wordsworth's Addenda to Godwin." *University of Toronto Quarterly* 44, 1 (Fall 1974), 56–65.

Punter, David. *The Literature of Terror. A History of Gothic Fictions from 1765 to the Present Day*. London: Longman, 1980.

———. "Fictional Representation of the Law in the Eighteenth Century." *Eighteenth Century Studies* 16, 1 (Fall 1982), 47–74.

Quarterly Review 18 (January 1818), 379–85. Review of [Mary Shelley], *Frankenstein*.

Rabkin, Eric S. *The Fantastic in Literature*. Princeton: Princeton University Press, 1977.

Radcliffe, Ann. "On the Supernatural in Poetry." *New Monthly Magazine* 16 (1826), 145–50.

Railo, Eino. *The Haunted Castle.* London: Routledge, 1927.

Rajan, Tillottama. "Wollstonecraft and Godwin: Reading the Secrets of the Political Novel." *Studies in Romanticism* 27, 2 (Summer 1988), 221–51.

Redfield, Marc W. "Pynchon's Postmodern Sublime." *PMLA* 104, 2 (March 1989), 152–62.

Reijen, Willem van, and Veerman, Dick. "An Interview with Jean-François Lyotard." *Theory Culture and Society* 5, 2–3 (June 1988), 277–309.

Restuccia, Frances L. "Female Gothic Writing: 'Under Cover to Alice.'" *Genre* 18 (Fall 1986), 245–66.

Richter, David H. "Gothic Fantasia: The Monsters and the Myths. A Review Article." *The Eighteenth Century. Theory and Interpretation* 28, 2 (Spring 1987), 149–70.

Rieger, J. "Dr. Polidori and the Genesis of *Frankenstein.*" *Studies in English Literature* 3 (Autumn 1963), 461–72.

Riely, John. "*The Castle of Otranto* Revisited." *The Yale University Library Gazette* 53 (July 1978), 1–17.

Riffaterre, Michael. "The Intertextual Unconscious." *Critical Inquiry* 13, 2 (Winter 1987), 371–85.

Roberts, David. "Marxism, Modernism, Postmodernism."*Thesis 11* 12 (1985), 53–63.

Roberts, Robin. "The Paradigm of *Frankenstein*: Reading *Canopus in Argos* in the Context of Science Fiction by Women." *Extrapolation* 26, 1 (Spring 1985), 16–23.

Robson-Scott, W. D. "Georg Forster and the Gothic Revival." *The Modern Language Review* 101, 1 (January, 1956), 42–48.

Rothstein, Eric. *Systems of Order and Inquiry in Later Eighteenth-Century Fiction.* Berkeley: University of California Press, 1975.

———. "Allusion and Analogy in the Romance of *Caleb Williams.*" *University of Toronto Quarterly* 37 (October 1967), 18–30.

Rubinstein, Marc A. "My Accursed Origin: The Search for the Mother in *Frankenstein.*" *Studies in Romanticism* 15 (Spring 1976), 165–94.

Rutherford, Andrew, ed. *Byron: The Critical Heritage.* London: Routledge and Kegan Paul, 1970.

Sadleir, Michael. "The Northanger Novels." English Association Pamphlet, No. 68. London: Oxford University Press, 1927.

Said, Edward W. "The Problem of Textuality: Two Exemplary Positions." *Critical Inquiry* 4, 4 (Summer, 1978), 673–714.

———. *Orientalism*. Harmondsworth: Penguin Books, 1985.
St. Clair, William. *The Godwins and the Shelleys*. London: Faber and Faber, 1989.
Salgado, Gámini, ed. *Three Jacobean Tragedies*. Harmondsworth: Penguin Books, 1965.
Sambrook, A. J. "A Romantic Theme: The Last Man." *Forum for Modern Language Studies* 2 (1966), 25–33.
Schofield, Ann Mary, and Macheski, Cecilia. *Fetter'd or Free? British Women Novelists 1670–1815*. Athens, Ohio: Ohio University Press, 1986.
Scott, Jonathan. *Piranesi*. London: Academy Editions, 1975.
Scrivener, Michael. "*Frankenstein's* Ghost Story: The Last Jacobin Novel." *Genre* 18 (Fall 1986), 299–318.
Searle, J. R. "The Logical Status of Fictional Discourse." *New Literary History* 6, 2 (Winter 1975), 319–32.
Sedgwick, Eve Kosofsky. "The Character in the Veil: Imagery of the Surface in the Gothic Novel." *PMLA* 96, 2 (March 1981), 255–70.
———. *Between Men: English Literature and Male Homosocial Desire*. New York: Columbia University Press, 1985.
Sekler, Patricia May. "Giovanni Battista Piranesi's *CARCERI:* Etchings and Related Drawings." *The Art Quarterly* 25, 4 (Winter 1962), 331–63.
Shapiro, Gary. "From the Sublime to the Political: Some Historical Notes." *New Literary History* 16, 2 (Winter, 1985), 213–35.
Sharpe, Eric J. "Some Western Interpretations of the Bhagavadgītā 1785–1885." *Journal of Studies in the Bhagavadgītā* 1 (1981), 1–28.
Sherburn, George. "Godwin's Later Novels." *Studies in Romanticism* 1, 2 (Winter 1962), 65–82.
Sherwin, Paul. "*Frankenstein*: Creation as Catastrophe." *PMLA* 96, 5 (October 1981), 883–903.
Shipley, John B. "Horace Walpole: Some Mistaken Identifications." *Notes and Queries* 202 (1957), 475–77.
Showalter, Elaine. *A Literature of Their Own: British Novelists from Brontë to Lessing*. Princeton: Princeton University Press, 1977.
Siegel, Lee. *Sacred and Profane Dimensions of Love in Indian Traditions as Exemplified in the Gītagovinda of Jayadeva*. Delhi: Oxford University Press, 1978.
Silverman, Hugh J., and Aylesworth, Gary E., eds. *The Textual Sublime. Deconstruction and Its Differences*. Albany: SUNY Press, 1990.

Small, Christopher. *Mary Shelley's Frankenstein. Tracing the Myth.* Pittsburg: University of Pittsburg Press, 1973.

Smith, Curtis C. "Horror Versus Tragedy: Mary Shelley's *Frankenstein* and Olaf Stapledon's *Sirius.*" *Extrapolation* 26, 1 (Spring 1985), 66–75.

Smith, Warren Hunting, ed. *Horace Walpole, Writer, Politician and Connoisseur.* New Haven: Yale University Press, 1967.

Snyder, Robert Lance. "Apocalypse and Indeterminacy in Mary Shelley's *The Last Man.*" *Studies in Romanticism* 17 (Fall 1978), 435–52.

Spacks, Patricia Meyer. *The Insistence of Horror. Aspects of the Supernatural in Eighteenth Century Poetry.* Cambridge, Mass.: Harvard University Press, 1963.

Spark, Muriel. *Child of Light. A Re-assessment of Mary Wollstonecraft Shelley.* Hadleigh, Essex: Tower Bridge Publications, 1951.

Spatt, Hartley S. "Mary Shelley's Last Men: The Truth of Dreams." *Studies in the Novel* 7 (1975), 526–37.

Spivak, Gayatri Chakravorty. "Three Women's Texts and a Critique of Imperialism." *Critical Inquiry* 12, 1 (Autumn 1985), 243–61.

Stein, Jess M. "Horace Walpole and Shakespeare." *Studies in Philology* 31 (1934), 51–68.

Steinhauer, Harry. "Goethe's *Werther* After Two Centuries." *University of Toronto Quarterly* 43 (Fall 1974), 1–13.

Stephen, Leslie. "Hours in a Library. No. 5—Horace Walpole." *Cornhill Magazine* 25 (June 1872), 718–35.

———. "Godwin and Shelley." *Cornhill Magazine* 39 (January–June 1879), 281–302.

———. *Studies of a Biographer.* Three vols. London: Duckworth and Co., 1902.

Sterrenburg, Lee. "*The Last Man*: Anatomy of Failed Revolutions." *Nineteenth-Century Fiction* 33 (December 1978), 324–47.

———. "Mary Shelley's Monster." In Levine and Knoepflmacher, eds., *The Endurance of Frankenstein,* 143–71.

Stonum, Gary Lee. *The Dickinson Sublime.* Madison: University of Wisconsin Press, 1990.

Storch, Rudolf E. "Metaphors of Private Guilt and Social Rebellion in Godwin's *Caleb Williams.*" *ELH* 34 (1967), 188–207.

Sturrock, John, ed. *Structuralism and Since.* Oxford: Oxford University Press, 1979.

Suleri, Sara. *The Rhetoric of English India.* Chicago: University of Chicago Press, 1992.

Summers, Montague. *The Gothic Quest* (1938). New York: Russell and Russell, 1964.
Swingle, L. J. "Frankenstein's Monster and Its Romantic Relatives: Problems of Knowledge in English Romanticism." *Texas Studies in Literature and Language* 15, 1 (Spring 1973), 51–65.
Sypher, Wylie. "Social Ambiguity in a Gothic Novel." *Partisan Review* 12 (1945) 50–60.
Tafuri, Manfredo. *The Sphere and the Labyrinth. Avant-Gardes and Architecture from Piranesi to the 1970s.* Translated by Pellegrino d'Acierno and Robert Connolly. Cambridge, Mass.: MIT Press, 1987.
Tannenbaum, Leslie. "From Filthy Type to Truth: Miltonic Myth in *Frankenstein.*"*Keats-Shelley Journal* 26 (1977), 101–13.
Temkin, Oswei. *The Double Face of Janus and Other Essays in the History of Medicine.* Baltimore: Johns Hopkins University Press, 1977.
"Terrorist Novel Writing." *The Spirit of Public Journals for 1797*, vol. 1 (3rd ed.) London: James Ridgway, 1802, 227–29.
Thompson, E. P. *The Making of the English Working Class.* London: Victor Gollancz Ltd. 1965.
———. "Deterrence and 'Addiction.'" *Yale Review* 72, 1 (October 1982), 1–18.
Thompson, G. R., ed. *The Gothic Imagination.* Pullman: Washington State University Press, 1974.
Thompson, J. M., *The French Revolution.* Oxford: Basil Blackwell, 1962.
Tobin, Mary-Elisabeth Fowkes. "Bridging the Cultural Gap: *Tom Jones* and Post-Modernism." *Clio* 17, 3 (Spring 1988), 211–23.
Todd, W. B. "The Early Editions and Issues of *The Monk.*" *Studies in Bibliography* 2 (1949), 3–24.
Todorov, Tzvetan. *The Fantastic: A Structural Approach to a Literary Genre.* Translated by Richard Howard. Ithaca: Cornell University Press, 1975.
———. *Mikhail Bakhtin. The Dialogical Principle.* Translated by Wlad Godzich. Manchester: Manchester University Press, 1984.
Tompkins, J. M. S. *The Popular Novel in England 1770–1800.* London: Methuen, 1969.
———. *The Polite Marriage.* Cambridge: Cambridge University Press, 1938.
Tysdahl, B. J. *William Godwin as Novelist.* London: Athlone Press, 1981.

Varma, Devendra P. *The Gothic Flame* (1957). New York: Russell and Russell, 1966.

Vaughan, Charles Edwyn. *The Romantic Revolt.* Edinburgh: William Blackwood and Sons, 1907.

Veeder, William. *Mary Shelley and Frankenstein.* Chicago: University of Chicago Press, 1986.

Wasserman, E. R. "The Walpole-Chatterton Controversy." *Modern Language Notes* 54, 67 (1939), 460–62.

Watt, Ian. *The Rise of the Novel. Studies in Defoe, Richardson and Fielding.* Harmondsworth: Penguin Books, 1963.

Weiskel, Thomas. *The Romantic Sublime: Studies in the Structure and Psychology of Transcendence.* Baltimore: Johns Hopkins University Press, 1976.

Wellek, René. *A History of Modern Criticism: 1750–1950. Vol. I The Later Eighteenth Century.* London: Jonathan Cape, 1955.

Willey, Basil. *The Eighteenth Century Background: Studies on the Idea of Nature in the Thought of the Period.* London: Chatto and Windus, 1940.

Williams, Ioan, ed. *Sir Walter Scott. On Novelists and Fiction.* London: Routledge and Kegan Paul, 1968.

———, ed. *Novel and Romance 1700–1800. A Documentary Record.* London: Routledge and Kegan Paul, 1970.

Williams, Raymond. *Marxism and Literature.* Oxford: Oxford University Press, 1977.

———. *Culture and Society 1780–1950.* Harmondsworth: Penguin Books, 1963.

Wilson, Angus. "Evil in the English Novel." In Kerry McSweeney, ed., *Diversity and Depth in Fiction,* 3–24.

———. "William Godwin's Novels." In Kerry McSweeney, ed., *Diversity and Depth in Fiction,* 34–38.

Wilson, Rob. *American Sublime. The Genealogy of a Poetic Genre.* Madison: University of Wisconsin Press, 1991.

Wilt, Judith. *Ghosts of the Gothic. Austen, Eliot, & Lawrence.* Princeton: Princeton University Press, 1980.

Wolin, Richard, "Modernism versus Postmodernism." *Telos* 62 (1984–85), 9–29.

Wood, Theodore E. B. *The Word 'Sublime' and Its Context 1650–1760.* The Hague: Mouton, 1972.

Woolf, Virginia. "Two Antiquaries: Walpole and Cole." In *The Death of the Moth.* London: Hogarth Press, 1945, 45–51.

———. "The Rev. William Cole, A Letter." In *The Death of the Moth,* 52–55.

———. *Collected Essays.* Vol. 1. London: Hogarth Press, 1966.

Worringer, Wilhelm. *Form in the Gothic.* London: G. P. Putnam's Sons, Ltd., 1927.

———. *Abstraction and Empathy.* Translated by Michael Bullock. London: Routledge and Kegan Paul, 1948.

Yaeger, Patricia. "Toward a Female Sublime." In Kauffman, Linda, ed., *Gender and Theory,* 191–212.

Young, Robert, ed., *Untying the Text: A Post-Structuralist Reader.* London: Routledge and Kegan Paul, 1981.

Žižek, Slavoj. *The Sublime Object of Ideology.* London: Verso, 1989.

———. *Looking Awry. An Introduction to Jacques Lacan Through Popular Culture.* Cambridge, Mass.: MIT Press, 1991.

Index